SOURCES AND METHODS IN AFRICAN HISTORY:
SPOKEN, WRITTEN, UNEARTHED

ROCHESTER STUDIES in AFRICAN HISTORY and the DIASPORA

Toyin Falola, Senior Editor
The Frances Higginbotham Nalle Centennial Professor in History
University of Texas at Austin

(ISSN: 1092-5228)

SOURCES AND METHODS IN AFRICAN HISTORY: SPOKEN, WRITTEN, UNEARTHED

Edited by Toyin Falola and Christian Jennings

 UNIVERSITY OF ROCHESTER PRESS

First published 2003
by the University of Rochester Press

The University of Rochester Press
668 Mt. Hope Avenue, Rochester, NY 14620, USA
and at Boydell & Brewer, Ltd.
P.O. Box 9, Woodbridge, Suffolk 1P12 3DF, UK
www.urpress.com

ISBN 1–58046–134–4

Library of Congress Cataloging-in-Publication Data
Sources and methods in African history : spoken, written, unearthed /
edited by Toyin Falola and Christian Jennings.
    p. cm. — (Rochester studies in African history and the
diaspora, ISSN 1092-5228 ; v. 15)
    Includes bibliographic references and index.
    ISBN 1-58046-134-4 (acid-free paper)
    1. Africa—History—Methodology.   2. Africa—History—Sources.   I.
Falola, Toyin.   II. Jennings, Christian.   III. Series.
DT19.S68 2003
960´.01—dc21
                                                                      2003001197

British Library Cataloguing-in-Publication Data
A catalogue record for this book is available from the British Library

Designed and typeset by Straight Creek Bookmakers
Printed in the United States of America
This publication is printed on acid-free paper

For
Cheikh Anta Diop,
Joseph Ki-Zerbo,
Djibril Tamsir Niane,
and
Jan Vansina

CONTENTS

ACKNOWLEDGMENTS

This volume consists of selected and revised papers that were originally presented at *Pathways to Africa's Past*, a conference on sources and methods held at the University of Texas at Austin from March 30 to April 1, 2001. We are indebted to all who attended the conference for their spirited contributions and collegial attitude, which elevated both the tone and the fruitfulness of the proceedings incalculably. In addition, we are particularly grateful to Laura Flack, Kevin Roberts, Julie Sederholm, and Joey Walker for their help in organizing the conference, as well as to Barbara Harlow, who took on many roles during the conference, usually on short notice. We are also grateful for the participation and continued involvement of Timothy Madigan of the University of Rochester Press. And we are always inspired by the small but dedicated group of faculty and graduate students in African history at the University of Texas, including John Lamphear, Ann Cooper, Tyler Fleming, Ann Genova, Matt Heaton, Steve Salm, and Kirsten Walles, as well our recent graduates, Saheed Adejumobi, Joel Tishken, and Jacqueline Woodfork.

INTRODUCTION

Sources and methods have been an ongoing concern in African history since the early years of its development as a viable field of academic specialization. African scholars working at universities before and during the 1950s were aware of the strong traditions of oral historical consciousness developed in African societies over the course of centuries, but were constrained by the prevailing doubt and skepticism towards their use in historical research. Consequently, pioneer publications such as K. O. Dike's *Trade and Politics in the Niger Delta* and S. O. Biobaku's *The Egba and Their Neighbours* wrung as much information as possible from archival sources, while acknowledging the importance of oral sources and even using them to a limited extent.[1] Still, they and other African historians were enthusiastic about the potential for nondocumentary sources to expand the scope of their studies dramatically, and set themselves to the task of establishing oral tradition as a "legitimate" source for historical research. Jan Vansina did much of the work of developing a formal methodology for collecting oral traditions, as evidenced by his highly influential *Oral Tradition,* published in English in 1961.[2] African historians could now craft detailed historical narratives based on oral sources, such as Bethwell Ogot's *History of the Southern Luo,* or combine oral traditions with documentary sources, as in *Yoruba Warfare in the Nineteenth Century* by J. F. Ajayi and Robert Smith,[3] and have their works recognized for the serious scholarly efforts they were. Oral tradition had the additional benefit of providing a counterpoint to written colonial documents, which were seen as "tainted" with their creators' racism and cultural bias. Newly independent states in Africa were more than welcoming to such pro-African projects, and history departments across the continent set to the task of compiling nationalist narratives of their countries' precolonial past, colonial experiences, and resistance struggles. Perhaps the archetypal example of this nationalist approach to African history was the Dar es Salaam faculty, which included Terence Ranger and Walter Rodney, but equally vibrant and optimistic groups of historians converged at Ibadan with Dike and Ajayi, at Dakar with Cheikh Anta Diop, and elsewhere across the continent.

During the late 1960s and continuing through the 1970s, methodologies for African history continued to diversify and diverge. Oral tradition was soon complemented as a source by the development of methodologies for carbon dating, allowing new archaeological evidence to be used in reconstructing African history, and glottochronology, which opened new lines of inquiry for historical linguists. An insurgence of Marxist scholarship, exemplified by Walter Rodney's *How Europe Underdeveloped Africa*, drew upon economic models and sources for reconstructing a materialist narrative of the past.[4] Philip Curtin's meticulous study of the Atlantic slave trade, which prompted a skeptical response from J. E. Inikori, led to a healthy and contentious debate over sources and methods for calculating the numbers and ramifications of the African holocaust.[5] With the contributions of Joseph Miller, Paul Lovejoy, John Thornton, and others, this line of inquiry later flowered into a vibrant historiography on Africa's central role in the Atlantic world. At the same time, Africanist historians also pioneered methodologies for the study of religious, environmental, and gender history. David Henige founded the journal *History in Africa* in 1971 for the express purpose of tracking and critiquing these divergent methodologies, as well as advocating comparative studies, lest they become incommunicative with each other.

Spurred in part by the ongoing reevaluation of sources and methods in research, African historiography in the past two decades has been characterized by the continued branching and increasing sophistication of methodologies and areas of specialization, while at the same time following the discipline-wide shift to an emphasis on social and cultural history. The landmark publication in the early 1980s of the UNESCO *General History of Africa* provided a summation of the previous three decades' experiences in the development of African history.[6] Several scholars also pointed out that the UNESCO project provided an accessible map to the many points of narrative and methodological weakness that still remained. The late 1980s and 1990s saw an even further branching of methodology, as Africanist scholars employed strikingly different means to produce sophisticated histories of specific subjects. This diversity manifests itself in wide-ranging works: James Fairhead and Melissa Leach use ecological methods to study the historical dynamics of forest-savanna boundaries in Ghana; Onaiwu Ogbomo's *When Men and Women Mattered* offers a provocative look at the history of gender relations in Nigeria; John Lamphear has undertaken pioneering research on nineteenth-century East African military history; and Timothy Burke's history of soap in Zimbabwe demonstrates that no facet of material culture is insignificant when placed in its historical context.[7]

The rate of incorporation of new sources and methods into African historical research shows no signs of slowing, and the challenge ahead might be simply to keep these divergent branches rooted in some sort of shared foundation, a pleasantly different task from the struggle to gain acceptance for the use of oral traditions four decades ago.

Despite, or perhaps owing to, the ever-increasing methodological divergence in African history, scholars continue to maintain an insistence on foregrounding and debating the methods they use to collect their data. Thomas Spear's *Kenya's Past,* published in 1981 and long a popular text for undergraduate courses, is organized explicitly so that the reader develops an understanding of archaeological, linguistic, oral, and documentary sources for African history.[8] Toyin Falola and Michel Doortmont made the complete text of a primary documentary source—M. C. Adeyemi's 1914 history of the Yoruba—the centerpiece of an innovative essay for the *Journal of African History* in 1989.[9] A collection published in 1996, *In Pursuit of History,* edited by Carolyn Keyes Adenaike and Jan Vansina, is devoted solely to essays on the challenging experience of carrying out historical fieldwork in Africa.[10] And a recent collection edited by Luise White, Stephen Meischer, and David Cohen, provides keen critical insights into the practice of African oral history.[11] Perhaps inevitably, the past few decades have seen a reappraisal of the uses and limitations of oral tradition in historical research. Scholars have pointed out that oral traditions are imbued with political and ideological biases, not unlike the "tainted" colonial records they were purported to correct, and that they are often the products of selective recall on the part of their keepers. At the same time, a quick survey of recent issues of the *Journal of African History* reveals that African historians remain heavily indebted to colonial archives for their research.

Our volume, *African Historical Research,* is both a snapshot of current academic practice and an attempt to sort through some of the problems scholars face within this unfolding web of sources and methods. Perhaps more importantly, we hope this volume provides a space for Africanists to compare their diverse sources and methodologies, and to find common ground on which we might pose questions for future research and writing. The essays presented here range in tone from cautious optimism to well-meaning criticism, but they share a commitment to keeping the various divergent streams of African history mutually intelligible and interconnected. The book is divided into five sections, on archaeology, Africa and the Atlantic world, documentary sources, oral tradition, and innovative sources and methods. Each section begins with a short introduction by a distinguished Africanist scholar, which points out the particular contributions of the essays in the section and locating them within the broader context of the specializations and problems with which they are engaged.

The first section of the volume deals with archaeological contributions to historical research. Jim Denbow's introduction describes the possibilities for archaeology transcending its customary "validationist" role and becoming a method in its own right for proposing and testing historical ideas. However, the section's first chapter, by Christopher DeCorse and Gerard Chouin, draws from the title of a well-known Vansina essay on archeology and history to develop a cautionary statement about the misunderstandings and misuses of each discipline's methods and epistemologies by practitioners of the other. DeCorse and Chouin do not dismiss the potential for mutual benefit through shared research, but stress that historians and archaeologists must strive to fully understand each other's disciplines. In the next chapter, Laura Mitchell describes precisely the sort of well-informed interdisciplinary study that DeCorse and Chouin have in mind. Mitchell argues that an understanding of the archaeological record for the Late Stone Age in South Africa's Cedarberg Mountains forces historians to reconsider their assumptions about eighteenth-century interactions between indigenous Khoisan groups and European settlers. In contrast to Mitchell's relatively focused approach, Akin Ogundiran offers an example of the ways archaeological data and oral tradition can be combined to produce historical narratives spanning more than two millennia. Ogundiran demonstrates that the cultural history of the Yoruba-Edo region of western Africa can be divided into seven broad phases covering the years from 500 B.C. to A.D. 1900. Ed Wilmsen concludes the section by returning to the Khoisan in southern Africa, arguing that their involvement in regional commercial networks, and especially the slave trade, was much more complicated than previously assumed, and further, that their settlement in the area of Botswana and Namibia might have occurred as late as the seventeenth and eighteenth centuries. Where Ogundiran combines archaeology and history to establish a very long cultural history in one part of the continent, Wilmsen produces a study that challenges long-held stereotypes about a "primordial" group of people in another.

The second section, on Africa and the Atlantic world, examines the methodologies involved in deciphering historically accurate African ethnic identities from the records left by various actors in the transatlantic slave trade. Paul Lovejoy's introduction pauses to consider the various conceptions of ethnicity itself, and attempts to formulate a methodology for incorporating evidence of African ethnic formation and redefinition on both sides of the Atlantic. Matt Childs uses archival material from Cuba and

Spain to piece together the history of the *cabildos de nación,* Afro-Cuban voluntary mutual aid societies. The *cabildos* explicitly dealt with issues of ethnic identity, and while different ethnicities were represented within the same association, regulations often decreed that only members from particular ethnic groups were eligible for leadership positions. Russell Lohse, drawing on evidence from Costa Rican archives in which slaves themselves, rather than their owners, identified their ethnic affiliations, cautions that clear-cut ethnic identifications may be the exception rather than the norm. Lohse argues that slave owners in general had little clue about the ethnic origins of their slaves, often managing at best an educated guess as to the individual's port of embarkation; when slaves were asked directly about their ethnic affiliations, they often gave entirely different names than their masters had recorded for them. Kevin Roberts follows on this idea of ethnic misidentification with an example in which slaves themselves appropriated an ethnicity that clearly was not the one into which they were born. Bambara peoples from Senegambia represented only a minority of slaves imported into Louisiana, yet their cultural practices pervaded Louisiana slave culture to such an extent that both slaves and slave owners saw Bambara culture as the most widespread and influential ethnic identity. The essays in this section demonstrate the wide applicability and varied results obtainable from both local archives and the recently consolidated databases on transatlantic slavery.

The third section of the volume continues the previous section's theme of mining old documentary sources for new historical perspectives. The introductory essay by Thomas Spear focuses on the potential for Africanists to mine documentary sources, which they have traditionally avoided doing in favor of developing alternative methodologies. Despite the bias inherent in sources written by European observers, Spear argues that a critical-minded approach to these written sources produces substantive information that might otherwise be unavailable. Christian Jennings attempts one such examination of neglected documentary sources, using a close reading of early missionary records to produce a view of East African pastoralist history that is at odds with the model generally employed by scholars working solely with oral traditions. Based on the careful observations of the missionaries Krapf, Erhardt, and Rebmann, who have been largely neglected by twentieth-century historians, Jennings posits a late date for the development of a distinct Maasai identity, arguing that the Maasai emerged in the early nineteenth century from a larger group of pastoralists known collectively as Iloikop. Turning from missionary documents to court records, Kristin Mann presents a study of three court cases from late nineteenth-century Lagos, in which a wealthy patron and two of his clients struggled over their obligations to each other, using the British legal system to serve their own purposes. Mann demonstrates that these court records cast a valuable light on the shift from slave labor to patron-client relationships in the new palm-produce trade in colonial West Africa. Finally, returning to missionary records, Meredith McKittrick looks at reports of expansive violence in documents written by European missionaries and their African converts in late nineteenth-century northern Namibia. These accounts have often been dismissed as exaggerations by historians on the basis that they merely reflect the missionaries' desire to portray Africans as savages. But McKittrick argues that the African informants who helped to shape these accounts were reflecting a dire reality of expanding warfare and political centralization spurred by the penetration of the slave trade into the region.

The fourth section of the volume deals with the method most often associated with African historians, that of drawing historical data from oral tradition. In his introduction, Dennis Cordell locates each of the section's four essays within this historiographical tradition, noting the ways in which they each maintain, question, and modify the assumptions of earlier historians. Jan Jansen's essay is perhaps the most provocative in the entire volume, as it takes to task earlier interpretations of oral traditions surrounding the Mande trickster figure of Nfa Jigin. Jansen demands that oral tradition be subjected to the same cross-checking with other forms of evidence that scholars use to validate written sources. Where many scholars have taken Nfa Jigin narratives to represent a core of information handed down from antiquity, Jansen's comparison of these stories with other sources of external and internal evidence leads him to the conclusion that they are in fact are a product of nineteenth-century Mande thought. Constanze Weise offers a similar attempt to use oral tradition to write history that is grounded in empirical analysis and multilayered evidence. But where Jansen seeks to revive the use of oral tradition as history by pulling scholars towards a more accountable methodology, Weise attempts to revive the legitimacy of the method as a whole for the study of Nupe history. Weise argues that previous scholars who dismissed the historical value of stories about the mythical hero Tsoede overlooked their internal cohesion, their complexity, and their agreement with external sources of evidence, in this case the continued existence of the Ndakigboya cult, all of which confirm the existence of a precolonial and pre-Islamic kingship system in Nupeland. James Giblin pushes our reexamination of the methodology of oral tradition even further, asking whether historians unwittingly alienate history from their oral informants simply by the way they frame their interviews. Giblin's research indicates that rural communities in Njombe District of Tanzania have been engaged in a century-long struggle to preserve their own interpretations of the Maji Maji conflict. Historians may well be the latest in a series of outside authorities, including colonial and post-colonial administrations, to twist the meaning and context of Maji Maji for their own purposes. Jamie Monson takes this concern with preserving local interpretations of history and applies it to her own methodology in studying the experience of communities in the Kilombero valley of Tanzania with the construction of the TAZARA railway. Monson focuses on the local concept of *maisha,* which can mean "life," "livelihood," and "life cycle," attempting to reconstruct life histories through these three different meanings. Monson's research demonstrates the flexible ways in which individuals responded to the railway, and finds that the complexity of these experiences can reveal larger historical processes.

The fifth and final section of the volume is devoted to essays that present innovative sources and methods for African historical research. David Henige, in his introductory essay, notes that despite the frequently source-poor context of African history, scholars should be "willing to regard all evidence *from* the past as evidence *for* the past as well." The essays in this section offer a glimpse of the possibilities. Cynthia Brantley finds previously untapped historical value in the 1939 Nyasaland Nutrition Survey, which used scientific and anthropological research to describe a full agricultural cycle in three different villages. Brantley's careful, and critical, examination of these nutrition studies reveals that they offer valuable insight into local social and economic history, as well as the complexities of European colonialism in Africa. Catherine Coquery-Vidrovitch contributes a striking essay on the possibilities for turning economic sources into social history, focusing in this case on the history of electricity in Francophone West African cities. The introduction and uneven spread of electric power, Coquery-Vidrovitch argues, had profound implications for the lives of millions of Africans, changing daily life and social relations in the process. Steven J. Salm offers another view of changing urban social relations in his study of youth subcultures in Accra, Ghana, during the early years of independence. Drawing on newspapers, magazines, novels, and interviews, Salm pieces together a narrative of the "Bukom Boys," young Ghanaians who converged around the area of Bukom Square to take part in the dance culture associated with rock 'n' roll and high life music. Finally, Dennis Cordell's chapter points out that the voluminous social-science surveys undertaken during the past fifty years in Africa, usually concerned with contemporary problems, have inadvertently produced a valuable source of historical data. Cordell focuses here on a migration survey conducted during 1974–75 on Burkina Faso, which, when combined with complementary sources, actually provides a useful source for tracing the history of twentieth-century migration in West Africa.

Together, the essays in this volume represent the current state of the art in African historical research. While the contributing authors certainly extend the frontiers of knowledge in their respective specializations, pointing us towards new questions and new debates, they also reaffirm the primacy of fundamental standards, rigorous criticism from peers, and a constant commitment to the kind of history that reveals rather than conceals its subject. We have no doubt that African historians will continue to make a place for themselves at the forefront of their profession, continually producing innovative work, and demonstrating that a continent once thought devoid of historical significance has always been, in fact, at the very heart of all of human history.

Notes

1. K. O. Dike, *Trade and Politics in the Niger Delta, 1830–1885: An Introduction to the Economic and Political History of Nigeria* (Oxford: Clarendon Press, 1956); S. O. Biobaku, *The Egba and Their Neighbours, 1842–1872* (Oxford: Clarendon Press, 1957).

2. Jan Vansina, *Oral Tradition: A Study in Historical Methodology* (Chicago: Aldine, 1961).

3. B. A. Ogot, *History of the Southern Luo* (Nairobi: East African Publishing House, 1967); J. F. Ajayi and Robert Smith, *Yoruba Warfare in the Nineteenth Century* (Cambridge: Cambridge University Press, 1964).

4. Walter Rodney, *How Europe Underdeveloped Africa* (Washington, D.C.: Howard University Press, 1972).

5. Philip D. Curtin, *The Atlantic Slave Trade: A Census* (Madison: University of Wisconsin Press, 1969); J. E. Inikori, "Measuring the Atlantic Slave Trade: An Assessment of Curtin and Anstey," *Journal of African History* 17 (1976): 197–223; Philip D. Curtin, "Measuring the Atlantic Slave Trade Once Again: A Comment," *Journal of African History* 17 (1976): 595–605; J. E. Inikori, "Measuring the Atlantic Slave Trade: A Rejoinder," *Journal of African History* 17 (1976): 607–27.

6. UNESCO International Scientific Committee for the Drafting of a General History of Africa, *General History of Africa*, 8 vols. (London: Heinemann, 1981–).

7. James Fairhead and Melissa Leach, *Misreading the African Landscape: Society and Ecology in a Forest-Savanna Mosaic* (Cambridge: Cambridge University Press, 1996); Onaiwu Ogbomo, *When Men and Women Mattered: A History of Gender Relations among the Owan of Nigeria* (Rochester, N.Y.: University of Rochester Press, 1997); John Lamphear, (forthcoming); Timothy Burke, *Lifebuoy Men, Lux Women: Commodification, Consumption, and Cleanliness in Modern Zimbabwe* (Durham, N.C.: Duke University Press, 1996).

8. Thomas Spear, *Kenya's Past: An Introduction to Historical Method in Africa* (New York: Longman, 1981).

9. Toyin Falola and Michel Doortmont, "Iwe Itan Oyo: A Traditional Yoruba History and Its Author," *Journal of African History* 30 (1989): 301–29.

10. Carolyn Keyes Adenaike and Jan Vansina, eds., *In Pursuit of History: Fieldwork in Africa* (Portsmouth, N.H.: Heinemann, 1996).

11. Luise White, Stephen F. Meischer, and David William Cohen, eds., *African Words, African Voices: Critical Practices in Oral History* (Bloomington: Indiana University Press, 2001).

PART I

Archaeological Sources

1

SECTION INTRODUCTION
ARCHAEOLOGY AND HISTORY

James Denbow

From the nineteenth century, when Heinrich Schliemann set out to find the legendary city of Troy by following descriptions in Homer's *Iliad*, archaeology has often served history in a "validationist" role by seeking to "prove" the existence of events, places, or personalities found in historic documents—or even epic poems. For much of the twentieth century this was one of the principal methodological strategies and goals of archaeological excavations in the holy land and Mediterranean regions. Archaeology can play a much broader role in historical studies, however, by permitting an engagement and dialogue with historical materials that can facilitate not only a validation of historical records and traditions, but also a method whereby historical questions and statements can be tested, critiqued, expanded upon, and modified by new lines of evidence. Such methodologies are especially useful in Africa, where so much of the past, particularly in the interior regions, is still unknown.

While the general goals of historical and archaeological interpretation often overlap, the methodologies and data used to formulate and evaluate hypotheses differ. A new generation of archaeologists is now becoming aware of the need to be more sensitive to the biases, limitations, and reliability of historical documents. At the same time, historians are coming to grips with the nuances of archaeological data collection and its interpretation. As a result, once can expect to find fewer instances where, for example, the earliest from a broad range of radiocarbon dates for a site is selected as the only "correct" one for an event or occupation in question. Archaeological data also have their inherent biases and limitations; some of these are statistical, while others stem from the biological or cultural-interpretive realms from which the data were drawn and/or interpreted.

Each of the four papers presented here explores the use of archaeological and historical data in slightly different ways. Changes in settlement pattern, in population distribution, and in the spatial distribution and extent of trading networks, for instance, are all issues that are addressed in one form or another in each of the papers included here. One of the integrating features is that all to some degree use both archaeological and historical lenses to expand perspectives on the African past beyond what could be traditionally achieved by either discipline alone. As DeCorse and Chouin note, "what is often striking when considering the primary documentary records is the paucity of information and the lack of detail available on certain topics—topics that can be readily assessed through archaeological research."

Mitchell, for example, uses archaeological data on the prehistoric distribution of Late Stone Age foragers and herders to set the stage for comparisons with cadastral data that document early white settlement in the Cedarberg region of South Africa. Wilmsen, on the other hand, uses archaeological distributions of marine shells, glass beads, and other trade items to map the extent of the penetration of slave-trading networks far into the interior of southern Africa. In West Africa, DeCorse and Chouin emphasize the ability of archaeological reconnaissance to provide information on long-term changes in settlement patterns, especially in those areas away from the coast where European and other records are often less informative. Hard evidence about the effects of the slave trade on the far interior is usually not documented directly in historical records, but rather resides between the lines of explorers' itineraries and ship captain's logs. Archaeological investigations can foreground these implicit traces and, in some cases, provide a means for examining, testing, and modifying them. And as DeCorse and Chouin point out, African landscapes and their development are as much a cultural history in which landscapes are human "artifacts" as they are the product of natural and biological processes.

Using both cadastral records of land tenure and archaeological distributions of proto-historic sites, Mitchell concludes that access to grazing, water, and hunting rights was at the center of a struggle between Khoisan and Europeans in the mid-eighteenth to nineteenth centuries. Furthermore, she shows how archaeological data can be used to critique colonial records by providing evidence that there was a much greater precolonial intensity of land use in the Cedarberg region than is indicated by the colonial cadastral data. Furthermore, the mapping of archaeological data onto colonial land maps indicates "an overlap which suggests that violent confrontations between Khoisan and colonists in the eighteenth century were not only about competition for general resources and broad reaches of territory, but . . . access to specific features, such as springs, defensible shelters, and . . . mountain passes." Historians have long understood that conflicts over scarce resources often characterized colonial and indigenous relations. Archaeological data provides a means to add substance to such suppositions—whether they relate to conflicts over water and grazing rights in southern Africa, or shifts from dispersed to more urbanized settlements in West Africa during the period of the Atlantic slave trade. Such are the insights that can be derived from cognizance of the different data sets on which history and archaeology rest, and exploiting the advantages while understanding the limitations of each.

Changes in population distributions, trade networks, and their relation to transformations in political economy are used to good effect by Wilmsen and Ogundiran to discuss the effects of slave and other trading on the interior of Africa. While written documents provide details for some regions on the scope of trade, archaeological and oral histories can help to fill in blank places and, more specifically, map such relations onto geographic locations seldom mentioned otherwise. Ogundiran seeks to contextualize the meanings of material objects through an integration of historical narratives, ethnography, and archaeology. In his paper he outlines how beads and other so-called luxury or exotic items have functioned since early times in West Africa as paraphernalia of political authority. In contrast to European valorizations of such items, he argues that "the need for political control of production and distribution of red stone beads (whether at Ile-Ife, Old Oyo, or Oba-Isin) emanated from the fact that these beads constituted one of the most important and rarest badges of high political office in the Yoruba-Edu region during the Classical period. . . . More than anything else, the proliferation, expansion, and monopoly of brass and glass bead industries transformed Ile-Ife into prominence as an industrial and commercial center." His paper is an example of how a new generation of archaeologists in west Africa is moving beyond empirical-descriptive interpretive frameworks to grapple with the processes through which items of material culture become imbued with meaning, and how these meanings, and changes in them, may index other social, economic, and political transformations.

Wilmsen also reminds us that the material objects that archaeologists dig up need to be contextualized and valorized by African as well as European standards, arguing that, "material objects, even commodities, are socially inflected and, therefore, are differentially marked as manifestations of relations of production and consumption in different societies." To dismiss the trade beads, cloth, and other items brought to Africa as mere "trinkets" thus "carries a strong implicit devalorization of African labor and, correlatively, African mentality—while raising the value of that labor's product to European heights." His examination of archaeological and historical records indicates that by the mid-nineteenth century European trade had spread widely into the southern Angola-Okavango region. As a result of such developments, he argues that hunters and gatherers such as the Zhu or !Kung may be fairly recent arrivals in northern Botswana, where they have expanded since the seventeenth or eighteenth centuries as a result of slave raiding further north. If he is correct, then it is ironic that popular conceptions of the !Kung as a static icon of a primordial past have been biased by studies in which their "active roles have been devalued by an ethnography that insists upon their isolation from the historicity swirling about them." In this case archaeology moves to the forefront as a method for actively proposing historical hypotheses, rather than simply validating or invalidating the truth of earlier records.

2

TROUBLE WITH SIBLINGS: ARCHAEOLOGICAL AND HISTORICAL INTERPRETATION OF THE WEST AFRICAN PAST

Christopher R. DeCorse and Gerard L. Chouin

Contiguities between history and archaeology, real or imagined, often undermine the possibility of recreating and narrating the African past. Varying perceptions of the relative contribution of each discipline underscore dramatic differences in method and theory, the data sets employed, and underlying epistemologies. On one hand, recent debates reveal how historians often misinterpret or ignore insights into the vertiginous temporal depth provided by archaeology because they misconstrue the nature of the archaeological record and cannot evaluate archaeological data within their own, discipline specific, epistemological frameworks. On the other hand, archaeologists have long used the same written and oral sources as historians to build analogical systems of reference to make sense of the material record. Doing so, they frequently abuse these sources, ignoring, or misapplying the conceptual basis of historical criticism. Recognition of such problems does not mean that the contributions of the disciplines cannot be reconciled. Rather, cognizance of the data sets on which each discipline rests and the questions they can address can lead to productive inquiries of mutual benefit. We consider these issues in light on ongoing research in coastal Ghana.

The gulf between the disciplines of history and archaeology was highlighted by Jan Vansina's provocatively entitled article, "Historians, are archaeologists your siblings?" (Vansina 1995). Notably and, perhaps sadly, the article, published in *History in Africa,* was unread and uncommented on by most Africanist archaeologists. On the other hand, those of us that did read it were troubled by the perceived gulf between the disciplines. Many were puzzled and frustrated to realize that their sibling historians seemingly had almost no idea of the theoretical and epistemological debates within archaeology. The reaction of historians, those at whom the article was aimed, is difficult to assess, but appears to have been one of nonplussed ambiguity. The answer to Vansina's question is clearly a resounding, "Yes—archaeologists are historians' siblings."

Our point in this paper is not to underscore these differences in point of vantage, or to attempt to disentangle the relative contribution of each discipline. Rather, we celebrate the differences of each but recognize the potential of their intersection. The perceived disjuncture in the aims and objectives of history and archaeology is not unique to studies of the African past. It is an issue that has been explicitly confronted in the origins and growth of historical archaeology in the Americas, and it remains of fundamental concern today; there is a large literature relevant to this point (e.g. Beaudry 1988:1; Deagan 1982; Little 1994; Schuyler 1978). The primary tools of archaeologists and historians—the documentary past and the material record—clearly provide different types of data that are each better at assessing certain types of questions.

This is borne out by the fact that, in practice, most historians of Africa have made very limited use of archaeology, their data sets, and hence their interests, lying elsewhere. Some of the most truly interdisciplinary projects have focused on ethnoarchaeological research, a notable example being that of Schmidt—for example, his 1978 volume *Historical Archaeology: A Structural Approach to an African Culture*—Schmidt being one of the few Africanist archaeologists who have received training in oral historiography. The broader point here, however, is that Schmidt framed his research in terms of questions that would necessitate the use of archaeology, as well as other source material. For most researchers, anthropological, archaeological, and historical research have more often than not focused on questions that can be evaluated—rather, must be evaluated—through the use of individual categories of source material.

It is logical that researchers concentrate on those data best suited to address their particular research questions. It is not our contention that each historian should only proceed with an archaeologist at his side. Our concern is with the possible questions of interest to both the historian and the archaeologist, and to which both might contribute. In this chapter, we briefly consider some of the areas of inquiry we see as complementary to both disciplines from our work in the Central Region of coastal Ghana. This region has been the focus of the primary author's work since 1985, and it continues to be the focus of the Central Region Project, which now includes several archaeologists focusing on the material record of the past millennium (DeCorse et al. 2000, DeCorse 2001a).

In terms of European documentary records, coastal Ghana is among the best illustrated and best described regions of Africa. Documentary sources begin in the late fifteenth century, with increasing amounts of material available in succeeding centuries. The area has also been the focus of extensive analyses by historians, including Harvey Feinberg (1989), Paul Hair (1967, 1994b), Adam Jones (1983, 1990, 1994), David Henige (1973, 1974), and Larry Yarak (1986, 1989, 1990). Yet what is often striking when considering the primary documentary records is the paucity of information and the lack of detail available on certain topics—topics that can be readily assessed through archaeological research. The material record is, for example, particularly good at demonstrating the timing and kind of change that occurred in subsistence strategies, technology, and indigenous artistic traditions. It can also assess some of the specific types of goods—ceramics, glass, tobacco pipes, and firearms—that were traded and their temporal ranges, thus affording both a means of refining site chronology and insight into trade patterns.

Archaeology can, however, also contribute to broader historical and anthropological debate through examination of changes in artifact inventory, archaeological features, and settlement patterns that can be used to assess sociocultural and historical change. With regard to the post-European contact period in West Africa, perhaps the greatest potential contribution of archaeology lies in the delineation of the impacts and consequences of the Atlantic slave trade on African populations, not solely those on the coastal margins occasionally mentioned in documentary records, but also those in the vast hinterland from which many enslaved Africans originated (DeCorse 2001b). Many of these populations are virtually unmentioned in documentary sources or oral traditions until the late nineteenth or twentieth centuries. This vast topic has received limited attention, but there has been important work, some of which promises to change how historians as well as archaeologists perceive the past.

The real potential lies in the interdisciplinary study of both historical (documentary and spoken) and archaeological data. Use of different sources allows for a fuller interpretation of specific artifacts, sites, or sociocultural phenomena in a manner impossible using a single source. For example, well-dated archaeological specimens of *forowa* clearly expand our understanding of coastal Akan craft traditions. *Forowa* are vessels made from imported sheet brass, fastened together with rivets and decorated with *repoussé* and punch-work designs of animals and geometric forms. They are associated with the coastal Akan where they served in a variety of functional and ritual contexts. They have been regarded as a late product of the coastal and near-coastal Akan, with most production probably occurring between 1830 and 1930 (Ross and Garrard 1983). However, the discovery of several fragmentary examples from burial contexts at Elmina indicates that *forowa* were being produced by the mid-eighteenth century. Furthermore, the examination of these finds suggests the stylistic origins of the *forowa* may, in fact, rest with the earlier *kuduo*: cast brass vessels that date back to the origins of Akan casting in the fifteenth century (DeCorse 2001a 130–134).

At another scale, archaeology contributes to a much clearer understanding of West African settlement patterns and the long-term creation of cultural landscapes. We have no detailed documentary descriptions of the central Gold Coast at the time of contact and the precise changes that took place in African cultures over the past five hundred years will probably never be known. Detailed demographic information is regrettably limited. In fact, the specific locations, numbers, plans, and descriptions of coast and hinterland settlements are quite limited. Yet changes in the material record can be used to infer transformations in the sociocultural frameworks of which these features were part. The data from sites such as Elmina are illustrative of dramatic change, ranging from innovation in subsistence and diet, to urbanization and state formation.

From an archaeological standpoint, the first and most striking change in African societies in the Ghanaian coast and hinterland during the post-European contact period was increasing urbanization, the concentration of population into larger aggregates (DeCorse 2001 31–35; 44–56). This began as a gradual process during the fifteenth and sixteenth centuries, but culminated during the following centuries. On the eve of European contact settlements were scattered along all of coastal Ghana and throughout the adjacent hinterland. Most were likely small fishing villages or farming communities. This pattern would dramatically change in the following centuries. Population growth along the coastal margin and concomitant changes in sociopolitical structures characterize the post-European contact period.

During the fifteenth century, however, the larger population centers were still located in the West African interior and coastal settlements were small and dispersed. This view accords well with the documentary records that do exist. Describing coastal Ghana in 1479, de la Fosse noted Shama and Elmina as the only significant harbors. Even here it took four or five days for news of a ship's arrival to spread and for the merchants to gather (Hair 1994a: 129). Another fifteenth-century account of the trade comments that "when any of the [European] ships reached that land, the people of the land immediately summoned each other with trumpets because they lived in the countryside, and would all assemble at the ports to trade their gold" (Hair 1994a: 115).

Archaeological data from coastal Ghana suggest this pattern of dispersed settlement extends back at least a thousand years, probably much earlier. Pre-European-contact coastal sites are represented by low-density scatters of ceramics with occasional stone beads and iron artifacts. Some sites of these are quite sizable. At Brenu Akyinim and Coconut Grove, for example, pottery sherds can be found for almost a kilometer along the shore. This distribution, however, is likely the result of a series of small, shifting settlements over a long period of time rather than a single large occupation. Substantial midden deposits, large settlement mounds, or embankments—features that characterize later sites—are absent. Similar observations have been made for other parts of coastal Ghana. Archaeological data document the abandonment of these early sites and the expansion of larger trading enclaves, such as Elmina, as well as the growth the capitals of the Fanti states of the hinterland known from documentary sources, such as Eguafo, Asebu, and Efutu.

Current archaeological work promises to provide further insight into the sociocultural changes that occurred over the past five hundred years. There has not been a comprehensive survey of the Central Region, but data are accumulating. Seemingly pristine, forest reserves and sacred groves may afford particularly important insight. African environments have rarely been "understood as historically unique" (Nyerges and Green 2000: 273), while African societies have too often been perceived as restrictively shaped by their environment. Anthropologists have contributed to the realization that the history of ecological milieus has often been misinterpreted (Fairhead and Leach 1996, 1998). It is our opinion that archaeologists can establish a fruitful dialogue with historians such as Juhé-Beaulaton (1995, 1999), studying past vegetation cover, shifts in agricultural practices, and complex events of forest degradation and forest formation. Indeed, we have come to the realization that, in Africa like everywhere else, landscapes are anthropic formations; landscapes are artifacts and in this sense, the history of landscape belongs less to the realm of natural history than to archaeology.

The extraction of social history from such human landscapes can be illustrated by our examination of the processes of formation and use of sacred groves in the last millennium A.D. Sacred groves, which are scattered across the Ghanaian landscape, are often presented as primeval forests that escaped degradation by their integration into rituals. Thus, they are culturally sanctioned, "natural landscapes" and become, by definition, the domains of the botanist and of the cultural anthropologist. Few historians have attempted a social history of these forests, the only example coming to mind being Tom McCaskie's study of Nananompow, the main shrine of the historic Fante states (1990). Yet such so-called pristine landscapes are anthropic formations and can, therefore, be read as a palimpsest of long-term history. Many forest reserves actually cover archaeological remains. In the heart of the Kakum forest, for instance, we found evidence of early agrarian activities in the form of grooved rocks once used for the polishing and sharpening of stone tools. The same marks are to be found in many locations in coastal Ghana, often associated with the mythic origins of early states. Even more surprising, a number of sacred groves were, in fact, located on the sites of old cemeteries associated with abandoned settlements. At Eguafo, for instance, the capital of a coastal polity well known from sixteenth- to twentieth-century historical sources, recent archaeological survey and test excavations conducted by the Central Region Project suggest that the Dumpo—a sacred grove associated in oral traditions with the foundation of this coastal state—was indeed a settlement predating the 1600s. Elsewhere in the same polity, we have documented and we will soon excavate sacred groves associated with other early settlements and royal cemeteries that may help us to understand the dynamics of complexity in the forest fringes of West Africa in the last thousands years for the least (Chouin 1998, 2001).

We have much to learn from these landscapes, which can be read as palimpsests of the African past. Here, we see clear potential for the establishment of a dialogue between historians and archaeologists interested in the challenge of writing the long-term social history of African landscape formations, enlarging the scope of their hypotheses beyond the scope of view afforded by the documentary record. This, however, does not mean that archaeologists are concerned only with the far away past. Documenting much more recent events of the past is part of the holistic approach of archaeology, for the long-term, by definition, includes the present as much as the past. In fact, some of the forests became sacred only at the end of the nineteenth century. For instance, oral traditions and documentary resources allowed us to understand that in the small community of Nsadwer, near Elmina, these "new" sacred groves were a way of making sense of and reacting against traumatic events such as the spread of smallpox or military encounters in the last quarter of the nineteenth century (Chouin 1998). Here again, there are wonderful opportunities of dialogue and, personally, we would not have been able to make sense of these landscape features if historians had not guided us towards the complementary written records.

Finally, our point is that there are many possible ways for archaeologists and historians to communicate and integrate their data. Historians should be aware of the fact that history does not begin when documentary or oral sources become available. There is a deeper past that historians cannot ignore when they assemble the written fragments and pieces of the most recent centuries. Historians have to cross the epistemological channel and become more familiar than they are with our methods, assumptions, and language, and also with theoretical trends within our discipline. Similarly, archaeologists must become familiar with potential archival resources and be exposed to the principles of historical criticism. Personally, we have learned much from interacting with historians such as Paul Hair, Adam Jones, Larry Yarak, and Michel Doortmont. Archaeologists must also become familiar with the specificities of oral traditions and oral history and make use of them as data rather than as narratives to be inserted uncritically into discussion. Such intersection must occur at varying levels, with recognition of the differences in epistemology, as well as the style of presentation and discipline-specific explications. There is space for a fruitful interdisciplinary dialogue if we make the effort to learn each other's language, if we renounce writing only for our peers, and if we read and constructively criticize each other's work from the perspective of our own discipline. We should listen more than we ask. The archaeologist often surprises his interlocutors by showing interest for features, objects, technological savoir-faire, everyday ritual practices, and landscapes that are generally ignored by historians who focus on genealogies, biographies, and stool histories, or look for specific direct historical analogies to make sense of their other sources. Different questions and interests often open pathways to parts and pieces of memory that yield treasures when critically examined.

References

Beaudry, M. C., ed. 1998. *Documentary Archaeology in the New World.* Cambridge University Press.

Chouin, G. 1998. Looking through the Forest. Sacred Groves as Historical and Archaeological Markers in Southern Ghana: an Approach. 14th Biennial Conference of the Society of Africanist Archaeologists, 21–24 May 1998, Syracuse.

———. 2001. Pathways to the Social Shaping of Forest Landscapes: Archaeology, Sacred

Groves and the Dynamics of Socio-political Complexity in Coastal Ghana (1000–2000 AD). Changing Perspectives on Forests: Ecology, People and Science/Policy Processes in West Africa and the Caribbean, Workshop at the Institute of Development Studies, University of Sussex, 26–27 March 2001, Brighton.

Deagan, K. 1982. Avenues of Inquiry in Historical Archaeology. *Advances in Archaeological Method and Theory,* 5:151–155.

DeCorse, C. R. 2001a. *An Archaeology of Elmina: Africans and Europeans on the Gold Coast, 1400–1900 AD.* Washington, D.C.: Smithsonian Institution Press.

DeCorse, C. R. (editor). 2001b. *West Africa during the Atlantic Slave Trade: Archaeological Perspectives.* New York: Leicester University Press.

DeCorse, C. R., E. Carr, G. Chouin, G. Cook, and S. Spiers. 2000. Central Region Project, Coastal Ghana—Perspectives 2000. *Nyame Akuma,* 53: 6–11.

Feinberg, H. 1989. *Africans and Europeans in West Africa: Elminans and Dutchmen on the Gold Coast during the Eighteenth Century.* Philadelphia: Transactions of the American Philosophical Society, 79 (pt. 7).

Fairhead, J., and M. Leach. 1996. *Misreading the African Landscape: Society and Ecology in a Forest-Savanna Mosaic.* Cambridge University Press.

———. 1998. *Reframing Deforestation: Global Analyses and Local Realities: Studies in West Africa.* London and New York: Routledge, Global Environmental Change Programme.

Juhé-Beaulaton, D. 1995. Les paysages végétaux de la côte des Esclaves du 17e siècle à la veille de la colonization: essai d'analyse historique. Unpublished dissertation, Université de Paris-I.

———. 1999. Arbres et bois sacrés: lieux de mémoire de l'ancienne Côte des Esclaves. In *Histoire d'Afrique: Enjeux de Mémoire,* edited by J. P. Chrétien and J. L. Triaud, Paris: Karthala, 101–18.

Hair, P. E. H. 1967. Ethnolinguistic continuity on the Guinea Coast. *Journal of African History* 8: 247–268.

———. 1994a. The early sources on Guinea. *History in Africa* 21:87–126.

———. 1994b. *The Founding of São Jorge da Mina: An Analysis of the Sources.* African Studies Program, University of Wisconsin–Madison.

Henige, D. 1973. The problem of feedback in oral tradition: four examples from the Fante coastlands. *Journal of African History* 14 (2): 223–235.

———. 1974. *The Chronology of Oral Traditions: Quest for a Chimera.* Oxford: Clarendon Press.

Jones, A. 1983. *German Sources for West African History 1559–1669.* Studien zur Kulturkunde (66). Stuttgart: Franz Steiner Verlag.

———. 1990. *Zur Quellenproblematik der Geschichte Westafrikas 1450–1900.* Studien zur Kulturkunde (99). Stuttgart: Franz Steiner Verlag.

———. 1994. Drink deep, or taste not: thoughts on the use of early European records in the study of African material culture. *History in Africa* 21 (1994), 349–370.

Little. B. J. 1994. People with history: an update on historical archaeology in the United States. *Journal of Archaeological Journal and Theory* 1 (1): 5–40.

McCaskie, T. C. 1990. Nananom Mpow of Mankessim: An essay in Fante history. In *West African Economic and Social History: Studies in Memory of Marion Johnson,* edited by D. Henige and T. C. Caskie. African Studies Program, University of Wisconsin-Madison, 133–150.

Nyerges, A. E., and G. M. Green. 2000. The ethnography of landscape: GIS and remote sensing in the study of forest change in West African Guinea savanna. *American Anthropologist* 102 (2): 271–289.

Ross, D. and T. Garrard, eds. 1984. *Akan Transformations.* Monograph Series 21. Los Angeles: Museum of Cultural History.

Schmidt, P. 1978. *Historical Archaeology: A Structural Approach to an African Culture.* Westport, Conn.: Greenwood Press.

Schuyler, R. L. 1978. *Historical Archaeology: A Guide to Substantive and Theoretical Contributions.* Farmingdale, N.Y.: Baywood Publishing.

Vansina, J. 1995. Historians, are archaeologists your siblings? *History in Africa* 22: 369–408.

Yarak, L. 1986. The "Elmina note": myth and reality in Asante-Dutch relations. *History in Africa* 13: 363–382.

———. 1989. West African coastal slavery in the nineteenth century: the case of the Afro-European slaveowners of Elmina. *Ethnohistory* 36 (1): 44–60.

———. 1990. *Asante and the Dutch: 1744–1873.* Oxford: Clarendon Press.

3

MATERIAL CULTURE AND CADASTRAL DATA: DOCUMENTING THE CEDARBERG FRONTIER, SOUTH AFRICA, 1725–1740[1]

Laura J. Mitchell

If rocks could talk, in the Western Cape they would tell tales of violence, theft, and retribution. But not all the rocks of the region necessarily need be mute witnesses to the complex and contested process of colonization. Although technically voiceless, Paleolithic chips and stone canvases convey information—which is not news to archaeologists. This information, however, too rarely is considered by historians. More importantly, it is rarely used in any systematic way to challenge, corroborate, or interrogate history as reconstructed from documentary sources. This paper is a methodological exploration of the ways in which historians can use prehistoric archaeological data to understand events and processes in the historic era better. Integrating different kinds of data creates a direct confrontation between notions of what is historic and what is prehistoric. The result of such a collision is an opportunity to construct a new epistemological pathway to Africa's past.

The paper uses as a case study the process of European settlement in the Olifants River valley, situated in the Cedarberg Mountains roughly 250 km north of Cape Town. At the time when the colonial frontier began advancing as far north as the Olifants River, the Dutch East India Company had maintained a refreshment station for its trading fleets at the Cape of Good Hope for three-quarters of a century. Since the first Company outpost was established at Table Bay, Dutch demand for land, fresh water, and meat—in the form and cattle and sheep—had put the Europeans at odds with the indigenous hunters and herders of the region, known collectively as Khoisan.[2]

Previous historical studies of the relationship between Khoisan and colonists, as well as most treatments of colonial-era Khoisan, have relied exclusively on archival sources.[3] This study uses Late Stone Age archaeology to shed light on the European colonization of the Olifants River area in the Cedarberg. I argue that the archaeological record suggests a greater pre-colonial intensity of land use than is conveyed in the early Dutch East India Company records. Furthermore, specific sites in the landscape were more important to both Khoisan and colonists than others. Locating prehistoric hunting and herding sites at specific points in the landscape, and then comparing sites of earliest colonial penetration, reveals an overlap which suggests that the violent confrontations between Khoisan and colonists in the eighteenth century were not only about competition for general resources and broad reaches of territory, but were, in fact, about access to specific geographical features: perennial springs, defensible shelters, and control of mountain passes. Moreover, many of these sites had ritual significance to the Khoisan.

Disciplinary Disjunctures: The Historic Divide

This paper is a response to a challenge issued by historian Jan Vansina for historians and archaeologists to engage one another more directly in their respective efforts to understand and illuminate characteristics of the human past.[4] Vansina notes the disjuncture in time, subject, and approaches to the past between the work of historians and archaeologists. In accepting a definitive break between historic and prehistoric eras, historians and archaeologists have divided the past and claimed their respective terrains. Of course, historical archaeology bridges this chasm, using excavated material evidence in conjunction with documentary sources to create a more complete picture of the past than either archaeology or archivally based history could produce alone.

Embedded in historical archaeology, however, are implicit assumptions of "authorship," particularly in colonial studies. Except in cases explicitly looking at indigenous elements of colonial interactions,[5] the people producing and using the excavated material remains are assumed to be roughly the same people who produced the documentary evidence—not the same individuals, *per se,* but people participating in the same society, living under the same norms—people who might reasonably be expected have had some common ground for interaction if we were to assume a meeting between those who wrote the documents and those who handled the physical objects which have become evidence for subsequent scholars.

It is more complicated to try to correlate physical evidence with archival sources produced by two disparate groups of people. However, the remains of some colonial encounters produce the means to do so, thus breaching the chasm between historic and prehistoric and thereby confronting the greatest disjunctures between history and archaeology. Such an attempt presents a forceful reply to Vansina's challenge for historians and archaeologists to integrate their work more closely.

On one level, Vansina's challenge is an audacious one. Although history and archaeology both investigate the human past, the differences between the two are significant enough that an argument against disciplinary integration could be marshaled. The most prominent of these divisions is the issue of periodization. I contend, however, that the distinction between prehistoric and historic is spurious. The most important contribution of method that self-consciously integrates historical and archaeological approaches is to repudiate the notion that herders and hunters of the eighteenth century belong to a timeless, isolated, ahistorical past. The painters of rock and makers of stone tools were historical actors of the eighteenth century to the same degree as the colonial settlers so meticulously documented by the clerks of the Dutch East India Company.

Setting aside the question of periodization, there remain important differences of sources, the technical training of practitioners, and the demand among historians for specific dates.[6] These differences, rather than being seen as points of contention, can be used as starting points for more closely correlating the work of archaeologists and historians. To date, archaeologists have been more successful in this integrative endeavor than historians. In southern Africa, several studies use contemporaneous documentary evidence to contextualize and interpret Late Stone Age archaeology, rock art in particular.[7] Historians, however, have not begun to explore how Late Stone Age archaeological studies can contribute to the creation of historical narrative in ways that both complement and challenge the archival record, not to mention provide information in places where text is absent or inadequate on its own.[8] In a crude caricature, it would seem that historians see Late Stone Age evidence as "prehistoric," in which case the data and conclusions of archaeologists are useful for setting the stage of the historian's tale, but do not intervene directly in the narrative constructed from textual evidence. Thus the prehistoric-historic divide is maintained.

This caricature provides a neat conceptual division, but it is no help whatsoever in explaining what happened when "prehistoric" people and "historic" people collided. From the archival record we know they cooperated, collaborated, cohabited, procreated, and even married. They fought violently and transmitted virulent diseases. They transferred technology conceptually across millennia and spatially across the subcontinent of southern Africa.

When these various encounters are elaborated, for the most part historians tell the tale from the colonial perspective. Even in the hands of subtle and skillful historians, the effort to recover the voice of the Khoisan is mediated by the limits of the colonial records.[9] Meanwhile the archaeology sits mute. Admittedly filtered by time, deterioration, and the conceptual limitations of modern thinking projected onto an extinct *mentalité*, archaeological evidence is not distorted by the misunderstandings, the misapprehensions, or the contemporary objectives of colonial record keeping. Although undoubtedly influenced in its production by colonial encounters, the archaeological record of the hunter-gatherers and pastoralists of the Western Cape is mediated neither by foe nor ally. Hardly foolproof or completely objective, Late Stone Age archeological evidence does, nevertheless, provide historians with a useful—and heretofore untapped—source of information for understanding eighteenth-century human interactions in the Olifants River Valley and surrounding Cedarberg mountains of the western Cape in South Africa.

Populating the Cedarberg

The Olifants River cuts a valley through the Cedarberg, then flows across the coastal plain to join the Atlantic Ocean. The river valley has—and had before the river was dammed at Clanwilliam—several broad, flat reaches suitable for farming. The mountainous terrain on either side of the valley is steep and rocky, with thick, scrubby vegetation capable of supporting wildlife and domestic stock such as sheep and cattle. The climate is arid, though winter rains fill seasonal springs and streams. Place names—Rhenosterhoek, Zeekoe Valley, Elands Kloof, Tijgershoek, and the Olifants River—bear testimony to the wildlife that once inhabited the area.

Although not a fecund environment, the Cedarberg has accommodated human settlement for at least 10,000 years.[10] The region's numerous

rock art sites and Late Stone Age remains have attracted intense archaeological investigation for over 20 years, shedding new light on the relationship between hunter-gatherers and pastoralists and on the movements of
precolonial people.[11]

It is generally accepted that hunting populations, known as Bushmen
or San, predated herding populations, or Khoikhoi, at the Cape.[12] People
who subsisted predominantly by hunting and gathering used land and resources differently from people whose subsistence was based on pastoralism. Although archaeological, documentary, and ethnographic data is not
absolutely conclusive, it is strongly suggestive that the indigenous populations of the Cape had a strong sense of territoriality and regular ranges
through which different groups moved systematically. Groups gathered and
dispersed in response to climatic and economic stimuli.[13] Such movement
among people engendered both cooperation and conflict. Open hostility
and struggle for specific territory seems likely in the precolonial era, but it
appears as though the notions of individual land claims and land ownership arrived in the region with European settlers.[14]

Europeans first arrived in the Olifants River valley in 1660, at which
time Jan Danckaert saw the herds of elephants after which he named the
river. Europeans visited the river valley after that time on hunting expeditions, further exploratory treks, en route further northward in search of the
Copper Mountains, or to barter for cattle with Namaquas.[15] The expan-
sionary tendency of the Dutch East India Company colony began to affect
the region full-time in 1725, when the first grazing permit was issued.[16]
Stock farmers began regularly using the area from that point onward, and
by the late 1730s had instituted arable farming.[17]

Colonial land claims under the Dutch East India Company rule at
the Cape were based on a two-tiered system of permanent grants (freehold
property) and permits (loan farms). Settlement in outlying areas such as
the Cedarberg was based on loan farms, which were annual permits granted
by the Vereenigde Oost Indische Compagnie (VOC, the Dutch East India
Company) to free burghers. A loan farm gave a settler exclusive right to a
fixed tract of land in exchange for annual rent. The permit was renewable
indefinitely. Burghers could build, farm, hunt, and graze on their loan farms
without restrictions. There is some debate among historians of South Africa about the fixedness and permanence of the loan farms granted by the
VOC.[18] I agree with the compelling evidence presented by Botha and Guelke
that although the loan farm permits may have been legally temporary and
tenuous, in practice the grants conferred permanent, alienable property
rights on the permit holders.[19]

For the existing hunting and herding populations of the Cedarberg, the introduction of VOC loan farms meant intensified competition for access to land and resources such as water, grazing, and game. More importantly, settler loan farms represented the advent of a new land tenure regime based on notions of private ownership that was thus intrinsically inimical to Khoisan seasonal migration.

Khoisan response to colonial intrusion was uneven, consisting of various degrees of engagement, resistance, and flight. Toward the end of the late 1730s, violent resistance predominated, culminating in the fierce frontier war of 1739. Nigel Penn argues that the 1739 war effectively ended the possibility of independent existence for local hunters and herders in the region; crushed concerted, armed Khoisan resistance; and opened this portion of the frontier to more intensive colonial use.[20]

The Method: Integrating Khoisan Material Culture Remains with Settler Cadastral Data

To document the interactions between Khoisan and colonial settlers during the eighteenth century requires locating both groups of people at particular points in space and time. In this instance using archival documentation in conjunction with archaeological data to locate people in a landscape is both ideal and problematic. The method is ideal in that it forces a side-by-side comparison of artifacts left by two contemporaneous but distinct populations, thereby integrating a historian's archive with an archaeologist's Paleolithic finds. It is this very difference in the kind of available record that is problematic, however. This approach mirrors the prehistoric-historic divide, relegating the settlers to the documentary record and the Khoisan to pieces of rock. Despite this shortcoming, the approach is an improvement upon the traditional use of the Paleolithic as a backdrop to historical narrative because it self-consciously places both groups of people and both sets of evidence in the same time and place. Thus this study renders the eighteenth-century Cape as a crucial zone of interaction, fundamental for understanding both early colonial conflicts and the epistemological basis of our own historical interpretations.

In order to locate hunters and herders in the Cedarberg landscape, I relied on the site reports compiled by Spatial Archaeology Research Unit (SARU) at the University of Cape Town.[21] The reports span over a decade of field work, the result of repeated trips to the Cedarberg in search of rock art and other Paleolithic remains. Using the 1:50,000 series of topographi-

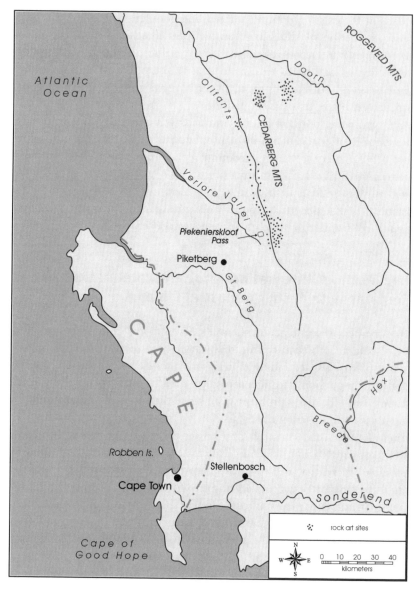

Figure 3.1. Map of Olifants River Area Rock Art Sites. Map by Bruce Moses.

cal maps published by the South African Surveyor General, I plotted the SARU-identified sites in the Olifants River valley, the surrounding mountain range, and adjacent valleys.[22] The majority of the sites identified by SARU in the Cedarberg consist of rock paintings. In plotting the sites I did not differentiate on the basis of quantity of material present, the type (whether painting or other artifact), or the content of painted images. I merely recorded the presence of a facet of Khoisan cultural remains.

Using the same set of SASG maps, I set out to locate early settler farms based on information in the South African Archives Cape Archives Depot (CA) and the Algemeenrijksarchief (ARA) in The Hague. The bulk of this archival data is from loan farm records and the *opgaaf* (census and taxation rolls). From these sources it is possible to know the land holder's name and the approximate location of his (or occasionally her) loan farm.[23] The *opgaaf* adds information about the land holder's spouse, children, livestock, and the productivity of the land.[24] Other archival sources such as freehold grants, magisterial reports, probate inventories, and criminal proceedings shed further light about the location of farms and the settler claims to the land.[25] I used published genealogies in addition to church records to ascertain family connections among landholders.[26] Thus I reconstructed the network of kin and neighbors among the first three generations of colonial settlers in the Cedarberg region. From the colonial perspective, I was able to get an idea of who had claim to the land; where it was; whether an individual or a family occupied the land seasonally, year-round, or not at all; and how land claimants were linked to the rest of colonial society. I plotted this archivally constructed network of settler farms on the SAGS maps using historical maps, place names, and the few detailed descriptions of farm locations that emerge in various archival records.[27]

The two sets of population data revealed a high degree of overlap. An early settler farm encompassed every dense cluster of Paleolithic sites. All of the first twenty loan farms claimed in the Cedarberg, which are enumerated in Table 3.1, encompassed material evidence of previous Khoisan use. The stock-rearing colonial settlers were claiming the very places used by the hunting and herding populations they were displacing.

This high degree of geographical overlap is not surprising. The Cedarberg is not a resource-rich area. People will choose to camp or settle in places where there is perennial water, natural shelter, and natural defenses or outlooks. It was advantageous to both settlers and Khoisan to be close to game trails and to have easy access to human trails, including river fords or mountain passes. Desirable spots in the landscape were limited

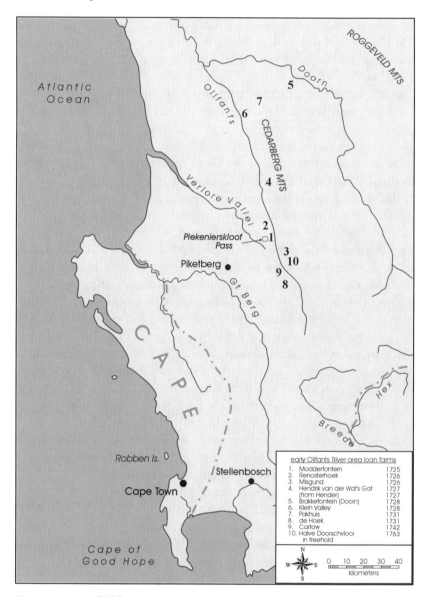

Figure 3.2. Map of Olifants River Area Loan Farms. Map by Bruce Moses.

Table 3.1: First Olifants River/Cedarberg Area Loan Farm Permits

Date	Permit Holder		Farm	CA: RLR Vol	Folio	*
1725	Johannes	Ras	Lange Valleij	6	58	
1725	Francois	Smit	Klein Valleij	6	54	
1725	Jurgen	Hanekoom	Modder Font	6	49	
1725	Arnoldus Johannes	Basson	Groot Valleij	6	53	
1726	Willem	Burger	Misgunt	6	88	
1726	Pieter Willemsz	van Eerden	Ratel Font	6	102	
1726	Daniel	Pheil	Zeekoe Valleij	6	90	
1726	Alewijn	Smit	Thien Rivieren	6	94	
1726	Jan	Steenkamp	Groene Valleij	6	96	
1726	Jan	Dissel	Renoster Hoek	6	85	
1727	Daniel Sr.	Pfeil	Brakkefontein	7	11	
1727	Johannes Lodewijk Pieters	Putter	Halve Dorschvloer	6	113	
1727	Jochem	Koekemoer	Hendrik van der Wats Gat	7	12	
1727	Hendrik	Vries de	Zeekoe Valleij	6	139	
1728	Andries	Kruger	Lange Valleij	7	45	r
1728	Jan Andries	Dissel	Groote Zeekoe Valleij en de Klein Valleij	7	54	
1728	Jochem	Koekemoer	Hendrik van der Wats Gat	8	133	r
1728	Hendrik	Cloete	Klein Valleij	8	142	
1728	Alewijn	Smit	Thien Rivieren	8	125	r
1728	Francois	Smit	Lange Fontien	7	58	
1728	Francois	Smit	Lange Fontien	8	159	r
1729	Jacob	Mouton	Berg Valleij	8	202	
1729	Andries	Krugel	Lange Valleij	8	223	r
1729	Johannes	Bota	Breede Rivier	8	261	r
1729	Guilliam	Visagie	Gonjemans Kraal	8	267	r
1729	Jan Andries	Dissel	Groote Zeekoe Valleij en de Klein Valleij	8	264	r
1729	Pieter Willemsz	van Heerden	Ratel Fontein	8	272	r
1729	Juff Anna	de Coning	Sonquas Cloof en het Kley Gat	8	303	r
1729	Jan Andries	Dissel	Renoster Hoek	8	308	r

* indicates the record is a renewal, not a new permit

Source: CA: Receiver of Land Revenue series and Leonard Guelke RLR data

and were equally attractive to both groups of people. It is no wonder the settlers and the Khoisan fought over the land.

The Results: A New Interpretation of Frontier Violence

An examination of the spatial distribution of both colonists and Khoisan in the Olifants River valley and the surrounding Cedarberg suggests that the brutal confrontation of 1739[28] might well have been about access to specific sites in the landscape, rather than a more generalized struggle over water sources and hunting or grazing terrain, as the existing historical literature suggests.[29] Archaeological studies reveal clusters of intensive precolonial activity, as evidenced by concentrations of rock art sites throughout the landscape (Figure 1).[30] Accepting the arguments that rock art expresses symbolic as well as literal meaning, and that rock art creation formed a part of important social ritual among hunter-gatherers, we can infer that places with high concentrations of rock art were important to the indigenous population not only for their resources or strategic location, but also for social and ritual reasons.[31] Although these points in the landscape may not have been—and most probably were not—sites of constant occupation, they were places in the landscape important enough to fight for.

Because these places of ritual significance coincide with advantageous terrain, these sites were attractive to the first colonists (Figure 2). Access to permanent springs, locations near water crossings or mountain passes, and defensible positions would have attracted hunters, herders, and frontier farmers alike. There is little evidence from contemporary written sources that early Dutch settlers had much awareness of—let alone knowledge about—the numerous rock art sites in areas of colonial expansion. Though difficult to substantiate, it is unlikely that migrant stock farmers looking for new grazing territory had an understanding of the ritual significance of any rock art they encountered, or a sense of the importance of that ritual meaning to hunter–gatherer social structure. Whatever encounters *trekboere* may have had with rock paintings, they left little trace of their observations in surviving written records.[32]

The lack of eighteenth-century documentation that refers to the abundant rock paintings in the Cedarberg suggests that the early settlers were uninterested in the practices of the hunters they were displacing. It is also likely that the settlers were unwilling to acknowledge these marks of territoriality in the landscape. Whether the farmers ignored the traces of precolonial inhabitants on rock faces, or were genuinely ignorant of most rock paintings and their significance, the advancing European frontier effectively monopolized access to economic resources in the environment. In so doing, the increasing exercise of colonial control over specific pieces of land also restricted access to sacred places important to the social cohesion of people already in crisis.

The first loan farms granted in the Olifants River valley coincide with points of intensive precolonial use as suggested by the frequency of Late Stone Age sites. Taking examples of loan farms granted between 1725 and the 1740s, it is clear that farmers were competing with hunters and herders for use of the same places. This argument is intuitive: the land is unequally endowed, so people and animals gravitate toward areas with the best quality or highest concentration of natural resources. Historians have long understood that conflict between colonists and the indigenous population had to do with contested resources. Using the archaeological record in conjunction with documentary evidence gives specific, tangible substance to that supposition. Incorporating an understanding of prehistoric hunters and herders derived from archaeological study into a historical narrative sheds new light on the nature of the conflict between colonists and the Khoisan. In the face of an advancing colonial frontier, the indigenous inhabitants of the western Cape fought not only for access to the means of economic subsistence independent from colonial service, they also fought to maintain the integrity of their social structures and belief system. Being denied access to sites of ritual importance was a devastating blow delivered to the Khoisan at the same time as they were being forced onto more marginal land or into colonial service.

The Implications: A Historian Relies on Her Siblings

Given how prolific rock painting sites are in the Cedarberg, it is incomprehensible that colonial settlers did not encounter irrefutable traces of their Khoisan neighbors on their farms. In fact, it would be difficult to make a land claim in the region and not include some Paleolithic remains. Thus the juxtaposed mapping of Late Stone Age sites and settler cadastral data could be seen as superfluous. Khoisan inhabited the Cedarberg for centuries before VOC settlers began to encroach upon the Olifants River Valley. The hunters and herders moved through the landscape and did not make permanent territorial claims. This combination of fluid range and time depth would naturally inscribe the terrain as Khoisan. Thus, wherever the settlers claimed land, the claim would challenge Khoisan land use and naturally include remnants of Khoisan material culture. Consequently, a method of mapping populations using two different sets of source material tells us nothing we would not already know from the archaeological record alone.

From a historian's perspective, however, this juxtaposition of material culture evidence with cadastral data challenges traditional notions of periodization. The colonial and precolonial collide. Historic and prehistoric cohabitate in the same narrative. Moreover, this narrative is more richly informed by the Khoisan voice. The irrefutable material evidence of widespread and long-standing Khoisan presence in the Cedarberg adds resonance to the colonial documentary accounts of brutal and desperate eighteenth-century battles.[33]

The eighteenth century in Southern Africa was a remarkable historic moment. The "prehistoric" confronted the historic. The "precolonial" confronted the colonial. And the colonial unfolded in all its messy complexity a century before the Age of Imperialism ordained that such interactions should take place. The eighteenth century in the Western Cape shakes up some of the received wisdom of African history. Colonization on an imperial model took place before the industrial revolution and the rise of social Darwinism. People with stone tool technology, no fixed abode, and no governmental structure succeeded in limiting the European colonial presence for a century in the Cedarberg.[34]

The scholarly disjuncture between what is historic and what is archaeological comes to the fore in the Cedarberg. This disjuncture is deeper than the lack of a shared vocabulary. It is not just that historians cannot tell the difference between a chip and a flake, as Vansina seems to suggest. Yes, historians get uncomfortable with relative dates and floating chronologies. But archaeologists also operate within their own fixed spheres of expectation.

The first years of the UCT SARU surveys in the Cedarberg did not record historic material. The teams were looking for rock art and stone tools. Remnant foundations and rotting wagon wheels were not in their purview. Colonial settlers were, however, in the purview of the Khoisan. Rock art exists in the Western Cape depicting settlers, ox wagons, and ocean-going ships.[35] For the past few years, SARU surveys now assiduously record historical as well as Paleolithic finds.

There is ample evidence of the extent to which the "precolonial" and the "colonial" overlapped throughout Africa. Stone age archaeologists who ignore what might be contemporaneous historical artifacts are guilty of emptying the landscape of a colonial presence that Khoisan themselves could not ignore. It is as though we have internalized the imperialist construct of the "empty landscape," then turned it upside down in a way that is neither revolutionary nor illuminating.

Thousands of Khoisan individuals lived in the historical era. Very few of them, however, survive in the historical record. Thus we approach them as archaeological artifacts and push their existence back in time. They are not people without history, or even people without records. Their legacy of graceful eland and stone adzes is difficult to correlate with census reports and property records, however.

This disjuncture points to other difficulties in correlating historical with archaeological methods. The disciplines use different vocabularies. More importantly, they ask different questions. Archaeology has a hard time responding to the concerns of a historian. For example, an inquiry into the eighteenth-century frontier wars of the Western Cape may inquire, "What is colonial?" Does the term *colonial* refer to a fixed time period? A mentality? A process? Archaeology also has difficulty incorporating the social historian's trinity of race, class, and gender. Gender, in particular is obscured in the archaeological record.

My own archival research reveals a lot about settler family structure; the importance of kin and neighbors in upholding property claims; and the role of women in anchoring extended family networks and transferring property (both land and slaves), even though VOC policy and Dutch custom recorded property ownership in the name of men. No matter how much work they do, my archaeologist colleagues cannot approach those questions of detail. Their material evidence does not permit it, and it is not the questions they are asking. Their evidence, does, however, enable me to incorporate Khoisan actors (though not as named individuals) firmly in a narrative about contested, sustained colonial interactions. Without the prolific, pervasive evidence of rock paintings and stone tools painstakingly collected by archaeologists, that narrative would be one of settler conquest rather than a multisided tale of contest.

As an historian looking at colonial encounters, I confront multiple points of conflict: hunter versus herder, Khoikhoi herder versus settler herder, Khoisan land use versus settler land use, and historical data versus archaeological data. Understanding how these conflicts played themselves out merits investigation, leading to a better integration of the "historic" with the "prehistoric," and of archaeology with history.

Notes

1. The research for this paper was supported by a Fulbright-Hays Dissertation Research Grant and by a Graduate Fellowship from the History Department at UCLA. I am grateful to Tony Manhire for so graciously sharing his time and data with me, and to John

Parkington and Nigel Penn for their comments on an earlier draft of this paper. The final product benefited greatly from the insights of my co-panelists at the Pathways Conference and from lively discussion from members of the audience.

2. A note on terminology: Khoisan is an elision of the terms Khoikhoi and San. The name survives as an imprecise but functional reference to hunting and herding populations of the Cape when precise nomenclature is not possible to ascertain. Early European travelers and settlers referred to the indigenous herders of the South Western Cape as Hottentots. This term acquired a derogatory connotation through its historical use. The term Khoikhoi is now the accepted convention. The hunter-gatherers of the region were known collectively as Bushmen. The modern appellation of San recently has been disputed, since it derives from a derogatory Khoikhoi term. In most cases, reference to specific groups of Khoikhoi and Bushmen are preferred, but this convention is not practical for general discussion. This paper will use the terms Khokhoi when referring specifically to pastoral peoples, Bushmen when referring to hunters, and the admittedly awkward Khoisan when referring to indigenous people when it is not possible to differentiate them.

3. Richard Elphick, *Kraal and Castle: The Khoikhoi and the Founding of White South Africa* (New Haven, Conn.: Yale University Press, 1977); V. C. Malherbe, "Diversification and Mobility of Khoikhoi Labor in the Eastern Cape Districts of the Cape Colony Prior to the Labor Law of 1 November 1809" (M.A. thesis, University of Cape Town, 1978); Nigel Penn, "The Northern Cape Frontier Zone, 1700–c.1815" (Ph.D. thesis, University of Cape Town, 1995).

4. Jan Vansina, "Historians, Are Archaeologists Your Siblings?" *History in Africa* 22 (1995): 369–408.

5. Patrice L. Jeppson, "Colonial Systems and Indigenous Responses: Black Material Expressions at a British Mission in South Africa," (paper presented at the Society for Historical Archaeology Conference on Historical and Underwater Archaeology, Richmond, Va., 9–13 January 1991).

6. Vansina, "Historians," 377–81, 384.

7. Colin Campbell, "Art in Crisis: Contact Period Rock Art in the South-Eastern Mountains of Southern Africa" (M.Sc. thesis, University of the Witwatersrand, 1987); Hannalie van der Merwe, "The Social Context of Rock Art during the Contact Period in the North-Western Cape and the Seacow River Valley" (M.A. thesis, University of Stellenbosch, 1990); Janette Deacon and Thomas A. Dowson, eds., *Voices from the Past: /Xam Bushmen and the Bleek and Lloyd Collection* (Johannesburg: University of the Witwatersrand Press, 1996).

8. Nigel Penn's work is informed by archaeological thinking, but his historical method does not self-consciously incorporate or challenge archaeological evidence or interpretation. See his articles "The Northern Cape Frontier Zone" and "The Frontier in the Western Cape, 1700–1740," in *Papers in the Prehistory of the Western Cape,* ed. John Parkington and Martin Hall, 2:462–503 (Oxford: BAR, 1987).

9. Richard Elphick and V. C. Malherbe, "The Khoisan to 1828," in *The Shaping of South African Society, 1652–1840,* ed. Richard Elphick and Hermann Giliomee, 3–65 (Cape Town: Maskew Miller Longman, 1989); Susan Newton-King, "The Enemy Within: The Struggle for Ascendancy on the Cape Eastern Frontier, 1760–1799" (Ph.D thesis, University of London, 1992); and Newton-King, *Masters and Servants on the Cape Eastern Frontier* (Cambridge: Cambridge University Press, 1999).

10. Tony Manhire, *Later Stone Age Settlement Patterns in the Sandveld of the South-Western Cape Province, South Africa* (Oxford: BAR, 1987); and John Parkington, "Time

and Place: Some Observations on Spatial and Temporal Patterning in the Later Stone Age Sequence in Southern Africa," *South African Archaeological Bulletin* 35 (1980): 73–83.

11. John Parkington, "Changing Views of Prehistoric Settlement in the Western Cape," in Parkington and Hall, *Papers in the Prehistory of the Western Cape,* ed. John Parkington and Martin Hall, 1:4–23; Tony Manhire, *Later Stone Age Settlement Patterns in the Sandveld of the South-Western Cape Province, South Africa,* Cambridge Monographs in African Archaeology, 21 (Oxford: BAR, 1987); and Richard Klein, "The Prehistory of Stone Age Herders in the Cape Province of South Africa," *The South African Archaeological Society Goodwin Series* 5 (1986): 5–11.

12. Andrew B. Smith, "Competition, Conflict and Clientship: Khoi and San Relationships in the Western Cape," *The South African Archaeological Society Goodwin Series* 5 (June 1986): 37.

13. R. B. Lee, *The !Kung San: Men, Women and Work in a Foraging Society* (Cambridge: Cambridge University Press, 1979); Klein, "The Prehistory of Stone Age Herders," 5.

14. For an overview of the literature on Khoisan land use and patterns of seasonal migration, see Laura J. Mitchell, "Contested Terrains: Property and Labor on the Cedarberg Frontier, 1725–c.1830." (Ph.D. dissertation, UCLA, 2001), chapter 3.

15. Pillipppus Lodewikus Scholtz, "Die Historiese Ontwikkelling van Die Onder-Olifantsrivier 1660–1902: 'n Geskiedenis van die Distrik Vanryhsdorp," *Archives Yearbook for South African History* (1966): 7–27. My thanks to Robert Ross for sharing his copy of Scholtz with me.

16. CA: Receiver of Land Revenue (RLR) series 6:58, *Oude Wildschutte Boeke,* 18 Oct. 1725. Permit issued to Johannes Ras at *Lange Valleij.*

17. For a detailed reconstruction of early settler land claims in the region, see Mitchell, "Contested Terrains," chapter 4.

18. L. C. Duly, *British Land Policy at the Cape 1795–1844: A Study of Administrative Procedures in the Empire* (Durham, N.C.: Duke University Press, 1968).

19. C. Graham Botha, *Early Cape Land Tenure* (Cape Town: Cape Times Limited, 1919. Reprinted from the *South African Law Journal,* May and August 1919). Leonard Guelke, "Early European Settlement of South Africa" (Ph.D. dissertation, University of Toronto, 1974).

20. Penn, "The Frontier in the Western Cape, 1700–1740," 492–93.

21. The original reports are housed at SARU. I have photocopies of relevant reports; in addition I have the information available as a database. I am grateful to Tony Manhire for sharing the original reports with me.

22. SASG 1:250,000 series: 3118, Calvinia, 1989; 3218, Clanwilliam, 1997; 3318, Cape Town, 1994. SASG 1:50,000 series: 3218 CA, Citrusdal, 1986; 3218 DD, Piketberg, 1975; 3218 DB, Eendekuil, 1986; 3218 BD, Oliewenboskraal, 1986; 3218 BB, Clanwilliam, 1986; 3219 CC, Keerom, 1986; 3219 AC, Wuppertal, 1986; 3219 AA. Pakhuis, 1986.

23. CA: RLR series, *Oud Wildschutte Boeke* records all loan farms granted by the VOC. I am grateful to Leonard Guelke, who kindly shared with me the RLR database he compiled. CA: Stellebosch Magisterial Records (1/STB) contain loan farm payment and renewal information, especially 1/STB 11/18 and 1/STB 11/19, *Register Grootboek van Leningsplase,* 1793 and 1794.

24. CA: J, *Opgaaf* for Stellenbosch and Drakenstein, various years; ARA: VOC 4097–4259, *Overgekomen brieven en papeiren,* 1725–1764. I am grateful to Hans Heese, Robert Shell, and Robert Ross, each of whom kindly shared their own compiled *opgaaf* data with me.

25. DO: Old Stellenbosch Freeholds Vol. 2, part 2 and Vol. 3. CA: 1/STB, Stellenbosch Magisterial District records. CA: MOOC, Master of the Orphan Chamber, for wills, auction rolls, and probate inventories. CA: CJ, Council of Justice, for criminal proceedings.

26. J. A. Heese and R. T. J. Lombard, *Suid-Afrikaanse Geslagregisters,* 5 vols. (Pretoria: Raad vir Geesteswetenskaplike Navorsing, 1986–99); (Protea Boekhuis, 1999); C. Pama and C. C. de Villiers, *Genealogies of Old South African Families* 2 vols. (Cape Town: A. A. Balkema, 1981); CA: G2 4/4 *Doop Register* 1765–1794.

27. Good descriptions of locations come, for example, in the testimony presented in criminal cases. CA: CJ 785.28, *Crimineel Sententie,* 10 January 1732. ARA: VOC 4158, *Overgekomen brieven en papieren,* 1743–1744. Vol. 2, Case 9 against Willem van Wijk. I am grateful to Robert Ross for drawing this case to my attention.

28. In 1739 there was a violent period of frontier conflict between settlers and Khoisan, interpreted as the last concerted effort at independent Khiosan political/social viability.

29. Leonard Guelke and Robert Shell, "Landscape of Conquest: Frontier Water Alienation and Khoikhoi Strategies of Survival, 1652–1780," *Journal of Southern African Studies* 18:4 (1992): 803–24.

30. Manhire et al., "A Distributional Approach to the Interpretation of Rock Art in the South-Western Cape," *The South African Archaeological Society Goodwin Series* 4 (1983): 29–33.

31. J. D. Lewis-WIlliams, *Believing and Seeing: Symbolic Meanings in Southern San Rock Painting* (London: Academic Press, 1981). Royden Yates and Anthony Manhire, "Shamanism and Rock Paintings: Aspects of the Use of Rock Art in the South-Western Cape, South Africa," *South African Archaeological Bulletin* 46 (1991): 3–11. Royden Yates, Jo Golson, and Martin Hall, "Trance Performance: The Rock Art of Boontjieskloof and Sevilla," *South African Archaeological Bulletin* 40 (1985): 70–80.

32. Royden Yates, Anthony Mahire, and John Parkington use this absence of historical reporting on rock painting to surmise that the practices associated with the finely detailed work had disappeared by the time of colonial contact: "Rock Painting and History in the South Western Cape," in *Contested Images: Diversity in Southern African Rock Art Research,* ed. Thomas A. Dowson and David Lewis-William (Johannesburg: University of the Witwatersrand Press, 1994), 54. Without disputing their chronology for the end of finely detailed rock painting, I would caution against using a lack of information contained in colonial documents as conclusive that the practice was no longer taking place.

33. Penn, "The Northern Cape Frontier Zone," chapters 3 and 5. Newton-King, *Masters and Servants,* chapters 4 and 6.

34. Mitchell, "Contested Terrains."

35. Yates, Manhire, and Parkington, "Rock Painting and History," 42–43.

4

CHRONOLOGY, MATERIAL CULTURE, AND PATHWAYS TO THE CULTURAL HISTORY OF YORUBA-EDO REGION, 500 B.C.–A.D. 1800

Akinwumi Ogundiran

Introduction

The topics of origins and intergroup relations in Yoruba-Edo region have attracted the attention of historians, archaeologists, and linguists alike, but the long-term chronological and cultural historical scheme needed to understand the origins, changes, and continuities of the cultural institutions in the region has been lacking (see Figure 4.1).[1] In fact, one can argue that the pre-nineteenth-century historiography of Yoruba-Edo region has been poor in research themes, in historical explanations of cultural innovations, and in long-term perspectives of structural change and continuity, partly because an historical periodization scheme that encompasses the region has yet to be defined. A major manifestation of this historiographical poverty is that the vision of the precolonial cultural history has been predominantly limited to the nineteenth century. This study brings the achievements of over fifty years of archaeological and historical research together for developing a long-term chronological scheme using archaeological data (chronometric dates and artifacts) and oral historical traditions.[2] The historical themes that define the periodization and cultural-historical schemes focus on factors internal to Yoruba-Edo region and not on the episodes of external contacts.[3] This study involves an integration of local and site-specific

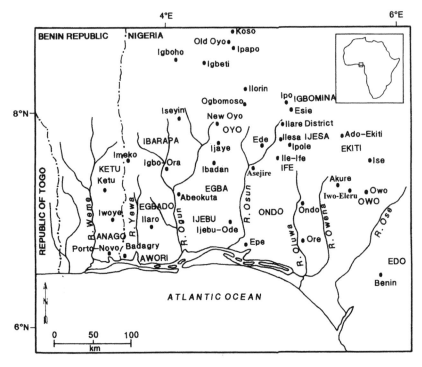

Figure 4.1. Yorubaland, showing areas mentioned in the text.

regional chronology, and the reworking of chronological schemes that were based on narrow or specific types of cultural behavior (e.g., artistic traditions) (see Table 4.1). Although background information is provided on the possibilities of much earlier human occupation in the region, the period covered in this study stretches from ca. 500 B.C. to A.D. 1800.

There are some justifications for this exercise. The general lack of long-term chronological and cultural historical frameworks for most regions of Africa especially for the vast period that is often referred to as "precolonial" or "Iron Age" has encouraged the wrong view of African cultural institutions as a fixed timeless past or a floating ethnographic present for which there is a *status quo ante.*[4] This chapter demonstrates that traditions have history and that archaeology provides a pathway to the understanding of the long-term history of these traditions (read: cultures and structures). In other words, the goal is to demonstrate that inherited artifacts, technology, ideas, values, institutions, sociopolitical organizations, and social actions of Yoruba-Edo region are "historically produced as organized and organizing schemes of action that are meaningful to the indi-

Table 4.1. Chronological and Cultural-Historical Schemes for Yoruba-Edo Region

Dates	Willett/Eyo's Scheme for Ile-Ife	Drewal's Scheme for Ile-Ife	Akinjogbin/Agbaje-Williams' Scheme for Yoruba	Connah's Scheme for Benin	Agbaje-William's Scheme for Old Oyo	Shaw's Scheme for Nigeria (including Yoruba-Edo)	Proposition for Yoruba-Edo Chronology/Periodization
400 B.C.	Pre-Classic/Pre-Pavement					Early Contact	Archaic
200 BC							
AD 0							
200							
400							
600		Archaic	Pre-Dynastic/Pre-Urban				Early Formative
800		Pre-Pavement		Early Period	Early Period		Late Formative
1000	Classic/Pavement	Early Pavement	Dynastic/Urban			Northern Contact	Classical
1200		Late Pavement			Intermediate Period		
1400		Post-Pavement		Middle Period			Intermediate
1600	Post Classic/Post Pavement	Stylized Humanism Era		Late Period	Late Period	Southern Contact	Atlantic
1800							

viduals (and societies) involved," just as historical experience is also culturally mediated.[5] Structures are therefore seen as the vehicle through which
meaning and collective experience are forged, reproduced, and sometimes
transformed.[6] The aspects of cultural history emphasized in this study are
the linkages between the formal and stylistic properties of material culture,
including iconographic, on the one hand and changes in the structures of
sociopolitical organization, ideologies of political power, and regional interactions on the other. The study draws attention to how archaeological
data and their contextual meanings can be a basis for understanding the
long-term history of cultural traditions in Yoruba-Edo region. This emphasis on material culture derives from the perspective that objects "are
internally constituted by the changing script of social relations . . ."[7] and
that "the production and use of objects have the capacity to transform situations as well as people" through the choices made by human agency.[8] Since
objects are repositories of meaning and value, these meanings and values
would change as objects move from one context to the other in new places,
times, and situations. This process gives us the opportunity to view the life
history of objects as life history of peoples, ideas, and structures,[9] and it
allows us to situate the properties of material culture in the contexts of
sociopolitical changes and in a regional perspective.[10] The changing relations among the social units that made up the interacting sphere in Yoruba-
Edo region, and the material imprints of these transformations constitute
the central mode of explanation. Although objects and features obtained
through systematic archaeological research are at the core of the study, the
repertoire of material culture belonging to the non-archaeological domains
are also discussed and the contextual meanings of these objects are sought
in the historical ethnography. By focusing on the cultural contexts of the
objects, an attempt is made to generate a cultural historical scheme that
integrates archaeological data with oral historical narratives and historical
ethnography.

   This chapter is an offshoot of recent historical-archaeological investigations in Ilare district (Ijesaland), a study that was aimed, in part, at understanding the trajectories of regional interactions in central Yorubaland
between the thirteenth and nineteenth centuries.[11] The study at Ilare district was conceived as a comparative archaeology of Yoruba-Edo region,
and it was geared at explaining how the events that originated in the me-
tropolises of Ile-Ife, Benin, and Old Oyo shaped the local historical trajectories in Ilare district. The comparative framework of the study at Ilare
district is expanded here, and by building upon the local chronological and
cultural historical sequences that have been defined for a few areas in Yoruba-

Edo region (Table 4.1), six cultural historical phases are delineated for Yoruba-Edo region between the middle of the first millennium B.C. and the eighteenth century. The periods are the Archaic (500 B.C.–A.D. 500), Early Formative (A.D. 500–800), Late Formative (800–1000), Classical (1000–1400), Intermediate (1400–1600), and the Atlantic (1600–1800).[12] Before we go into the details of each of these cultural historical phases, let us examine the nature of the archaeological evidence for the earliest human occupation in the region.

Early Human Occupation in Yoruba-Edo Region

The entire span of the African Stone Age, south of the Sahara, has been divided into three techno-temporal periods: Early Stone Age (ESA): ca. 3 million–35,000 B.C.; Middle Stone Age (MSA): 35,000–15,000 B.C.; and Late Stone Age (LSA): 15,000–500 B.C.[13] Although the possibility that human occupation of Yoruba-Edo region began during the ESA or MSA has been raised, the evidence is so far tenuous and controversial because all the stone tools that are supposedly associated with these two periods have come from secondary depositions, especially from the gravel and terrace deposits of the Osun and Ogun river valleys (Fig. 1).[14] Recent archaeological investigations in Ajíbóde area, northern section of Ibadan city, have uncovered what might turn out to be a primary context of ESA or MSA occupation. According to the principal investigators, the ancient (ESA/MSA) land surfaces of Ajíbóde are preserved by encrusted laterite; and the exposed old ground surface of the area are marked by rich deposits of choppers and scrapers.[15] The work at Ajíbóde is still at a very preliminary stage, and we are not sure whether the stones identified as choppers and scrappers were shaped by weathering processes or by human actions.

The most certain evidence for the earliest human occupation in the Yoruba region comes from Iwò Elérú rock shelter, about 24 kilometers from Àkúré. Human remains were found at the lower deposits of the site in a context dated to 11,000 YBP (years before the present). Associated with the human remains is an assemblage of LSA tools characterized by crescent-shaped, triangular, and trapezoidal microliths.[16] The possibility that the microliths were used for cutting plants and for food collecting activities is indicated by their polished edges with sickle-sheen characteristics.[17] The upper horizon of the cave reveals the evidence that pottery and ground stone implements were adopted at the site ca. 5000 YBP.[18] There are indications that between 1000 and 500 B.C., all the ecological niches of Yoruba-

Edo region were occupied by LSA populations with a subsistence that was based on the cultivation of palm oil and yam, hunting, and fishing, and possibly domestication of sheep and goat.[19] The archaeological evidence for these later LSA occupations has been found at Itaakpa cave in Iffe-Ijumu area of Kogi State,[20] Mèjírö rock shelter in Old Oyo,[21] Àyànbándélé rock shelter, 40 km from Ile-Ife,[22] and the coastal areas in Badagry/Porto-Novo area.[23]

The Archaic Period (500 B.C.–A.D. 500)

It is difficult to place the end of the Late Stone Age in Yoruba-Edo region at a specific date, but the transition from lithic to iron technology took place sometime between 500 B.C. and A.D. 500. This 1000–year period is referred to as the Archaic period because the rudiments of sociocultural structures that would in the later centuries became the indices of Yoruba-Edo societies were emerging at that time. Unlike the LSA period that persisted for at least 9000 years and provided a set of stable artifact and socioeconomic categories, the advent of iron technology marked the beginning of a rapid pace of cultural development and marked regional differences in West Africa as a whole. The earliest evidence for the adoption of iron technology has so far come from the northeast part of the region, in Iffe-Ijumu area.[24] The simultaneous occurrence of iron slag and tuyères (a clay pipe through which air is pumped into an iron-smelting furnace), and an iron arrowhead in the lower stratum of Oluwaju rock shelter indicates that both the use and manufacturing of iron tools started at about the same time in northeast Yorubaland.[25] Although the lower level of Oluwaju was dated to ca. A.D. 160, the proximity of Iffe-Ijumu to the southeastern edge of the Nok culture area, where the advent of iron production is dated to ca. 500–300 B.C., suggests that the technology was possibly adopted first in northern Yoruba-Edo region before the beginning of the first millennium A.D. through the interaction networks that connected different societies in central Nigeria with the Nok culture area.

The stylistic similarities in the ceramics of the upper LSA deposits and of the earliest iron-bearing levels have been identified as evidence of some cultural continuity during the technological transitions of the period between 500 B.C. and A.D. 500. These transitions not only witnessed the shift from stone technology to iron but there was also an overlap of the two technologies in Yoruba-Edo region.[26] The continuity of ceramic stylistic attributes is best demonstrated at Iffe-Ijumu, where we have not only continuous stratified sequences of occupation from the LSA deposits (> 300 B.C.) to the beginning of iron-using era (ca. A.D. 160) but also similar ceramic attributes in the two technological phases. The ceramic characteristics that show continuity are inverted rims, twisted cord roulette, multiple grooves, and incisions. Thus, it has been suggested, at the risk of equating pottery with people, that the same cultural group was responsible for the LSA and the metal-using traditions in Iffe-Ijumu area.[27] Moreover, there was no sharp break in the shift from stone to iron technology in the region. Although the production of iron is attested at Iffe-Ijumu during the second century A.D., ground stone axes and microlithic tools continued to be a major component of the agricultural tool kit until about A.D. 500.[28]

The archaic period was both a technological and a sociocultural transition period. It was remarkable not only for the adoption of iron technology but also for the complete shift in settlement pattern from rock shelter dwelling to open hamlet and village settlements. The preferred choice of open-area settlements during the archaic period is attested at both Iffe-Ijumu in the north and savanna belt and at Ile-Ife in the central and rainforest belt of the region.[29] In view of the wide gaps in the archaeology of the Archaic Period, only tentative inferences can be made at this point on the nature of social organization of the period. The general preferences shown for open-site settlements and the propensity for nucleated villages indicate a steady population increase, an increase in the head counts that constituted a family unit, and the development of formal genealogical structure. While dispersed homesteads (Houses or extended family groups) were possibly the dominant form of settlement organization, the formal aggregation of homesteads into village corporate groups were likely also taking place during the Archaic period both as a natural consequence of population increase by birth and the decrease in the contiguous farmland relative to the increase in family sizes, and as a result of the need for defense and cooperation against the forces of nature and human aggressions. Whereas the Houses served as the units of biological reproduction and economic/ food production, the villages were primarily the organization units for defense. Moreover, while corporate identity and mutual co-residence on a clearly defined tract of land would have been the basis for defining the membership of the emerging village units, the membership in the Houses and the homesteads were probably defined only on the basis of shared unilineal descent.

Although defense concerns facilitated the aggregation of Houses and the nucleation of settlements, the most important resource that would have been coveted during the period was not agricultural land but people, especially people with skills in iron technology. Access to sites with good iron ores would also have been very important. The impact of iron on demographic changes and on sociopolitical formations during this period is poorly understood in Yoruba-Edo region, but the myths, legends, and other genre of oral traditions often associate the origins of societies with the advent of iron technology. Although the superiority of iron tools and weapons over those made of stones should not be exaggerated, iron cutlasses, axes, and hoes are more efficient agricultural tools than stone axes and digging sticks in terms of productivity, and iron spears and arrows would have increased the efficiency in hunting and warfare over stone missiles, clubs, and arrowheads. The central role of iron in increased food production and better defense capability, the high skills needed for iron production, and the relative scarcity of iron tools would have created a high social valuation for iron products. We do not know whether iron became a form of social capital used as a means of having access to political power or as repositories of value and social payment as was the case in Equatorial Africa.[30] But the oral traditions in Yorubaland direct our attention to the importance of iron and the specialists with iron-using skills (especially, hunters) in the process of economic specializations and the making of compact village settlements at least for the purpose of defense and access to iron resources.[31]

The poor archaeological visibility of the Archaic material remains may account for the terse information that is currently available for the period. The investigations at Iffe-Ijumu however indicate that it would take a systematic research agenda to uncover the archaeological sequence of the 1000 years that straddle 500 B.C.–A.D. 500 in Yoruba-Edo region. A particular ecological and geological niche that is not yet explored for the Archaic sites in the region are the valleys that meander through the Yoruba hills in Ife-Ijesa-Ekiti area. Given the importance of water to the settlement location decisions of early agricultural cultures, the archaeological survey of these areas may be highly rewarding for uncovering the settlements and activity areas of the Archaic period.

The Early Formative Period (A.D. 500–800)

The Early Formative period (EFP) was marked by the proliferation of iron-using communities and the development of large compact villages as the common type of social organization in Yoruba-Edo region. These sociopolitical transformations were imprinted on the landscape by the prolific construction of embankments to demarcate settlements and land boundaries. These embankments, mostly low banks with ditches, have been documented mainly in the Esan and Benin areas where an intricate network of over 16,000 kilometers of banks and ditches enclosing a 4000 square kilometer area has been surveyed. It has been noted that these ditches and banks became deeper and larger as settlements grew in size and sociopolitical complexity. These earthworks provide a broad landscape perspective to understanding the history of social formation in the area.[32]

There are richer oral historical and archaeological information for the EFP than the archaic period but yet the archaeological data are terse and many of the gaps can be filled only by oral historical traditions. The general historical process of sociopolitical development during the EFP is best described in the rich oral traditions of Ile-Ife. At least 13 autonomous village polities are said to have developed in the area of Ile-Ife before A.D. 800.[33] These are Ìdó, Ìdèta Òkò, Iloran, Iloromu, Ìjùgbè, Imojubi, Ìráyè, Ìwìnrìn, Odun, Òkè Àwo, Òkè-Ojà, Omológun, and Parakin.[34] Each village-complex comprised of quarters or villages, or even hamlets (each forming a House). Ìjùgbè, for example, is said to have comprised of four major contiguous quarters or villages: Eranyiba, Igbogbe, Ipa, and Ita-Asin. Each quarter, headed by a titled priestly chief, had its own contiguous farmlands and all the quarter heads had to report to Obaléjùgbè, the Lord of Ijugbe. Similarly, the Ideta complex was made up of three settlement units: Ilale, Ilesun, and Ilia headed by Obalale, Obalesun, and Obalia respectively. The three heads were in turn under the political leadership of Obàtálá, the paramount ruler of Ideta.[35] Each village-complex was made up of smaller village units, and each of these village units was in turn an amalgamation of extended family units (Houses) that served as the unit of biological reproduction and economic/food production. But the House of the LFP was likely different from the House of the EFP. Whereas the later reckons genealogy in terms of biological relations, the former includes both biological and social relations in a way that the reckoning of family membership and relations became all-inclusive and fictive.[36] The sizes of the village and extended family units of LFP must have varied depending on their age, the charisma of the House head to attract and recruit membership, and the extent of the fortune in reproduction. It seems that sometime between A.D. 500 and 800, these village complexes began to aggregate into loose associations or confederacies with an administrative council made up of the heads of the complexes.[37] Although each council member seems to have had control over his/her village complex or political unit, the ideology for the unity of the council was based on the adoption of a common deity.[38]

The head of the council (possibly chosen by his/her peers) presided not only over the secular matters affecting the confederacy as a whole but also over the rituals and ceremonies associated with the worship of a common deity.[39] Oral traditions indicate that the constituent polities maintained a profound autonomy and that the nominal head of the confederacy only enjoyed a *primus inter pares* status. The Ile-Ife confederacy was therefore a loose political alliance short of political integration, with no central chieftaincy hierarchy, powerful royal dynasties, centralized governments, or urban capital. The development of dense, compact village polities in Ile-Ife area was paralleled by similar formations in Edo area. Among these polities were Efa, Ego, and Udo but it is not certain whether these polities formed a confederacy similar to that of Ile-Ife.[40] It is difficult to ascertain how widespread these multiple village confederacies were but we can only speculate at this point that prosperous village units with charismatic political leaders would have been more successful in attracting Houses or family units than the weaker villages. In such a situation where wholesale relocation and absorption of new Houses was a common phenomenon, the ever-shifting demography would have created the need to define a specific geographical space whose boundaries were clearly defined, in this case by ditches and ramparts). The rise and fall in the size of the population would have, however, subjected these boundaries to continuous adjustments. The prolific construction of embankments during the EFP should therefore be seen both as land demarcation strategy and as a mechanism for organizing common defense and security. The loose confederacy that developed from these village complexes in Ile-Ife was probably a strategy to mitigate the social stress and potential conflicts associated with population buildup in the area. But the confederacy was by itself a phenomenon of internal social transformation, an innovation in sociopolitical organization. The sociopolitical structure that developed during the Early Formative period has been the enduring framework for the organization of societies in Yoruba-Edo region.[41]

Historical ethnography indicates that the paraphernalia of political authority, such as crowns and shell beads, developed during the Early Formative period as a means of distinguishing the hierarchies of sociopolitical leaders and title-holders.[42] The symbol of authority for the confederacy chairman was the *Àdrè* crown and "Whoever had the *Àdrè* among the lineage heads . . . had the mandate to act as head of the confederacy."[43] Likewise, the advent of erecting commemorative stone monoliths, such as the Oranmiyan Staff and the Oke Mogun monoliths at Ile-Ife, was associated with this new sociopolitical formation. The "massiveness and figurative minimalism" of these monoliths testifies to the emerging transformations in the structure and iconography of worldview, religious worship, and sociopolitical relations.[44] The Oranmiyan staff, for example, is a 19–foot tall granite and almost its entire length is studded with spiral-headed iron nails in a fork-like arrangement. The labor and knowledge involved in the carving and the dressing of the granite with nails before raising the mono-lith to position is indicative of a complex ritual-religious knowledge backed by a consolidated sociopolitical formation. The granite/iron association during the EFP possibly laid the foundations for the elaborate ritualization of iron at the community level. The elaboration of the rituals and religious symbolism associated with iron would have derived from the importance of iron to the emerging sociopolitical communities, especially for agricul-tural production, and offensive and defensive warfare. The need to have access to sustainable food production and to win wars was crucial to ensur-ing population growth and strengthening the political base of the commu-nities. It is also possible that divination corpus developed during the EFP as indicated by the fork-like arrangement of the iron nails studded into the Oranmiyan stelae, a symbolic pattern whose meaning is now lost.[45]

Late Formative Period (A.D. 800–1000)

The Late Formative period (LFP) witnessed social transformations along the path of increased political centralization. It was a transition period be-tween village polities and village confederacies on one hand and a central-ized political system with an urban capital on the other. The period is syn-onymous with what has been identified as the Oduduwa era in Yorubaland and the Ogiso period in Edo area.[46] At Ile-Ife, where we have the best-preserved oral traditions, LFP was a period marked by factional conflicts between the loyalists of the confederacy and the harbingers of centralized political structure that sought to displace the power and influence of the confederacy potentates. The historical narratives of this sociopolitical ten-sion have received attention from a host of scholars.[47] Suffice it to state here that the Late Formative period witnessed the birth of a new political struc-ture centered around the personality of a king (Ooni or Oghene) who laid claim to supreme spiritual and political status among the political and reli-gious elite. This claim, or the attempt to make the claim, and the political actions that followed it led to intense sociopolitical turmoil, as the harbinger(s) of the new political structure attempted to destroy or weaken the independence, authorities, and powers of the Early Formative village-level potentates. Although these political actions are personified as a con-flict between Obatala and Oduduwa in the oral traditions, it is certain that the two personalities were factional representations of two different cultural ideals. The former was associated with the Early Formative and the later became the cornerstone of the Classical period. These factional groups represented different ideologies of political structures and social relations, and they seem to have engaged in moietal opposition throughout the 200 years of the Late Formative period.

A model proposed by Akin Mabogunje and Paul Richards invites us to see the factional disputes that shaped the sociopolitical transformations of the LFP and the advent of the Classical period as struggles between two economic interests.[48] According to this model, the Obatala group possibly represented the farming interests, peoples whose ideologies were related to the land and nature, whereas the Oduduwa group represented individuals who were preoccupied with commerce and foreign exotic goods. The latter, sometimes referred to as the foreigners, possibly had little investment in land just as the Obatala faction (represented as the autochthonous Igbo group in the oral traditions) had little or no investments in long-distance trade. The eruption of conflicts between the two groups would have emanated from both the economic potentials of Ile-Ife relative to long-distance trade, and from the need to have access to the political power that would ensure the control and regulation of the flow of export and import goods. The culmination of these struggles in the Classical period, a period marked by long-distance trade with the Middle Niger as shown below, seems to suggest the triumph of the merchant faction over the farming faction, at least in ideological and economic terms.

As the EF political structures were dismantled by the Oduduwa group, many settlements in Ile-Ife area were abandoned.[49] The displaced populations moved to the new settlement identified with the Oduduwa group while some moved further away from Ile-Ife area. The impact of the LF sociopolitical transformations in Ile-Ife on the surrounding areas of Yoruba-Edo region is not yet well understood. The annual rituals of origins in Ijesa and Ekiti areas, where the events associated with the foundations of towns and dynasties are often reenacted, indicate that some of the groups that moved away from Ile-Ife succeeded in establishing new settlements and polities or integrated into the preexisting ones in different parts of the Yoruba region. In the area of Ijesaland, for example, among the potentates and polities that likely developed as a result of these migrations out Ile-Ife are the Ita of Ilemure, Ajalorun Oro of Ilare, and Ologo of Ogo.[50] But much more important, the new enclave of power around Iremo area in Ile-Ife is said to have been the major recipient of the populations that were displaced from the village-polities.[51] By A.D. 1000, this area was on its way to becoming the nucleus of the first known urban center in Yoruba-Edo region.

Another significant development that took place during the LF era was the transformation in religious worship and ideology, with the accompanying emergence of minimalist figurative human sculptures. The Oramfe cult/deity that had held together the loose sociopolitical confederacy of the Early Formative polities in Ile-Ife ceased to be the nexus of political ideology and religious worship.[52] Rather, an elaborate and hierarchical ritual structure developed and the royal personality rather than the physical landscape became the focus of religious activities at the community level. Although natural phenomena such as hills and rivers continued to play important roles in religious worship, not only did royal rituals become the core of public participation but also the institutions of these rituals became a major source of patronage of arts and of religious and social values.

The use of stone as a medium of figurative representation of human personalities commenced during this period, especially in Ile-Ife and Ekiti areas.[53] This advent of minimalist humanism and realism in the artistic representation of the elite personalities during A.D. 800–1000 was likely related to the sociopolitical development of the LFP. The practice of making idealized sculptures, carved stones in this case, in honor of deceased political figures possibly began during the LFP. Obatala, the most prominent and the last of the rulers that derived their political mandate from the sociopolitical structures of the Early Formative period, is associated with these early trends of humanism in artistic representations and he personifies artistic creativity in the Yoruba worldview.[54] This association suggests that the artistic innovations of the LFP were derived in part from the structural contexts of the preceding EFP and in part from the factional conflicts that pervaded the LFP. In fact, the figurative human stone sculptures from Ile-Ife are associated in the oral traditions and religious worship with the political leaders that belonged to the Obatala factional group: Obatala, Oreluere, and Ijugbe. It seems that the emergence of humanism-realism in stone sculptures, especially in the rendition of the political figures of the Late Formative period, was an innovation that developed in the context of the shifts in political cleavages that narrowed the apparatus of decision-making to few personalities. The pervading conflicts of the period most likely accentuated the visibility of leaders with charismatic and strong personalities. The leadership skills and talents of these individuals, as administrators and warriors, earned them ascribed supernatural qualities that formerly applied to only the non-human entities such as Oramfe hill. These deified personalities therefore became the focus of religious worship and artistic representation.

Four human sculptures, two apiece from Ore grove in Ile-Ife and from a site near Esure (100 km northeast of Ile-Ife) are very illustrative of this early manifestation of figurative human sculptures in Yoruba-Edo region. We see in these stone sculptures the representation of paraphernalia of authority such as beaded necklace and anklets, and elaborately tied sash that dangles down from the hip. Moreover, just as nails were inserted into the phallic monoliths of the Early Formative period so are nails inserted into the heads of the human sculptures. The two stone sculptures from Ore grove in Ile-Ife, *Idena and Oreluere,* provide a very useful indication of the style of outfit of the eighth- to tenth-century period. Both figures "are bare-chested, wear heavy necklaces with globular beads, bracelets, and wrappers . . ."[55] Since no glass beads or copper/bronze metals have been identified in the pre-eleventh-century archaeological contexts of Yoruba-Edo region, the beads and bracelets of the Late Formative period were most likely made of stone, clay, bone, shell, and possibly of the silica iron slag. The use of these objects for ornamental purposes certainly extended into the much later periods as demonstrated at Ilare district and Isoya, where bone, clay, and shell beads have been recovered from the archaeological deposits of the thirteenth to nineteenth centuries.[56]

Classical Period (A.D. 1000–1400)

The political crisis and strivings of the Late Formative period at Ile-Ife gave way to political consolidation, stability, and material culture efflorescence during the eleventh century. The repertoire of complex material culture, technological innovations, and new political culture that serve as the hallmarks of the Classical period not only began at Ile-Ife but it was there that they were mostly elaborated. An urban capital with concentric embankments (possibly incorporating the pre-Classical ones), a royal dynasty, and an elaborate network of hierarchical political and ritual officials, are among the sociocultural markers of the Classical period. The archaeological indicators of this period include roads and courtyard houses paved with ceramic tiles (potsherds), glass beads, detailed naturalistic life-size terracotta and copper/bronze sculptures with idealized naturalism, and deposits of complex ceremonial and burial rituals.

The technological innovations that heralded the Classical period are most noticeable in the manufacture of glass beads and brass casting. These innovations began simultaneously with the emergence of a strong centralized political institution that revolved around the king (Ooni) and his large retinue of political and religious officials. The importance of beads as insignia and paraphernalia of elite, especially royal status, is illustrated in the prolific association of beads with naturalistic terracotta, stone, and brass sculptures of important personalities in Ife, Benin, and Esie during the Classical period. And, for the first time, the royal personalities and other political elite were represented in brass sculptures.

Beads as Badges of Political Office: Status, Social Formation, and Long-Distance Trade

The evidence that glass beads were manufactured at Ile-Ife in the early phase of the Classical period comes in form of fragments of crucibles whose interiors are often fused with glass in rich variety of blue, green, red, olive-brown, and turqouise colors. A substantial part of the activities associated with glass bead production took place at a site now known as Olokun grove, about two-and-a-half kilometers north of the center of Ile-Ife. Although the area is now a sacred and religious center dedicated to the worship of Olokun,[57] the grove is also an important archaeological site. The artifacts that have come from this site include glass-fused crucibles and furnaces, glass beads, glass droppings, pieces of iron-smelting tuyères, iron objects and slag, pottery, and terracotta and brass sculptures.[58] The remains at the site suggest that the grove was an extensive production center not only for beads but also for pottery, iron, and probably copper-alloy metals. A glass-smelting crucible containing beads was also found at Ita Yemoo site in the eleventh-to-thirteenth-century archaeological deposits, and the excavations at Woye Asiri and Obalara site (Ile-Ife) have led to the discovery of glass beads and bead crucibles dated to the thirteenth to fifteenth centuries.[59] The other evidence of bead manufacture that has been found at Ile-Ife consists of grooved or dimpled stones used for grinding and polishing stone beads, of which the most valuable are the red cylindrical jasper and carnelian beads.[60]

Although the production of glass beads was probably limited to Ile-Ife, there were two other centers for the making of the highly valued cylindrical red beads (*okùn*) of jasper and carnelian (red chalcedony) stones during the Classical period. The archaeological investigations at Oba-Isin (Oba) site have exposed evidence of stone bead manufacture in form of complete and fragments of stone beads and stone bead polishers.[61] The matrices where these cultural materials were found at Oba-Isin have been radiocarbon dated to the thirteenth century.[62] Archaeological, oral, and documentary evidence also demonstrates that Old Oyo was a center for the production of the red jasper/carnelian beads. Jasper beads and the stones used for grinding and polishing the beads into their characteristic cylindrical shapes been found in archaeological contexts at Old Oyo;[63] and it is likely that the industry was brought under the royal control in about the thirteenth century.[64] We are not sure whether jasper and carnelian stones were locally quarried at Old Oyo, but the recent history of bead production at Ilorin indicates that these crypto-crystalline silica were quarried close to River Niger.[65]

The proximity of Old Oyo to the natural deposits of red chalcedony and jasper rocks made it an ideal site for the red stone bead industry. It is likely that the demands for the jasper/chalcedony beads stimulated the earliest trading contacts between Ile-Ife and the village polities in the Old Oyo area and around the River Niger during the Late Formative and early Classical periods. The profits from this commercial traffic, due to its middleman position in the trading highway between the rainforest belt and the Middle Niger, were probably a prime factor in the political centralization of Old Oyo in the thirteenth century. The need for the political control of production and distribution of the red stone beads, whether at Ile-Ife, Old Oyo, or Oba Isin, emanated from the fact that these beads constituted one of the most important and rarest badges of high political office in Yoruba-Edo region during the Classical Period.[66] The burgeoning social complexity and kingdoms across the region during the period would have increased the need and the demands for these emblems of political authority. Although Ile-Ife seems to have had some initial success in controlling the regional distribution of these stone beads, especially to its rainforest belt neighbors, oral narratives and archaeological evidence indicate that Old Oyo became a prominent exporter of jasper/chalcedony beads and stones between the thirteenth and fifteenth centuries. The product formed a particularly important part of the royal trading exchanges between Old Oyo and Benin.[67] Nevertheless, Old Oyo, Benin, and other polities of the Classical period depended on Ile-Ife for the procurement glass beads, especially the blue dichroic beads, which, unlike the red jasper/chalcedony beads, were used, among other things, as markers of affluence.[68]

Terracotta, Stone, and Brass Sculptures

The media for sculptural arts expanded during the Classical period from stone to terracotta and brass. Terracotta was, however, the most popular medium of sculptural arts in Ile-Ife. The earliest evidence for the use of the lost wax technique for casting life-size brass masks and portrait-like heads of important personalities began in the eleventh or twelfth century at Ile-Ife. This technology also began in Benin during the fourteenth or fifteenth century. The oral traditions of Benin not only credit Ile-Ife as the source of this technology but a brass figurine rendered in the Classical Ife artistic style, and possibly originating from Ile-Ife, has also been found in Benin.[69] Unlike terracotta figures which depicted a broad range of themes: people of different social statuses and conditions (including ailments), animals, and objects (e.g., stools), brass figures were made of only the elite personalities. Moreover, although stone sculptures became more refined at Ile-Ife during the Classical period, it seems that they became more associated with non-human subjects such as stools. Outside Ile-Ife, however, stone sculptures in naturalistic human forms continue to be made, as is evident in Igbomina area, where soapstone human forms belonging to the same style have been found at Esie, Ofaro, Ipo, and Ijara.[70] The majority of these stone sculptures, about 800 in total, have been found in Esie. Although the archaeological contexts for these stone figures have not yet been defined, it has been speculated that they belonged to a cultural milieu whose foundations were laid independent of Ile-Ife between A. D. 800 and 1000.[71] In contrast, Adepegba, by comparing the surface decorative patterns on the Esie and Ife sculptures, has argued that the style of Esie sculptures derived from that of Ile-Ife during the middle of the Classical period.[72] The veracity of any of these different claims awaits archaeological investigations.

Courtyard Architecture, Ceramic Tiles, and Potsherd Pavements

In addition to technological changes in the elite material culture, there were also changes in the domestic and religious architectures from simple rectilinear to courtyard or impluvium structures during the Classical period. The most basic courtyard structure has a quadrangular layout with rooms that open onto a veranda and then to into a central atrium. While rectilineal structures possibly dated to the Early Formative period,[73] the multiple-courtyard houses proliferated during the Classical period as a result of the integration of disparate family units into residential structures with multifamily (extended family) apartments in an urban or township social space bounded by embankments and walls. The courtyard style architecture was replicated at different parts of the region as autonomous villages were displaced and their populations were integrated into the new townships that rapidly developed across the Yoruba-Edo area in the thirteenth century.

Tiles, in the form of ceramic disks, for decorating walls and columns, have been identified in the rubbles of elite houses and shrines/temples at Ile-Ife and Ilare district.[74] The tiles are circular sherds ground uniformly around the edges, usually less than 1 cm thick and 2.0–3.1 cm in diameter, and they are often decorated with carved basket-work and fine cord roulettes. These disks were "set in the surfaces of mud walls or other vertical features, especially columns, as a continuous 'mosaic' finish or in decorative patterns."[75] The use of these tiles seems to have continued until the middle of the twentieth century in different parts of Yoruba-Edo region.[76]

Like the terracotta and bronze sculptures, potsherd pavements formed part of the material ensembles of cultural efflorescence in the region between the eleventh and fifteenth centuries. Again, we have the most extensive occurrence of potsherd pavements at Ile-Ife, where not only courtyard floors but also roads were paved with potsherds arranged on their edges in herringbone pattern; it is likely that almost all roads within the city walls of Ile-Ife were paved with potsherds during the Classical period.[77] Given the intense labor involved in constructing potsherd pavements, it has been suggested that only an effective centralized political leadership would have made the mobilization of labor for public projects such as road construction and paving possible, a phenomenon attested to in the oral traditions at Ile-Ife.[78] All the calibrated radiocarbon dates associated with the potsherd pavement sites in Ile-Ife are in the range of the twelfth to the fifteenth centuries: Ita Yemoo, twelfth to fourteenth centuries; Odo-Ogbe, twelfth century; Woye Asiri, twelfth to fifteenth centuries; and Obalara site, fourteenth century.[79] Radiocarbon dates have also been obtained from charcoal samples that are associated with potsherd pavements at Old Oyo, Benin, and Itagunmodi (Ijesaland). Three successive levels of potsherd pavements at Old Oyo dated to the thirteenth to fourteenth centuries.[80] At the Museum site in Benin, a charcoal sample above one of the pavement rubbles yielded a calibrated date of the fourteenth century.[81] Similarly, at Itagunmodi, a settlement 15 km northeast of Ile-Ife, a charred palm kernel seed associated with potsherd pavement has been dated to the fourteenth century.[82]

While the aesthetic and utilitarian use of potsherds for paving house floors and roads has a broad geographical and temporal distribution in Africa,[83] potsherd pavements have also been found in specific ritual and religious contexts in Yoruba-Edo region. In these religious contexts, potsherd pavements were documented to be associated with buried jars and flasks. The evidence at Ile-Ife, Ila-Orangun, and Ilare district indicates that the pots may have been buried either in an upright or capsized position, usually with the bases of the pots removed before burial. The lips of the pots are often at the same level as the pavement surface, with the ceramic tiles radiating from the buried pots.[84] These open-ended pots and pot-necks served as altars and receptacles within the potsherd pavement matrices for libations and other sacrificial activities. The buried pots served as metaphorical and symbolic "routes" connecting the Yoruba earthly world with the underworld where, according to the Yoruba worldview, all the ancestors and deities—the receptors of the sacrifices—reside. The excavations of architectural features in Ile-Ife, Benin, and Ilare district indicate that beginning from the Classical period, these altars formed an intrinsic part of domestic structures.[85] The rooms and the courtyards that were utilized as altars in these structures were often paved with potsherd pavements, and the foci of sacrifices, offerings, and libations were marked with a solid earth erection or with a buried pot with broken base.

Ile-Ife and the Birth of the Yoruba-Edo "World" System

The sociopolitical transformations in Ile-Ife, especially the upsetting of the dynamic equilibrium of village polities and their culmination in the advent of the Classical period, triggered chain reactions that had far-reaching implications for Yoruba-Edo region as a whole. But these impacts were slow to take shape for it was not until the thirteenth century that the sociopolitical and material culture innovations associated with the Classical period spread across Yoruba-Edo region in rapid successions. For example, historical and archaeological evidence shows that the thirteenth century marked a region-wide replacement of autonomous small-scale village polities by new dynasties and political structures. The iconography of political authority, the structure of kingship institution, the ideology of social relations, and the layout of the new townships that appeared in the region during the thirteenth century all point to Ile-Ife as the source of inspiration (Table 4.2). Population movements and intersocietal networks through elite social exchanges, economic relations, and cultural imitations played important roles in the structural reproduction of the sociopolitical, ideological, and material components of the innovations at the regional level between the thirteenth and fourteenth centuries. The adoption and adaptation of the Ife-centered innovations indicate the attempt by the former village polities in the region to increase their efficiency.

Ceramic stylistic attributes are so far the most ubiquitous class of archaeological artifacts that illustrate the fact that there was a mass adoption of Ife's cultural innovations at regional level beginning from the thirteenth century.[86] The emergence of homologous ceramic iconic-stylistic elements along the Ife-Benin corridor during the thirteenth century indicates the existence of a regional cultural and interacting system that linked central and eastern Yorubaland with the Edo areas. In other words, the expansion of the Ife ceramic sphere to Ilare, Owo, and Benin in the thir-

Table 4.2: Distribution of Radiocarbon Dates at Sites Mentioned in the Text*

Place/Site, C14 Dates, & Lab. #	2-sigma Calibration (Age range)	Cal. Average Age	Cultural Period
University Agricultural Site, Ile-Ife (Eyo 1974a)			Archaic (500 B.C.–A.D. 500)
2360+/-120 YBP (N-346)	798–125 B.C.	400 B.C.	
Itaakpa, Iffe-Ijumu (Oyelaran 1998)			
2210 ± 80 (Oxa-1150)	403–45 B.C.	352–210 B.C.	
Oluwaju, Iffe-Ijumu, (Oyelaran 1998)			
1840 ± 125	95 B.C.–A.D. 434	A.D. 134–209	
Orun Oba Ado, Ile-Ife (Willett 1973)			Early Formative (AD500–800)
1390±150 YBP (BM 265)	A.D. 360–979	656	
Addo, Iffe-Ijumu, (Oyelaran 1998)			
1110 ± 80	A.D. 694–1148	902–962	
Orun Oba Ado, Ile-Ife (Willett 1973)			Late Formative (A.D. 800–1000)
1150±120 YBP (BM 2114)	A.D. 656–1158	892	
Site 00/1, Old Oyo (Agbaje-Williams 1983)			
1185±90 YBP (I. 12345), 1160±90 YBP (I. 12353)	A.D. 660–1021, A.D. 665–1025	780–880, 890	
Orun Oba Ado, Ile-Ife (Willett 1973)			Classical (A.D. 1000–1400)
1010±150 YBP (BM 2116), 960±130 YBP (BM 264)	A.D. 686–1287, A.D. 779–1291	1020, 1034	
Ita Yemoo, Ile-Ife (Willett 1973)			
1100±120 YBP (M2121), 990±130 YBP (BM 261)	A.D. 665–1209, A.D. 734–1283	904–976, 1023	
800±200 YBP (M 2119), 790±130 YBP (M 259)	A.D. 782–1469, A.D. 997–1413	1256, 1259	

Table 4.2: *(continued)*

Place/Site, C14 Dates, & Lab. #	2–sigma Calibration (Age range)	Cal. Average Age	Cultural Period
Woye Asiri, Ile-Ife (Garlake 1977)			
1165±75 A.D. (N 1688), 1135±85 A.D. (N 1687)	A.D. 1040–1382, A.D. 1023–1379	1260, 1220	
1280±75 A.D. (N 1685), 1405±85 A.D. (N 1689)	A.D. 1219–1415, A.D. 1284–1482	1300, 1410	
Obalara, Ile-Ife (Garlake 1974)			
1190±85 A.D. (N. 1392), 1325±75 A.D. (N1393)	A.D. 1044–1395, A.D. 1266–1431	1270, 1310–1380	
1370±60 A.D. (N 1391)	A.D. 1287–1435	1400	
Odo Ogbe, Ile-Ife (Eyo 1974b)			
855±95 YBP (I.4670),	A.D. 998–1299	1190–1210	
Clerks' Quarters, Benin (Connah 1975)			
1180±105 A.D. (N. 377), 1230±105 A.D. (N. 376)	A.D. 1023–1402, cal A.D. 1041–1420	1270, 1290	
1385±100 A.D. (I. 3622), 1310±90 A.D. (I. 2722)	A.D. 1268–1487, A.D. 1219–1438	1400, 1300–1380	
Ogba site, Benin, (Connah 1975)			
1340±105 A.D. (N. 379)	A.D. 1219–1455	1320–1390	
Museum Site, Benin, (Connah 1975)			
1305±105 A.D. (N. 378)	A.D. 1277–1408	1300–1380	
Site 00/1, Old Oyo (Agbaje-Williams 1983)			
900±80YBP (I. 12343), 810±80 YBP (I. 12343)	A.D. 989–1281, A.D. 1027–1379	1160, 1220–1240	
Site 0075/3A, Old Oyo (Soper 1977)			
855±110 YBP	A.D. 982–1384	1200–1210	
Site 0074/IGV (Soper 1977)			
655±80 YBP	A.D. 1222–1429	1300–1380	

Table 4.2: *(continued)*

Place/Site, C14 Dates, & Lab. #	2-sigma Calibration (Age range)	Cal. Average Age	Cultural Period
Site 1, Iloyi, Ilare district (Ogundiran 2000a)			
715 ± 145 YBP (GX-24000), 730 ± 155 (GX-23998)	A.D. 1021–1447, A.D. 998–1448	1290, 1280	**Intermediate** (AD 1400–1600)
Olupefon, Igbomina (Usman 2000)			
510 ± 80 YBP (Beta-88413)	A.D. 1293–1615	1422	
Gbagede Ib, Igbomina (Usman 2000)			
320 ± 60 YBP (Beta-88414)	A.D. 1441–1667	1525–1629	
Apateki, Igbomina (Usman 2000)			
(50 ± 60 YBP (Beta-88411)	A.D. 1433–1658	1507–1615	
Site 1, Iloyi, Ilare district (Ogundiran 2000a)			
485 ± 65 (GX-23999)	A.D. 1326–1620	1430	
Igbo 'Laja, Owo (Eyo 1976)			
515 90 YBP	A.D. 1291–1625	1420	
Odo Ogbe, Ile-Ife (Eyo 1974b)			
320±95 YBP (I.4669)	A.D. 1420–1948	1530–1630	
Ita Yemoo, Ile-Ife (Willett 1973)			
480±100 YBP (M 2117)	A.D. 1295–1642	1434	
Obalara, Ile-Ife (Garlake 1974)			
1470±95 AD (N 1390)	A.D. 1292–1638	1430	
Clerks' Quarters, Benin (Connah 1975)			
1490±90 AD (I. 2723)	A.D. 1301–1641	1440	

Table 4.2: *(continued)*

Place/Site, C14 Dates, & Lab. #	2–sigma Calibration (Age range)	Cal. Average Age	Cultural Period
Usama Site, Benin, (Connah 1975) 1500±105 AD (N. 380)	A.D. 1298–1654	1440	
Igbo 'Laja, Owo (Eyo 1976) 195 90 YBP	A.D. 1482–1955	1670–1800	**Atlantic** (A.D. 1600–1800)
Sekunde, Ife Area (Eluyemi 1976) 240±120 YBP; 150±75 YBP	A.D. 1433–1955, A.D. 1660–1951	1670, 1680–1950	
Obaloyan II, Igbomina (Usman 2000) 290 ± 60 YBP (Beta-88415)	A.D. 1454–1946	1640	
Ofaro I, Igbomina (Usman 2000) 220 ± 70 YBP (Beta-88412)	A.D. 1491–1951	1661	

*All the radiocarbon dates are calibrated using CALIB software (Stuiver and Reimer 1993) and based on the 2–sigma standard error limits rather than 1–sigma. In the later, the chances are 1 in 3 that a given measurement will not straddle the true age value of the samples, whereas the chance of missing the true date with 2–sigma is reduced to 1 in 20 (McIntosh and McIntosh 1986: 416). The calibrated average age represents the closest date of the C14 age and it is calculated from the intercepts of the radiocarbon age and standard deviation. It should be noted that the dating of sites to the Atlantic period is mostly achieved by cross-dating of imported object such as cowry shells, smoking pipes, and other European imports.

teenth century is an evidence of the regional acculturation to the material and cultural forms of the established polity with the longest history of sociopolitical complexity. The Ife ceramic sphere along the Ife-Ijesa-Owo-Benin corridor can therefore be viewed as a material correlate of an interacting system in which different subgroups and areas in central and eastern Yoruba-Edo region had access to a coherent system of "ideological structures that established and organized their place in the social world."[87] In contrast to the ceramic homologies in the Ife-Benin corridor, however, a different ensemble of diagnostic elements characterized the ceramic assemblages in the northern areas of Yoruba-Edo region, especially Old Oyo, Igbomina, and Okun areas.[88] Although Old Oyo adopted some of the iconographic symbols and ideological elements of Ife kingship institution during the second half of the Classical Period, Old Oyo and other parts of northern Yorubaland were not incorporated into the ceramic sphere.

As social relationships became more complex and codified in the ideology of kingship institution as the mainpost of social relations, structure, and worldview, the ensemble of artifacts needed to support and advance those relationships became more diversified. The iconographic elaboration, artistic versatility, and material culture diversification that heralded the Classical Period were as much instruments of political strategies used to create a new vision of the world as they were manifestations of economic prosperity and cultural efflorescence in Ile-Ife. More than anything else, the proliferation, expansion, and monopoly of brass and glass bead industries transformed Ile-Ife into prominence as an industrial and commercial center. The current evidence indicates that Ile-Ife monopolized glass bead production and converted glass beads into objects of social value just as it did for the red jasper/chalcedony beads during the ninth to eleventh centuries. The production of stone beads was however carried out at other centers by the thirteenth century, and Ile-Ife was not the only polity in Yoruba-Edo region with economic ties to the Niger Valley termini of the Saharan trade routes, from where it obtained the materials crucial to its royal art industries—glass and copper products. Economic factors cannot therefore be invoked as the primary basis for the regional prominence of Ile-Ife during the Classical period.[89] Rather, the emergence of Ile-Ife as the regional political and cultural center derived from the ideologies, knowledge, and information that the beads, copper-alloy/terracotta sculptures, and the iconic signs embodied. The materialization of the new ideas, philosophies, and structures in the form of jasper/chalcedony beads, glass beads, brass sculptures and jewelry, and terracotta sculptures was crucial to the development of Ile-Ife as the primary center of Yoruba-Edo region. This process of materialization involves the following:

> The transformation of ideas, values, stories, myths, and the like into physical reality . . . can take the form of ceremonial events, symbolic objects, monuments, and writing. It is the process by which culture is created, codified, and contained. Ideas and objects unite and are inseparable; ideas, unconnected to the objects of worlds, have no means of being communicated, experienced, used, and owned. Ideas must be materialized to become social, to become cultural things. Our ideas are private and powerful for ourselves, but their materialization brings them into the public arena.[90]

The social and ideological valuation of the objects of long-distance trade, in the form of converting them to objects that have relevance to sociopolitical formation and the maintenance of power, therefore seems to have transformed copper and beads into the material basis for validating Ile-Ife as the metropole of Yoruba-Edo region during the Classical period. As the most prolific center for the production of the paraphernalia and symbols that served as the identity tokens for kingship and elite personalities in the region, many harbingers of dynastic institutions in the region visited and allied with Ile-Ife to establish and validate their political power. By the twelfth or thirteenth century, Ile-Ife had become a major center for the "sale" or distribution of beads, beaded regalia, brass sculpture, and the skills associated with the technical production and the religious and ritual functions of these commodities to the other Yoruba-Edo polities. Thus, in Benin as well as in Ijebu-Ode and Obo-Aiyegunle (northern Ekiti), oral historical traditions indicate that the knowledge of brass casting was introduced from Ile-Ife by the fourteenth or fifteenth century.[91]

The universal cosmology espoused by the politico-religious institutions at Ile-Ife, through the elaboration of ideas of kingship and the complexity of religion, rituals, and worldview, made it the center of the Yoruba-Edo world system and a magnet for the populations of the surrounding region. As a professed guarantor of order, through its complex and elaborate politico-religious system (including divination system) and military prowess, Ile-Ife was involved as an arbiter in the factional conflicts of its neighbors. It is within this context that we should, for example, assess the historical claims that Ile-Ife played the role of an arbiter in the factional conflict that bedeviled Benin area from about the tenth to the twelfth century.[92] The invitation or the intrusion of Ile-Ife into the local politics of Benin, and its impact on restoring order to the troubled area by the twelfth or early thirteenth century derived from the universal claim (mythical origins) of Ife's cult and ideology of power and material innovations. All these factors favored Ile-Ife to serve as the court of appeals when the local cults and factional leaders of Ogiso, for example, could not satisfy their adherents and followers. One would expect that Ile-Ife played a similar role in other parts of Yorubaland. The *primus inter pares* position of Ile-Ife during the Classical Period was not only a testimony to the political and economic differentiation of Yoruba-Edo region but also the establishment of an ideological system that pulled a diverse body of separate localities and autonomous polities under a single cultural system. Through networks maintained by the ties of ritual interdependency, elite goods transactions, "trade, tribute, patronage, clientship, and migration," Ile-Ife succeeded in integrating diversified political process into an unequal economic exchange.[93]

The political centralization, material culture elaboration, and high artistic highmarks associated with the Classical period took place in a milieu of economic and political networks that were tied to the trans-Saharan commerce via the Middle Niger. There is direct evidence that the glass beads and the copper products, crucial to the political economy of power in Ile-Ife, were imported from across the Sahara, via the Middle Niger.[94] Chemical analyses have ascertained that the glass beads excavated at Ile-Ife sites are of two chemical groups: potassium and sodium. The potassium glass beads, also high in calcium, are generally comparable to the medieval European glass; and the sodium glass beads are characteristic of the medieval Islamic glass. On the basis of this evidence, Frank Willett affirms that glass and glass beads of both medieval European and Islamic sources reached Ile-Ife through the termini of the trans-Saharan trade on the Middle Niger between the eleventh and fifteenth centuries.[95] Indeed, the most common of the glass beads found in Ile-Ife, the blue dichroic beads, usually "blue in reflected light and green in transmitted light,"[96] have been found at other areas: Ilare district, Old Oyo, Gao, Koumbi Saleh, and Tedaghoust all from contexts that date to between the eleventh and fifteenth centuries.[97]

Although the Middle Niger had emerged as an entrepot of the Western Sudanese and the trans-Saharan commerce during the second half of the first millennium A.D., the increased demands across the Sahara for gold and kola intensified the Middle Niger's lucrative commercial status throughout the first half of the second millennium, corresponding to the Yoruba-Edo Classical period. The role of the Middle Niger as the link between the peoples and polities of the rainforest belt and the Mediterranean-Arab world was particularly important to the expansion of the long-distance trade networks in the subcontinent between the eleventh and thirteenth centuries.[98] Although Ile-Ife seems to have been drawn, at least indirectly, to the area of River Niger by the Early Formative period, especially for the red carnelian/jasper stone beads, it was not until about 1000–1100 that Ile-Ife began to tap into the material resources of the Middle Niger. How much role this pull of the northern trade played in the sociopolitical transformations at Ile-Ife during the Late Formative and Early Classical periods is difficult to assess at this point. In other words, we are not sure whether the extension of the Middle Niger trade to the rainforest acted as a catalyst for sociopolitical changes in Yoruba-Edo region. But one would be on a firmer ground to suggest that the political centralization that took place in the region, especially at Ile-Ife during the Late Formative period stimulated the need for elaboration in the elite material culture. This development created the push to acquire prestige goods, and it led to the establishment of economic relations with the peoples of the Middle Niger by the eleventh-twelfth century. The sociopolitical innovations and the regional long-distance trade expansions therefore coincided in ways that allowed the new elite at Ile-Ife to convert the prestige, foreign, and exotic goods into political capital. To conclude this section, the Classical Period can be subdivided into two phases. The first lasted between 1000 and 1200, and was mainly defined by the development at Ile-Ife. The second phase, from 1200 to 1400, attests to the region-wide adoption of sociopolitical innovations of Ile-Ife as township settlements, kingship institutions, and ideologies of social relations based on the model at Ile-Ife proliferated during the thirteenth century. The artifacts and iconographies that were formerly used in the years between about 1000 and 1200 to represent these new institutions at Ile-Ife now became central to the continuation of the social relations, structures, and new visions of the world that rapidly gained currency throughout the region between 1200 and 1400.

Intermediate Period (ca. 1400–1600)

The Intermediate period was a transitional period between the waning of Ile-Ife's political influence as the center of the Yoruba-Edo regional system and the time when the region became involved in Atlantic commerce, with new ideologies of political organization and control. The period witnessed an increase in the number of sociopolitical formations and economic centers at the regional level, an intense spirit of political centralization, emergence of hegemonic ambitions, diffuse regional interaction networks, and ideological innovations. All these developments were to some extent stimulated by a general population increase in the region, and by population movements made more intense by the process of frontier migrations due to factional competitions and conflicts.[99] As the new polities grew in number and some in size, peer polity competitions intensified, and the old cleavages of regional hierarchies began to give way to new configurations. It has been observed that the fifteenth century was the period when the foundations for hegemonic states of Old Oyo and Benin were laid, and therefore the century when the peer-polity and *primus inter pares* ideologies began to be challenged, eroded, and replaced by military expansion and hegemonic domination. The Intermediate period heralded increased militarization and hegemonic-type political entities that were different in style and structure from the patrimonial sociopolitical networks that Ile-Ife developed during the Classical period. Around the two major hegemonic polities that emerged during this period—Old Oyo and Benin—a plethora of smaller polities developed in a matrix of intensified factional warfare as peer-polities jockeyed for superior positions.[100]

Transatlantic commerce in the Bight of Benin, begun in the late fifteenth century, was by the early sixteenth century replacing the trans-Saharan trade termini in the Niger bend as the focus of regional long-distance trade networks. The changes in the topography of trade networks created new routes, market centers, and new forms of sociopolitical alignments that culminated in drastic changes in the configuration of regional political power as new polities, dynasties, and political entrepreneurs emerged after the systematic destruction or weakening of olderones. It was within this transitional context of new opportunities that strong economic relations developed between Old Oyo and Benin in the fifteenth century, with adverse effects on the economic base of Ile-Ife. Gaining from its location at the intersection of the Middle Niger trans-Saharan trade termini and Yoruba-Edo region, and its sociopolitical consolidation between the thirteenth and fifteenth centuries, Old Oyo was by the early sixteenth century on its way to becoming a formidable economic, cultural, and political center.[101] Likewise, the ambitions for the political expansion of Benin were well underway by the mid-fifteenth century under its militarily inclined ruler, Ewuare.[102] As the economy of Ile-Ife depended on a punctuated distribution of resources and on external demands for its locally produced preciosities, the shifts in the regional reliance on Ife products and the establishment of direct access by other polities to the Middle Niger trade entrepot, as demonstrated by the Old Oyo/Benin trading relations, played a major role in weakening the economic and political position of Ile-Ife in the region. The Intermediate period therefore heralded Old Oyo and Benin as pacesetters for the political and cultural transformations in the region.

Archaeological evidence shows that the bead and brass industries at Ile-Ife became less prolific and naturalistic sculptures became rare at the onset of the sixteenth century.[103] However, as the courtly splendor and royal art of Ile-Ife were waning, those of Benin were increasing in the fifteenth and sixteenth centuries. It was in Benin royal art that we see the themes of warfare and courtly splendor intertwined for the first time in the region. The iconography of warfare depicted on Benin bronze plaques included warriors in military gear and a wide range of weapons, "javelins, spears, rapiers, bows, and poisoned arrows. . . ."[104] Beginning in the sixteenth century, sword and spear also became important iconographic symbols of power and authority in Ijesa and Owo, a reflection of the increased militarization as hegemonic control became an integral part of sociopolitical formation and a common means of political control.[105] In fact the proliferation of these weapons in the arts of Benin indicates that part of the cultural transformations of the Intermediate period were innovations in weaponry and, possibly, the techniques of warfare. It should also be noted that during this period equestrian images, usually associated with iron weaponry, also became incorporated into the iconography of Benin and Old Oyo art as a symbol of military power and domination. Although military conquest played some role in the establishment of the Classical polities, it was in the Intermediate period that military attacks and conquests were organized on large scales for the sole purpose of economic subjugation. Hence, the meaning of warfare seems to have expanded to include political and territorial expansion, and economic predation of the subjugated polities. The prolific rendition of military conquests on the commemorative plaques has prompted a scholar of Benin history to suggest that "military conquest was one of the pillars of Benin's prosperity" in the fifteenth and sixteenth century.[106] Following Benin's conquests of several sociopolitical units along the coast as far as Lagos and Mahin, and its forays into the eastern Yoruba region, Benin became a major metropolis in Yoruba-Edo region.

The second half of the Intermediate period marked the beginning of Atlantic commerce in Yoruba-Edo region, but the commercial relationship with the Portuguese was limited to Benin. This southward shift in the focus of long-distance trade began to bring the riverine and coastal areas that had operated at the periphery of the socioeconomic networks during the Classical period into prominent positions during the fifteenth century. The trade opportunities with the Europeans on the coast stimulated a rapid trend of population buildup in the area, and it is therefore not surprising that many traditions of origins of the dynasties and settlements of the present-day coastal area can be dated with some accuracy to the late fifteenth or sixteenth century. Harbingers of the Atlantic trade, the Portuguese first established cultural and diplomatic relationships with Benin, a position that Benin monopolized for the most part of the sixteenth century. From this time onwards, the images of the Portuguese as "the bearer of wealth and supporters of the king" became prolific in the royal commemorative bronze plaques. The importance of the Atlantic Ocean as the abode of wealth also began to be represented in the arts of Benin during the Intermediate period. Hence, not only did the iconographies associated with the Oba (king) of Benin include the European material culture, but the imagery of the Atlantic Ocean also became part of the royal representation. For example, the Maltese cross was incorporated into the elite material culture, and the royal robes were adapted from the Catholic Priest vestment during the sixteenth century. Likewise, the king began to be represented "as a fish-legged figure . . . in a dompting pose," which Paula Ben-Amos considered "as a cosmological image symbolizing the correspondence between the Oba of Benin, ruler over the dry land, and the deity of Olokun, king of the great waters."[107]

One of the most important historical motifs of the Intermediate period was the political pressure imposed on the eastern wing of Yoruba-Edo region by the hegemonic ambitions of Benin and the autocratic rule of its monarchs during the sixteenth century. These two related political developments stimulated emigration from Benin, a process that had far-reaching regional impacts in terms of intensive population movements and demographic reshuffling. New alliances and new sociopolitical formations, and new cleavages of power developed as migrants from Benin area settled in new communities, especially in Owan, Esan, and Akoko-Edo areas.[108] The other historical motifs that the Intermediate period represents were economic decline at Ile-Ife, the north-to-south shift in the direction of long-distance trade, hegemonic political system and increased militarism, and the advent of the Atlantic commerce.

Atlantic Period (1600–1800)

Most parts of the region lived in the shadows of Benin and Old Oyo hegemony from 1600 to 1800 in a milieu of economic transactions that were tied to the Atlantic trade. The Atlantic period witnessed the region's entry into a European-dominated world capitalist economy. Although the societies were not transformed into capitalist economies, the organization of economic production and socioeconomic relations were drastically impacted.

The Benin and Old Oyo hegemonies and the Atlantic socioeconomic conditions shaped the cultural transformations and the trends in material consumption in the region. The consolidation of new inland market and production centers under hegemonic political control and the strengthening of the powers of the new political and economic entrepreneurs, polities, and dynasties took place across the region. As trade routes and market centers proliferated, the major concern among the polities of the period was to expand and protect their core and periphery boundaries. The period witnessed the region-wide emulation of Benin's elite subculture, especially the style and forms of its royal and ritual material culture. This is best evident in eastern and southern Yoruba country, especially in Ijebu-Ode, Ode-Itsekiri, Ondo, Owo, and Eko (Lagos) as well as in Urhobo, Isoko, and Esan in the Edoid region, where the regalia of the kings and chiefs were adapted from those of Benin.[109] The excavations at Igbo'laja, a site dedicated to royal ritual in Owo, have shown the convergence of the naturalist Classical Ife art styles and the idealized styles and iconography of Benin court art during the seventeenth century.[110] Even polities that were outside the ambit of Benin's political control, such as Ilesa and Ila-Orangun, sought to forge an alliance with the new center of political power, economic wealth, and military prowess in the region.[111]

Almost all the archaeological deposits dating to this period bear the material imprints of the Atlantic trade. The three most common material indices of this period are cowry shells (especially moneta species); clay pipes of both local manufacture and European imports; and imported iron objects. The occurrence of these artifacts in the archaeological deposits of Yoruba-Edo region during the seventeenth and eighteenth centuries is a testimony to the integration of the region into the Atlantic commerce. Iron tools became a major part of the English and Dutch imports to Yoruba-Edo region in the seventeenth century.[112] The archaeological evidence that these iron imports were traded as far as 150 km inland was recently found in Ilare district, where imported iron-boring tool and pivots were present in a 1600–1750 context.[113] There is also documentary evidence that African blacksmiths were employed by the Europeans on the coast in the early seventeenth century to recut imported iron bars to smaller lengths for the purpose of local trade.[114] The iron imports, especially the Dutch iron bars, fed the local blacksmithing industries and soon became the main source of domestic agricultural tools and of weaponry. These imported iron bars provided a cheaper and alternative source of iron in relation to local iron-working industries and led to the expansion of accessibility to iron products in the region. The impact of imported iron products on the demise of local iron production in West Africa has been noted by a number of scholars,[115] but the impact on the local agricultural production, craft specialization, and warfare has hardly been studied. The proliferation of iron-tool types during the Atlantic period no doubt expanded the repertoire of meanings and knowledge associated with the object and its patron-deity, Ogun.[116] There has been a lack of systematic study of the political economy of iron production during the Atlantic period. Such a study would be important to understanding the ways in which the development of Ogun-iron-war complex was related to the organized military-warfare-hegemonic culture of the Atlantic period as permanent military career, preoccupation with the construction of defense structures, and hegemonic expansion became the norms of the societies. In fact, the equestrian imagery that first appeared in Benin as the symbol of domination became prevalent in the rainforest belt, especially in Ijesaland and Owo, polities whose military power was less dependent on cavalry.

It was also during the Atlantic period that cowries became the currency unit for commercial transactions in Yoruba-Edo region. Of all the transatlantic imports into West Africa, cowry was the most common and the one known best to the vast majority of the Yoruba-Edo people during the Atlantic period. The adoption of cowries as the unit for price measurement and for the conduct of economic transactions stimulated standardized and more formalized conditions for production and exchange systems. Although cowries were known to Yoruba-Edo region during the Classical period, possibly obtained through the trans-Saharan trade, their distribution was limited, and they functioned primarily in the contexts of aesthetics, ritual signification, and royal/political iconography. The first shipment of cowry imports to the Bight of Benin arrived from Lisbon in 1515. The importation was certainly based on the knowledge gained during the earlier trips by the Portuguese that there was a market for cowry in Benin area.[117] The advent of the Atlantic trade created for the first time a dependable source for the supply of cowries. Partly for its long-distance origins, steady supplies, accessibility, and its Classical sociocultural attributes as an object of intrinsic ornamental and ritual value, cowry rapidly became in the seventeenth century a socioeconomic currency and index of wealth that symbolizes value in both social meaning and economic exchange.[118] Prior to the importation of cowry shells via the transatlantic commerce, the red stone beads and the red and blue glass beads were the ultimate material manifestations of royalty, wealth, and status. The conversion of cowry from aesthetic objects and curios to currency during the Atlantic period seems to be an adaptation from the commoditization of glass and stone beads as means of indexing "social wealth" and status. It has been argued that the cultural contexts in which cowries were used and the meanings imposed on those contexts and objects best illustrate the Yoruba cultural translation of their Atlantic experience; that is, the way the Yoruba sought to understand their world in relation to the Atlantic economy.[119]

The elaborate cultural repertoire of wealth accumulation, storage, distribution, and credit that developed as a result of the institutionalization of cowries as the unit of currency and economic exchange led to major changes in interpersonal and social relationships, and in ideological definitions of commerce and political mobilization. These changes even led to the creation of new deities, redefinition of the old ones, and restructuring of the pantheons in order to accommodate the new economic conditions within the parameters of the Yoruba-Edo cosmology. Aje, Olokun, Obatala, and Esu were among the deities that were redefined as patrons of commerce, wealth, profit, and market, and they were accorded new meanings within the contexts of the transatlantic trade and wealth.[120] The ocean, *òkun,* began to feature more prominently in the Yoruba-Edo cosmology of trade and wealth because of its role as the immediate source of the wealth and riches of the Atlantic Period—cowries. The period also witnessed the incorporation of *òkun* into the names of a number of the potentates that became prominent after the fifteenth century. Three of such names are:

(1) Obalokun ("the king of the ocean"): the king of the city-state of Old Oyo reputed to have established trading relations with the Europeans on the coast.[121]
(2) Obokun ("the one who fetches the ocean water"): political-military hero who laid the foundation for the Obokun dynasty in Ijesaland, ca. late sixteenth century.
(3) Atakunmosa ("the one who knows the ocean and the lagoon"): second king of the Ilesa city-state, ca. seventeenth century; he established diplomatic mission with Benin and spearheaded the hegemonic expansion of Ilesa.

The centrality of women to the Atlantic economy and the immense profits that accrued to them from their domination of the hinterland production and commercial networks that supported the coastal trade explain why all the deities associated with the Atlantic commerce in Yorubaland are of female identity.[122] Although the slave trade component of the Atlantic trade in West and Central Africa as a whole was a catastrophic human tragedy, the Atlantic economy also stimulated expansion in the manufacturing and agricultural sectors, especially in cotton cultivation, cloth weaving, and dye manufacture in the Yoruba-Edo hinterlands. These new productions were dominated by women, and the wealth accrued by them became an important weapon in challenging the dominant patriarchal ideologies that began to develop during the Intermediate period as a result of the hegemonic orientation of political organization and the intense militarization of the polities. Onaiwu Ogbomo has drawn attention to the fact that the economic wealth enjoyed by women during the seventeenth and eighteenth centuries in northern Benin areas revived women's hopes for greater equality.[123] Gender struggles were therefore energized by the Atlantic economy much more so because of the erosion in the social standing of women following the institutionalization of male-dominated ideologies at the onset of the Intermediate period. In this regard, the revival of an elaborate queen mother political office and the support given to her cult in the kingdom during the eighteenth century was possibly an effort by the Benin monarchy to win female support, a reflection of the important economic status of women as producers of one of the key exports of the kingdom—cloth—and as facilitators of commerce.[124]

No doubt, the trade opportunities that the Atlantic commerce brought expanded the local trade networks in the region, so also did the new crops, especially maize and cassava—mainly cultigens from the New World—revolutionize the agricultural practice, broaden the foods and cuisines, and transform the foodways of Yoruba-Edo region, as in other parts of the subcontinent. The process by which these foods were adopted and the impacts they had on the health, eating habits, birth scheduling, feasting, and on the population in general remains unknown. The Atlantic period, with the vast importation of cowry shells brought into the region, was indeed an era of transformations in the sociocultural conception of money, transaction, wealth, and power. The ensembles of material culture and the meanings they were imbued with provide a rich fodder of information for understanding the transformations of the ideas of social valuation during the seventeenth and eighteenth centuries.[125] A major improvement in the archaeological conceptualization of material culture is needed in order for archaeologists, with their unique access to different cultural contexts and time depths, to open a new vista of knowledge on the changes associated with the incorporation of the region into the European-centered capitalist economy. Among these changes are the impacts of New World crops on the organization and methods of agricultural production and on sociocultural reproduction, and the impacts of European mercantilism on technological production capabilities. Also of importance is how the social valuation of cowry laid the groundwork for the ideas of monetization, transactions, and material wealth between ca. 1600 and 1800.

The century that followed the *terminus ad quem* of this study has been called a "Revolutionary Century" because many events of the period were great leaps from the norms and traditions of the preceding era.[126] The material correlates of these transformations would be found more in documents, material culture, and oral traditions than in archaeological data. Of all the periods and centuries in Yoruba-Edo history, possibly with the exception of the twentieth century, the nineteenth century has received the most thorough study because of the availability of more accessible sources (oral traditions and documentary) than the preceding centuries.[127] These studies have covered, for the first half of the nineteenth century, the collapse of the Old Oyo Empire and the subsequent panregional internecine warfare; the emergence of new political formations; massive dislocation of populations from the north to the south; and extensive enslavement and transportation of war captives to the New World, especially the Caribbean, and Central and South America. The momentous events associated with the second half of the nineteenth century were the introduction of Christianity ideologies, the advent of the so-called legitimate trade (exports of agricultural commodities other than human cargo to Europe after 1860), and the advent and impacts of the British colonial rule. The nineteenth century constitutes a different historical era in the sociopolitical and cultural lives of Yoruba-Edo region. As much as it was a turbulent century, the period also represents the emergence of new social identities and social affiliations. As Christianity, western education, and colonial rule made inroads into the region during the nineteenth century, the Yoruba-Edo encounter with Western "modernity" began in earnest, and new forms of culture, worldview, and new yardsticks for measuring social order (civilization) took hold in the consciousness and expectation of the region's peoples.[128]

Summary and Conclusions

An attempt has been made to define some of the diagnostic materials that characterize each of the cultural-historical phases, but the features that have been used to define each period are not exhaustive. The obvious exclusion of many aspects of cultural and chronological indicators has risen not from deliberate neglect but from the focus on the available evidence and the quest for coherence of the narratives. After all, as a doyen of African history puts it, "the reconstruction of all facets of history is an impossibility."[129] The study, however, moves beyond a mere cataloging of the objects, styles, and forms that are associated with a particular period. As demonstrated above, the meanings and functions of the objects, and why and how these changed over time are important to understanding the innovations and the emergence of new structures that distinguish the periods from one another. The historical reconstruction and the periodization scheme offered above have focused on institutions, sociopolitical processes, economy, technological innovations, ideas, ideology, and social valuation. The interconnections among these facets of history have been examined in order to define the unique characters of each period, but the emphasis on each facet has varied according to its importance in each period. There are gaps in the narrative, and hypotheses have been offered in a bid to fill some of the gaps. The agenda for the future research is to verify or falsify these propositions. This is particularly true for the early periods for which we have the most acute limited information due to the very little archaeological focus on the pre-tenth century contexts. It is hoped that archaeological investigations will redress these lacunae. Admittedly, the regional diversity of historical experience and material culture has been obscured in the narrative. This is inevitable given the fact that the goal was to define broad temporal categories that will allow us to comprehend the sociohistorical trajectories at the regional level.

The cultural historical narrative outlined in this chapter indicates that stone-using agricultural homesteads dotted the landscape of Yoruba-Edo region before 500 B.C. These homesteads were located both in rock shelters and also in open sites. The populations cultivated yam and palm oil, gathered wild plants, and hunted animals around their settlements. At the onset of the Archaic period, there was a widespread adoption of iron technology, and open-air homesteads became more common and many of these coalesced or grew into hamlets and multi-family villages. As population increased, and village settlements became the preferred unit of social organization, the ideologies of unilineal descents became elaborate for the purpose of access to farmland and defense. Iron-using communities proliferated during the Early Formative period, and large compact villages developed as the common type of social organization in Yoruba-Edo region. The prolific construction of embankments to demarcate settlements and land boundaries at this period indicate that the concern for defense and access to land was accentuated by population increase which was due less to large-scale migrations but to natural increase by birth. There is evidence at Ile-Ife that thirteen of these village complexes organized themselves in a federation headed by a titular leader. The unity of the confederation was emphasized by the adoption of common deities, such as Oramfe, and the conduct of specialized rituals in which the heads of the village complexes and other political elite performed. New political visions that favored the reorganization of the different village complexes under a central government heralded the Late Formative period. Although the changes took place in Ile-Ife between 800 and 1000, the consequence had reverberating effects in Yorubaland due to the massive migrations from Ile-Ife to other parts of Yoruba-Edo region. The LFP also witnessed the commencement of the use of stone as a medium of figurative representation of important personalities.

The repertoire of material culture, technological innovations, and political institutions that have served as the hallmarks of Yoruba-Edo culture developed during the Classical period. An urban capital with concentric embankments, a royal dynasty, and an elaborate network of hierarchical political and ritual officials are among the sociocultural markers of the period. Although Ile-Ife pioneered this development, it was not until the thirteenth century that the sociopolitical and material culture innovations associated with the Classical period spread across Yoruba-Edo region in rapid successions. A pan-Yoruba-Edo regional system and cultural identity were created through the sociopolitical networks that Ile-Ife developed across the region. It is noted that the political centralization, material culture elaboration, and the high artistic marks associated with the Classical period took place in a milieu of economic and political networks that were tied to the trans-Saharan commerce via the Middle Niger. The ideology of political relationships that sustained the regional system of interaction and peer-polity relationships began to be challenged during the Intermediate period as Benin and Old Oyo rose into regional hegemonies and the political influence of Ile-Ife began to dwindle. These changes were associated with the inauguration of Atlantic commerce and the decline in the industries that had sustained the political capital of Ile-Ife—beads and copper. Warfare assumed new meanings as a means of political and territorial expansion, and economic predation. New artistic forms and iconography developed during this period to justify and illustrate the new hegemonic political institutions. The changes in the topography of trade networks created new routes and market centers, and new forms of sociopolitical alignments that culminated at that time. The regional political powers were reconfigured as new polities, dynasties, and political entrepreneurs emerged mainly through the systematic destruction or weakening of the pre-1500 ones. Hence, the sixteenth century marked a second wave of sociopolitical formations as migrations intensified and the coastal areas became important economic hubs. The incorporation of the region into the Atlantic economy beginning from 1600 created new forms of material accumulation, new forms of wealth, and new forms of exchange on a scale and with characteristics that the region had never experienced. Although the Benin and Old Oyo hegemonies shaped the political topography of the region, the Atlantic socioeconomic conditions generated most of the cultural transformations that took place between 1600 and 1800, in terms of material consumption, technology, religion, ideology of gender, and social relations. Any study of local history in Yoruba-Edo region would be meaningful only with adequate accounting for this Atlantic experience.

The foregoing demonstrates that historical periodization allows us to see the major currents underlying the changes and continuity in the history of a people, a region, a culture, and even an idea. By this endeavor, new research questions are brought forth, and techniques and procedures for answering the questions are refined. Archaeological data provide us with the kinds of information needed for defining the long-term historical periods for Yoruba-Edo region, but, as demonstrated in this paper, the complex meanings of these mute materials can be better understood when we assess them in relation to oral-ethnographic historical data, cultural contexts, and panregional events. The six chronological periods proposed above, covering a broad sweep of time between ca. 500 B.C. and A.D. 1800, are informed by the view that objects are ultimately connected to time-specific sociohistorical processes, and to the change from one type of social experience to another. This study is only a beginning of an ongoing project aimed at understanding the long-term cultural history in Yoruba-Edo region with emphasis on the formation and transformations of ideas, and sociopolitical institutions, and how regional interacting systems acted on cultural historical reproduction and changes at the local levels. Students of Yoruba-Edo history are invited to begin to examine the different pathways of cultural historical themes such as political history, the shifting cleavages of regional interactions, technological history, settlement history, migrations, ethnogenesis, and even the history of ideas, e.g., of monetization, social valuation, etc., within these chronological categories. Since this is only a first attempt at developing a cultural historical scheme for Yoruba-Edo region, it is expected that our inferences will be refined in the future as we collect more data and subject them to systematic evaluation and interpretation.

Notes

1. For a review of the discussions on the Yoruba and Edo relationships, see Babatunde Agbaje-Williams, "Ife, Old Oyo, and Benin: A Chronological Consideration in the Light of Recent Aarchaeological Work at Old Oyo," *Nigeria Magazine* 55 (1987): 23–31; S. O. Babayemi, "The Oyo, Ife, and Benin Relationship Reconsidered," *African Notes* 8, 2 (1981): 15–26; see Ekpo Eyo, "Recent Excavations at Ife and Owo, and Their Implications for Ife, Owo, and Benin Studies," 3 vols. (Ph.D. dissertation, University of Ibadan, Nigeria, 1974); Akinwumi Ogundiran, "Filling a Gap in Ife-Benin Interaction Field (A.D. 13th–16th centuries): Excavations and Material Culture in Iloyi Settlement, Ijesaland," *African Archaeological Review* 19, 1 (2002): 27–60; A. F. C. Ryder, "A Reconsideration of the Ife-Benin Relationship," *Journal of African History,* 6, 1 (1965): 25–37. John Thorton, "Traditions, Documents and the Ife-Benin Relationship," History in Africa 15 (1988): 351–62.

2. Taking a cue from studies that have demonstrated cultural interdependency between the Yoruba and Edo areas as a result of migrations and interactions over the past seven hundred years, Yoruba-Edo region is regarded here as a coherent unit for historical analysis. Although the cultural geography of the region crosscuts Nigeria, Benin Republic, and Togo, the focus is on southwest Nigeria. Archaeological information is drawn largely from the areas of Ile-Ife, Old Oyo, Ijesa, Owo, and Benin. The other areas are Badagry and Igbomina.

3. For the use of external contact scheme to delineate periodization in Nigerian history, see Thurstan Shaw, "Prehistory," in *Groundwork of Nigerian History,* ed. O. Ikime (Ibadan: Heinemann Educational Books, 1980), 25–53.

4. For a critique of this cultural stasis view, see Jane Guyer "Introduction: The Currency Interface and Its Dynamics," in *Money Matters: Instability, Values, and Social Payments in the Modern History of West African Communities,* ed. J. Guyer (Portsmouth, N.H.: Heinemann, 1995), 36; Ann Stahl, "Change and Continuity in the Banda Area, Ghana: The Direct Historical Approach," *Journal of Field Archaeology* 21 (1994): 182. For notable and most recent exceptions that are based on studies ranging from historical linguistics to archaeology, see Christopher Ehret, *An African Classical Age: Eastern and Southern Africa in World History, 1000 B.C. to A.D. 400* (Charlottesville: University Press of Virginia, 1998); I. Pirikayi, *The Zimbabwe Culture: Origins and Decline in Southern Zambezian States* (Walnut Creek, Calif.: Altamira Press, 2001); Jan Vansina, *Paths in the Rainforests: Toward a History of Political Tradition in Equatorial Africa* (Madison: University of Wisconsin Press, 1990).

5. Ian Hodder, "The Contribution of the Long Term," in *Archaeology as Long Term History,* ed. I. Hodder (Cambridge: Cambridge University Press, 1978), 1–8.

6. Ann Stahl, *Making History in Banda: Anthropological Visions of Africa's Past* (Cambridge, Cambridge University Press, 2001), 5.

7. Michael Shank and Christopher Tilley, *Re-constructing Archaeology* (Cambridge: Cambridge University Press, 1987).

8. Kris L. Hardin and Mary Jo Arnoldi, "Introduction: Efficacy and Objects," in *African Material Culture,* ed. M. J. Arnoldi, C. M. Geary, and K. L. Hardin (Bloomington and Indianapolis: Indiana University Press, 1996), 1.

9. Igor Kopytoff, "The Cultural Biography of Things: Commoditization as Process," in *The Social Life of Things: Commodities in Cultural Perspective,* ed. Arjun Appandurai (Cambridge: Cambridge University Press, 1986), 64–91.

10. For an exemplary work in this genre that focuses on the relationships between royal art and historical changes of kingship power, see P. Ben-Amos, *Art, Innovation, and*

Politics in Eighteenth-Century Benin (Bloomington and Indianapolis: Indiana University Press, 1999).

11. Akinwumi Ogundiran, *Settlement Cycling and Regional Interactions in Central Yorubaland, AD 1200–1900: Archaeology and History in Ilare District, Nigeria* (Ph.D. dissertation, Boston University, 2000).

12. Most of the terms, no doubt, have similarities to the ones that have been used in North and Central America to characterize the Olmec, Maya, Inca, and Aztec cultures. Christopher Ehret, in *An African Classical Age,* has also recently used similar terminologies such as Formative and Classical to characterize the cultural historical trajectories in eastern and southern Africa. These similarities are only utilitarian and are adopted in this study because of their descriptive and explanatory qualities. They are not intended to represent cultural historical comparability between the Yoruba-Edo area and any other region.

13. T. Shaw, "The Prehistory of West Africa," in *History of West Africa,* ed. J. F. A. Ajayi and M. Crowther (Ibadan: Longman, 1985), 58.

14. Bassey Andah, "The Earliest Human Occupation and Settlement in West Africa," *The Epistemology of West African Settlements, West African Journal of Archaeology* (Special Issue) 25, 1 (1995): 10; Philip Allsworth-Jones, "The Earliest Settlement in West Africa and the Sahara," *West African Journal of Archaeology (W.A.J.A.)* 17 (1987): 87–128.

15. B. Andah and K. Momin, "New Palaeolithic Finds in Ajibode and Environs, N. E. Ibadan, Oyo State," *W.A.J.A.* 23 (1993): 215–18.

16. Microliths are small flint tools, usually flaked in at least two directions as blades and arrowheads.

17. David Phillipson, *African Archaeology* (Cambridge: University of Cambridge Press, 1993), 104.

18. Thurstan Shaw and S. G. H. Daniels, *Excavations at Iwo Eleru, Ondo State, Nigeria, West African Journal of Archaeology* (Special Issue) 14 (1984).

19. Philip Oyelaran, "A Preliminary Report on Palaeoenvironmental Investigations in Iffe-Ijumu, Southern Nigeria," *Papers from the Institute of Archaeology* 4 (1993): 1–8; Merrick Posnansky, "Yams and the Origins of West African Agriculture," *Odu–A Journal of West African Studies* 1 (1969): 101–7; M. A. Sowunmi, "The Beginnings of Agriculture in West Africa: Botanical Evidence," *Current Anthropology* 26, 1 (1985): 127–29; Ann Stahl, "Intensification in the West African Late Stone Age: A View from Central Ghana," in *The Archaeology of Africa: Food, Metals, and Towns,* ed. T. Shaw et al. (London: Routledge, 1993), 261–73.

20. See Philip Oyelaran, "Archaeological and Palaeoenvironmental Investigations in Iffe-Ijumu Area of Kwara State" (Ph.D. dissertation, University of Ibadan, Nigeria (1991); and Philip Oyelaran, "Early Settlement and Archaeological Sequence of the Northeast Yorubaland," *African Archaeological Review* 15, 1 (1998).

21. Frank Willett, "Investigation at Old Oyo 1956–57: An Interim Report," *Journal of Historical Society of Nigeria* 2, 1 (1960): 59–77.

22. A. Fatunsin, "Ifetedo: A Late Stone Age Site in the Forest Region of Southwestern Nigeria," *W.A.J.A.* 26, 1 (1996): 71–87.

23. Raphael Alabi, "Apa: A later Stone Age Occupation Layer in the Southwestern Coast of Nigeria," *Nyame Akuma* 53 (2000): 29–33.

24. See Oyelaran, "Archaeological and Palaeoenvironmental Investigations."

25. Oyelaran, "Early Settlement," 72.

26. P. Allsworth-Jones, "Continuity and Change in Yoruba Pottery," *Bulletin of the School of Oriental and African Studies* 59, 2 (1996): 312–22; Fatunsin, "Ifetedo: A Late Stone Age Site."

27. Oyelaran, "Early Settlement," 73.

28. Graham Connah, *The Archaeology of Benin: Excavations and Other Researches in and around Benin, Nigeria* (Oxford: Clarendon Press, 1975); Patrick Darling, *Archaeology and History in Southern Nigeria*, 2 vols., Cambridge Monographs in African Archaeology 11 (London: Archaeopress, 1984).

29. Eyo, *Recent Excavations at Ife and Owo*, 1:81; Oyelaran, "Early Settlement," 77; Paul Ozanne, "A New Archaeological Survey of Ife," *Odu*, New Series 1 (1969): 32.

30. Vansina, *Paths in the Rainforests*, 60.

31. According to a popular tradition of Yoruba origins, Ogun, the deity of iron, was credited to have used his iron cutlass to cut the paths for other deities that Olodumare, the High God, sent to perform the task of creating the world. According to the oral traditions in the Ifa divination corpus, the advent of iron technology marked a revolutionary phase in the Yoruba cultural history: "[A]s society became more settled and populated, there came another age which the verses of Ifa refer to as the age of Oba jegi jegi [the age of the king who ate wood]. This was an age of iron which belongs to Ogun, the . . . divinity of war, iron, manufacture, and creativity. It was Ogun who fabricated the iron implements with which violence was done to the rest of creation. Ogun allied with Oduduwa to bring about a time in Yoruba mythology when society became more specialized and when agriculture, hunting, and manufacture started." Wande Abimbola, *Ifa Will Mend Our Broken World: Thoughts on Yoruba Religion and Culture in Africa and the Diaspora* (Boston: Aim Books, 1997), 20.

32. Patrick Darling, "A Legacy in Earth: Ancient Benin and Ishan, Southern Nigeria," in *Historical Archaeology in Nigeria*, ed. Kit W. Wesler (Trenton, N.J.: Africa World Press 1997), 143–97.

33. The use of the term "polities" in this context refers to sociopolitical units irrespective of their scale of complexity. The term should therefore not be construed to represent "state" or any other category of sociopolitical formation.

34. Omotoso Eluyemi, "The Role of Oral Traditions in the Archaeological Investigation of the History of Ife," in *Yoruba Oral Traditions*, ed. W. Abimbola, Proceedings of the Conference on Yoruba Oral Traditions (University of Ife, Dept. of African Languages and Literature, 1975), 120–21.

35. For details, see Biodun Adediran, "The Early Beginnings of the Ife State," in *The Cradle of a Race: Ife from the Beginning to 1980*, ed. I. A. Akinjogbin (Lagos: Sunray Publications, 1992), 80; and Ade Obayemi, "The Phenomenon of Oduduwa in Ife History," in *The Cradle of a Race*, ed. I. A. Akinjogbin, 70.

36. These extended family units are akin to what Jan Vansina calls "Houses" in Equatorial Africa: A House was "the establishment of a big man. Often it lasted beyond its founder's death and was taken over by another big man among its members. . . . Membership included kinfolk of the big man, but also friends, clients, and various dependents. . . . The ideology of the House was based on the fiction that it was a family." See Vansina, *Paths in the Rainforests*, 74–75.

37. Ade Obayemi, "The Yoruba and Edo-Speaking Peoples and Their Neighbours before 1600," in *History of West Africa*, ed. J. F. A. Ajayi and M. Crowther, 3rd ed. (Oxford: Oxford University Press, 1985), 255–322.

38. The deity of Oramfe was the religious and political ideological focus of the Ife confederacy. The abode of the deity is associated with a rocky hill north of the outskirts of the modern city of Ile-Ife.

39. Isola Olomola, "Ife before Oduduwa," in *The Cradle of a Race*, ed. I. A. Akinjogbin (Lagos: Sunray Publications, 1992), 55.

40. Obayemi, "The Yoruba and Edo-Speaking peoples," 302.

41. Ibid., 261

42. Titi Euba, "The Ooni of Ife's Are Crown and the Concept of Divine Head," *Nigerian Magazine* 53, 1 (1985).

43. Adediran, "The Early Beginnings of the Ife State," 86.

44. H. J. Drewal et al., *Yoruba: Nine Centuries of African Art and Thought* (New York: The Center of African Art and H. Abrams, 1989), 49.

45. Drewal et al., *Yoruba: Nine Centuries of African Art and Thought.*

46. Jacob Egharevba, *A Short History of Benin*, 4th ed. (Ibadan: Ibadan University Press, 1968); Obayemi, "The Yoruba and Edo-Speaking peoples."

47. I. Akinjogbin and E. Ayandele, "Yorubaland before 1800," in *Groundwork of Nigerian History*, ed. O. Ikime (Ibadan: Heinemann Educational Books, 1980), 121–43; Ulli Beier, "Before Oduduwa," *Odu: Journal of Yoruba and Related Studies* 3 (1956): 25–32.

48. A. Mabogunje and P. Richards, "Land and People—Models of Spatial and Eecological Processes in West African History," in *History of West Africa*, ed. J. F. A. Ajayi and M. Crowther (Ibadan: Longman, 1985), 1:12.

49. Adediran, "The Early Beginnings of the Ife State."

50. A. Ogundiran, "Factional Competition, Sociopolitical Development, and Settlement Cycling in Ilare District (ca. 1200–1900): Oral Traditions of Historical Experience in a Yoruba Community," *History in Africa*, 28: 20–40.

51. Eluyemi, "The Role of Oral Traditions," 122.

52. Adediran, "The Early Beginnings of the Ife State," 82.

53. Drewal et al., *Yoruba: Nine Centuries of African Art and Thought.*

54. O. B. Lawuyi, "The Obatala factor in Yoruba History," *History in Africa* 19 (1992): 369–75; Frank Willett, *Ife in the History of West African Sculpture* (London: Thames and Hudson, 1967), 122–23.

55. H. J. Drewal et al., *Yoruba: Nine Centuries of African Art and Thought*, 58.

56. Omotoso Eluyemi, "Excavations at Isoya," *West African Journal of Archaeology* 7 (1977): 97–115; Ogundiran, *Settlement Cycling and Regional Interactions.*

57. Olokun is the first bead-maker and the goddess of beads, wealth, and ocean in the Yoruba traditions; see Frank Willett, *Ife in the History of West African Sculpture* (London: Thames and Hudson, 1967), 27. In Benin traditions, however, Olokun is referred to as the "king of the waters," "god of the sea," and "god of wealth"; see Norma Rosen, "Chalk Iconography in Olokun Worship," *African Arts* 22, 3 (1989): 44.

58. O. Eluyemi, "The Technology of the Ife Glass Beads: Evidence from the Igbo-Olokun," *Odu* 32 (1987): 200; Willett, *Ife in the History of West African Sculpture*, 24.

59. Frank Willett, *Baubles, Bangles and Beads: Trade Contacts of Medieval Ife* (Thirteenth M. J. Herskovits Memorial Lecture delivered at the Center of African Studies, Edinburgh University, February 24, 1977), 16; Peter Garlake, "Excavations on the Woye Asiri Family Land in Ife, Western Nigeria," *W.A.J.A.* 7 (1977): 89.

60. These red stone beads, used as anklets and necklace, are up until today the markers of chieftaincy/political status in the region.

61. Obayemi, "The Yoruba and Edo-Speaking Peoples," 291.

62. Jonathan Aleru (personal communication, May 3, 1997).

63. F. Willett, "Investigation at Old Oyo 1956–57: An Interim Report," *Journal of Historical Society of Nigeria* 2, 1 (1960): 63, 74.

64. A. O'Hear, "Ilorin Lantana Beads," *African Arts* 29, 4 (1986): 37. H. J Drewal and John Mason have noted that political centralization and red stone beads are "intimately associated with Sango, the deified fourth king Oyo and deity of thunder, and his wife Oyo, the deity of River Niger, whirlwind, and storm." The advent of Sango on the political landscape of Old Oyo took place sometime between the thirteenth and fifteenth century: *Beads, Body, and Soul: Art and Light in the Yoruba Universe* (Los Angeles, Calif.: UCLA Fowler Museum of Cultural History, 1998), 47.

65. O'Hear, "Ilorin Lantana Beads," 36–37.

66. The artistic representations of these cylindrical beads indeed abound in the portrait-like terracotta and brass sculptures of the elite at Ile-Ife and Esie beginning from the eleventh-twelfth century. The painting of these bead motifs in terracotta sculptures was a common practice in Ile-Ife during the Classical period; see Peter Garlake, "Excavations at Obalara's Land, Ife, Nigeria," *West African Journal of Archaeology* 4 (1974): 131; and Willett, *Ife in the History of West African Scuplture,* 70.

67. Drewal and Mason, *Beads, Body, and Soul,* 47; Willett " Investigation at Old Oyo."

68. H. J. Drewal et al., *Yoruba: Nine Centuries of African Art and Thought,* 149.

69. William Fagg, *Nigerian Images* (Lagos: National Commission for Museums and Monuments, 1963), 32.

70. Phillips Stevens, *The Stone Images of Esie* (Ibadan: Ibadan University Press, 1978); Aribidesi Usman, "Soapstone Figurines Revisited: New Evidence from North-Central Yorubaland," *Nyame Akuma* 44 (1998): 13–18.

71. H. J. Drewal et al., *Yoruba: Nine Centuries of African Art and Thought,* 88

72. C. O. Adepegba, "Ife Art: An Enquiry into the Surface Patterns and the Continuity of Art Tradition among the Northern Yoruba," *W.A.J.A.* 12 (1982): 95–109.

73. There have been speculations that circular dwellings preceded the rectilineal and courtyard architectural forms in Yoruba-Edo areas but this is not yet confirmed; see Eyo, *Recent Excavations,* 171; I. Omokhodion, *Oyo Ile Pottery Analysis.* M.Sc. thesis (Dept. of Archaeology, University of Ibadan, 1978), 11.

74. Eyo, *Recent Excavations*; Garlake, "Excavations on the Woye Asiri Family Land"; Ogundiran, *Settlement Cycling and Regional Interactions,* 425; Willett, *Ife in the History of West African Scuplture.*

75. Garlake, "Excavations on the Woye Asiri Family Land," 71–72.

76. Eyewitness accounts indicate that the use of these ceramic disks for decorating the adobe walls of Yoruba structures survived until the mid-twentieth century in Ilesa and at Ahara village near Ilorin: Baba Adeyeye, pers. comm. July 2, 1997; Dr. Olawale Albert, pers. comm. Apr. 15, 1997.

77. Adisa Ogunfolakan, *Archaeological Survey of Osun North-East, Osun State, Nigeria,* M.Sc. thesis (University of Ibadan, Ibadan, Nigeria, 1994). The extensiveness of potsherd pavements between the twelfth and fifteenth centuries informed Ekpo Eyo's insistence that the period should be called Potsherd Pavement Era, see Eyo, *Recent Excavations* (see also Table 1).

78. Babatunde Agbaje-Williams, "Potsherd Pavements and Early Urban Sites in Nigeria, Yorubaland: A Consideration," Paper Presented at the 14th Biennial Conference of

the Society of Africanist Archaeologists, Syracuse University, Syracuse, New York, May 20–24, 1998.

79. E. Eyo "Excavations at Odo Ogbe Street and Lafogido, Ife, Nigeria," *W.A.J.A.* 4 (1974): 99–109; Garlake, "Excavations at Obalara's Land," 111–48, "Excavations on the Woye Asiri Family Land"; Willett, *Ife in the History of West African Scuplture.*

80. R. Soper, *Archaeological Works at Old Oyo,* Unpublished Report on File at Dept. of Archaeology and Anthropology (Ibadan, Nigeria: University of Ibadan, 1975).

81. Connah, *The Archaeology of Benin,* 32, 35.

82. Babatunde Agbaje-Williams, *Archaeological Investigation of Itagunmodi Potsherd Pavement Site, Ijesaland, Osun State, Nigeria, 1991/92* (Ibadan, Nigeria: IFRA Publication, Institute of African Studies, University of Ibadan, 1995).

83. N. Nzewunwa, "Prehistoric Pavements," *W.A.J.A.* 19 (1989): 93–116.

84. Eyo, *Recent Excavations*; Garlake, "Excavations at Odo Ogbe"; Garlake, "Excavations at Obalara's Land"; Garlake, "Excavations on the Woye Asiri Family Land"; Ogundiran, "Potsherd Pavements in Ilare-Ijesa, Yorubaland: A Regional Perspective," *Nyame Akuma* 53 (2000): 35–41; Ogunfolakan, *Archaeological Survey of Osun North-East.*

85. Garlake "Excavations at Obalara's Land," 65, 69–71; A. J. H. Goodwin, "Archaeology and Benin Architecture," *Journal of Historical Society of Nigeria* 1, 2 (1957): 69; Ogundiran, *Settlement Cycling and Regional Interactions,* 242.

86. Garlake "Excavations at Odo Ogbe," 131; Ogundiran, "Filling a Gap in Ife-Benin Interaction Field (A.D. 13th–16th centuries): Excavations and Material Culture in Iloyi Settlement, Ijesaland," *African Archaeological Review,* 19, 1 (2002): 27–60; Willett, *Ife in the History of West African Scuplture,* 70, 83, 86, 87, 144; Eyo, "Igbo'Laja, Owo," *W.A.J.A.* 6 (1976): 43–45. The diagnostic decoration indices of the sphere are applied bosses, cordons, keloid forms, cowryform motifs; hyphenated cross-hatched incisions; stamped geometric-shape impressions, circular stylus motifs; reliefs of guilloche and rosette designs; rustication; and red-on-rims/lips. The diagnostic value of these decorations, as indices of cultural-historical relationship, is illustrated by their association with both ceramics and the "classical" terracotta sculptures between the twelfth and sixteenth centuries. For example, red paint is found on the lips and rims of vessels and on the facial parts of the classical terracotta human figures in Ile-Ife. The occurrence of rustication, and applied motifs of cowryform, bosses, keloids, and cordons are pervasive symbols in the iconographic expressions of the Ife ceramic sphere. These motifs are found not only on ceramic vessels but also on terracotta figures. The cordon motifs that are applied and etched on the shoulders of bowls in Iloyi, Ife, Owo, and Benin, for example, are also represented as beads on the crowns, ankles, and wrists of the terracotta figures in Ile-Ife and Owo between the twelfth and sixteenth centuries. Likewise, herringbone and hyphenated cross-hatched incised motifs were used at Ife, Owo, and Benin during the same period to decorate ceramic vessels and terracotta sculptures of human and animal figures and stools. At Ile-Ife and Ilare district, cowryform motifs were represented on ritual clay vessels, terracotta stools, and terracotta sculptures during the Classical period. A vivid example from Ile-Ife dating to the eleventh-fifteenth century is a piece of terracotta with a relief of ram's head (symbol of power, leadership, and royalty) and a representation of woven fabric (carved basket-work roulette) with a fringe of cowry shells. The other iconographic representations, found mainly in the ritual and religious contexts and on objects associated with political power at Ile-Ife, Ilare district, Benin, and Owo during the Classical period, are stylized mudfish and snake images.

87. S. MacEachern, "Symbolic Reservoirs and Inter-Group Relations: West African Examples," *The African Archaeological Review* 12 (1994): 207.

88. The northwest and north-central areas of the region are particularly character-ized by the following surface and decoration patterns: burnishing, basting, brush marking, carved rouletted chevron (zig-zag) motifs, dot punctates, shell-edge impressions, perpen-dicular incisions, and incised geometric symbols consisting of cross, triangular, and square motifs. See Babatunde Agbaje-Williams *A Contribution to the Archaeology of Old Oyo,* Ph.D. dissertation (University of Ibadan, Ibadan, Nigeria, 1983); Omokhodion, *Oyo Ile Pottery Analysis,* 11; Willett, "Investigation at Old Oyo 1956–57".

89. Robin Horton, "The Economy of Ife from c. A.D. 900—c. A.D. 1700," in *The Cradle of a Race,* ed. A. Akinjogbin (Lagos: Sunray Publications, 1992), 122–47.

90. Timothy Earle, *How Chiefs Came to Power: The Political Economy in Prehistory* (Stanford, Calif.: Stanford University Press, 1997), 151.

91. David Aremu, "Early History of Metal Working among Northeast Yorubas in Kwara State," in *Historical Archaeology in Nigeria,* ed. Kit W. Wesler (Trenton, N.J.: Africa World Press, 1997), 75–98.; Drewal et al., *Yoruba: Nine Centuries of African Art and Thought,* 117; Fagg, *Nigerian Images.*

92. Egharevba, *A Short History of Benin.*

93. Mabogunje and Richards, "Land and People," 9.

94. Willett, *Baubles, Bangles and Beads,* 16

95. The possibility that glasses were locally produced at Ile-Ife from the local quartz-silica minerals rather than solely obtained via the trans-Saharan trade has been suggested by a number of scholars, e.g., O. Eluyemi, "The Technology of the Ife Glass Beads," 213; William Fagg, *Yoruba Beadwork: Art of Nigeria* (New York, Pace Editions and Rizzoli, 1980), 10; Horton, "The Economy of Ife," 132.

96. Drewal and Mason, *Beads, Body, and Soul,* 39.

97. Ogundiran, *Settlement Cycling and Regional Interactions,* 175; Willett, *Baubles, Bangles and Beads,* 16.

98. Merrick Posnansky, "Aspects of Early West African Trade," *World Archaeology* 5 (1973): 149–62; Stahl, *Making History in Banda,* 82–84.

99. Igor Kopytoff, "The Internal African Frontier: The Making of African Political Culture," in *The African Frontier,* ed. I. Kopytoff (Bloomington and Indianapolis: Indiana University Press, 1987), 3–84.

100. Some aspects of these sixteenth century factional and moietal conflicts have been discussed in relation to Ijesaland, see Ogundiran, "Factional Competition."

101. Robin Law, *The Oyo Empire c. 1600–c. 1836: A West African Imperialism in the Era of the Atlantic Slave Trade* (Oxford: Oxford University Press, 1977).

102. Egharevba, *A Short History of Benin.*

103. Robin Horton, in "Ancient Ife: A Reassessment," *Journal of Historical Society of Nigeria* 9, 4 (1979): 84–85, suggests that the internal political corruption at Ile-Ife possibly led to local disaffection, massive emigrations to the hitherto client polities—Old Oyo and Benin, and economic and political decline in the fifteenth and sixteenth centuries.

104. Ben-Amos, *Art, Innovation, and Politics,* 54.

105. It should be noted that the royal and political iconography of the Classical period is devoid of images of military actions and weaponry, and that the royal personalities were depicted holding a scepter as the symbol of authority. The scepter is usually a hollowed

ivory, a carved anthropomorphic figure, or a ram's horn filled with portent materials. It is the emblem of *Ase,* the life force or the divine energy upon which all existence, power, and authority are dependent, see Drewal et al., *Yoruba: Nine Centuries of African Art and Thought,* 16; John Pemberton and F. S. Afolayan, *Yoruba Sacred Kingship* (Washington, D.C.: Smithsonian Institution Press, 1996), 89.

106. Ben-Amos, *Art, Innovation, and Politics,* 57.

107. Ibid.

108. Onaiwu Ogbomo, *When Men and Women Mattered: A History of Gender Relations among the Owan of Nigeria* (Rochester, N.Y.: University of Rochester Press, 1997), 168.

109. Drewal et al., *Yoruba: Nine Centuries of African Art and Thought.*

110. Eyo, "Igbo'Laja, Owo."

111. J. D. Y. Peel, *The Ijeshas and Nigerians—the Incorporation of a Yoruba Kingdom, 1890s–1970s* (Cambridge: Cambridge University Press, 1983), 20–21; Pemberton and Afolayan, *Yoruba Sacred Kingship,* 66.

112. Horton, "Ancient Ife," 137.

113. Ogundiran, *Settlement Cycling and Regional Interactions,* 241.

114. Goucher, "Iron is Iron 'til It Is Rust: Trade and Ecology in the Decline of West African Iron-Smelting," *Journal of African History* 22 (1981): 186.

115. E.g., Frank Anozie, "An Archaeological Study of Ironworking at Umundu, Nigeria: The Decline and Continuity of an Indigenous Tradition," in *Historical Archaeology in Nigeria,* ed. Kit. W. Wesler (Trenton, N.J.: Africa World Press, 1998); Goucher, "Iron is Iron 'til It Is Rust."

116. Sandra Barnes, "The Many Faces of Ogun: Introduction to the First Edition," in *Africa's Ogun: Old World and New,* ed. S. Barnes (Bloomington and Indianapolis: Indiana University Press, 1997), 1–26.

117. According to Pacheco Pereira, the Benin people used cowries to buy everything, "and he that has most of them is the richest" cited in J. Hogendorn and M. Johnson, *The Shell Money of the Slave Trade* (Cambridge: Cambridge University Press, 1986), 19. There are reports that cowries were found in pre-sixteenth century archaeological deposits at Benin but evidence for their extensive usage as currency is not yet confirmed in the archaeological contexts; see Connah, *The Archaeology of Benin*; I. Omokhodion, *Northwest Benin Sites and Socially Determined Artifact Distribution,* Ph.D. dissertation (Ann Arbor, Mich.: UMI Press, 1988).

118. Earle, *How Chiefs Came to Power,* 73

119. Akinwumi Ogundiran, "From Beads to Cowry Shells: A Cultural History of Social Valuation in the Bight of Benin, with Emphasis on Yorubaland," Paper Presented at the 44th Meeting of the African Studies Association, Houston, Texas, p. 13.

Akinwumi Ogundiran, *Beads, Cowries, and Cultural Translations of the Atlantic Experience in Yorubaland, 1600–1850,* Discussion Papers in the African Humanities, Number 36 (2002). African Studies Center, Boston University.

120. Bernard Belasco, *The Entrepreneur as Culture Hero: Preadaptations in Nigeria Economic Development* (New York: Praeger Publishers, 1980); Norma Rosen, "Chalk Iconography in Olokun Worship," 44.

121. Samuel Johnson, *The History of the Yorubas* (Lagos: CSS Bookshop 1921), 168.

122. These goddesses include Olokun (goddess of the Ocean), Osun (goddess of a river that linked the Yoruba interlands with the coast, and also the patron deity of Osogbo,

the most important center for the production of cloth that were sent to the coastal trade), Yemoja (goddess of another river that connected the hinterland with the coast), and Aje (goddess of trade and profit).

123. Ogbomo, *When Men and Women Mattered,* 166.

124. Although Oba Esigie, a sixteenth century king of Benin, first created the office of queen mother and appointed his mother to fill the position, the practice gained currency only during the eighteenth century, partly because the seventeenth century was a period of internal strife and weak monarchies in Benin. However, at the onset of the eighteenth century, the queen mother (iyoba) images became the major stimulus for artistic innovations. They "appear widely on ivory tusks, brass alterpieces, brass . . . plaques, and other types of sculpture, but new forms were [also] created specifically in honor of Iyobas." The queen mother office was a senior chief in the order of Town Chiefs, and the a king's success to fill the position served to bolster the legitimacy of the ruling family's descent as well as to provide a sanction for the Oba's access to a potential source of political and supernatural power. For an excellent treatment of this subject, see Ben-Amos, *Art, Innovation, and Politics,* 66.

125. Karin Barber, "Money, Self-Realization, and the Person in Yoruba Texts," in *Money Matters: Instability, Values, and Social Payments in the Modern History of West African Communities,* ed. J. Guyer (Portsmouth, N.H.: Heinemann, 1995), 205–24; Belasco, *The Entrepreneur as Culture Hero*; Sara Berry, "Stable Prices, Unstable Values: Some Thoughts on Monetization and the Meaning of Transactions in West African Economies," *Money Matters,* 299–313; Ogundiran, *Beads, Cowries, and Cultural Translations.*

126. S. A. Akintoye, *Revolution and Power Politics in Yorubaland, 1840–1893: Ibadan Expansion and the Rise of Ekiti Parapo* (London: University of London Press. 1971).

127. For reviews, see Ajayi and Akintoye, "Yorubaland in the Nineteenth Century," in *Groundwork of Nigerian History,* ed. O. Ikime (Ibadan: Heinemann Educational Books, 1980); Toyin Falola, "A Research Agenda on the Yoruba in the Nineteenth Century," *History in Africa* 15 (1988): 211–27.

128. For an exposition of this process for the Yoruba, see J. D. Y. Peel, *Religious Encounter and the Making of the Yoruba* (Bloomington: Indiana University Press, 2000).

129. Vansina, *Paths in the Rainforests,* 251.

5

FOR TRINKETS SUCH AS BEADS: A REVALORIZATION OF KHOISAN LABOR IN COLONIAL SOUTHERN AFRICA

Edwin N. Wilmsen

> . . . denen sie für Kleinigkeiten, wie Glas- und Porzellanperlen, Tabak und so fort, Elfenbein, Wachs, Honig und gedörrtes Wildfleisch austauschen.
>
> —Ladislaus Magyar (1860) in *Petermann's Geographische Mitteilungen* 6:228.

Glass beads,[1] cloth, tobacco, even guns and ammunition were cheap for nineteenth-century European traders in Africa, who often thought that Africans must place a similarly low value on these commodities and thus were ignorant and irrational to acquiesce in the adverse terms of trade offered for their cattle, ivory, and other products. Chapman ({1850s} 1971 1:113–16)[2] wrote that he obtained some items in trade for a "trifle of beads," and that, in 1853, the natives "will do any mean thing to obtain beads" including prostitute their women (p. 77). Gordon-Cumming ([1850] 1904:254) and Andersson (1854:31), however, record that the initially high value of beads did not last long. At Lake Ngami already in 1853, Andersson noted that "beads were not sought after with the avidity they used to be, such quantities having been imported of late into the lake country, that (to use a vulgar, but very emphatic expression of Letcholatebe) 'the women grunt under their burdens like pigs.'" In other words, Africans rationally assessed the worth of beads to them as they assessed other commodities according to their desire for a product, its availability, and its cost to them. Nevertheless, sentiments such as those expressed by Chapman and Ladislaus Magyar's dismissal as "Kleinigkeiten" (trinkets) of the merchandise he stocked carry a strong implicit devalorization of African labor—and, correlatively, African mentality—while raising the value of that labor's product to European heights.

But material objects, even commodities, are socially inflected and, therefore, are differentially marked as manifestations of relations of production and consumption in different societies. Thus, just as African ivory was inscribed with status as piano keys and billiard balls in bourgeois Europe, so was European glass in the form of beads inscribed by Africans as an element in the construction of objects of value.

Magyar, in the quoted passage, was referring to a particular group of Khoisan people, !Kung-speakers he called "Ka-ssekel oder, wie man sie im Süden nennt, Mu-kánkála"[3] among whom he lived in central Angola in the 1840s–50s; today we call them Sekele and Kwankala (sometimes with Va or Ova prefix). Magyar, like many of his contemporaries (though not all, cf. Chapman [1868] 1971 1:185), devalorized Khoisan labor more thoroughly than that of other Africans, although he, like they, appreciated the value of the product of that labor.

Thus, my continuing revalorization of the place of Khoisan peoples in the political economy of southern Africa has led me to a closer reading of earlier historical documents as well as to a synthetic analysis of the later archaeological record that is now available for the region. Both contain substantial evidence for the penetration of Portuguese-inspired Kongo-Angola trade into what is now Botswana and Namibia beginning in the seventeenth century. This trade from the north entered the region through long established pathways that are archaeologically visible as early as the eighth century C.E. at Divuyu in the Tsodilo Hills in the form of two Atlantic marine shells of the family *Cerithiidae* commonly found around the Congo river mouth and ceramic designs developed in that region 400 years earlier. From the mid-nineteenth century, European traders based in Cape Town and Grahamstown increased the intensity of trade several fold; they, too, used paths of communication—these from the south—over which indigenous peoples had maintained political and economic relations for a very long time. These channels would have been ready-made routes not only for material but also for relatively nonaggressive deployment of peoples able to take advantage of the new commerce. In order to stress indigenous agency in these transforming events—especially that of Khoisan-speaking peoples, whose active roles have been devalued by an ethnography that insists upon their isolation (whether voluntary or imposed by a hostile environment) from the historicity swirling about them—it is necessary to look at the interrelated activities of all peoples in the region.

Trade

As a preliminary step to considering the subcontinent as a whole, I concentrate attention on the Angola-Botswana-Namibia border country (a rather large area which I designate for my present purpose to encompass central Angola through central Namibia plus Ngamiland in Botswana) and limit myself to the approximate time period 1650–1912. There are twenty-five archaeological sites in this region that have yielded European material dated by radiocarbon analysis to this period; eleven other sites have pottery assignable to this same time range, but no European items.

The earliest dateable European items are five Indian-red-on-green-core (IROG) glass beads. Two of these were recovered along with 180 other glass beads at VunguVungu near the confluence of the Cuito and Cubango Rivers (Sandelowsky 1979:60). The reported radiocarbon date, 320±45 (Pta-236): C.E. 1630 (Sandelowsky 1979:55), falls within the early period of these beads. One IROG bead was also recovered from a level in this time range at Xaro on the apex of the Okavango Delta; both sites also yielded clay tobacco pipes that appear to have been locally made on European models. A fourth IROG bead is radiocarbon dated to the mid-eighteenth century (C.E. 1755) at Kgwebe Hills. The late-seventeenth-century date obtained by Yellen and Brooks (1988) at CaeCae is not directly associated with an IROG bead excavated there by me but does suggest that the occupants of this place were linked to the networks through which these beads were distributed. Beads of this kind were manufactured in the Netherlands beginning in the seventeenth century and are known to have been imported into East Africa by C.E. 1750, but seem to date somewhat later at the Cape (Saitowitz and Sampson 1992:101). However, they occur in large numbers at #Khîsa-|gubus, dated C.E. 1702–1780, and one was recovered at Khaeros, C.E. 1650–1750; both sites are near Walvis Bay on the central Namibian coast (John Kinahan 1991:120, 155). Thus, the Namibia-Ngamiland specimens appear to be somewhat earlier than are those at the Cape (perhaps because repercussions of the Portuguese mid-Atlantic trade were more readily felt closer to its Kongo-Angola epicenters) and may be considered to indicate indigenous association with that trade from about the second quarter of the eighteenth century or possibly slightly before.

Nine locations (including CaeCae, Kgwebe, Xaro, and the NyaeNyae pans adjacent to CaeCae[4]) have yielded 36 oyster white, blue cylinder, and blue faceted beads dateable to the century between 1750 and 1850 (John Kinahan 1991:120; Saitowitz and Sampson 1992). Jill Kinahan (2000:70) argues convincingly that "combinations of bead types can be more reliable chronological indicators for a particular area," thus supporting my use of such combinations when they can be identified in archaeological assemblages. Several eyewitness accounts are available for this period. Blue faceted beads like those from CaeCae are shown dangling from the hair (along with red beads) of a man in a watercolor sketch made by one Captain Thompson near Walvis Bay in 1786 (reproduced on the cover of John Kinahan 1991); John Kinahan (p. 99) says the sketch was probably made at #Khîsa-|gubus where several of these beads were found. Brink described similar blue beads which he saw in central Namibia in 1761; he was told that these beads were obtained from peoples to the north, some of whom were "of a yellow or tawny hue and were named Sandamrocquas" (Mossop 1947:51). These tawny people must have been Khoisan, almost surely Khoé-speaking; they also are specified by Wikar as being engaged in trade in southern Namibia during the 1770s (Mossop 1935:29–79). In 1837 near Windhoek, Alexander ([1838] 1967 1:172) was told by Ovaherero of their trade at an inlet of the sea north of the Cunene with Europeans, from whom they obtained cowries, copper, and iron in exchange for cattle. Gibson (1962:62) identifies this place as Baia dos Tigres in what is today southern Angola. In 1851, Carl Hugo Hahn (1984:510) was near the Cunene with Galton while Cotton Oswell (1900 2:230, 245) and Livingstone ([1858] 1912:65) were at Linyanti on the Zambezi near Victoria Falls; all reported well-established trade with Portuguese and their agents. Four years later, Green (1857:535–39 [Wilmsen 2003]) reported the same at Libebe on the Okavango; Ladislaus Magyar (1860:227–31) was one of the traders to whom these reports referred. Also in 1855, Andersson ([1875] 1967:182–83) at Otjikoto noted extensive trade between Khoisan and Ovambo, and shortly thereafter, Carl Hugo Hahn (1867:285–86) remarked on the far-flung extensions of this trade to the north. Thus, from the far west all the way to the east at the Falls, all the early European traders along the border country report established, flourishing trade. Taken together, these archaeological and historical records confirm each other and reveal a consistent picture of European trade spread over a very large area; until about 1855 the European input into this Namibia-Ngamiland trade came mainly from the north.

The picture changed dramatically after Oswell and Livingstone in 1849 made the southern routes to Ngamiland known to European traders and the full effect of Alexander's exploration of central Namibia took hold; the most significant of these effects for our present purpose is Andersson's (1854) 1853 survey of the Orlam road from Walfish Bay to Lake Ngami. From 1850 or so onward, two-thirds of all presently known archaeological sites in the region contain European goods, and the metal objects at the others might well prove to be derived from introduced sources (Alexander, Galton, and Carl Hugo Hahn all remark on the indigenous demand for European iron and copper). Neutral white now replaced oyster white beads while various pink, pale blue, and striped beads mark the earlier part of this period; Theophilus Hahn (see below), among others, specifies these colors along with green and the timeless black. Chapman ([1868] 1971 1:127) remarks on the popularity of a pink-and-blue striped bead in 1853. Ruby-red-on-white and pale-pink-on-white were introduced in 1875 (Saitowitz and Sampson 1992). Jill Kinahan (2002:61) has confirmed that this combination of bead forms and colors characterizes the second half of the nineteenth century in our region. Carl Hugo Hahn ({1850s} 1984:510) describes continuing heavy trade with Portuguese across the Cunene and remarks particularly on white, red, and blue beads; Galton ([1853] 1971:199) estimated that Ovaherero still obtained half their iron from this source in 1851.

There is abundant evidence for other European activity in Namibia-Ngamiland beginning in 1850; a decade or so later, hunters and traders frequented all inhabited areas of the region, even those ethnographically described as remote. For example, Frederick Green informed his outfitter Charles John Andersson in December 1865 that he intended hunting to the southeast of the Omuramba Sheshoongoo. Green's map of this trip delineates a route into the Dobe-NyaeNyae area, as evidenced by three place names: Large reed ft[n] (Karakuwisa: Nama *!ara,* reed + *!kuwis,* vley); 2nd Palm ft[n] (Konambikus: Nama *!unib,* palm + *!ous,* spring); and Makgow (the Herero and Tswana name for the plant *Dichapetalum cymosum,* which is deadly to cattle in the rain season [Wilmsen 2003]).

Green suggests that James Todd and Robert Lewis had used this route before. It was a route often traveled in part or in whole by Europeans beginning in the late 1860s and routinely by Batawana beginning at least by the 1870s. Serton (1954:177) notes, in reference to several entries in Gerald McKiernan's dairies, that the route transecting Dobe-NyaeNyae and Tebra was on "the route through the Kaukauveld to the Epukiro, and then along this dry river-bed to its origin near Otjiarua." A branch at Epukiro went down to Ghanzi through Rietfontein; Boltmann's (1901) map has the notation "Weg n[ach] Transvaal" at the point where the route stems off at

Karakuwisa, thus indicating its incorporation within trade networks which, indeed, went on to Transvaal—as well as Walvis Bay and the Cape—from Ghanzi. Anonymous (1906) plots the entire route from Karakuwisa to Rietfontein, which was a well-worn track by the time Schinz went over it in the mid-1880s. It was along this route that a cowrie shell (*Cypraea annulus*, along with six Indo-Pacific land shells of the family *Helicinidae*) collected by Dyson in 1951 must have been brought to Gautsha in the NyaeNyae area from the south, where it is commonly found in the waters of the Natal Coast, especially Algoa Bay, where the Grahamstown traders had their supply port. A cowrie shell with iron and copper ornaments found at #Gi near Dobe probably is assignable to this time (Brooks and Yellen 1979:28)

Tabler (1973:111–12) relates that "Todd, Lewis and Kruger hunted elephants successfully till 27 May 1866 at a fountain about 45 miles [75km] northeast of Otjituo"—about 80km west of NyaeNyae. Lewis is remembered at CaeCae by his Herero name, Karobbie. And it is likely that Todd is remembered there—under the name Dowtli—by a Zhu woman, Wanxa,[5] as the employer of her mother's father who came from far to the south and spoke Nama (Wilmsen 1989:217, 342). This man married a Zhu woman of the area; their daughter, Wanxa's mother, would have been born about 1870, give or take a few years. This coincides with Todd's activities in Zhu country.

Both Bantu and Khoisan peoples continued active participation in these trading networks right up until the beginning of World War I, even though European traders had long reduced their activity in the area (Wilmsen 1989:123–29). The following quotes, selected from among many, convey the scope of continuing indigenous trade as it tapped into more distant European sources.

Theophilus Hahn (1895:614–15) describes some details of San trade in the 1890s:

> The Gabe Bushmen of ||Nuis shewed me beautiful embroideries of their own make from white, pink, blue, black and green beads, which they said they had bartered from the Ghanse or !Ai Bushmen, and these had again bartered the beads from the Batoanas of the Lake for ostrich feathers, leopard and jackal skins.

CaeCae people have described the same route to me and told me that it extended, as far as their grandfathers' dealings were concerned, through Qangwa and Tsodilo to the Hambukushu at Ncamasere and Muhembo on the Okavango (1989:116). Passarge (1907:40) in 1896–1898 found beads in abundance in the western sandveld: "Als Schmuck dienen ²Chore-Ketten, sowie weisse, rote, blaue Glasperlen, die in Ketten um den Hals getragen werden oder in die Haare geknüpft sind und in Form einer Schlinge auf der Stern herabhängen;" he also found cowrie shells, which led him to exclaim "Welche Geschichte mögen die Kowriemuscheln hinter sich haben!"[6]

It was, however, a time of transition; the heyday of the hunters had passed with the virtual elimination of elephants from the region and the catastrophic reduction in cattle herds by rinderpest. Lugard (1897:24) records that in defense against the latter, the "Germans have very stringent rules regarding the rinderpest. . . . Cattle have been removed Westwards, and the now depopulated condition of the Geikhana district (West of Reidfontein)" was abetted by a policy of killing the resident Khoé population. As a result, Baumeisters Laubschat (1903:681) observed:

> Zum Okavango sind deutsche Händler selten gekommen; aber auch die Portugiesen scheinen diese Gegend nicht häufig zu besuchen, weil der Handel bei dem geringen Viehbestand wenig lohnend ist. Gangbare Handelsartikel, wie Elfinbein und Kautschuk, sind nur in geringen Mengen vorhanden.[7]

But it was not simply commodity reduction that brought about this hiatus in European trade; political factors were equally critical. I (1989:134–39) have examined the Batawana, British, and German policy reasons for reducing activity in the border area; these had to do on the one hand with conflicts between the Tawana Kgosi, Sekgoma Letsholathebe, and the Kwanyama Omahona, Nyanganda, which came to a head in 1903. In the late 1890s, Sekgoma felt he could extend his territory at the expense of Nyanganda, and this led to a series of cattlepost raids on the German-British border and the killing of a German trader, Pasch, and his family. Khoisan are recorded to have been full participants in these affairs, which had their roots in the competition over reduced trade in the region (Wilmsen 1989:134–39 synthesizes the evidence).

A second factor was brought about by increased movement of Ovaherero back to the NyaeNyae and Ghanzi pans in order to escape intensifying German harassment. Both European administrations were aware that a local German-Herero conflict appeared imminent and that a major war between their countries was increasingly likely; both wished to avoid antagonizing the other, so all cattleposts were removed from the area in 1903, and trading there by Europeans was discouraged. Tommy Kayes, who came to Ngamiland in 1913 with his father (who had traded in the South West for years), told me that German authorities began advising his father "some years" before their move to make arrangements to go to British territory so as to be safe from German arrest in the event of war (Wilmsen 1985).

Trade among native peoples continued, however, and continued to be directed toward European commodity outlets—now by taking the goods to the trade centers. Nine years after Laubschat, in 1912, Stabsartz Kahle (Müller 1912:539–40) provided some details of this continuing trade among Khoisan and Bantu peoples:

Was sie [Batawana] nicht selbst schiessen, erhandeln sie von Buschleuten . . . fertig zum Verfand! . . . Die Buschleute scheinen aber gut Freund mit den Betchuanen zu sein. . . . Ich bin der festen Überzeugung, dass das Gewehr von dem Kapitäin Garu auch von den Betchuanen stammt, und das diese ihm auch regelmässig für Jagdzwecke Munition verkaufen.[8]

This refers to NyaeNyae (in German territory) in 1912, where Hauptmann Müller says trade (due to the economic and political restrictions just enumerated) was relatively light, as Laubschat had noted. Indeed, Müller's mission was, in part, to capture or expel any herders or traders he found in the area; Kahle (1912:539–40) makes it clear that there were many such:

In jedem Jahr, bald nach der Regenzeit, erscheinen sie [Batawana] mit Pferden, Reitochsen, und Wagen. . . . In Tsumkui, Gautscha, Garu und Nama zuegten frischer Kraal und frischer Ochenmist von ihrer Unwesenheit. . . . Leider sind wir um vier Wochen zu spät gekommen, sonst hätten wir die schwartze Jagdgesellschaft . . . noch gefasst.[9]

Trading was not, however, interdicted in Bechuanaland. For Dobe (in British territory), Müller and Kahle had this to say:

Ferner hören wir, dass in Lewisfontein, das schon auf englischem Gebiet liegt, ein Viehposten der Betschuanen sei. [Müller 1912:535] . . . von andere Seite her sesst die moderne Kultur ein. Unsere Nachbaren haben mit den Buschleuten bereits Handelsbeziehungen angeknüpft. (Kahle in Müller 1912:537).[10]

Nonetheless, Kahle recorded many trade items at the NyaeNyae pans: "Kauriemuscheln kamen vor. Glasperlen, Eisenperlen, und Kupferringe waren häufiger. . . . Auch Ovambomesser waren häufig" (Kahle in Müller 1912:539).[11]

Tommy Kayes supplies many details of this trade in the prewar years of this century, including the value placed upon salt and gunpowder by Kaukauveld peoples—Damara and Herero as well as Zhu (Wilmsen 1985).

Slavery

> In alter Zeit kamen sie, um Warenbündel einzutauschen. Sie kamen zu den Kxoé am Lùyánà. Auf verschiedenen Wegen kamen sie auch nach Búma. . . . Sie kamen und kauften mit den Warenbündel Kxoé-Kinder. Manchmal verkaufte ein Grossvater seinen Neffen an die Tchimbàrè. Manchmal verkaufte er den Sohn seiner alteren Schwester, manchmal den Sohn seiner jungeren Schwester— (meist) ein Kind, das sich immer weiter weigerte, wenn es auf einen Weg geschickt wurde—an die Tchimbàrè-Männer. Auch ein Vater tauschte seinen Sohn bei den Tchimbàrè-Männern gegen (gewebten) Stoff ein. Und auch die Mutter war einverstanden, um aus den dem Stoff einen Vorderschurz zu binden. Der Junge weinte zwar, ging aber mit [Köhler 1989:434–44].[12]

We have in this oral text (which refers to the mid-nineteenth century) collected from an old Kxoé man by Oswin Köhler (1989:444) not only direct evidence of participation by Khoisan speakers in the slave trade but also clues to the social organization through which the trade was carried on. Reports of such trade date back to the 1850s, when mentions of slavery in the Angola, Botswana, Namibia border country were common; Hahn ({1850s–60s} 1984:510), Livingstone ([1857] 1912:65), Oswell (1900 2:230, 245), Green (1857:537), Magyar (1860:227–31)—all of whom were in the region between 1851 and 1855—speak of this trade, as does McKiernan in the 1870s (Serton 1954). Indeed, Magyar, a Hungarian who lived and traded with Angolan !Xu (the source of the ethnographic label !Kung)[13] from about 1840 (Fodor 1983; Wilmsen 1978) seems to have been involved in the trade with his Mbari partners. A trickle of reports continued into this century; there are the direct observations of Gibbons (1904:202) among Barotse and Hambukushu, Passarge (1907:97–98) concerning Naro-Khoé, and Seiner ([1913] 1977:34) among ||Anikhoé. Historians have long confirmed the activity of Mbari (Tchimbàrè of Köhler's Kxoé), Mbwela, and Mbukushu slaving in the region before 1850 (Gray and Birmingham 1970; Miller 1976); however, Nettleton's (1934:358) claim that Arab traders operated on the northern Ngamiland border cannot be substantiated (see Slade 1962 for nearest Arab zone of operation in the Congo).[14]

More recently, Estermann (1976, 1:125) describes ekongo slave raiding among nineteenth–century Ovambo and Ovakwanyama, and Lee (1979:77–78) recounts how Batswana put Zhu "under the carrying yoke" and subjected them to "rough frontier justice" when they moved into the lands of these Khoisan-speaking people. Tlou (1985) and Chirenje (1977) evaluate much of this material, while Gadibolae (1985) and Mautle (1986) document the pervasive extent of *bolata* (indigenous Tswana slavery), involving subjugated peoples, including Khoisan. What began as a reciprocal relation for production between Batswana and Khoisan in a hunting and pastoral partnership changed during the nineteenth century into one of servitude in which Khoisan first served the evolving Tswana states and later became the private property of Tswana masters (Meirs and Crowder 1988:173; Wilmsen 1989:96–157). Morton (1990, 1994) argues that, to a comparatively small but not negligible degree, Batswana extended their domestic practice in the nineteenth century to deal in slaves with Boers and Portuguese; he cites evidence that Hendrik Van Zyl—active in the Dobe-NyaeNyae area during the 1860s (Tabler 1973:114)—dealt in slaves from Namibia and Ngamiland. Gewald (1991) examines Namibian sources.

Although they mention the participation of many peoples, the primary sources just cited do not give thick descriptions of slaving in the region; indeed, the fact of the existence of slavery is usually noted in the same manner as the presence of a particular species of tree, as if the only new information needed concerning a commonly known phenomenon was about its distribution. I think it was this offhand manner of recording—plus the isolationist stance of those then crafting the modern classical Bushman canon—that diverted 1960s ethnographers of Khoisan peoples from an examination of these sources. To be sure, the Okavango region was the interior frontier of Atlantic slave trade, and no claim can be made that the long human lines chained toward the coast, common not far to the north, were ever seen in the region. But Miller (1988:10, 17), in his *Way of Death,* shows the frontier at the Delta in the second quarter of the nineteenth century, a position confirmed by Tlou's (1985:14) oral histories, which say that the Mbukushu chief, Disho, was trading slaves from the Okavango to Benguela on the Atlantic coast about 1820. Köhler (1989:426, 441) suggests that his informants indicated that the Mbari traders who came to them were from "Benguela and its hinterland" but estimates no date when this may have happened.

Further indication of the trade at this early date is found in another of Köhler's (1989:441) oral texts, which states that the first Mbari carried cowhide shields and raided Kxoé with flint-locks (*Steinschlossgewehren*); although a few of the latter weapons remained as relics for decades, shields

were abandoned soon after guns became readily available. We can also surmise that more than one person with !Kung ancestry, !Xu and/or Zhu, fell
into line—for in 1980 in New York City a man presented with a rare,
recessive CEA abnormality so far found only in persons of !Kung ancestry
(Jenkins 1979:79). It is not necessary that anyone with stereotypical
"Khoisan" physique or who spoke only a !Kung language was taken as a
slave to the Americas. It is only necessary that some persons who carried
this recessive gene, which, as far as we now are able to tell, could have been
acquired only from !Kung ancestors, were taken, and that descendents of
these met and had children, some of whom acquired the dominant characteristic. In the light of data regarding the extent of !Kung-Bantu intermar-
riage now coming to our attention, it is probable that a not insignificant
number of such recessive carriers were transported.

Indeed, Köhler's (1989:426) texts specifically include Wald-!Xu (Zhu)
among those frequently captured and traded by Kxoé to Mbwela and Portuguese; "So nahmen die Mbwélà-Männer oft Kxoé und Wald-!Xu
gefangen."[15] Zhu, in turn, are reported to have captured Kxoé children for
exchange with Mbari;

> Die !Xu-Männer kamen und überfielen die Kxoé-Leute. Sie überfielen die
> Kxoé, um Warenbündel dafür zu tauschen. So hielten sie die Kxoé-Kinder
> fest, um bei den Anda etwas gegen sie einzutauschen. Als die Kxoé-Männer
> dies sahen, gerieten sie in Wut und Zorn und entrissen den !Xu-Männer die
> Kxoé-Kinder. So machten sie es. Die !Xu-Männer schossen auf die Kxoé. In
> Búma schossen sie mit vergifteten Pfeilen (Köhler 1989:344).[16]

It is, thus, worthwhile to look more closely at Khoisan participation
in the slave trade; Köhler's texts provide an opportunity to do so.

I shall begin by unwrapping the bundle that the grandfather received
for a slave. It contained blankets, cloth, clothing, guns, gunpowder and
lead, percussion caps and balls, copper bangles, [glass beads], and marine
shells (Köhler 1989:426). Glass beads are not mentioned in Köhler's texts,
but they are frequently listed in the other bundle inventories. This inventory is remarkably congruent with those found all across the Angola-Congo
slaving zone (*African Repository* 1853:343; Nettleton 1934:358; Miller
1988:56, 66–67; Vansina 1990:205). That this inventory should have become the conventional packet is not surprising, for Miller (1988:56) notes
that copper and shells possess the necessary durability and uniformity required of standard units of exchange, while cloth was cut in lengths "appropriate to garb a person" (Miller 1988:67, 1986).

At this point a digression about the value of these goods throughout the history of the region is appropriate. Glass beads appear to have been valued from an early date and are found in archaeological sites in the region dating to the eighth century (these are from East Coast ports associated with the Indian Ocean trade) and again from the sixteenth-century Atlantic trade to the present. Cowrie shells, too, have a long history of value in the region; they appear as early as C.E. 800/900 and are found in archaeological sites of different time periods from then on into the nineteenth century, when they are reported to have had high value (Wilmsen 1989:115–17, citing Alexander, Passarge, and Vedder). Meillassoux (1991:47–48) records that cowries were a major currency in the slave trade in North Africa. Cloth also has a long history of value in the region, although its perishability makes its presence difficult to establish; Phillipson (1977:193) notes that a scrap of India cloth was found at Ingombe Ilede (sixteenth century), preserved by contact with copper.

Vansina (1990:94, 180, 205) shows that the slave bundle was but a contemporary transformation of centuries-old trade bundles which contained raffia cloth, mats, copper and iron, marine products, dyewoods, beads, salt, and other items. This congruence reveals the standardization of values in a vast material and human commodity market as well as the stability of these values over space and time; it also underwrites the credibility of Köhler's (1989:426) native historians' memories:

> "Diese Sachen habe ich gebracht, um damit einen Sklaven zu kaufen." So spricht der Mbwélà-Mann zu dem Kxoé. . . . Nachdem der Alte (Herr des Wohnplatzes) dies gehört hat, (anwortet er): "Wenn es so ist, habe ich gewiss einen Sklaven. Bring mir das Bündel!" . . . Der Alte hebt es auf. . . . Dann schneidet er das Tuch (in Stücke). . . . Hat er dies getan, verschenkt er das ganze Tuch an die Leute des Wohnplatzes.[17]

We have here additional insights into the social organization of the trade. Although we must await the appearance of Köhler's volume 4 to learn the specific details of Kxoé kinship and marriage, we may rely on Barnard's (1988:29–50, cf. 1991) conclusion that "the deep structure of all Khoé kinship systems is essentially the same." Hence, we may provisionally surmise that Khoé slaving operated in extension of the principle that a man and his sister's son (potential husband of his daughter) were bound by reciprocal social and material obligations similar to the Nama mother's-brother/sister's-son *xnurixas* relationship of cattle snatching and unbalanced transfer of possessions from a man to his sister's son, who thereby acknowl-

edged avuncular authority. This was by no means unusual: Gibbons
(1904:202) recorded that in 1898 the Mbukushu Chief, Libebe, sold children of his subjects, claiming them to be his children, no doubt in extension of the eponymous principle that he was the father of his following.
Khoé residential arrangements were also organized along extended affinal-
kinship lines; thus, the "grandfather-headman" of the homestead, in his
capacity as elder avuncular in-law, may have been in a position to extract
especially strong demands from his sisters' sons (possibly classificatory as
well as actual). Indeed, as marriage between Kxoé and Mbwela slavers seems
to have been common—"Mein Neffe lebt bei den Mbwéla. Er hat eine
Mbwélà-Frau geheiratet. . . . Meine beiden Neffen . . . heirateten Mbwélà-
Frauen"[18] (Köhler 1989:427)—this may have been looked upon as an ex-
pectable kinship transaction. It may also have been looked upon as only a
temporary loss, given the widespread notion that gunpowder was the bone-
ashes of sent-off slaves returned to its people (Miller 1988:86). When this
notion is compared with another held by African slaves in the Caribbean
who believed that the spirits of their dead returned to Africa, an affective
communication across the sea of complex dimensions is revealed.

Moreover, Kxoé-Mbwela marriages were simply an extension of long-
standing affinal relations among peoples of the region. So pervasive were
marriages between Kxoé and !Xu that their ||Anikhoé neighbors sometimes
refer to Kxoé as !Xu (Köhler 1989:184). In 1898, Passarge (1907:21) found
that the headman at Tsodilo was the son of a Khoé man and a Zhu woman
and grew up at CaeCae; twenty years earlier, in 1878, the Boer Trekkers
found a Khoé-speaking headman in the NyaeNyae area (Prinsloo and Gauche
1933:29–30, they called him a Bergdamara). These relationships, and others like them at CaeCae, appear in my (1989:204–5) genealogies and reflect
multiple links between Zhu and Khoé. Such links were widespread in the
region, as in Nyaneka otyisoko kinship among omaanda descent groups, through
which a man could "obtain the possession of a person to serve him as a slave"
(Estermann [1957] 1976 2:126–27). Among Herero, Khoisan "retainers" could
be taken into oruzo and eanda descent reckoning and their children, thus,
become full social equals (Vedder 1928:193). Clearly, the whole fabric of
Okavango slave practice contradicts Meillassoux's (1991:35) assertion of
"the slave's juridical inability to become kin" and that "the exploitation of
slaves necessitates the establishment of social relations which are the social
and juridical antithesis of kinship relations." Indeed, it seems clear that
Okavango peoples, Bantu- and Khoisan-speaking, employed just exactly
those long-existing social and juridical relations that were well understood
within the community to sanction the sending of kin into slavery.

Okavango slaving did, however, include brigandage—"the practice of abducting captives *from within the same community,* among relatives and neighbors" (Meillassoux 1991:143, original emphasis—this seems contradictory in light of the previous quote), as the following text from Köhler (1989:425–26) testifies.

> Hat er indes keinen Sklaven, nimmt er das Warebündel entgegen und legt es nieder. Hat man dann alle Sachen (zum Aufbruch) bereitgelegt, sammelt er die Kxoé-Männer um sich. Sie gehen dann hintereinander. . . . Sie jagen die Kinder und die Frauen und nahmen sie fest . . . und kehrten mit ihnen zum Wohnplatz zurück. . . . Dann nahm er einen Sklaven und gab ihn dem Mbwélà-Mann. Damit war es zu Ende.[19]

There is evidence that "Bushmen" in the area below the Okavango were also subject to being raided by slavers, although almost surely at a very low rate and perhaps only for the indigenous rather than the Atlantic system. In 1878, McKiernan recorded that a posse was formed to avenge the murder of C. L. Thomas by Ovakwanyama on the Okavango just north of Lion Fountain; among the traders in the vicinity at the time,

> [Robert] Lewis [with James Todd (Tabler 1973:68)] and others agreed to come after they could collect their people . . . [and] Lewis came at the appointed time with 9 horsemen and 20 Bushmen, who are willing enough to fight the Ovampos who make slaves of them (Serton 1954:167).

It is crucial to notice here that Lewis and Todd went to collect "their" people for assistance in a grave matter and that among their people were Khoisan. From Lion Fountain, they could only have gone generally southward to collect these people; given the available evidence, primarily that there are no habitable places between, it is probable that Lewis went to Dobe-NyaeNyae, most likely to Green's first Palm fountain (see also Köhler 1989).

Although all people within the reach of any group were targets for raiding, there were affiliate connections that were thought ought not to be broken, as expressed in the following account from 1898: "I belong to Lewanika; so do they. It is not good that the children of one father should quarrel and fight" (Gibbons 1904:238). Even though slaving in the region continued into the first decade or so of this century—"Als Kxyáró (noch) ein Kind war [about 1905–10], nahmen sie immer wieder Wald-!Xu gefangen"[20] and sold them as slaves (Köhler 1989:426; see also Seiner 1977)—it brought ever smaller returns after 1900.

Red Rubber

From the 1870s, however, rubber became increasingly important as an export commodity (Vansina 1990:209); in the final quarter of the nineteenth century, Benguela became a port of transit for this wild plant commodity (Miller 1988:227) and thus opened the Okavango region to its profitable exploitation. In 1896–98, Passarge (1907:121 [Wilmsen 1997:204]) listed Wurzelkautschuk (root-rubber) as a tributary item paid by northern Kalahari[21] Bushmen to the Tawana Kgosi, who traded it to the Portuguese in Angola from whence it went on to sheath the electrical wires then being strung across Europe. This rubber is derived from the root of *Landolphia camptoloba* (White 1962:349) as well as two species of *Carpodinus*; its production was the basis of King Leopold's ruthless subjugation of the Congo (Vansina 1990:242). Its high price pushed the search for sources into the Okavango region. Köhler (1989:439) was told that "Sie [die Tcìmbúndù] gruben dir Wurzel des kàmbúngò-Baumes[22] aus und klopften sie weich. War die Wurzel weich, wurde es zu Gummi."[23] This was a labor intensive process requiring about sixty man-hours to produce a kilogram, worth about four square yards of cloth at the turn of the century (Hobson [1960] 1974:493). Gibbons (1904:240–42) noted that rubber production was a major industry along the Cubango and Cuito rivers in 1898. At the same time, in 1896–98, Passarge (1907:7 [Wilmsen 1997:131) recorded the engagement of Khoisan in this production; he cites several reports of "Makwengo" (Kxoé) on the north bank of the Cubango (as the Okavango is called in Angola) at the confluence of the Cuito where "Sie sind Sklaven der Kovale bezw. Owakwangari und müssen für ihre Herren Wurzelkautschuk suchen."[24] Five years after Passarge, Baum (1903) recorded *Landolphia* on the Angolan side of the Okavango, and Laubschat—who described the production process he observed—noted it was produced in small quantities in this same vicinity on the South West side: "Handelsartikel, wie Elfenbein und Kautschuk, sind nur in geringer Mengen vorhanden."[25]

Transition

Preliminary outlines of geographical movements of peoples can be discerned in this brief outline of the social organization of trade. Köhler's (1989:349) oral texts are again helpful; they state that !Xu and Zhu formerly lived where Kwankala were found by the first Europeans (and are found today), and that Gciriku (who also live there) came in from the north in mid-eighteenth century. This date features in the movement histories of numbers of peoples in the region (prominently Hambukushu and Ovaherero); by this time, slavers had been active in the Benguela hinterland around the headwaters of the Cunene and Cubango for nearly a century, and consequent displacements of peoples had been set in motion (Miller 1988:148–49). There is also substantial archaeological evidence for the penetration of Portuguese trade items into northern Botswana and Namibia already in the seventeenth century (Denbow and Wilmsen, forthcoming). I (1989) have argued that these materials entered the region through long established trade relations, relations that would have included marriage alliances and trade-friend networks. These channels would have been ready-made routes not only for material and human commerce, but for the relatively nonaggressive deployment of peoples able to take advantage of that commerce. Wiessner (1995) discusses the social channels along which this could be accomplished by Zhuchoasi.

I suggest that this process brought Zhu to their present locations in Botswana-Namibia during the seventeenth/eighteenth centuries; we know that they moved into the Tsodilo Hills and Delta-Lake Ngami margins as a result of engagement with European trade and Tswana hegemony only at the end of the last century (Passarge 1907:22–27 [Wilmsen 1997:140–44]; Lee 1979:81; Wilmsen 1989:205–7; Campbell, Denbow, and Wilmsen 1994:155). Today the Kwankala-Sekele-!Xu linguistic relatives of Zhu live in a large contiguous part of Angola spanning almost the entire east-west extent of the center of the country including the Cunene-Cubango-Cuito-Cuando drainages. There is evidence that they were much farther north and perhaps east in recent centuries. Magyar, himself, was in the headwater area of those rivers when he first mentioned Sekele. At about the same time, in 1847, members of a Portuguese expedition to the Bulozi describe a people on the northern Angola-Zambia border whom they called "Cassaqueres . . . os Bacancala e os Bacassequeres. . . . Uma outra designação para este grupo . . . é de Cunques [*!kung*]" (Madeira Santos 1986:335, 387).[26] As Kubik (1984:131) remarks, "Die Erinnerung an die 'Vasekele' im Lucazi-Sprachschatz ist ein Hinweis darauf, wieviel weiter nördlich es früher Khoisan-Gruppen gegeben haben muss."[27] Today the Zhu in Namibia-Ngamiland form a short, narrow wedge into an otherwise solid band of Khoé speakers between 16° and 23° south latitude extending from the Atlantic eastward beyond Victoria Falls. Within this wedge, many place-names remain Khoé (Wilmsen 1989:334), a fact recognized a century ago by Passarge (1907:23), who concluded—correctly, I think, in light of the foregoing presentation of evidence—that this must imply comparatively recent movement of Zhu into the area, beginning perhaps in the seventeenth/eighteenth centuries in conjunction with the initial penetration of Portuguese-inspired Congo-Luanda trade into the interior.[28]

We have seen in this discussion a catalog of cattleposts, commodity trade, and multi-community relations among agents of commerce, including Khoisan peoples, combing Namibia-Ngamiland on a regular, routine basis over a period of several generations. That is, Khoisan peoples represented as simply foraging "Bushmen" were engaged as labor in production for a world market; producing primary commodities (copper ore, feathers, hides, horns, ivory, dye-wood, salt, slaves), manufacturing containers for delicate items (slip cases for feathers), adding value to products (processing hides and salt), delegating time for these purposes, and coordinating activities with other links in the market economy. Although it goes beyond the central scope of this paper, I should note that there was a deep trade recession in the area during the 1930s–1950s, associated with world depression and war. It was at the end of these depressed decades with their atypical economic conditions that modern ethnographies of disengaged Khoisan foragers were written. When Botswanacraft, a parastatal crafts purchasing organization, began buying local products again for a revived world market in the early 1970s, local economies recovered to some extent and several Khoisan families prospered modestly by investing craft sales profits in livestock.

Notes

1. Magyar also mentions porcelain beads, but the latter are not known to have been traded into the subcontinent. He probably thought that the large opaque-oyster white and neutral white beads highly favored in the region were porcelain—as observers sometimes do today.

2. For works published long after the observations upon which they are based were made the date of observation is given in { }; for reprints, the date of original publication is given in [ ].

3. "Ka-ssekel or, as one calls them in the south, Mu-kánkála."

4. The NyaeNyae material was collected by Robert Dyson in 1951 when he was a member of the Marshall Expedition.

5. In keeping with usual practice in Botswana, I use Tswana orthography for clicks in personal names—c = | (dental) and # (alveolar), x = | (lateral), q = ! (palatal)—(cf. Dickens 1994:353–56).

6. "As jewelry there are necklaces of white, red, and blue glass beads worn around the neck or stuck in the hair so that they hang in loops across the forehead. . . . What histories these cowries must have behind them."

7. "German traders seldom come to the Okavango, and it seems the Portuguese also visit this region infrequently because the trade for the small number of cattle is worth little. Acceptable trade items, such as ivory and rubber, are available only in small quantity."

8. "What they do not shoot themselves, they trade from the Bushmen [he mentions ostrich feathers in *Grewia* stem slip-cases, horn, hides] . . . ready to be delivered! . . . The Bushmen appear to be on good terms with the Batswana. . . . I am of the firm opinion that Captain Garu's gun came from the Batswana and that these also regularly sell him ammunition for hunting purposes."

9. "Every year, soon after the rain season, they appear with horses, ride-oxen, and wagons. . . . At Tjùm!kúí, Aòchà, Garu, and Nama fresh kraals and fresh cow dung gave evidence of their presence. . . . Unfortunately, we came about four weeks too late, otherwise we would have seized the black hunting party."

10. "We heard further, that there is a Tswana cattlepost at Lewisfontein, which already lies in English territory . . . on [that] other side, modern culture is established. Our neighbors [Batswana/British] have ensconced trade relations with the Bushmen."

11. "Cowries are in evidence. Glass beads, iron beads, and copper bracelets are more abundant. . . . Ovambo [metal] knives are common."

12. Oral text 1.2.3.3–3: "In the old days, they came with bundles of goods to exchange. They came to the Kxoé on the Luiana. They also came to Búma along different routes. . . . They came and bought Kxoé children with the bundles of goods. Sometimes a grandfather exchanged his nephews to the Mbari. Sometimes he exchanged the son of his older sister, sometimes the son of his younger sister—(mostly) a child that always refused when sent along the way—to the Mbari. Also a father exchanged his son for (woven) cloth from Mbari men. The mother also agreed, in order to put on an apron of cloth. The boy cried it's true, but went with."

13. I think that !Kung should be restricted to use as a general term to refer to Bleek's (1929) Northern Bush languages which include Kwankala, Sekele, Zhu, and !Xu; this is parallel to the current practice of using Khoé as the term applied to Bleek's Central Bush languages. I use the term in this sense when speakers of one of these particular languages cannot be identified, but employ the appropriate ethnonym whenever possible. Both Zhu and !Xu mean 'people' and may be cognate in these closely related languages. Khoé also means "people." Kxoé is Köhler's spelling of the ethnonym of a particular group of Khoé-speaking peoples in the Okavango region who are also known by their Tswana designation, Makwengo.

14. It is, however, probable that middlemen, both Bantu- and Khoisan-speakers, engaged in trade with Okavango peoples that connected through a series of links with Arabs in the Congo headwaters region; archaeological evidence for such links extends to C.E. 800/900 (Denbow and Wilmsen 1986, forthcoming). Other than Nettleton's, whose inventory of the slave-trading bundle is consistent with others, I am not aware of any reference to slaving as a possible part of this trade; the matter needs attention.

15. Oral text 1.2.3.2–2c: "In this way, Mbwela men often took Kxoé and Zhu."

16. Oral text 1.2.1.2.1–1: "Zhu men came and seized Kxoé people. They seized Kxoé to exchange for the bundle of goods. So they held the Kxoé children tightly, to exchange them for something with the |Anda. When the Kxoé men saw this they reacted with rage and anger and snatched the Kxoé children from the Zhu men. That's the way they did it. The Zhu men shot at the Kxoé. In Búma, they shot with poisoned arrows."

17. Oral text 1.2.3.2–2b: "These things I have brought with which to buy a slave; so spoke the Mbwela man to the Kxoé. . . . When the elder, the grandfather, (headman of the

homestead) heard this he said, if this is so I have a slave for you. Bring me the bundle! The grandfather took it; then he cut the cloth into uniform pieces . . . when he had done this, he distributed all of the cloth to the people of the homestead."

18. Oral text 1.2.3.2–3: "My nephew lives with the Mbwela; he has married an Mbwela woman. . . . My two nephews have married Mbwela women."

19. Oral text 1.2.3.2–2: "If [the grandfather-headman] had no slave available, he took the trade-bundle and stashed it. When all had been secured, he gathered the Kxoé men; they went single-file . . . they hunted children and women and captured them and took them back to their place. . . . Then [the grandfather] took a slave and gave it to the Mbwela man. That was the end of it."

20. Oral text 1.2.3.2–2c: "When Kxyáró was still a child, they frequently took Zhu captive."

21. The present Angola-Namibian border is roughly the division line between Passarge's Northern and Central Kalahari.

22. The Mbundu name for *L. camptoloba*. White (1962) gives the Shona name, mubungu—which is the same; he also confirms that the vine extends into the Kalahari sands of Botswana.

23. Oral text 1.2.3.3–1: "The Mbundu dig up the roots of kàmbúngò and beat them soft; when the roots are soft, they produce rubber."

24. "They are slaves of the Kowale and/or Ovakwangari, and they must search for root-rubber for their masters."

25. "Trade goods, such as ivory and rubber, are available only in small quantities."

26. "Cassaqueres . . . the Bacancala and the Bacassequeres. Another designation for this group is Cunques (*!Kung*)." Cassaqueres and Bacassequeres would seem to be (Ka/Va)sekele and Bacancala to be (Ova/Va)kwankala. I am grateful to Achim von Oppen for leading me to literature on former !Kung distributions.

27. "The recollection of the Vasekele in Lucazi vocabulary is an indication of how much further north Khoisan groups must have been found in the past."

28. Rainer Vossen (personal communication) suggests that this makes sense from a linguistic perspective.

References

African Repository. 1853. "Interior Africa—Progress of Discoveries," vol. 29, 343.

Alexander, J. 1967. *An Expedition of Discovery into the Interior of Africa, through the Hitherto Undescribed Countries of the Great Namaquas, Boschmans, and the Hill Damaras* [1838]. Cape Town: Struik.

Andersson, C. J. 1854. "A Journey to Lake Ngami, and an Itinerary of the Principal Routes Leading to It from the West Coast; With the Latitudes of Some of the Chief Stations." *South African Commercial Advertiser and Cape Town Mail,* 22 May.

———. 1856. *Lake Ngami.* London: John Murray.

Anonymous. 1906. *Die Kämpfe der deutschen Truppen in Südwestafrika. Erster Band: Der Feldzug gegen die Hereros.* Berlin: Mittler.

Barnard, A. 1988. "The Deep Structure of Khoé Kinship." *Africa* 58: 29–50.

———. 1991. *Hunters and Herders of Southern Africa: A Comparative Ethnography of the*

Khoisan Peoples. Cambridge: Cambridge University Press.

Baum, H. 1903. *Kunene-Sambesi-Expedition.* Berlin: Kolonial Wirtschaftlichen Komitees.

Boltmann, (none given). 1901. "Reise des Oberleutnants Boltmann nach dem Okavango." *Deutsches Kolonialblatt* 12: 866.

Brooks, A., and J. Yellen. 1979. "Archaeological Excavations at #Gi." *Botswana Notes and Records* 9: 21–30.

Campbell, A., J. Denbow, and E. Wilmsen. 1994. "Paintings Like Engravings." In *Contested Images: Diversity in Southern African Rock Art Research,* ed. D. Lewis-Williams and T. Dowson, 131–58. Johannesburg: University of Witwatersrand Press.

Chapman, J. 1971. *Travels in the Interior of Africa* [1868]. 2 vols. Cape Town: Balkema.

Chirenje, J. 1977. *A History of Northern Botswana: 1850–1910.* Rutherford N.J.: Fairleigh Dickenson University Press.

Denbow, J., and E. Wilmsen. 1986. "The Advent and Course of Pastoralism in the Kalahari." *Science* 234: 1509–15.

———. Forthcoming. *Cattle, Copper, and Capital in the Transformation of Southern African Communities.*

Dickens, P. 1994. "English-Juǀ'hoan/Juǀ'hoan-English Dictionary." *Qwellen zur Khoisan Forschung/Research in Khoisan Studies* 8.

Estermann, C. 1976. *Ethnography of Ssouthwestern Angola.* 3 vols. Translated and edited from *Ethnográfia do sudoesteo de Angola* by G. Gibson [1957]. New York: Africana Press.

Fodor, I. 1983. *Introduction to the History of Umbundu.* Budapest: Akadémiai Kiadó.

Gadibolae, M. 1985. "Serfdom (Bolata) in the Nata Area." *Botswana Notes and Records* 17: 25–32.

Galton, F. 1971. *The Narrative of an Explorer in Tropical South Africa* [1853]. New York: Johnson Reprint.

Gewald, J.-B. 1991. "Untapped Sources: Slave Exports from Southern and Central Namibia up to the Mid-Nineteenth Century." Paper presented at the conference on The Mfecane Aftermath, University of Witwatersrand—Johannesburg.

Gibbons, A. 1904. *Africa from South to North through Marotseland.* Oxford: Bodley Head.

Gibson, G. 1962. "Bridewealth and Other Forms of Exchange among the Herero." In *Markets in Africa,* ed. P. Bohannan and G. Dalton, 617–39. Evanston, Ill.: Northwestern University Press.

Gordon-Cumming, R. 1904. *The Adventure of a Lion Hunter in South Africa* [1850]. London: John Murray.

Gray, R., and D. Birmingham. 1970. *Pre-Colonial African Trade.* Oxford: Oxford University Press.

Green, F. 1857. "Narratives of an Exploration to the Northwest of Lake Ngami." *Eastern Province Monthly Magazine* 1: 537.

Hahn, C. 1867. "Neueste deutsche Forschungen in Süd-Afrika: Von Karl Mauch, Hugo Hahn und Richard Brenner, 1866 und 1867." *Petermann's Geographische Mitteilungen* 8: 281–98.

———. 1984. *Carl Hugo Hahn Tagebücher, 1837–1860.* Edited by B. Lau. Windhoek: Archeia 4.

Hobson, R. 1974. "Rubber: A Footnote to Northern Rhodesian History." *Occasional Papers of the Rhodes-Livingstone Museum* 1–16: 489–538.

Jenkins, T., and A. B. Lane. 1979. "The Red Cell Adenosine Deaminase Polymorphism in

Southern African Populations, with Particular Reference to the !Kung of Tsumkwe, Southwest Africa/Namibia." *Inborn Errors of Specific Immunity* 73: 91.

Kinahan, Jill. 2000. "Cattle for Beads: The Archaeology of Historical Contact and Trade on the Namib Coast." *Studies in African Archaeology* 17. Uppsala: University of Uppsala and Windhoek: Namibia Archaeological Trust.

Kinahan, John. 1986. "Settlement Patterns and Regional Exchange: Evidence from Recent Iron Age Sites on the Kavango River, Northeastern Namibia." *Cimbebasia* 3: 109–16.

———. 1991. *Pastoral Nomads of the Central Namib Desert.* Windhoek: New Namibia Books.

Köhler, O. 1989. *Die Welt der Kxoé-Buschleute,* Vol. 1: *Die Kxoé-Buschleute und ihre ethnische Umgebung.* Berlin, Dieter Reimer.

Kubik, G. 1984. "Das Khiosan-Erbe in süden von Angola." *Wiener Ethnohistorische Blätter* 27: 125–55.

Laubschat, Baumeister. 1903. "Bericht über eine Reise nach dem Norden des deutsch-südwestafrikanischen Schutzgebietes." *Deutsches Kolonialblatt* 14: 614–16, 641–46, 678–82.

Lee, R. 1979. *The !Kung San.* Cambridge: Cambridge University Press.

Livingstone, D. 1912. *Missionary Travels and Researches in South Africa.* [1857] London: John Murray.

Lugard, F. 1897. "Report No. 3: July 1st to September 30th 1896." Bodleian Library, Oxford University, MSS.Brit.Emp.s.56.

Madeira Santos, M. E., ed. 1986. *Viagems e apartamentos de un Portuense em Africa,* vol. 1. Coimbra: Junta de Investigaçoes do Ultamar.

Mautle G. 1986. "Bakgalagadi-Bakwena Relationships: A Case of Slavery, c.1840–c.1930." *Botswana Notes and Records* 18: 19–32.

Meillassoux, C. 1991. *The Anthropology of Slavery.* Chicago: University of Chicago Press.

Meirs, S., and R. Roberts. 1988. *The End of Slavery in Africa.* Madison: University of Wisconsin Press.

Miller, J. 1976. *Kings and Kinsmen.* Oxford: Oxford University Press.

———. 1988. *Way of Death.* Madison: University of Wisconsin Press.

Morton, B. 1990. "'Black Wool': The Ngamiland-Transvaal Slave Trade, 1850–77." Indiana University, African History Seminar Paper.

———. 1994. "Slavery in the Kalahari." In *Slavery in South Africa: Captive Labor on the Dutch Frontier,* ed. E. Eldredge and F. Morton, 214–35. Boulder, Colo.: Westview.

Mossop, E. 1935. *The Journal of Hendrik Jakob Wikar (1779)* (English translation by A. van der Horst) and *The Journals of Jacobus Coetse Janz (1760) and Willem van Reenan (1791).* Cape Town: The Van Riebeck Society.

———. 1947. *The Journals of Brink and Rhenius.* Cape Town: The Van Riebeck Society.

Müller, Hauptmann. 1912. "Ein Erkundungsritt in das Kaukau-Veld." *Deutsches Kolonialblatt* 23: 530–41.

Nettleton, G. 1934. "History of the Ngamiland Tribes up to 1926." *Bantu Studies* 8: 343–60.

Oswell, W. 1900. *William Cotton Oswell.* 2 vols. London: Heinemann.

Passarge, S. 1904. *Die Kalahari.* Berlin: Dieter Reimer.

———. 1907. *Die Buschmänner der Kalahari.* Berlin: Dieter Reimer.

Phillipson, D. 1977. *The Later Prehistory of Eastern and Southern Africa.* London, Heinemann.

Prinsloo, J., and J. Gauche. 1933. *In die woeste Weste.* Pretoria: de Bussy.

Saitowitz, S., and G. Sampson. 1992. "Glass Trade Beads from Rock Shelters in the Upper Karoo." *South African Archaeological Bulletin* 47: 94–103.

Sandelowsky, B. 1979. "Kapako and VunguVungu: Iron Age Sites on the Kavango River." *South African Archaeological Society, Goodwin Series* 3: 52–61

Schinz, H. 1891. *Deutsch-Südwest-Afrika: Forschungreisen durch die deutschen Schutzgebiete Gross-Nama-und Herereroland, nach dem Kunene, dem Ngami-See und der Kalaxari, 1884–1887.* Oldenburg and Leipzig: Schulzesche Hof.

Seiner, F. 1977. "Die Buschmänner des Okawango und Sambesigebietes der Nord-Kalahari." Translated from the 1913 German original by H. Vierich-Esche. *Botswana Notes and Records* 9: 31–36.

Serton, P. 1954. *The Narrative and Journal of Gerald McKiernan in South West Africa, (1874–1879).* Cape Town: The Van Riebeck Society.

Slade, R. 1962. *King Leopold's Congo.* Oxford: Oxford University Press.

Tabler, E. 1973. *Pioneers of South West Africa and Ngamiland: 1738–1880.* Cape Town: Balkema.

Tlou, T. 1985. *A History of Ngamiland, 1750–1906.* Madison: University of Wisconsin Press.

Vansina, J. 1990. *Paths in the Rainforests.* Madison: University of Wisconsin Press.

Vedder, H. 1928. "The Herero." In *The Native Tribes of South West Africa,* ed. C. Hahn, H. Vedder, and L. Fourie, 153–208. Cape Town: Frank Cass.

White, F. 1962. *The Forest Flora of Northern Rhodesia.* Oxford: Oxford University Press.

Wiessner, P. 2002. "Historical Dimensions of Ju|'hoan hxaro." In *Qwellen zur Khoisan Forschung/Research in Khoisan Studies* 15, ed. R. Ross, R. Vossen, and E. Wilmsen.

Wilmsen, E. 1978. "Prehistoric and Historic Antecedents of an Ngamiland Community." *Botswana Notes and Records* 10: 5–18.

———. 1985. "Conversations with Mr. Tommy Kayes of Maun." *Botswana Notes and Records* 17: 175–78.

———. 1989. *Land Filled with Flies.* Chicago: University of Chicago Press.

———. 1997. "The Kalahari Ethnography of Siegfried Passarge." *Qwellen zur Khoisan Forschung/Research in Khoisan Studies* 13.

———. 2003. "Some Lessons in Kalahari Ethnography and History." *History in Africa* 30.

Yellen, J., and A. Brooks. 1988. "The Late Stone Age Archaeology of the !Kangwa and /Xai/Xai Valleys, Ngamiland." *Botswana Notes and Records* 20: 5–27.

PART II

Africa and the Atlantic World

6

SECTION INTRODUCTION
METHODOLOGY THROUGH THE
ETHNIC LENS:
THE STUDY OF ATLANTIC AFRICA[1]

Paul E. Lovejoy

Ethnic Identities as Historical Filters

The essays by Matt Childs on Cuba, Russell Lohse on Costa Rica, and Kevin Roberts on Louisiana explore the methodological issues that arise from a consideration of ethnicity in the historical context of the circum Caribbean. They suggest that ethnic identities can serve as historical filters, and that the process of deciphering the meaning of ethnicity in historical context involves a methodology that is important to the historian's craft. Who people are, how they identify themselves, and how they are identified by others are questions that are shaped by the contexts of forced migration and slavery. Childs shows how specific *cabildos* (associations) in Cuba had ethnic and historical meaning, which can only partially be reconstructed at this point but which nonetheless reveal a complex world of ethnicity and identity. Lohse draws on the records of two slave ships to reveal the close interconnection between events in West Africa and the forced relocation of people to the Americas as slaves, and in this case, the fugitives who were not lucky in their *marronage* (escape from slavery), but in their capture have left a bewildering ethnic trail. Roberts considers the well-documented records of emigration to eighteenth-century Louisiana, in which there was a preponderance of enslaved Africans from Senegambia and, secondly, the

Bight of Benin. Roberts examines surviving narratives to find clues that flesh out the demographic data on ethnicity. These case studies suggest that the definition of ethnicity in historical context had to be flexible. Because they consider events on both sides of the Atlantic, their studies reveal the methodological potential of deconstructing the interpretations imposed on ethnic concepts through an examination of the empirical record.

The meaning and use of "ethnicity" have to be considered carefully. Much of African historical studies has assumed that concepts of ethnicity in Africa are very old, and for this reason there has been an implicit ordering that is based on ethnic factors (e.g., Songhay, Hausa, Wolof, Swahili, etc.). However, "ethnic" is usually employed loosely, because it is recognized that distinctions among ethnicity, language, and political structures are not always clear. In particular, the distinction between ethnicity and language is often blurred. Nonetheless, the primacy of ethnicity is highlighted in the formation of such associations as Mansa (the Mande Studies Association) and the Akan Studies Council, and the respective journals associated with these "ethnohistorical" associations. (*Mande Studies* does indeed treat ethnic studies, although the Akan Studies Council was transformed into the Ghana Studies Council, with an interdisciplinary journal *Ghana Studies,* so that it became national rather than ethnic.) What ethnicity actually means in the context of the history of Africa and the African diaspora in the Americas is worthy of examination, but for the moment let us just establish its importance so that we can extend the generalized use of ethnicity in the Africanist context to the study of the diaspora in the Americas. In order to do so, it is necessary to distinguish between an "Africanist" or "Afro-centric" approach from the manner in which ethnicity is often treated in studying the African diaspora and the history of slavery in the Americas.

Despite the tradition of ordering African history along ethnic lines, the focus in the African diaspora emphasizes the importance of ethnic re-definition and formation in diaspora, and sometimes it is even suggested that the concept of ethnicity among peoples of African descent was a creation of the diaspora itself, in part because the number of African ethnicities was so great and in part because ethnicity in Africa might change. It has even been argued that ethnicity was *not* especially important in the African context, or at least less important than most Africanists seem to have thought, and most perhaps still do.[2] As an example, I refer you to the oft-repeated statements that certain African "ethnicities," such as Yoruba and Igbo, first developed in the diaspora of Atlantic Africa.[3] The theory behind such propositions emphasizes the genesis of ethnicity in the diaspora.

If this theory of "diasporic genesis" is the case, then we have to ask what was the nature of the homeland that spawned such spontaneous expressions and reflections of self and group identity only in diaspora? Except in the case of the Jewish diaspora, where there was no occupied "homeland," diaspora is usually associated with an ethnic homeland that is real and in which people of common origin actually live. The people in dispersion may be cut off from that homeland, and indeed long separated, but its existence is real. On the basis of a homeland, the sense of ethnic identification can be intensified in diaspora, but the identity itself is not created there. As in the homeland, the conception and practice of ethnicity is subjected to change, and from different pressures, so that existing ethnic identities are reformulated or submerged in ways that might or might not have happened in the homeland itself.

There are many issues that arise from this apparent contradiction between those who emphasize ethnic formation in diaspora versus those whose reconstruction of African history is implicitly and often explicitly based on assumptions of ethnic homogeneity, struggle, and interaction. There appear to be two diametrically opposed views of the importance of ethnicity in Africa and the nature of ethnicity in the African diaspora. In this introduction, my purpose is to focus on Atlantic Africa, including both sides of the Atlantic, attempting to reconcile these apparently conflicting views of ethnicity.

The questions I am asking relate to the meaning of ethnicity as articulated during the period of transatlantic slavery.[4] I am less interested in the essentialist questions of whether or not ethnic groups existed here or there, but rather I want to concentrate on the various references to things that are sometimes called "ethnic" as a means of accessing the historical record and assisting in its reconstruction. In this sense, I am using ethnic designations as a lens through which to view the past, questioning the meaning of terms and markers and thereby suggesting a "methodology of ethnicity." From an Africanist perspective, the evidence suggests a much closer link between developments in homeland and the responses of people in diaspora than has often been allowed, and that in fact ethnic change and redefinition occurred in tandem on both sides of the Atlantic.

Specifically, this methodology is based on the assumption that the experience of enslaved Africans in the Americas has left a trail of historical evidence that is relevant not only for an understanding of the history of slavery in the Americas but also for the reconstruction of the African past. The analysis which follows in the essays by Childs, Roberts, and Lohse only makes sense in the attempt being made to determine precisely where and when people moved, and who they were. Their analysis, although limited by the current state of historical knowledge, nonetheless considers historical events on both sides of the Atlantic. Their evidence reflects the reality of an Atlantic world, where source material for historical reconstruction exists in the Americas that can assist in the analysis of African history, which in turn has ramifications for the study of slavery in the Americas. It is now possible for a broader interpretation of African history that includes the diaspora; the defining boundaries of Africanist history can now incorporate Atlantic Africa.

Databases and Historical Reconstruction

The methodology of the "ethnic lens" in the study of ethnicity in Atlantic Africa is quantitative, and requires the construction of databases that can be manipulated in digital form. As the following essays demonstrate, this is not to suggest that this type of source manipulation is the only way to approach the study of ethnicity. It is possible to create various types of databases, including ones based on text and visual representation. Statistical databases, such as the voyage database developed by David Eltis, David Richardson, Stephen Behrendt, and Herbert Klein is an invaluable tool, as demonstrated below, but it cannot address certain types of questions relating to ethnicity and culture, at least not directly.[5] Hence the construction of other databases that are not just statistical will undoubtedly affect our analysis of ethnicity and change. Databases, of course, are not new, but what is different in the present context is the extent and scope of database construction, a byproduct of the digital revolution in data storage and management. In the reconstruction of Atlantic Africa, there is a great quantity of data, scattered in dozens of countries and hundreds of repositories. These essays discuss a methodology that is currently in the process of definition and implementation.

The assumption here is that ethnicity is not fixed, but rather a problematic and contradictory method of classification, and that the distinction between ethnic groups, on the one hand, and racial categories, on the other, is not always clear. Perceptions of ethnicity often seem to reflect a closed, ordered world of insiders armed against a hostile world. The appearance can suggest biological isolation and cultural purity, when in fact ethnic boundaries, however defined, are more or less sieve-like, letting individuals and, more important, aspects of culture pass through, although for various reasons and motives and with varying impact. As Frederick Barth has argued, ethnicity has no meaning without boundaries, and hence the key to understanding how ethnicity is being interpreted at any time and in any place is the identification of the boundaries that are imposed, by whom, and for what purposes.[6] Time and place matter in the identification of the specific context.

There are merits in emphasizing ethnic boundaries, but ethnicity is also an artificial construct, a box arbitrarily shaped to include some people and exclude others for a great variety of purposes. When people were moved arbitrarily from Africa to the Americas, ethnic factors assumed a specific set of ambiguities. Ethnicity was redefined in significant ways in the Americas that allowed people to "cross ethnic boundaries," to quote Barth, with the emergence of pan-ethnic groups within a colonial world.

Racialized slavery in the Americas was a colonial project, in which ethnicity had specific functions. The situation of enslaved Africans in colonial America is worth comparing with the pioneering work of Ludwig White and Leroy Vail on ethnicity in southern Africa. Their analysis of ethnicity emphasizes the key role of colonialism in developing mechanisms of labor extraction and social control.[7] To some degree, colonialism and ethnicity interrelate in ways not unlike the slave condition in the Americas. However, in southern Africa ethnicity defined the migrant labor system within the colonial state. The movement of enslaved Africans to the plantations of colonial America was also in a colonial context, but the source of labor was external to the colonies, in territory entirely independent of European control, except in small parts of Angola and a few other places. In southern Africa, ethnicity was a means of assuring that labor would be kept on the move, tied to a homeland. Under slavery, the work force was, of course, totally separated from the homeland, and indeed the homeland(s) themselves remained outside the colonial state. Despite these contrasts, ethnic distinctions characterized both labor regimes and social formations, but the relationship between homeland and diaspora was remarkably different, and hence the meaning of ethnicity was historically specific. In both cases, however, an analysis of the meaning of ethnicity is a mechanism for isolating factors that the historian can use.

As is clear in the sources for Brazil and Hispanic America, especially, there are hundreds of terms that were used as ethnic labels in the seventeenth and eighteenth centuries.[8] Some of these are discussed in the essays that follow. A few are well known and "easy" to identify in an essentialist sense. "Nago" means Yoruba in Brazil, while "Lucumi" is the Cuban and

Central American term for the same;[9] "Aussa" is clearly Hausa, and so forth. These simple identifications tell us about as much as distinctions between French, German, and English do. They have meaning in a general sense, and their use in the sources immediately calls forth questions that, if answerable, qualify each term, uncovering more refined and historically specific meanings.[10]

Much of the information on ethnicity is in forms derived from the methods of classification convenient for the slave-owning elite and the colonial state.[11] Perhaps the best known is Gwendolyn Hall's database on eighteenth-century Louisiana, which is reassessed in Roberts' essay below.[12] There are similar databases being constructed on the slave population of Central America by Rina Cáceres Gómes, in Colombia by Renée Soulodre-La France, and in Brazil by Mariza de Carvalho Soares. Although there is evidence of self-ascription in these materials, most official records on the enslaved population more or less reflect the perceptions of the slave owners and colonial officials, of course, and therefore like all data have to be used carefully, a point that is emphasized by Lohse.

The second type of data being assembled relates to individuals, not categories of ascription based on perceived differentiation,[13] and this means a focus on text.[14] Biographical information exists in a variety of forms, most richly in the numerous narratives and autobiographies that are peculiarly common in North America, fugitive slave advertisements, announcements of slave sales, probate records and other inventories, etc. Biographical data are most complete for the nineteenth century, and while there are earlier accounts they are rare and tend to become more superficial the more distant in time. However, the numerous databases that are currently being constructed suggest that there is an extensive amount of source material that has previously not been used, at least not exhaustively.[15] Similar information can be gleaned from fugitive slave advertisements, slave sales, baptism records, and marriage certificates, and databases derived from such sources are being constructed in many parts of the diaspora.[16]

These various database projects will greatly augment the existing materials that exist on slavery and the slave trade. The interface between databases has to be bridged to allow further study, especially with respect to ethnic identification. The juxtaposition of statistical databases, such as the voyage database and biographical databases, will allow a much more detailed consideration of the general patterns and the deviations of specific individuals, between structures of trade and economy, and the lives of the many individuals entrapped in slavery.

Images of Ethnicity (and Race)

The visual representations of race and ethnicity during the slavery era can be found in a variety of forms, including contemporary paintings and other means of visual expression in Europe, as well as the facial and body scarification and tattooing to be found on many of the bodies of the enslaved Africans brought across the Atlantic. These types of visual images represent two extremes. On the one side, images in European art represent the "other," often stylized and otherwise depicting racial and implicitly as well ethnic differences from perceived European norms, such as in the work of Viktoria Schmidt-Linsenhoff on visual images in European and in that of Joseph Adande on art objects in Africa, and the relationship of these images to the attitudes of Europeans and Africans about themselves and each other.[17]

Facial and body scarification characterized those who were born in Africa, although some people did not practice scarification, even when their neighbors did. The Fulbe at least did not practice scarification, or did they? While not all Africans had permanent scarification on their faces or bodies, many of the enslaved, particularly Igbo, Yoruba, Akan, Gbe, and Muslims other than Fulbe/Fulani all used marks, and so did their neighbors. Consequently, these markings, if they could be mapped, would be highly informative of ethnic distinctions. By contrast, many of the enslaved from the regions inland from Kongo and Angola do not seem to have had marks, although they used tattoos, hairstyles, and other signs as distinguishing markings. An examination of the facial and body markings of the African-born population would refine the analysis of identity that is examined here, but as yet this information is not available.

An indispensable tool in reading the "ethnic map" of facial body markings is the construction of a visual database of enslaved Africa.[18] Among the most important collections of facial and body markings: Johann Moritz Rugendas, Jean Baptiste Debret, Eduard Hildebrandt, and Francis de Castelnau.[19] In North America, illustrations of the people who were rescued from the Amistad provided a good sample of markings from the interior of Sierra Leone.[20] There is also information on markings in fugitive slave advertisements and other descriptions of individuals. When combined with illustrations, these descriptions may in fact have hidden meanings that can be revealed through the creation of an ethnic map. The images portray stereotypes that reflect as much about the observer and those who observe the illustrations as about the subject of the images themselves.

Nonetheless, facial markings convey various meanings that can be compared with more recent information and images.

"Country marks" displayed visual distinctions among enslaved Africans that were clear markers distinguishing the African-born from the "creole" generations born in the Americas. As Michael Gomez has poignantly expressed the transition under slavery, Africans came to the Americas with "country marks" like those in the illustrations from nineteenth-century Brazil, and they exchanged those marks for the ones branded on their bodies as if they were livestock.[21] The "country marks" of the second generation of slaves were applied with the branding iron. This transformation in the meaning of scarification defined the "creole" generation. It also wiped out previous identifications. Hence the demise of the practice of self-identification through scarification was thereby destructive of the collective past of individuals, and by extension, their elimination destroyed historical evidence. Nonetheless, thousands of examples of facial and body markings have survived that date to the eighteenth and nineteenth centuries.

The enslaved also used different hairstyles and tattoos as signs of fashion and identification, and this was particularly characteristic of the creole generation, as Brazilian illustrations demonstrate. Like the permanent scarification of the African-born generation, hairstyles, jewelry, tattoos, and clothing were indicative of self-identification and often involved the conscious association with a group, sometimes ethnically determined but not always. The visual representation in this case is intended for insiders, not always or easily understandable to outsiders. Self-perception was represented in physical markings that were transformed under racialized slavery. Such images are important as historical sources that can allow further examination of ethnicity in the areas affected by the slave trade.

The development of racial distinctions also reflected historical change whose images can be recorded and through digitization can be subjected to complex analysis. In Mexico, at least fifty-three racial/ethnic distinctions had emerged by the end of the eighteenth century, and such distinctions and methods of classification can then be compared with the data from Costa Rica and Cuba that are examined by Lohse and Childs.[22] The gradation in skin color was also a factor in identification elsewhere, of course, but not to such a degree. Individuals could cross between categories to avoid taxation or otherwise act in their own interests, suggesting parallels with ethnicity. Indeed, the distinctions between ethnic categories, on the one hand, and racial categories, on the other, are not always clear.

Through the Lens of Ethnicity

Masters did display preferences for slaves of different backgrounds, although the significance of these preferences and how they changed over time is a subject of dispute and is open to study. Slave preferences are stated in planter statements about what can be conceived of as ethnic signifiers, e.g., Igbo and suicide, Akan and rebelliousness, "Soudanese" and greater intelligence, etc. Ethnicity, language, religion, and culture show correlations, concentrations, and conflicts within each category/classification. When such preferences and stereotypes came into existence may be important, and establishing a distribution based on time and geography for specific stereotypes or other ethnic markers may offer clues that are important historically.

The way in which gender and ethnicity were intertwined affected ethnic distinctions because of the differential numbers of women who were available to procreate. After all, it is women who bore the children, and indeed appear to have performed the major share of child rearing under slavery. The flow of women across ethnic boundaries reveals ways in which culture was transmitted, including language. The trajectory of enslaved women highlights the sex ratios of the imported enslaved populations. Because women were in a minority among new arrivals, they were particularly prized. It is important to recognize, moreover, that they did not come randomly; there were proportionately more Igbo than Muslim women. Indeed there were very few Muslim women. The relative numbers, backgrounds, and occupations selected for women have to be taken into consideration in understanding the alienation of the labor of women, which was certainly a factor in the types of occupations they tended to dominate (domestics, including sexual services, and field hands). The gender division of labor also affected western Africa, where polygyny seems to have become more prevalent among the political and commercial elite that benefited from the slave trade and slavery. While ethnicity is often associated with patterns of resistance and accommodation, the gender component is often overlooked in the analysis of ethnic factors.

While the suggestion here is that a "methodology of ethnicity" can be identified, it is important to contrast this approach to ethnicity from the way the "ethnic" factor is sometimes used. The strategy being advocated here deconstructs the meaning of ethnicity in historical context. The aim is to uncover the complexities and contradictions of identity, and how these change. Ethnic signifiers can be deconstructed to reveal cleavages and change arising from interaction, choice, and coercion. Then, ethnicity has value as a means of looking into history. Deciphering the meanings of particular ethnic and other forms of identification addresses issues of conceptualization and methodology.

An examination of ethnic factors raises questions about the relationship between ethnicity and homeland, and hence how diasporas are constructed and how they are interpreted by participants, as well as observers, both contemporary and modern. What are the differences between race and ethnicity, when both rely on visual signs, ethnicity on artificially constructed markers, and race by markers that are perceived to be "biological"—skin color, hair, facial features. Diasporas are "ethnic" when they are Yoruba, Irish, and Jewish; are they "racial" when "African" and "European?" Childs, Lohse, and Roberts demonstrate that ethnic data are worthy of careful study, both because of the information revealed on the African and transatlantic dimension of culture change and also because of the reassessment that such an approach offers to an understanding of the adjustments under slavery when the creole population became dominant and the interaction between diaspora and homeland became more complex.

Notes

1. The research for the paper has benefited from my association with the York/UNESCO Nigerian Hinterland Project at York University. I wish to thank the Social Sciences and Humanities Research Council of Canada, and particularly its Major Collaborative Research Initiatives program for its support.

2. J. Lorand Matory, "The English Professors of Brazil: On the Diasporic Roots of the Yoruba Nation," *Comparatives Studies in Society and History* 41, 1 (1999): 72–103; David Eltis, *The Rise of African Slavery in the Americas* (Cambridge, Cambridge University Press, 1999); David Eltis and David Richardson, eds., *Routes to Slavery*, special issue of *Slavery and Abolition,* 18:1 (1997).

3. On Yoruba, see especially J. Lorand Matory, "The English Professors of Brazil: On the Diasporic Roots of the Yorùbá Nation," *Comparative Studies in Society and History* 41, 1 (1999): 72–103; on Igbo, see Douglas Chambers, "'He Is an African But Speaks Plain': Historical Creolization in Eighteenth-Century Virginia," in *The African Diaspora*, ed. Alusine Jalloh and Stephen E. Maizlish (College Station, Tex.: Texas A&M University Press, 1996), 100–33; Douglas Chambers, "'My Own Nation': Igbo Exiles in the Diaspora," *Slavery and Abolition,* 18:1 (1997): 72–97; and Paul E. Lovejoy, "Tracing Igbo into the Diaspora," in *Identity in the Shadow of Slavery,* ed. Paul E. Lovejoy (London: Continuum, 2000).

4. This issue is pursued more fully in Paul E. Lovejoy, "Ethnic Designations of the Slave Trade," Byrne Lecture, Vanderbilt University, 26 March 2001.

5. In particular, the voyage-based database developed by David Eltis, David Richardson and Stephen Behrendt, from records of 27,000 slaving voyages, has revolutionized the study of the slave trade and the transatlantic migration of enslaved Africans. See David Eltis,

Steven Behrendt, David Richardson, and Herbert Klein, *The Transatlantic Slave Trade: the W.E.B. Du Bois Database on CD-Rom* (Cambridge: Cambridge University Press, 1999). In addition, the team has developed other databases relating to shipboard violence, health conditions of the enslaved population, and ethnic origins of 68,000 individuals liberated by the British anti-slave trade patrols after 1807. See David Eltis, *The Rise of African Slavery in the Americas.*

6. Frederik Barth, "Introduction," *Ethnic Groups and Boundaries* (Bergen, Universitetsforlaget, 1969), 10–11. Also see Stephan Palmié, "Ethnogenetic Processes and Culture Transfer in Afro-American Populations," in *Slavery in the Americas,* ed. Wolfgang Binder (Wurzburg: Königshausen & Hermann, 1993), 337–63; and Lovejoy, "Ethnic Designations of the Slave Trade."

7. Leroy Vail and Ludwig White, eds., *The Creation of Tribalism in Southern Africa* (London: Currey, 1989).

8. Particularly important is Alonso de Sandoval, *Un Tratado Sobre la Esclavitud (1627), Introduccion, transcripcion y traduccion de Enriqueta Vila Vilar* (Madrid: Alianza Editorial, 1987). For various studies of ethnicity that draw on this work, see Frederick Bowser, *The African Slave in Colonial Peru, 1524–1650* (Stanford, Calif.: Stanford University Press, 1974), 42–44; Stephan Buhnen, "Ethnic Origins of Peruvian Slaves (1548–1650): Figures for Upper Guinea," *Paideuma,* 39 (1993): 57–110; Jean-Pierre Tardieu, "Origins of the Slaves in Peru: The Lima Region (Sixteenth and Seventeenth Centuries)," unpublished paper, Colloque International, La route de l'esclave, Ouidah, Benin, 1994. For a discussion of Sandoval's work, see Vila Vilar, "En torno al padre Sandoval, autor de un tratado sobre la esclavitud," in *Eglise et politique en Amerique* (Burdeos, 1984), 65–67, and John Thornton, *Africa and Africans in the the Making of the Atlantic World,* 2nd ed. (Cambridge: Cambridge University Press, 1998).

9. Biodun Adediran, "Yoruba Ethnic Groups or a Yoruba Ethnic Group? A Review of the Problem of Ethnic Identification," *Africa: Revista do Centro de Estudos Africanos da USP* 7 (1984): 57–70; and Robin Law, "Ethnicity and the Slave Trade: 'Lucumi' and 'Nago' as Ethnonyms in West Africa," *History in Africa* 24 (1997).

10. In order to analyze this type of source, a team of scholars, under the coordination of Rina Cáceres and associated with the York/UNESCO/SSHRCC Nigerian Hinterland Project, is constructing a database in which all references to ethnic, linguistic, and geographic terms are being incorporated, noting date and place of reference, with textual information in a form that replicates the original documentation. Such a database also requires a qualitative guide that explains and quotes what is known about contemporary interpretations of terms. See *African Diaspora Newsletter,* No. 4, York/UNESCO Nigerian Hinterland Project (http://www.yorku.ca/nhp).

11. Billy G. Smith and Richard Wojtowicz, eds., *Blacks Who Stole Themselves: Advertisements for Runaways in the Pennsylvania Gazette, 1728–1790* (Philadelphia: University of Pennsylvania Press, 1989); Graham Russell Hodges and Alan Edward Brown, eds., *"Pretends to be Free": Runaway Slave Advertisements from Colonial and Revolutionary New York and New Jersey* (New York: Garland, 1994); Lathan A. Windley, ed., *Runaway Slave Advertisements: A Documentary History from the 1730s to 1790,* 4 vols. (Westport, Conn.: Greenwood Press, 1983); P. A. Bishop, "Runaway Slaves in Jamaica, 1740–1807: A Study Based on Newspaper Advertisements Published during That Period for Runaways," M.A. thesis (University of the West Indies, Mona, 1970).

12. Gwendolyn Hall, *Databases for the Study of Afro-Louisiana History and Genealogy,* 1699–1860 (Baton Rouge, La.: Louisiana State University Press, 1999).

13. Paul E. Lovejoy, "Biography as Source Material: Towards a Biographical Archive of Enslaved Africans," in *Source Material for Studying the Slave Trade and the African Diaspora*, ed. Robin Law (Stirling, University of Stirling, 1997).

14. The Text and Testimony Collective is centered at the University of the West Indies (Mona) and is focused on the collection and dissemination of texts and oral data, and the Collective is linked with other initiatives, including the Nigerian Hinterland Project, and is under the direction of Hilary McD. Beckles, Verene Shepherd, and David Trotman.

15. The biographical database of the Nigerian Hinterland Project draws heavily on missionary accounts and existing published narratives; the project emphasizes the primacy of text, as well as database construction; see <http://www.yorku.ca/nhp>. Also, David Eltis and Ugo Nwokeji are developing a database from the records of 68,000 recaptives taken off slave ships by the British anti-slave trade patrols; see G. Ugo Nwokeji and David Eltis, "The Roots of the African Diaspora: Methodological Considerations in the Analysis of Names in the Liberated African Registers of Sierra Leone and Havanna," unpublished paper.

16. José Cairus is assembling information on individual Muslims in Brazil in newspaper accounts and the trial records of the 1835 uprising in Bahia. João Reis, Paul E. Lovejoy, and Neuracy Moreira are constructing a database derived from probate records for eight parishes in Bahia between 1780 and 1823, which notes ethnicity, racial features, age, gender, value, and other distinctions for slaves in the central sugar districts, a manioc region, a mining area, and a frontier zone of cattle and cotton production. Finally, the Underground Railroad project carries this biographical approach forward into a sphere of the African diaspora for which there is extensive, but widely scattered, data. It builds on the existing corpus of biographical information of individual African Americans, which includes hundreds of published biographical accounts, as well as extensive oral testimony, and descriptive accounts. For details, see <http://www.yorku.ca/nhp>.

17. See Viktoria Schmidt-Linsenhoff, "Sklaverei und Männlichkeit um 1800," in *Projektionen: Rassismus und Sexismus in der Visuellen Kultur*, ed. Annegret Friedrich, Birgit Haehnel, Viktoria Schmidt-Linsenhoff, and Christina Threuter (Marburg: Jonas, 1997); "Vergessen, Verschieben, Verkörpern. Repräsentation der Sklaverei in der orientalistischen Malerei des 19. Jhh, erscheint in dem Tagungsband 'Körper-Konzepte,'" in Claudia Opitz, ed., (forthcoming 2002).

18. Mariza da Carvalho Soares is constructing such a database examining visual images of individuals in Brazil, drawing on illustrations from the nineteenth century. Also see her *Devotos da cor. Identidade étnica, religiosidade e escravidão no Rio de Janeiro, século XVIII* (Rio de Janeiro: Civilização Brasileira, 2000). For earlier use of such materials, see Mary Karasch, *Slave Life in Rio de Janeiro, 1808–1850* (Princeton: Princeton University Press, 1987).

19. Johann Moritz Rugendas, *Voyage pittoresque dans le Brésil, por Maurice Rugendas* (Paris: Engelmann & cie., 1835, trans. M. de Golbéy [Paris: Engelmann & cie., 1835]); *Negro de Corpo e Alma, Black Body and Soul, Edemar Cid Ferreira, Presidente* (São Paulo: Fundação Bienal de São Paulo, 2000), 90–93. Also see Jean Baptiste Debret, *Voyage pittoresque et historique au Brésil: Séjour d'un artiste français au Brésil*, 3 vols. (Rio de Janeiro: New York Distribuidora Record Contenental News, 1965 [1834]); Paulo Cesar de Azevedo and Mauricio Lissovsky, eds., *Escravos Brasileiros do século XIX na fotographia de Christiano Jr.* (São Paulo, Ex Libris,1988); and Francis de Castelnau, *Renseignements sur l'Afrique centrale et sur une nation d'hommes à queue qui s'y trouverait, d'après le rapport des nègres du Soudan, esclaves a Bahia* (Paris: P. Bertrand, 1851). Also see Gilberto Ferrez, *O Brasil de Eduard*

Hildebrandt (Rio de Janeiro: Distribuidora Record de Serviços de Imprensa, 1988); and the discussion in Robert M. Levine, "Faces of Brazilian Slavery: The Cartes de Visite of Christiano Júnior," *Americas,* 47, 2 (1990): 137.

20. These drawings are at Yale University.

21. Michael Gomez, *Exchanging Our Country Marks* (Chapel Hill: University of North Carolina Press, 1998).

22. Teresa Castello Yturbide, "La indumentaria de las castas del mestizaje," in *Artes de Mexico,* La Pintura de Castas, Número 8, 1990, 72–79.

7

PATHWAYS TO AFRICAN ETHNICITY IN THE AMERICAS: AFRICAN NATIONAL ASSOCIATIONS IN CUBA DURING SLAVERY*

Matt D. Childs

The Atlantic slave trade and its legacy represents one of the strongest currents that shaped and continues to influence identities in the Americas. The largest forced migration in human history uprooted more than ten million Africans from their home communities and scattered them throughout the Americas. Although ownership of human beings in one form or another had been a feature common to most societies of the world until about 1800, the racial component of slavery in the Americas, whereby people of white European ancestry owned people of black African ancestry, made the institution distinct from its Old World precedents. As a result, over time, the identification as black or white often defined the boundaries that separated slave and free, rich and poor, employer and employee, and ruler and subject. In this chapter, I shift the attention away from racial identities shaped by New World slavery to examine how Africans identified themselves in their new Cuban surroundings. Africans recognized that a white ruling class of European ancestry governed Cuban society and that all people of the African diaspora shared a common association with racial oppression. However, Africans did not define themselves only in racialized terms of European derivation.

Africans in Cuba voluntarily formed associations based upon a common ethnicity that often reflected a shared geographic origin, language, and common culture. Prevalent in colonial society, these collective organizations became known as *cabildos de nación* to reflect the voluntary grouping by common ethnic identity of the numerous African "nations" forcibly imported to Cuba. The Spanish term *cabildo* represents the English language equivalent of a town council or a town government. Consequently, the labeling of these societies as *cabildos* provides some indication of how they functioned as representative bodies for African nations by providing political, administrative, social, and cultural services.[1] Almost all the activities of the *cabildos* revolved around the ownership of a home that served numerous functions vital to the society: a boarding-house which rented rooms; a conference center for holding meetings and reunions; a school for education and training in the artisan trades; a bank by collecting membership dues, offering loans, and even purchasing the freedom for slaves; a restaurant through food services such as the "plate of the day"; a theater for dances; and even a funeral parlor. The *cabildo* house provided a sacred space for ethnic solidarity in a society increasingly divided along racial lines between slavery and freedom.

The example of Cuban *cabildos* illustrates the necessity for scholars to address not only how Africans identified themselves in contrast to masters through New World racial terms, but also how they defined who they were among themselves and among other Africans. This chapter begins by addressing the common appearance of African nations in the Americas, followed by an analysis of the relationship between the slave trade and African ethnicity in the New World, and then a detailed examination of the role of *cabildos de nación* in shaping African identity in Cuba.

African Nations in the Americas

The formation of ethnic groups based upon African nations represented a common feature of slave societies in the Americas. Masters throughout the New World recognized that Africans did not represent an undifferentiated mass of laborers, but brought with them forms of social organization and cultural differences that they perpetuated and refashioned in the Americas as survival strategies. Robert Jameson, a British observer in Cuba, recognized how both master and slaves identified Africans by nations in the early nineteenth century: "The different nations to which the negroes belonged in Africa are marked out in the colonies both by the master and the slaves; the former considering them variously characterized in the desired qualities, and the latter joining together with a true national spirit in such union as their lords allow."[2] Masters often stereotyped certain nations for possessing distinguishing characteristics that some historians regard as offering a few "glimmers of truth" about African cultural traits.[3] Regardless of what masters' stereotypes can tell us specifically about African identity in the New World, it is clear that profits depended on an awareness of cultural differences. Historian David Eltis has soundly observed, "While the planters' basic requirement was slave labor from anywhere in Africa, no one can read the transatlantic correspondence of the early modern slave systems without recognizing the importance of African nationhood in the shaping of the plantation regimes."[4]

Depending on the nature of documentation and the quality of reporting, the existence of societies based upon African nationhood can be found throughout the Americas for the whole period of slavery. For the slave societies of Anglo-America, the action of Africans grouping themselves by nations normally became known in the context of a rebellion. In the 1650s Richard Ligon reported visiting a Barbadian planter who "feeds daily two hundred mouths, and keeps them in such order, [as] there are no mutinies amongst them; and yet of several nations."[5] Over ten years later the Barbadian Governor reassured that a rebellion uniting all the slaves would not occur because "the blacks' . . . different tongues and animosities in their own Country have hitherto kept them from insurrection, but I fear the Creolian generation now growing up."[6]

The nations may have militated against the formation of a broad racial identity, but that hardly prevented rebellions. In 1675 Barbadian officials discovered a plot among numerous Coromantee or Gold-Coast slaves to rebel against their masters led by an "ancient Gold-Coast Negro called Cuffe" who had been chosen as king of the movement.[7] More than fifty years later British officials on the nearby island of Antigua discovered an elaborate island-wide conspiracy in 1736 led again by Coromantee slaves where national associations proved crucial to planning the rebellion.[8] In 1760 the Coromantee once again led a rebellion, but this time on the much larger island of Jamaica that may have eventually included 30,000 followers.[9] Even in the eighteenth- and nineteenth-century United States, where creolization had been much more important to understanding slave culture, African nations shaped notions of identity. In 1712 a revolt broke out in New York City, led by the nations of the Coromantee and Pappa, according to contemporary account.[10] Fourteen years after the end of the African slave trade, an Igbo column led by Monday Gell from the Bight of Biafra reportedly played a leading role in the Denmark Vesey Conspiracy of 1822 in Charleston, South Carolina.[11]

For the Iberian slave societies of the Americas we have a better understanding of the daily functions of African nations compared to the Anglo colonies in the New World. The Portuguese colonies in Brazil and Africa often recognized African nations through religious ceremonies. As historian Linda Heywood has argued, "African folk Christianity" thrived among Lisbon's black population of the sixteenth century and in the Portuguese colonies of Africa and Brazil because, in part, the church established ethnic-based confraternities.[12] In Brazil, slaves imported from the Catholic territories of the Kingdom of Kongo and Angola flocked to the Brotherhood of Our Lady of the Rosary. The common appearance of Angolan and Kongolese ethnicity among African and Afro-Brazilian Catholic brotherhoods likely indicates religious traditions slaves took with them and transformed when they crossed the Atlantic.[13] For example, "Angolan Kings and Queens" received payments for directing the brotherhood of Our Lady of the Rosary in Recife.[14] The presence of African nations could also be found on plantations and mines throughout Brazil. In 1849 the superintendent of a British-owned gold mine worked by slave labor told the House of Lords that masters grouped Africans by nations "for the purpose of preserving peace on the establishment. [Otherwise] They would be able to league together."[15] According to Tomás Treolar, who worked at the same mine, Africans chose "kings and queens to watch over the interests and welfare of their respective nations."[16]

Spanish America appears to follow the same general pattern as Portugal of recognizing national differences among Africans through the church. At least a century before the conquest of the New World, the sub-Saharan African population in Seville had been firmly established by slavery. Municipal authorities appointed a steward to settle disputes between slaves and masters and allowed the African population the right to gather on feast days and perform their own dances and songs. In addition, black congregationalists established religious brotherhoods.[17] These practices were then carried to the Americas and expanded when introduced to a larger African slave population. By 1560 over half the population of Lima, Peru (the most important city for the Spanish Empire in South America) could claim African ancestry. Unsurprisingly, sodalities in Lima often reflected African ethnicity, such as the Dominican brotherhood for the "negros Congos," and the brotherhood of Nuestra Señora del Socorro for Angolans.[18] Catholic brotherhoods that catered to the specific needs of African members could be found throughout Spanish America.[19] In addition, organizations formed along lines of African ethnicity expressed the desire to separate from church control. In Buenos Aires, for example, Africans in the nineteenth century regularly petitioned the police department to form societies based upon their common national backgrounds to better serve their spiritual, cultural, and financial needs.[20] Whether through the church, informal organizations on plantations and mines, or by state-sanctioned societies, Africans in Ibero-America grouped themselves along lines of African ethnicity and culture.

In Cuba the presence of Catholic brotherhoods that included the participation of people of African ancestry can be traced back to the sixteenth century. In 1573 the town council of Havana reported that Africans took part in the procession of Corpus Christi, and several wills indicate they regularly made donations to sodalities.[21] Unfortunately, the Catholic church (along with the entire first three centuries of Cuban history) has long been neglected by scholars, so we cannot know with certainty the role of these brotherhoods for people of African ancestry. In 1755 the recently appointed Bishop Morell de Santa Cruz commented: "these *miserables* [slaves and free people of color] have been left totally abandoned as if they were not Christians and incapable of salvation"; this comment supports the generally accepted argument that the Catholic church played a weak role in Cuban society.[22] In particular, the Bishop was appalled at the "scandalous and grave disorders" created by the "*cabildos* . . . when they congregate on festival days."[23] Apparently, during the span of the sixteenth and seventeenth centuries, some *cabildos* had separated from the brotherhoods and taken on a social role independent of the church. The Bishop planned to bring the "lost sheep of the flock to the Good Shepherd [by] . . . administering to the *cabildos* the sacrament of confirmation, reciting the Holy rosary," and appointing lay religious officials to supervise and instruct the nations.[24] Despite the Bishop's protest, it does not appear the nations became "converted to temples of the living God," as he optimistically predicted.[25] The secularizing trends of the eighteenth-century Bourbon state likely undercut any attempts by the Catholic church to reclaim authority over the *cabildos*. For example, although the *cabildo* Karabali Induri affiliated itself with the Catholic Church Nuestra Señora del Buen Viaje, it does not appear from the internal documents of the nation that any religious officials oversaw their activities or settled disputes among the members.[26] By the mid-eighteenth century, if not earlier, *cabildos* likely outnumbered brotherhoods.[27]

Various scholars have traced the origins of the *cabildos* to religious holidays and Catholic brotherhoods of Spanish origin, but Philip Howard has pointed out that analogous societies were common to West and Central Africa.[28] At the port of Old Calabar and surrounding regions in the

Bight of Biafra, an all-male secret society known as Ekpe formed as early as the second half of the seventeenth century. Identified with the leopard, Ekpe members paid dues assessed by their rank in the organization. According to historians Paul Lovejoy and David Richardson, Ekpe society created an "interlocking grid of secret associations [that] served to regulate the behavior of members."[29] The secret organization crossed the Atlantic and resurfaced in nineteenth-century Cuba through an altered form in the Abakuá society.[30] In the Yoruba Kingdom of Oyo there existed a semisecret organization known as the Ogboni society, that advised the King on religious and political matters. Scholars disagree about the founding date of the Ogboni society and the extent of its influence. However, it is almost certain that because the war-torn region of Yorubaland funneled thousands of Africans to Cuba in the nineteenth century some knowledge of the organization likely crossed the Atlantic and influenced the *cabildos*.[31] Associations, organizations, and secret societies in West and Central Africa provided an institutional framework that enslaved and free Africans could mold to their New World surroundings.

Various other societies could be found in West and Central Africa that performed charitable, recreational, political, and economic functions for members who often shared the same language, ethnicity, and nationality. The collective and communal organizing principles of these organizations, though not necessarily egalitarian, often translated into mutual-aid societies in the Americas. The African-born and American-born population of African descent displayed a strong tendency to socialize and regularly meet with their fellow nationals by forming some sort of organization, formally or informally, to keep in touch with and look out for each other. In Cuba and elsewhere in the Americas, the association of Africans who shared a common language, culture, history, and identity often functioned as a mutual-aid society that linked the more fortunate and well-placed members with their poorer and severely exploited co-nationals through patron-client networks.[32] The Yoruba in West Africa, for example, operated mutual-aid societies as early as the eighteenth century through the Ajo and Esusu saving institutions. Each member paid dues into a collective fund that would then be made available for individual loans. When Yoruba slaves began to be exported across the Atlantic, the Esusu savings association emerged in the Caribbean.[33] Spanish colonial administrators and Catholic priests regarded African *cabildos* in Cuba as an extension of religious sodalities with their origins in Europe. The organizations for Africans, however, surely did not represent something entirely of Spanish or Cuban origin, but an Old World institution modified in a New World setting.

The Atlantic Slave Trade and African Nationhood in Cuba

Ever since the publication of Philip Curtin's monumental *The Atlantic Slave Trade* (1969), our knowledge of the migratory process linking the Americas and Africa that spanned four centuries has greatly expanded.[34] In recent years, scholars have turned their attention away from elaborating and revising Curtin's figures (although this continues as well), to focus on tracing the African origins and American destinations of slaves. As a result of collaborative efforts, computer assistance, and the construction of data sets, it has become easier for scholars to eschew the generic nondescriptive terms "Africa" and "African," and identify more precisely the origins of slaves and their New World destinations. David Eltis, David Richardson, Stephen D. Behrendt, and Herbert S. Klein have compiled an easily accessible database of more than 27,000 slaving voyages that now makes it possible to trace the Old World origins and American destination of Africans with greater precision than ever before.[35] For example, historians utilizing the database have been able to demonstrate that two out of every three slaves imported into the British Caribbean from roughly 1650 to 1710 left from a 200–mile stretch of territory on the Gold/Slave Coast of Africa.[36] Brazil has shown clearly defined migration patterns as a result of the Portuguese control of the slave trade at African ports of origin and New World destinations. Nearly three-quarters of the slaves leaving South-East Africa arrived in South-Central Brazil to work in gold mines and on coffee estates, while nearly sixty percent of the Bight of Benin's emigrants arrived in Bahia to labor on sugar plantations. In the French Caribbean, half of the slaves crossing the Atlantic could trace their origins to Senegambia.[37] At least two salient problems face the scholar studying African ethnicity, the Atlantic slave trade, and the diaspora in the Americas: first, most records reveal only the ports where ships left from, not the origin of slaves brought to the African coast; and second, the documents were authored by Europeans who, while cognizant of ethnic differences, often confused one group with another.

Tracing African ethnicity in Cuba through census data from the Atlantic slave trade remains difficult because no single region provided more than thirty-one percent of the migrants. The most recent scholarship derived from the Trans-Atlantic Slave Trade Database has shown that "[o]f all the receiving areas in the Americas, Cuba received the greatest mix of African peoples."[38] As a result, the authors of the Trans-Atlantic Slave Trade Database have suggested that the "Cuban African population had the potential for the greatest loss of culture and language specific to particular regions."[39] Examining African ethnicity through the formation and operation of Cuba *cabildos* in the era of the Atlantic slave trade provides an opportunity to study the diaspora in the Americas with an emphasis on African cultural origins from an angle other than migration records. As Africans formed *cabildos* and defined their own ethnicity, these sources provide a rare view into how they identified themselves instead of relying on European descriptions of African culture or census records from the slave trade. Salvador Ternero who served as the leader of the Mina Guagni *cabildo* of Havana from 1790 to 1800, for example, did not need to know the percentage of Mina Guagni slaves imported to Cuba to understand how the slave trade shaped ethnic identities in his *cabildo*. He simply recognized that "when they founded the *cabildo* in 1731 there had not come those from Ethiopia that want to join today."[40] The increase in the slave trade and the rapid spread of sugar plantations in Cuba after 1790 strengthened the importance of Mina Guagni fraternity for people who shared a common language, culture, ancestry, and identity by their growing numbers.

The same process occurred in the Yoruba *cabildo,* known in Cuba as Lucumi, that had been founded "many years ago," as one member stated vaguely. As the war-torn region of Yorubaland began to funnel slaves to Cuba at the end of the eighteenth century with the disintegration of the Kingdom of Oyo, a "confederation of black creoles" formed within the *cabildo,* representing the sons and daughters of the original, founding members. Cuban-born Manuel Blanco of Lucumi ancestry attempted to prevent the sale of the *cabildo* house that his parents had helped purchase. The marked increase of *bozal* (African-born) Lucumi members, however, resulted in the Africans winning the case to sell the house by their numerical superiority.[41] Cuba (along with Brazil for that matter) represents somewhat of an anomaly for African identity transformation in the Americas during the late eighteenth and nineteenth centuries. In other parts of the New World, a broad-based racial identity began to eclipse African ethnicities with the ending of the slave trade, the growth of a creole slave population, and the gradual abolition of slavery. In Cuba, however, the continuous importation of slaves strengthened African ethnicities.

Charting the overall growth of the number of *cabildos* and the membership in each nation proves difficult because no single governmental institution supervised the associations for the early nineteenth century. As a result, a concentrated corpus of records on the societies has yet to be found by historians. While quantifying the growth of *cabildos* remains difficult, qualitative sources indicate a noticeable increase in these societies from 1750 to 1820 that corresponded with the rise in Atlantic slave trade imports. In 1753 the Bishop of Cuba wrote to the king of Spain complaining of the "noisy shouting of males mixed with females amusing themselves in extremely clumsy and provocative dances . . . of the Ethiopians of both sexes that sanctify the festivals in this city." The Bishop counted "twenty-one houses that have served the devil": the Karabalies owned five; the Minas three; the Lucumies two; the Araras two; the Kongos two; the Mondongos two; the Gangas two; the Mandingas one; the Luangos one; and the Suangos one.[42] Scattered references to more than thirty *cabildos* found in civil disputes for the years spanning 1790 to 1820, along with frequent mentions of associations in official correspondence and criminal proceedings, suggests the number of societies increased to at least fifty by the early nineteenth century.[43]

A qualitative indication of the growth of *cabildos* as a result of what Mina-Guagni Cabildo leader Ternero described in the 1790s as the "arrival of those from Ethiopia that want to join today," is reflected by the division of several nations. In the 1780s a dispute surfaced within the Lucumi *cabildo* between the diverse ethnicities that claimed membership. One member recalled that "the *cabildo* was erected by the Lucumi nations, specifically the Nangas and the Barbaes."[44] By the seventeenth century Yoruba culture and language had become a lingua franca along the Western African Coast, promoting what John Thornton has described as "cultural intercommunication."[45] In Cuba, this process apparently expanded the cultural boundaries of inclusion that facilitated the collaboration of several nations under a broad Lucumi identity. The Lucumi *cabildo* was founded by cooperation among Nangas and Barbaes. In addition, Chabas and Bambaras such as free black Pedro José could join as well despite not sharing the ethnicity of the founders.[46] Near the end of the eighteenth century, however, with the increase of slaves from Yorubaland, the society divided into separate *cabildos* represented by the Nangas and Barbaes in one house and the Chabas and Bambaras in another. A similar division emerged in the *cabildo* Kongo Musolongo in 1806, indicated by their request to separate into two different societies.[47] Likewise, as a result of a contested election, Juan Gavilan and a group identifying themselves as the Karabali Osso desired to separate from the Karabali Umugini *cabildo* despite "fourteen years more or less of unity."[48] The division of *cabildos* as membership increased indicates how the Atlantic slave trade fundamentally shaped African ethnicity in Cuba. Further, the ability to incorporate members from different nations at one moment and then at another draw lines of exclusion, demonstrates the flexibility of African ethnicity and culture in the New World.

Cuban slaveowners clearly understood the important functions of *cabildos* in a slave society dependent on the Atlantic slave trade. The existence of societies sharing a common language and culture served to slightly mitigate the horrific experience of the middle passage through collective solidarity, even as they also prepared slaves for their new lives as unpaid laborers. In 1789 the King of Spain issued a slave code that sought to protect slave marriages, limit work hours, specify food and clothing rations, and prohibit excessive punishment. In addition, the code held implications for the activities of the *cabildos* by emphasizing the need for slaves "on holidays to . . . be instructed in the Christian doctrine" and prevent the "uniting with others . . . in simple and natural diversions [and] to avoid excessive drinking."[49] Cuban slaveowners immediately protested all the provisions that clipped their authority as masters, yet these same slaveowners defended the rights of slaves and free people of color to form *cabildos* and perform their dances. Diego Miguel de Moya authored a petition signed by "all of the masters of sugar plantations in this jurisdiction." In reference to the *cabildos,* he argued by "taking away now the slaves' right to holidays that they count on to leave slavery, would for certain be an infallible principle of their resentment."[50] Cuban slaveowners, obviously, did not mean that all the slaves who participated in *cabildos* became free. Rather, they recognized that some slaves survived the brutal daily life of slavery with the hope that participation in a nation could lead to liberation.

Masters also revealed more than they realized. Participation in *cabildo* functions allowed slaves, however briefly, to temporarily "leave slavery" and the confines of master dominion. Further, while masters described the "inclined diversion of the Blacks is to dance in the barbarous style of their countries," they recognized "that if this [right] is denied them, it will cause an irresistible pain and produce bad consequences."[51] Cuban masters convinced themselves that by providing slaves and free people of color with a limited sense of autonomy they would not rise in rebellion. Indeed, in 1809, the town council of Havana reasoned that French slaveowners destroyed by the Haitian Revolution only encouraged insurrection by "making slaves work on holidays."[52] In a society fueled by the forceful importation of thousands of Africans every year, slaveowners quickly realized the benefits of according limited privileges to depolarize master-slave relations.

The Different Ranks of Cabildo Membership

Cabildo membership served to strengthen networks and resources weakened by living in a slave society that showed little hesitation about destroying kin relations. *Cabildos* served as a surrogate for an incomplete family structure; members often described each other with familial connotations. Francisco Alas, the "emperor" of a Mina and Mandinga *cabildo* in Bayamo, described a meeting attended by his "*parientes* (relatives), free Blas Tamayo, slave Mateo and his wife, and the slave Candelaria Dolores."[53] One member of a *cabildo* reported that while he "was sick, all of his relatives had come to visit him."[54] José Caridad Perera, a free black of Karabali ethnicity, ate dinner during festival days in "the house of Antonio José Barraga the Captain General" of the *cabildo* together with "other various relatives."[55] Other *cabildos* simply referred to members as part of one family. Cristóbal Govín, the 2nd captain of the *cabildo* Karabali Oquella, complained of the new discord caused by an election "between a family that has always carried on with the utmost peace and harmony."[56] Still others described their fellow *cabildo* members with the more general *compañero* (companion) that conveyed a sense of shared camaraderie from being part of a community.[57] Whether described as "family" members, "relatives," or "companions," *cabildos* provided a widened network of associations that fostered collective solidarity.

Salvador Ternero's dispute with the Cuban-born creoles in the Mina Guagni *cabildo* indicates that within a nation, the rights and benefits accorded to "family" members, "relatives," or "companions" could vary widely. While African ethnic identification tended to define who could be counted on *cabildo* membership lists, evidence from various nations suggests the treatment of mulattos, Cuban-born creoles, and slaves depended on the regulations and customs of each society. Contemporary documents leave little indication that mulattos participated in *cabildos*. Given that nations in Cuba based their membership on a shared African ethnicity, *cabildos* may have excluded mulattos. Cuban officials may have also prevented them from joining *cabildos* as they sought to separate blacks and mulattos from making a common cause, further revealing the precarious position of a mixed race population in a society divided essentially between people of European and African ancestry. Despite these tendencies that would work to exclude mulattos, some may have participated in the nations or attended *cabildo* houses during festival days. On 25 February 1811, authorities arrested José Montero, Felipe Santiago, and Rafael Rodríguez, all soldiers in the free mulatto militia, for attending a meeting at a "*cabildo* of Blacks."[58] Other than this brief reference, there is no evidence to conclude that mulattos regularly participated in *cabildo* functions, just as there is no evidence to argue that the nations specified their exclusion.

While there are few references of mulatto participation in *cabildos*, ample evidence suggests that Cuban-born blacks regularly participated in the nations. For example, free creole Juan Bautista Valiente, known as "el

Cubano," participated in the Mina *cabildo*.[59] The *cabildo* Musolongo allowed creole participation and recognized Juan Ruíz as a member, "even though he is a creole, son of a father and a mother of the nation, and married to a free black of the nation."[60] Regardless of Salvador Ternero's bitter dispute with Manuel Vásquez over creole voting rights, he recognized their membership as "children of the same" nation, and never proposed their expulsion.[61] While the differences between African-born and Cuban-born members could lead to rivalries within *cabildos,* colonial officials acted more alarmed than the nations that the two groups fraternized. Judicial authorities chastised free black Clemente Chacón's parenting skills for allowing his son Juan Bautista "a free black Creole, to play the drums with the Kongo nation."[62]

While some creoles actively participated in the nations as membership increased, providing a heightened significance to African ethnicity in Cuba, others began to separate themselves from the African-born population. Leaders of the Lucumi *cabildo* complained of the formation of a creole group that opposed the interest of the bozales. As Cuban authorities settled divisions within *cabildos* and became cognizant of creole participation in the associations, they came to suspect that "there had formed a *cabildo* of black creoles." Free black José Herrera denied any association with the society, and insisted that he had no knowledge that his "sister-in-law Manuela González had been elected Queen of the creole *cabildo*." Further, Herrera, elaborated that "should one [*cabildo*] form, he would not join, because he was not a man of *cabildos* . . . and could not make the movements of the bozales." Rather, Herrera emphasized, he was somebody who "danced the minuet, as is the custom of creoles."[63] Herrera's contrast between the minuet and *cabildo* performances drew a clear distinction between African and creole dances. He also revealed, perhaps simplistically, the degree to which some creoles defined themselves in contradistinction to *bozales,* and the complexity of racial and ethnic identity in Cuba.

Slaves and creoles alike had limited rights and privileges in *cabildos*. As Salvador Ternero explained, slaves of the Mina Guagni nation participated in cabildo functions, but it was not by "a right that they have, but by voluntary permission."[64] The *cabildo* Karabali prevented slaves from voting for leaders; the organization's electoral roster listed only free members.[65] Likewise, other societies prevented slaves from participating in elections and deciding the financial expenditures of the nations.[66] Given that the distinction between free and slave represented the primary division of Cuban society, as well as the prevalence of slavery in Africa, it should not be surprising that *cabildos* defined membership rights based upon legal status.

Although they are rare in comparison with the entire scope of Cuban slavery, Afro-Cuban historian Pedro Deschamps Chapeaux has identified numerous people of African ancestry who owned slaves, representing what he describes as the interests of the "bourgeoisie of color."[67] A few *cabildo* members even owned slaves. In 1807, Antonio Ribero, a member of the Lucumí Llane nation, purchased a slave for 500 pesos. The transaction caught the attention of the *cabildo* not because they opposed the purchase on moral grounds, but because they suspected Ribero had bought the slave with money stolen from the nation.[68] In 1804 Cristobal Govin, capataz of the Karabali Oquella nation, opposed remodeling several dilapidated rooms of the *cabildo* house, including his own. Govin protested that "I would have to transfer my habitation during the construction" to the one of "Rafaela, slave of Teresa Barreto who lives in another room of the same house."[69] When Salvador Ternero assumed the title of *capataz* of the Mina Guagni *cabildo,* the nation authorized him to administer "whatever quantities of *maravedíes,* gold pesos, silver pesos, jewelry, slaves, merchandise, agricultural products, and other goods."[70] Although nations fostered ethnic identification and a community beyond the immediate supervision of white masters, the ownership of slaves by some *cabildo* members and the limited voting rights extended to human chattel illustrates how slavery pervaded every aspect of Cuban society.

Whereas some nations limited the participation of slaves in *cabildo* functions because of their servile condition, others attempted to overcome the barriers that blocked active participation. Festival days represented crucial events that allowed for a collective solidarity to be expressed through ceremony and dance. While numerous masters might grant permission to participate in *cabildos* as a reward, they also benefited from such participation.[71] The nation Karabali Osso recognized the important participation of slaves in *cabildo* functions. In 1803 their account book recorded the entry "payment for slaves' daily wages of our nation" to masters in order to secure their participation at *cabildo* events.[72] The Karabali Osso nation, in effect, hired the attendance of its enslaved members by paying wages to their masters. As slavery represented obstacles to full participation, generated additional expenses by paying wages to masters, and undermined collective strength, *cabildos* often provided loans to emancipate members.[73] The *cabildo* Kongo, for example, reported that Cayetano García owed "80 pesos of the 200 that he was given for his freedom."[74] Free members could not only participate more actively in *cabildos* than slaves, but as the rightful owners of their own labor they could contribute more generously to the nation's financial resources.

Some societies accepted members from different nations. Authorities assumed the free black Antonio from Bayamo was Karabali because he participated in the nation's festival days and "lived among them," but he described his ethnicity as Kongo.[75] Although the Mina and Mandinga could trace their nations to the distinct geographic areas of the Gold Coast and the Upper Niger Valley respectively, they formed a joint *cabildo* that extended membership to both groups.[76] Members of different nations could even gain considerable authority within a *cabildo* with which they did not share a common ethnicity. On 17 July 1803 the cabildo Karabali Induri elected Juan Echevarría to the position of 2nd capataz by an overwhelming majority. Jesús Sollazo, the leader of the *cabildo,* immediately declared Echevarría's election "null . . . because he is not of the nation Induri . . . for which he should not be admitted." The Captain General of Cuba decided to uphold the election because "the majority of the individuals of the *cabildo* Karabali Induri agreed upon" Juan Echevarría for the position of 2nd capataz.[77] Echevarría's election reveals both the flexibility and rigidity of African ethnicity in Cuba. Although not an African-born member of the Karabali Induri nation, he apparently had enough supporters within the *cabildo* who did not define leadership qualities exclusively by ethnicity. For the leader of the nation, however, it was precisely his lack of African ethnicity that made him unsuitable to serve as an elected officer.

The Captain General sided with Echevarría because he had won the election outright, and by "the fact that he had been admitted to the *cabildo*" long before the election took place.[78] *Cabildos* routinely extended membership to people of diverse ethnicities, but as with creoles and slaves, tended to restrict their voting rights. As described previously, Salvador Ternero dismissed Manuel Vásquez's complaint as "not having legitimate representation of the nation" because he was a creole and had the support of only one slave. In addition, Ternero emphasized that among Vásquez's supporters was "María de la Luz Romero who is of a different nation."[79] The Karabali Apapa, like other nations, did not limit membership to only one ethnicity. When a dispute divided the *cabildo* over buying a new house, however, only those members of Karabali Apapa ethnicity and those who had been extended voting rights could debate the purchase. The leaders of the *cabildo* explained that members of different ethnicities "do not have representation in the *cabildo* according to the resolutions of this government, without obtaining the right and permission of us, and the others who make up the nation."[80] Voting rights in nations appear to have been universally granted to free African-born members who represented the ethnicity of the *cabildo*. For creoles, slaves, and *cabildo* members of distinct ethnicities from the dominant group, generalizations prove elusive, because the practices and custom of each nation tended to differ, illustrating the diverse experiences of people of African ancestry in Cuba.

Although *cabildos* often restricted participation in their associations along ethnic lines, they also recognized commonalties with larger cultural groups common to areas of the slave trade. Manuel Blanco explained to authorities that the division of the Lucumies into separate nations reflected the different homelands of the members, while recognizing their common Yoruba culture. According to Blanco, "the truth is that among the blacks who call themselves Lucumies, some are Chabes, others Barbaes, Bambaras and Nangas. . . . [A]ll of them take the name Lucumi, but some are from one homeland and the others from another." The same recognition of a larger shared culture can be observed among the different groups of Kongolese in Cuba. Blanco observed that "there are many Blacks who call themselves members of the Kongo nation, but as they are from diverse homelands they have in this city diverse *cabildos.*" Blanco recognized the common culture of the Kongolese, yet pointed out that the "Kongos Luangos" and the "Kongos Mondongos" have their own *cabildos.*[81] The Karabali also identified themselves as part of a larger cultural group, but divided their *cabildos* ethnically to a specific homeland. In addition to choosing leaders for each Karabali *cabildo,* they also elected "José Aróstegui as the *capataz* of the five Karabali nations" to coordinate activities among the organizations.[82] The Lucumies, Kongoleses, and Karabalies formed associations based upon a broad shared cultural identity rooted in Africa. They then limited *cabildo* membership to reflect the same nation and homeland of those they described as their "*paisanos*" (countrymen).[83] The ability for Africans in Cuba to narrow their fraternal societies to reflect both a common nation and homeland supports John Thornton's argument that "slaves would typically have no trouble finding members of their own nation with whom to communicate."[84]

Within each *cabildo,* several members held administrative positions that strengthened the *capataz*'s leadership. The *cabildo* Karabali, located in the city of Matanzas, elected Rafael their new leader in 1814. They then decided upon a general staff that resembled a King's court. They agreed that Rafael's wife would serves as Queen mother; María Rosario Domínguez as princess; Diego as first minister, Nicario as second minister; Bernardo as first captain, Miguel de la Cruz as second lieutenant; Manuel del Portillo and Felipe as musicians; and Francisco as treasurer.[85] In addition to these titles, other *cabildos* created positions such as governor, emperor, sergeant of arms, queen of war, and captain of war.[86] Although denied voting rights within *cabildos*, slaves often attained leadership roles. The slave Patricio served as "captain of the Karabali slaves," and Alonzo Santa Cruz held the position of "King of the Kongo slaves."[87] The Captain General of Cuba attempted to prevent the establishment of an elaborate leadership structure and recommended that "there should not be positions other than first, second, and third *capataz*."[88] Despite the limited influence of *cabildos* beyond their own nation, the Captain General realized the possible dangers of allowing slaves and free people of color to create their own hierarchical structures and select their own leaders.

Cuban authorities remained torn over how to deal with the leadership organization created by *cabildos*. They recognized the important role of *cabildos* for a rapidly expanding slave society, as they provided crucial cultural adjustment for slaves recently imported from Africa. Further, a single leader provided the important function of an intermediary between colonial officials and African laborers. Nonetheless, the Cuban government continually voiced concerns over the power that came with being a *capataz* or captain of a *cabildo*. In 1759 the Captain General of Cuba informed Spanish officials that "as a precaution for certain disorders, it has been established by this government to name for each [*cabildo*] a Captain to watch and supervise their functions and meetings, who is of the same nation, and of old and mature age."[89] By the late eighteenth century and early nineteenth century, the previous policy of appointing leaders by the colonial government had been replaced by the *cabildos* electing their own leaders. *Cabildo* elections ultimately required approval of the colonial government, which, in turn, shaped who would and would not be an acceptable candidate. However, there are not any extant examples of authorities overturning an election. The change in policy from government-appointed to *cabildo*-elected leaders reflects the ability for nations to create a leadership structure acceptable to colonial officials. *Cabildos* expanded their restricted autonomy to determine the internal affairs of their societies by selecting leaders who did not attract the government's close scrutiny.

While government officials referred to *cabildo* leaders as *capataz* or captain, some nations came up with their own titles. The free black José Caridad Herrera described Antonio José Barraga, the leader of the Karabali *cabildo*, having the title "Captain General."[90] Authorities learned that "inside the house" of the Kongo nation members called Joaquín "the Kongo King."[91] The difference between the government-given title of capataz or captain and the chosen title by some *cabildo* leaders of Captain General or King probably did not represent any vast difference in the function of nations. Nonetheless, the distinction does reveal the tension that informed the process of identification and self-identification. The decision by the Kongolese to give their leader the title of King might be considered as something more than a generic reference to monarchical authority. Throughout the eighteenth century, one of the central claims to legitimate rule in the Kongo region was made by asserting "I am the King of the Kongos."[92] Civil wars split the Kingdom of Kongo into various camps by claiming adherence to a military King or a blacksmith King that may have informed who became selected as a leader of a nation in Cuba. Some *cabildos* eschewed the leadership titles of *capataz* and captain provided by the colonial government. Perhaps they did so in reaction to how colonial society disproportionately shaped the discourse of identity from stripping Africans of their birth names to deciding what titles could be given to *cabildo* leaders.

Cabildo leaders tended to be influential members of the free colored community tied to the militia. Francisco Alas, the "Emperor" of the Mina and Mandinga *cabildo* in Bayamo and member of the black militia, owned with his wife a small plot of land, three horses, two mares, seven pigs, a gold ring, and over a hundred pesos.[93] Domingo Acosta, the *capataz* of the Karabali Apapa nation, drew upon his connections as a "retired soldier . . . of the Black militia battalion" to request that a military court settle a dispute within the *cabildo*.[94] Captain General Someruelos recommended that the investigation into the financial affairs of the Mina Guagni nation be handled by a "military tribunal" after Esteban Torres and Salvador Ternero emphasized their militia service.[95] When Manuel Blanco became involved in a property dispute with the *cabildo* Lucumi over selling the nation's house, he hoped to win the case by stressing his volunteer militia service "without receiving a salary or any gratification."[96] The selection of *cabildo* leaders from the ranks of the colored militia served to present colonial authorities with individuals they regarded as loyal subjects of the Spanish crown. By electing leaders acceptable to government officials, the *cabildos* would suffer less scrutiny. In addition, some nations became entitled to the special privileges of military courts available to their leaders. By selecting militia soldiers for the position of *capataz, cabildos* could address the conflicting goals of earning approval from a government that sought to maintain a racial social hierarchy while at the same time bettering the conditions of those who shared a common African ethnicity.[97]

An examination of the electoral process indicates that female members often guided the affairs of the nation, not the elected *capataz,* as Cuban officials believed. Because of their numerical superiority among the *cabildo's* voting members, women often decided the selection of new leaders. Forty-two eligible voters participated in the *cabildo* Karabali Oquella elections of 1804; thirty-one were women.[98] Although the majority of males cast their votes for Cayetano García as the new *capataz* for the *cabildo* Kongo Macamba in 1807, Antonio Diepa won the election because of six females' votes.[99] Of the forty-seven votes cast in favor of Juan Echevarría for the position of 2nd *capataz* of the *cabildo* Karabali Induri, thirty-two came from women, guaranteeing his margin of victory by a ratio of two to one. The *capataz* of the *cabildo* Jesús Sollazo attempted to overturn Echevarría's election on the basis that he was not of Karabali Induri ethnicity, "but also because the general customs observed in the *cabildos* of this city for the elections of *capataz* do not admit the votes of women."[100] The Captain General ruled against the attempt "to not accept women's votes" for *capataz* because it was "contrary to what is daily observed." The Captain General's investigation concluded that Sollazo's protest simply represented a tactic to nullify an unfavorable election.[101] The *capataz* of the Karabali Oquella, Cristobal Govin, shared Jesús Sollazo's opinion that female participation in *cabildos* should be limited because Lázaro Rodríguez won the election with "only the assistance of Teresa Barreto's supporters."[102]

While some *cabildo* leaders felt threatened by the authority women could exert in shaping the leadership of African societies, others recognized their important role in maintaining the unity of nations. In 1805 José Aróstegui of the *cabildo* Karabali Osso informed the Captain General of the death of Rita Castellanos, who held the leadership position among the female members of the nation. Shortly thereafter, Barbara de Mesa "occupied her place with all the support of the nation for her recommendable" characteristics. Aróstegui requested that the Captain General "give his recognition to Barbara de Mesa as *capataza*" so that she could "govern the women of said *cabildo* with authority" to insure "perfect peace and harmony."[103] Other *cabildos* not only recognized the important role of women in governing female members, but acknowledged that they maintained the unity of the entire nation. The leaders of the Kongo Macamaba nation attributed their inability to resolve disputes by themselves and the need for government officials to intervene because since "the death of Rafaela Armenteras, Queen of the nation, the disorder has increased."[104]

Not only did females in nations exhibit considerable authority in determining the *cabildos*' leaders, but they also influenced financial expenditures. Through membership dues, renting rooms, collecting alms, and hosting festivals, *cabildos* normally held savings in cash that varied from 300 to 1,000 pesos. These savings represented a significant amount, given that the prices for slaves in Havana newspapers usually ranged from 300 to 500 pesos.[105] The important duty of guarding the safe that contained the *cabildo*'s money usually fell upon the Queen. When the *cabildo* Karabali Osso became involved in a dispute that required paying a legal fine, the neighborhood commissioner went to the house of Barbara de Mesa to "request the safe." José Castillo reported that Barbara de Mesa would not turn over the safe "until she had been threatened with prison."[106] When members of the *cabildo* Karabali Oquella challenged the financial expenses of the *capataz,* the whole nation went "to the house of Teresa Barreto, queen of said *cabildo*" to count the money in the safe. The *cabildo* leaders pulled from the safe "a bag full of money and in the presence of the nation . . . counted 946 pesos."[107]

Most *cabildos* entrusted the Queen of the nation to guard their money, but they took precautions to insure that it would take more than one person to open the safe. With banks unavailable to guard the money of *cabildos,* they generally used a safe that required three different keys to prevent one person from making a withdrawal.[108] According to the *Cabildo* Karabali Induri, their safe opened with "three different keys." The "First *Capataz*" received a key, "the Second *Capataz* another, and an elected person in consultation with all the nation" held the third key. The three key holders could open the safe only in the presence of "twenty people, men or women, of the nation" to explain the purpose of the withdrawal.[109] Likewise, the *cabildo* Kongo Macamba also required their safe to be opened in the presence of its members to "avoid future disputes, objections, and suspicions of the *capataz.*"[110] Money often disappeared despite such measures to regulate the opening of the safe. Tomás Paveda of the *cabildo* Karabali Osso suspected the *capataz* had withdrawn money without consulting the nation by acquiring the other two keys.[111] The required presence of three key holders could sometimes work too effectively in preventing access to the *cabildo*'s money. On one occasion, a safe could not be opened because the keyholder worked "in the countryside."[112] Unsurprisingly, one *cabildo* required that keyholders "should not be absent from the city without leaving the key with a person of known confidence."[113]

Female leaders of *cabildos* often received the duty of guarding the safe, but they did not hold the keys to open it. The Kongo Macamba nation stated very clearly that whoever "takes on the task of treasury" would have to be a "black male."[114] Cristóbal Govín, the *capataz* of the *cabildo* Karabali Oquella, feared that "the funds of the *cabildo* held by Teresa Barreto, a rebellious women with bad ideas" would jeopardize the stability of the nation.[115] Govin never suggested that Barreto be stripped of her duty to guard the safe, but believed she should be watched closely. According to Govin, Barreto supported "Lázaro Rodríguez for second *capataz* . . . with the design to place him later in the position of first [*capataz*]." Govin warned that if this would occur, she "could maneuver . . the common money of the nation." Despite Govin holding the title of *capataz,* he recognized the power of Teresa Barreto in deciding the affairs of the *cabildo* when he described her as the person "who moves all of these machinations."[116] Whether through deciding elections or guarding the safe, females decisively shaped *cabildo* functions.[117]

The *cabildos* showed remarkable flexibility at maintaining an overall sense of unity despite their divisions. While it is important to emphasize distinctions of ethnicity, place of birth, legal status, and gender, given that they were made by the members of the nations themselves, it is just as important to recognize that *cabildos* continued to support the collective efforts of the nation as a whole. As with many organizations representing lower-class interests in a society controlled by a powerful elite, the tension between the specific needs of individual members and the unity of the *cabildos* created friction within the nations. Nations could recognize and address dissent within their own ranks without causing the complete dissolution of their societies. This fact indicates that collective needs often superseded individual interests. The nations represented the only institutions that permitted the voluntary grouping along ethnic lines for Africans and creoles, men and women, and slaves and freedpersons in Cuba. For a colony rigidly divided between white European masters and black African slaves, *cabildos* stood in contrast to the racial slave-free paradigm that defined the circles of inclusion and exclusion for most of Cuban society.

Members of *cabildos* chose to join associations to define themselves in cooperation with others who shared a similar ethnicity. In this sense, they show the importance of understanding that Africans in the Americas did not immediately or exclusively adopt a racialized identity of blackness. Although notions of blackness and whiteness undoubtedly represent the most important legacy of slavery in the New World, it cannot be considered the single defining characteristic from the very beginning or even as late as the nineteenth century. The African population in Cuba defined itself, and became defined by others, by cultural, geographic, and linguistic criteria that tended to militate against a broad racial identity. While *cabildos* above all emphasized ethnic identity, they did not ignore that whites were not slaves and the ruling class of Cuba was not African. At meetings inside *cabildo* houses when nations discussed the needs of their members, they surely addressed the problems their organization faced of existing in a society based upon a racial hierarchy that privileged the European over the

African. Although the functions of *cabildos* did not concentrate exclusively on attacking racial inequalities, the nations sought to remedy, in one way or another, the grossly unequal position of its members that was common to all people of the African diaspora. As a result, African ethnic identity was not necessarily in conflict with a New World racial identity of blackness. By providing a network of alliances and an institutional structure that offered a limited sense of familiarity for Africans in Cuba, *cabildos* helped their members to survive in a society based upon racial oppression.[118] Africans in Cuba could define themselves by simultaneously emphasizing both their Old World ethnic nation and their New World racial identity, revealing the strength—not the weaknesses colonial officials assumed and some present-day observers fear—of cultural diversity.

Notes

*The author gratefully acknowledges financial support from the Conference on Latin American History, the Southwest Council of Latin American Studies, the Institute of Latin American Studies at the University of Texas at Austin, the Ford Foundation, the Johns Hopkins University, the Fulbright-Hays Program, and the Social Science Research Council to conduct research in Cuba and Spain.

1. Historian Philip A. Howard states the societies were "known as cabildos de naciones de afrocubanos." *Changing History: Afro-Cuban Cabildos and the Societies of Color in the Nineteenth Century* (Baton Rouge: Louisiana State University Press, 1998), xiv. I found the societies described as "cabildos de nación" only in documents from the 1790s to 1820s.

2. Robert Francis Jameson, *Letters from the Havana during the Year 1820; Containing an Account of the Present State of the Island of Cuba and Observations on the Slave Trade* (London: John Miller, 1821), 21.

3. See most recently Michael A. Gómez, "African Identity and Slavery in the Americas," *Radical History Review* 75 (1999): 118; and John K. Thornton, "The Coromantees: An African Cultural Group in Colonial North America and the Caribbean," *Journal of Caribbean History* 32, 1–2 (1998) 161.

4. David Eltis, *The Rise of African Slavery in the Americas* (Cambridge: Cambridge University Press, 2000), 244.

5. Richard Ligon, *A True and Exact History of the Island of Barbadoes* (1657; reprint, London: Frank Cass and Company, 1970), 55.

6. Quoted in Eltis, *Rise of African Slavery,* 230.

7. Michael Craton, *Testing the Chains: Resistance to Slavery in the British West Indies* (Ithaca: Cornell University Press, 1982), 108–10.

8. David Barry Gaspar, *Bondsmen & Rebels: A Study of Master-Slave Relations in Antigua: With Implications for Colonial British America* (Baltimore: Johns Hopkins University Press, 1985).

9. Craton, *Testing the Chains,* pp. 125–39.

10. Thornton, "Coromantees," 161, 173.

11. Trial of Peter, 21 June 1822, in *Designs against Charleston: The Trial Record of the Denmark Vesey Slave Conspiracy of 1822,* ed. and intro. Edward A. Pearson (Chapel Hill: University of North Carolina Press, 1999), 176; Douglas R. Egerton, *He Shall Go Out Free: The Lives of Denmark Vesey* (Madison, Wisc.: Madison House, 1999), 133; and Michael A. Gómez, *Exchanging Our Country Marks: The Transformation of African Identities in the Colonial and Antebellum South* (Chapel Hill: University of North Carolina Press, 1998), 3.

12. Linda M. Heywood, "The Angolan-Afro-Brazilian Cultural Connections," *Slavery & Abolition* 20, 1 (April 1999): 10.

13. Ibid., 19; Elizabeth W. Kiddy, "Ethnic and Racial Identity in the Brotherhoods of the Rosary of Minas Gerais, 1700–1830," *The Americas* 56, 2 (Oct. 1999): 238–43; João José Reis, *Slave Rebellion in Brazil: The Muslim Uprising of 1835 in Bahia,* trans. Arthur Brakel (Baltimore, Md.: Johns Hopkins University Press, 1986): 149–51, 153; João José Reis, "Différences et résistances: Les noirs à Bahia sous l'esclavage," *Cahiers d'études africaines* 32, 1 (1992): 19, 21; Patricia A. Mulvey, "Slave Confraternities in Brazil: Their Role in Colonial Society," *The Americas* 39, 1 (July 1982): 46, 49; A. J. R. Russell-Wood, "Black and Mulatto Brotherhoods in Colonial Brazil," *Hispanic American Historical Review* 54, 4 (Nov. 1974): 582–83; Mary C. Karasch, *Slave Life in Rio, 1808–1850* (Princeton, N.J.: Princeton University Press, 1987), 84–85, 358–59.

14. See the numerous documents reprinted by Robert C. Smith on an Angolan brotherhood, "Manuscritos da igreja de Nossa Senhora do Rosário dos homens pretos do Recife," *Arquivos* (Recife) 4–10: 7–20 (Dec. 1951): 53–120; Robert C. Smith, "Décadas do Rosário dos pretos: Documentos da irmandade," *Arquivos* (Recife) 4–10: 7–20 (Dec. 1951): 143–70.

15. Great Britain, House of Lords, "Report from the Select Committee of the House of Lords, Appointed to Consider the Best Means Which Great Britain Can Adopt for the Final Extinction of the African Slave Trade," *Sessional Papers, 1849–50, Slave Trade,* 24 May 1849, vol. 9, par. 2493, p. 171.

16. St. John d'el Rey Mining Company, *Circular to the Proprietors of the St. John d'el Rey Mining Company,* (London: R. Clay, 1850), p. 39, in St. John d'el Rey Mining Company Archive, Nettie Lee Benson Latin American Collection, University of Texas at Austin.

17. Ruth Pike, "Sevillan Society in the Sixteenth Century: Slaves and Freedmen," *Hispanic American Historical Review* 47, 3 (Aug. 1967): 344–46.

18. Frederick P. Bowser, *The African Slave in Colonial Peru, 1524–1650* (Stanford, Ct.: Stanford University Press, 1974), 249–50, 339.

19. Leslie B. Rout, Jr. *The African Experience in Spanish America, 1502 to the Present Day* (Cambridge: Cambridge University Press, 1976), 136.

20. George Reid Andrews, *The Afro-Argentinies of Buenos Aires, 1800–1900* (Madison: University of Wisconsin Press, 1980), 142–51.

21. Fernando Ortiz, *Los cabildos y la fiesta afrocubanos del Día de Reyes* (1921; Havana: Editorial de Ciencias Sociales, 1992), 6; Carmen Victoria Montejo-Arrechea, *Sociedades de instrucción y recreo de pardos y morenos que existieron en Cuba colonial* (Veracruz: Instituto Veracruzano de Cultura, 1993), 14–16.

22. "El Obispo Morell de Santa Cruz oficializa los cabildos africanos donde nació la santería, convirtiéndolos en ermitas," Havana, 6 Dec. 1755, in Levi Marrero, *Cuba: Economía y sociedad, del monopolio hacia la libertad comercial (1701–1763)* (Madrid: Editorial Playor, 1980), 8:159.

23. Ibid.

24. Ibid., 159–60.

25. Ibid., 159.

26. "Diligencias sobre cuentos del cabildo de la nación Induri pos su capataz Nicolas Veitia," (1800), Archivo Nacional de Cuba, Havana, fondo Escribanía Antonio D'aumy (hereafter ANC-ED), leg. 398, no. 23, fols. 1–5.

27. This date is earlier than Howard's who argues by "the beginning of the nine-teenth century, cabildos . . . outnumber[ed] cofradías." *Changing History*, 26–27.

28. Antonio Bachiller y Morales, *Los Negros* (Barcelona: Gorgas y compañía, 1887), 114–15. Ortiz, *Los cabildos,* 4–6; Montejo-Arrechea, *Sociedades,* 12–13; Pedro Deschamps Chapeaux, "Cabildos: Solo par esclavos," *Cuba* 7, 69 (Jan. 1968): 51; Pedro Dechamps-Chapeaux, "Sociedades: La integración de pardos y morenos," *Cuba* 7, 71 (Mar. 1968): 54; Howard, *Changing History,* 21–25.

29. Paul E. Lovejoy and David Richardson, "Trust, Pawnship, and Atlantic History: The Institutional Foundations of the Old Calabar Slave Trade," *American Historical Review* 104, 2 (April 1999): 347–49.

30. Paul E. Lovejoy, "Identifying Enslaved Africans in the African Diaspora," in *Identity in the Shadow of Slavery,* ed. Paul E. Lovejoy (London: Continuum, 2000), 8; Howard, *Changing History,* 48, 53, 68–69, 109–10. The classic treatment of the Abakuá in Cuba remains Lydia Cabrera, *La Sociedad Secreta de Abakuá, narrada por viejos adeptos* (Havana: Ediciones C. R., 1959).

31. Peter Morton-Williams, "The Yoruba Ogboni Cult in Oyo," *Africa* 30 (1960): 362–74; J. A. Atanda, "The Yoruba Ogboni Cult: Did it Exist in Old Oyo?" *Journal of the Historical Society of Nigeria* 6, 4 (1973): 365–72; Robin Law, *The Oyo Empire, c. 1600–c. 1836: A West African Imperialism in the Era of the Atlantic Slave Trade* (Oxford: Clarendon Press, 1977), 61.

32. Thornton, "Coromantees," 163, 169.

33. Toyin Falola and Adebayo Akanmu, *Culture, Politics, & Money among the Yoruba* (New Brunswick, N.J.: Transaction Publishers, 2000), 131–39.

34. Philip D. Curtin, *The Atantic Slave Trade: A Census* (Madison: University of Wisconsin Press, 1969).

35. David Eltis, David Richardson, Stephen D. Behrendt, and Herbert S. Klein, eds., *The Trans-Atlantic Slave Trade: A Database on CD-ROM* (Cambridge: Cambridge University Press, 1999).

36. Eltis, *Rise of African Slavery,* 251–54

37. Philip D. Morgan, "The Cultural Implications of the Atlantic Slave Trade: Afri-can Regional Origins, American Destinations and New World Developments," *Slavery & Abolition* 18, 1 (April, 1997): 125–26.

38. David Eltis, David Richardson, and Stephen D. Behrendt, "Patterns in the Trans-atlantic Slave Trade, 1662–1867: New Indications of African Origins of Slaves Arriving in the Americas," in *Black Imagination and the Middle Passage,* ed. Maria Diedrich, Henry Louis Gates, Jr., and Carl Pedersen (Oxford: Oxford University Press, 1999), 30.

39. David Eltis and David Richardson, "The Structure of the Transatlantic Slave Trade, 1595–1867," (unpublished paper presented to the Social Science History Meeting, 1995), quoted in Morgan, "Cultural Implications," 127.

40. "La nación mina guagni contra Salvador Ternero sobre cuentas," (1794–97), ANC-ED, leg. 893, no. 4 , fol. ? [It is not possible to cite the specific folios of many pages of this document and others in the fondo Escribanía because the pagination has been de-stroyed by deterioration.]

41. "La nación lucumi contra Dn. Manuel Blanco y otros sobre propiedad del terreno en que se halla fundado el cavildo de nación," (1777–1781), ANC, fondo Escribanía Cabello (hereafter ANC-EC), leg. 147, no. 1, fols. 50–53v.

42. Bishop of Cuba to His Majesty, Havana, 6 Dec. 1753, Archivo General de Indias, Seville, fondo Audiencia de Santo Domingo (hereafter AGI-SD), leg. 515, no. 51, quoted in Fernando Ortiz, *Los negros curros* (Havana: Editorial de Ciencias Sociales, 1986), 212–13.

43. Estimate derived from documentation found in: ANC-EC, leg. 6, no. 6; leg. 47, no. 1; ANC-ED, leg. 336, no. 1; leg. 398, no. 23; leg. 439, no. 16; leg. 548, no. 11; leg. 583, no. 5; leg. 610, no. 15; leg. 660, no. 8; leg. 673, no. 9; leg. 893, no. 4; ANC-Escribanía de Gobierno (hereafter ANC-EG), leg. 28, no. 4; leg. 123, no. 15; leg. 123, no. 15–A; leg. 125, no. 3; leg. 277, no. 5; ANC, fondo Escribanía Ortega, (hereafter ANC-EO), leg. 3, no. 8; leg. 6, no. 1; leg. 65, no. 11; leg. 494, no. 2; ANC- Escribanía de Valerio (hereafter ANC-EVal), leg. 671, no. 9873; ANC-Escribanía de Varios (hereafter ANC-EVar), leg. 211, no. 3114; Archivo Nacional de Cuba, Havana, fondo Asuntos Políticos (hereafter ANC-AP), leg. 11, no. 37; leg. 12, nos. 9, 14, 17, 27; leg. 13, no. 1; leg. 14, no. 1; ANC-Donativos y Remisiones (hereafter ANC-DR), leg. 542, no. 29; Archivo General de Indias, Seville, fondo Papeles de Cuba (hereafter AGI-PC), leg. 1433–B, and 1667.

44. ANC-EC, leg. 147, no. 1, fol. 53v.

45. John Thornton, *Africa and Africans in the Making of the Atlantic World, 1400–1800,* 2nd. ed. (Cambridge: Cambridge University Press, 1998), 190.

46. ANC-EC, leg. 147, no. 1, fol. 82.

47. "Pedro José Santa Cruz solicitando nombramiento de Capataz al Cabildo de la nación Congos Musolongos," (1806), ANC-ED, leg. 660, no. 8, fols. 1–4.

48. "La nación Caravali Umugini sobre división con la Osso y con la misma Umugini, y liquidación de cuentas con el capitán Pedro Nolasco Eligió," (1805–6), ANC-EG, leg. 123, no. 15–A, fol. 9.

49. "Real cédula de su magestad sobre la educación, trato y ocupaciones de los esclavos, en todos sus dominios de indias, e islas filipinas baxo las reglas que expresan," Aranjuez, 31 May 1789, Biblioteca Nacional José Martí, Havana, Colección Vidal Morales y Morales (hereafter BNJM-Morales), leg. 79, no. 3, fol. 7.

50. Diego Miguel de Moya to His Majesty, Havana, 19 Jan. 1790, ANC-Real Consulado y Junta de Fomento (hereafter ANC-RCJF), leg. 150, no. 7405, fol. 11.

51. Ibid., fol. 18v.

52. Archivo de la Oficina del Historiador de la Ciudad, Havana, fondo Actas Capitulares (hereafter AOHCH-AC), leg. 76, Cabildo Minutes, Havana, 2 Mar. 1809, fol. 73v.

53. "Autos criminales obrados en razón de la insurrección que contra los blancos tenían proyectada en Bayamo los negros vosales," (8 Feb. 1812), ANC-AP, leg, 12, no. 9, fol. 9v.

54. Ibid., fol. 22v.

55. Ibid., fol. 30v.

56. "Expediente seguido por Cristoval Govin, capataz de la nación Oquella contra Lázaro Rodríguez, capataz del la Agro, sobre cuentas," (1799), ANC-EO, leg. 6, no. 1, fol. 62.

57. ANC-AP, leg. 12, no. 9, fol. 23v.

58. Francisco Alonzo de Morazan to Someruelos, Havana, 28 June 1811, AGI-PC, leg. 1667.

59. ANC-AP, leg. 12, no. 9, fols. 86–87.

60. "Cabildo musolongo sobre nombramientos de Capataz," (1806) ANC-ED, leg. 548, no. 11, fols. 15v–16.

61. ANC-ED, leg. 893, no. 4, fol. ?.

62. ANC-AP, leg. 12, no. 14, fol. 12.

63. "Incidente a los autos sobre la conspiración de José Antonio Aponte contra José Herrera y otros por complicidad en aquella," (19 Mar. 1812), ANC-AP, leg. 14, no. 1, fols. 182v–183v. According to contemporary J. M. Pérez, the minuet was the most popular dance in 1800. "Siglo XIX: Costumbres de Cuba en 1800 por J. M. Pérez," AOHCH, fondo José Luciano Franco (hereafter AOHCH-JLF), leg. 214, no. 31.

64. ANC-ED, leg. 893, no. 4, fol. ?.

65. ANC-AP, leg. 12, no. 9. fol. 109.

66. ANC-ED, leg. 893, no. 4, fol. 46; "La nación Caravali Induri sobre nombramiento de capataz del cavildo del Santo Cristo de Buen Viaje," (1802–6), ANC-EG, leg. 125, no. 3, fol. ?; ANC-EO, leg. 65, no. 11, fol. 72.

67. Pedro Deschamps Chapeaux, *El negro en la economía habanera del siglo XIX* (Havana: Unión de Escritores y Artistas de Cuba, 1971), 47–86; also see Rafael Duharte, *El negro en la sociedad colonial,* (Santiago: Editorial Oriente, 1988), 91–115.

68. "Juan Nepomuceno Montiel y Rafael Aróstegui como apoderados en la nación Lucumi Llane contra Agustina Zaraza y Antonio Ribero sobre la extracción de pesos que hicieron de la caja de la nación," (1807–1810), ANC-EC, leg. 64, no. 6, fols. 13–15.

69. ANC-EO, leg. 6, no. 1, fol. 59.

70. ANC-ED, leg. 893, no. 4, fol. ?

71. Eugene D. Genovese adeptly describes how certain privileges bestowed to slaves such as garden plots and holidays became transformed into rights, *Roll, Jordan, Roll: The World the Slaves Made* (New York: Vintage, 1974), 30–31, 314–15, 535–85, esp. 539, 569, 575. Emília Viotti da Costa explores the battle between master-awarded privileges and slaves' rights within the context of an extensive slave revolt, *Crowns of Glory Tears of Blood: The Demerara Slave Rebellion of 1823* (New York: Oxford University Press, 1994), pp. 84–85.

72. ANC-EG, leg. 123, no. 15–A, fol. 21.

73. Howard, *Changing History,* 48.

74. "José Antonio Diepa, capataz del cabildo nación Congo, sobre que se recojía los memoriales que promovió Cayetano García y socios para despojarlo del encargo de capataz del cabildo nación Congo Macamba," (1808–09), ANC-ED, leg. 439, no. 16, fol. 51v.

75. ANC-AP, leg. 12, no. 9, fols. 68v–69v.

76. Ibid., fols. 13, 44v.

77. ANC-EG, leg. 125, no. 3, fols. 106–15.

78. Ibid., fol. 115.

79. ANC-ED, leg. 893, no. 4, fol. 47.

80. "José Xavier Mirabal y consortes contra Domingo Acosta y socios sobre pesos, trata del cabildo de Apapa," (1808–30), ANC-ED, leg. 583, no. 5, fols. 82–82v [emphasis in original].

81. ANC-EC, leg. 147, no. 1, fol. 54v.

82. "Tomás Poveda, Clemente Andrade, Antonio de Prucia, Joaquin de Soto y Antonio María Lisundia contra el moreno José Aróstegui sobre que cuentas de caja del cavildo," (1805), ANC-ED, leg. 336, no. 1, fol. 40.

83. ANC-EO, leg. 6, no. 1, fol. 60v.

84. Thornton, *Africa and Africans*, 199.

85. "Expediente relativo a la renovación de cargos de un cabildo de nación ante las autoridades en la ciudad de Matanzas," ANC-DR, leg. 542, no. 29, fol. 1; some of the documentation for the Matanzas Karabali cabildo is published in "Constitución de un cabildo Carabali en 1814," *Archivos del folklore cubano*, 1, 3 (1925), 281–83.

86. ANC-AP, leg. 12, no. 9, fols. 45, 68v, 73.

87. Ibid., fol. 36v; ANC-AP, leg. 13, no. 1, fol. 101.

88. ANC-EG, leg. 125, no. 3, fols. 115–115v.

89. Pedro Alonso to ?, Havana, 10 Oct. 1759, AGI-SD, leg. 1352, published in Ortiz, *Los negros curros*, 214.

90. ANC-AP, leg. 12, no. 9, fol. 30v.

91. ANC-AP, leg. 12, no. 27, fol. 12v.

92. John K. Thornton, "'I Am the Subject of the King of Congo': African Political Ideology and the Haitian Revolution," *Journal of World History* 4, 2 (Fall 1993): 186–98.

93. Archivo Histórico de la Provincia de Granma, Bayamo, fondo Protocolos, (hereafter AHPG-Protocolos), leg. 11, libro 1 (1810), fol. 116v.

94. ANC-ED, leg. 583, no. 5, fol. 24.

95. ANC-EO, leg. 65, no. 11, fol. 55.

96. ANC-EC, leg. 147, no. 1, fol. 41; also see Howard for the link between militia soldiers and cabildo activities, *Changing History*, 31–36.

97. Kimberly S. Hanger observed that in New Orleans the town council often rejected petitions by blacks to hold dances, "but when the free black militia, represented by four officers, submitted its request in 1800" authorities approved it. *Bounded Lives, Bounded Places, Free Black Society in Colonial New Orleans, 1769–1803* (Durham, N.C.: Duke University Press, 1997), 132.

98. "Expediente seguido por los de la nación Caravali Oquella sobre nombramiento de segundo y tercero capataces," (1804), ANC-EV, leg. 211, no. 3114, fols. 9v–12.

99. ANC-ED, leg. 439, no. 16, fol. ?.

100. ANC-EG, leg. 125, no. 3, fol. 108v.

101. Ibid., fol. 115.

102. ANC-EO, leg, 6, no. 1, fol. 60v–61.

103. ANC-ED. leg. 336, no. 1, fol. ?.

104. ANC-ED, leg. 439, no. 16, fol. ?.

105. See for example *Diario de la Habana*, 3 Feb. 1812, 3.

106. ANC-ED, leg. 336, no. 1, fol. 38v.

107. "Expediente de cuentas que produce Tomás Betancourt de las cantidades que han entrado en su poder del cavildo Caravali Oquella," (1804), ANC-EO, leg. 3, no. 8, fol. 7v.

108. Ibid., fol. 6v; ANC-EO, leg. 6. no. 1, fol. 8v.

109. ANC-ED, leg. 398, no. 23, fol. 3.

110. ANC-ED, leg. 439, no. 16, fol. ?.

111. ANC-ED, leg. 336, no. 1, fol. 5.

112. ANC-EO, leg. 6, no. 1, fol. 33v.

113. ANC-ED, leg. 398, no. 23, fol. 3.

114. ANC-ED, leg. 439, no. 16, fol. ?.

115. ANC-EO, leg. 6, no. 1, fol. 33.

116. ANC-EO, leg. 6, no. 1, fol. 30v.

117. Howard, *Changing History,* 40–42.

118. Howard identifies the same process whereby "members of these organizations manifested a 'consciousness of kind': an identity that mitigated, to a certain degree, differences of language, ethnicity, and customs, an identity that allowed them to discern the common problems all people of color confronted on a daily basis," *Changing History,* xvii.

8

SLAVE TRADE NOMENCLATURE AND AFRICAN ETHNICITIES IN THE AMERICAS: EVIDENCE FROM EARLY EIGHTEENTH-CENTURY COSTA RICA

Russell Lohse

Historians of the African Diaspora have welcomed the recent publication of a database on the transatlantic slave trade with great excitement.[1] Easily accessible data on more than 27,000 slaving voyages now make it possible to trace the Old World provenances of Africans in the New World with greater specificity than ever before; a far-reaching reassessment of the role of African identities in the Americas has been predicted. On the basis of some general findings of the *Trans-Atlantic Slave Trade* database, a "new orthodoxy" has emerged among certain Africanist historians, which sees slaves in the Americas "forming identifiable communities based on their ethnic or national pasts."[2] In his influential *Africa and Africans in the Making of the Atlantic World,* John K. Thornton has contended that European slavers drew "extremely homogeneous" human cargoes, usually from a single African port, and the slave trade "did little to break up cultural groupings." Once on New World estates, "slaves tended to cluster around members of their own nation," further reinforcing cultural similarities.[3]

This paper draws on sources from Costa Rican archives as well as the new database to raise a methodological challenge to this "new orthodoxy." By tracing the ethnic nomenclature—the *casta* names—attributed to the human cargoes of two Danish slave ships, from the time they embarked on the coast of West Africa through their enslavement in Costa Rica, I will show that much of the evidence that Africanists have used to make "ethnic-based" arguments suffers from an inherent unreliability. First, Spanish slavemasters generally categorized African slaves by their imputed port of embarkation. They sometimes made demonstrable mistakes in guessing the ports at which Africans embarked. Second, even when the names of the ports were correct, they did not necessarily bear any relationship to the ethnic identity of the slaves boarded there. Third, Spanish slavemasters often ethnically classified and reclassified the same African-born individuals several times in their lifetimes, casting strong doubts on the consistency or degree of accuracy with which they recorded African ethnic origins. Fourth and most important, when asked directly about their ethnic origins, slaves often volunteered a different name than that used by their masters. On the basis of the Costa Rican evidence, I will argue that historians of the African Diaspora must examine a larger body of documentary sources than they have to date before convincing arguments can be advanced regarding the importance or unimportance of specific African ethnicities in the New World.

In December 1708, two ships of the Danish West India and Guinea Company left Copenhagen for a voyage to West Africa and St. Thomas, Denmark's colony in the eastern Caribbean.[4] They arrived at the Danish trading station at Christiansborg, near modern Accra, Ghana, in mid-April 1709.[5] West of the Danish fort, the *Fredericus Quartus* loaded 11 slaves at Cape Three Points (Cabo Três Pontas) and 24 at Kormantin, then 357 slaves at Christiansborg before sailing east to fill the rest of its cargo, embarking 54 slaves at unidentified points east of Accra, and 105 at Keta on the upper Slave Coast.[6] The *Christianus Quintus* obtained the whole of its cargo on the Slave Coast in the Bight of Benin, embarking 60 slaves on the upper Slave Coast, including at Popo, and 323 at Ouidah.[7]

The Africans on board the *Fredericus Quartus* embarked not at one port—allegedly the norm—but at least five: Cape Three Points, Kormantin, Christiansborg, Keta, and a minimum of one undetermined point recorded only as "the coast." The *Christianus Quintus* took its captives from at least one port along the upper Slave Coast, then stopped at Popo, and loaded the bulk at Ouidah. True, most of the captives boarded on a stretch of coast between Accra and Ouidah less than 200 miles in length, yet these ports themselves displayed a great deal of ethnic diversity, and exported slaves from a wide catchment area. With few exceptions, only a general idea of the origins of slaves shipped through these ports can be established. The 323 men, women, and children loaded onto the *Fredericus Quartus* at Christiansborg almost certainly included Akan-speaking Kwawu and Ga-

and Adangme-speakers from around Accra, all taken prisoner that year in wars with Akwamu, then the dominant power in the region.[8] The ethnic origins of Africans embarked at the other ports must remain more speculative. The upper Slave Coast, including the ports of Keta and Popo, was an area of exceptional ethnic diversity, including the indigenous Gbe-speaking Hula and Anlo-Ewe; Ga- and Adangme-speaking immigrants originally from the area of Accra, a smaller community of Fante-speaking merchants of Gold Coast origin; and Akan-speaking Akwamu administrators.[9] To the north lived the Ana, the westernmost Yoruba-speaking subgroup, and beyond them, the Borgu or Bariba.[10] The 219 slaves embarked in this region doubtless included a combination of people from these linguistic and cultural groups.

The captives taken on at Ouidah may have been of similarly diverse origins. In 1709, the port of Ouidah was the single largest exporter of slaves in all of Africa, and the *Christianus Quintus* took on another 323 slaves there.[11] According to a French observer around 1715, only 5 percent of the slaves sold at Ouidah originated within that kingdom.[12] Most slaves exported through Ouidah came from the neighboring kingdom of Allada, but Allada itself was in large part a re-exporter of slaves from states further in the interior, such as Dahomey and Oyo.[13]

Thus, the 767 men, women, and children who sailed from Africa on the *Christianus Quintus* and *Fredericus Quartus* included members of a variety of linguistic and cultural groups. Because they steered wrong by a full three degrees latitude, the ships never arrived at St. Thomas. By 18 February 1710, disease, dehydration, and starvation had claimed the lives of 135 Africans.[14] More than 1200 nautical miles off course and desperately short of provisions, the ships finally landed at "Punta Carreto," at modern Cahuita, Costa Rica, on 2 March 1710.[15] The ships' provisions almost completely exhausted, the crews mutinied, breaking open the ships' gold chests, and on 4 March 1710, put ashore the surviving slaves to spare what provisions remained.[16] According to information later supplied by the Danes, 650 Africans escaped into the bush that day.[17] Little is known with certainty of the vast majority. Historical linguist John Holm has endorsed the later view of a British observer, who wrote in 1757 that many African survivors of two shipwrecked "Dutch" slavers had been assimilated by the Miskito Indians.[18] For some 105 of the Africans put ashore, relatively detailed knowledge of their fates in Costa Rica can be reconstructed.

A week after the Danish ships landed at "Punta Carreto," Costa Rican colonists captured a first group of 24 Africans near Moín on the Matina coast, some 50 km to the north. Their Spanish captors described the men and women of this group as belonging to three different *castas,* or "nations": *arará* (26), *mina* (2), and *carabalí* (2).[19] That is, they were believed to come from the Slave Coast, the Gold Coast, and the Bight of Biafra. The Spanish slave-catchers immediately set about searching the nearby cacao haciendas for an African slave who could serve as interpreter, and had little difficulty finding one in Francisco, a slave of *casta arará* who translated with the express permission of his mistress.[20]

Some weeks later, on 23 April, a sentinel at Moín reported that he had seen "many people on the beach marching toward Matina." This second group of Africans had been captured by some 20 Miskito Indians, who later explained that they were guarding the Africans for their British allies, who had gone to Jamaica for a ship. After a brief struggle, the Spaniards disarmed the Miskitos and took possession of a group of 45 Africans.[21] When brought to the colonial capital of Cartago on 11 May 1710, this entire group was described as of *casta mina,* from the Gold Coast.[22] Within the next few days, another contingent of Spanish colonists apprehended a third group of Africans. When Juan Francisco de Ibarra presented a group of 16 African men and women in Cartago on 11 June 1710, they were all described as members of the same *casta,* this time the unidentified *casta nangu.*[23]

On a first reading of these records of the *castas* of these newly arrived Africans, ample evidence would seem to exist for John Thornton's contention of a high degree of ethnic or "national" homogeneity among slaves arriving in the Americas. Despite the fact that the ships transporting these Africans obtained their cargoes from at least five ports, of the 89 Africans inventoried and assessed to that point, only four *castas* were mentioned in the documents: *mina* from the Gold Coast (45), *arará* from the Slave Coast (26), *nangu* (unidentified; 16), and *carabalí* from the Bight of Biafra (2). More than that, all were captured in groups demonstrating a high, if not absolute, degree of *casta* homogeneity: to some extent, the Africans had formed associations that evidently corresponded to their ethnic origins. And finding an African slave already in the colony who was able to communicate with some of the new arrivals posed little difficulty. On this evidence, there might indeed be grounds to suppose that these Africans formed "identifiable communities based on their ethnic or national pasts."[24]

Yet already in these initial documents, the *castas* as recorded raise some troubling issues. The presence of Africans of the *carabalí* "nation"— referring to Calabar in the Bight of Biafra, and usually identified with Igbo-speaking peoples—is difficult to explain, when we know with certainty that neither of the ships obtained slaves east of Ouidah. In fact, these two men were almost immediately reclassified with the name of another *casta:*

clearly, the Spaniards had made a mistake. Sixteen individuals of *casta nangu,* a name not encountered elsewhere in the literature, also provoke questions. It is tempting to identify *nangu* with Ningo, the Adangme-speaking polity east of Christiansborg, which was also written by contemporaries as "Nungo" and "Nungua," and very likely contributed to the cargo of the *Fredericus Quartus.*[25] But the *nangu* individuals came to be included not with other natives of the Gold Coast, but with *castas* of the Slave Coast and its hinterland. *Nangu* probably represents an early variant of the term *nago,* a Yoruba "subgroup" first attested in 1725 and later more broadly applied to Yoruba-speakers.[26] In any case, *nangu* does not appear again in Costa Rican documents with reference to these or other Africans. These 16 men and women were all reassigned to different *castas.*

Ethnic reclassification began almost immediately, and it is difficult if not impossible to infer the criteria used in this process. Bills of sale dated from January 1711 refer to five slaves apprehended on the beaches of Matina the previous year as belonging to a group of "black youths (*muleques*) of *casta mina* and *popo.*"[27] Did the inclusion of a fifth *casta popo,* reflect increased knowledge on the part of their Spanish captors?[28] Yes and no. Some of the Africans embarked on the Danish slavers were undoubtedly taken on at Popo, and the Spanish slavemasters had evidently learned that much. But the new name *popo,* again referring only to an imputed port of embarkation, was no more culturally or linguistically precise than other *casta* names. As might be expected from the complex ethnic mix of the upper Slave Coast, people described as of *casta popo* in Costa Rica included individuals from various cultural and linguistic backgrounds. How many of these languages were mutually intelligible, and how many enslaved individuals were bilingual or multilingual is an open question.[29]

Clearly, some were not. More than nine years after arriving in Costa Rica, when questioned by colonial officials, an African-born man known as Miguel Largo, reputedly of *casta popo,* could speak little Spanish. According to all who commented on him, Miguel was very "closed" (evidently meaning here "closed off" socially as well as "close-mouthed": *bozal y muy cerrado*).[30] Had Miguel been coached, or intimidated into silence by his master, as the governor alleged in other cases?[31] Other Africans more willing to talk with authorities all agreed that even "being of *casta popo* those of his same *casta* do not understand him."[32] It is quite possible that Miguel Largo was misidentified as *popo*; other documents described him as *mina.*[33] Yet neither could any of the more numerous *minas* (or *ararás*) in Cartago communicate effectively with him; in fact, Miguel Largo may have been of neither *mina* nor *popo* origin.

In several cases, the name *casta popo* was applied to individuals who claimed other ethnic origins. Described as *popo* when she was sold in 1716, Antonia identified her *casta* as *barbá* when questioned in 1719.[34] *Bariba* was the Yoruba-language name given by the Oyo to their neighbors in the kingdom of Borgu, including a western group in northern Benin and Togo.[35] While the name first appears in American documents as *barba* in 1627, further documentation of enslaved Borgu in the Diaspora has proved elusive for the period before 1750.[36] Antonia's presence in Costa Rica provides additional direct evidence of the early involvement of the Borgu in the Atlantic slave trade. Some of the Borgu slaves captured or purchased by Dahomey or Oyo were no doubt exported through Popo, plausibly explaining how Antonia came to be identified with the *popo* in Costa Rica, and illustrating the tendency of the Spaniards to identify members of small or unfamiliar *castas* with larger, more general categories associated with African slaving ports.[37]

On the other hand, another enslaved woman, described by her master and officials as a member of a smaller, more specific ethnic group, identified herself with the broader *casta popo*. Spanish officials and María's master generally identified her as of *casta aná,* a name that surely derived from the Ana, the westernmost "subgroup" of Yoruba-speakers in northern Togo and Benin.[38] But despite María's official identification with the *aná,* most blacks, whites, and *mulatos* in Cartago knew her as "María Popo," and when asked directly in 1719, María claimed the *casta popo* as her own.[39] Furthermore, in a clear example of the transmission of an African ethnic identity across generations, María's daughter Juana, although born in Costa Rica, also identified herself as of *casta popo.*[40] While it is uncertain how María became associated with *casta aná,* it is clear that in Cartago, most people identified her, and she identified herself, with the larger group of Africans called *popo*—and likely passed that identity on to her creole daughter.[41]

Like the variable usage of *casta popo,* the appearance of *casta aná* in the documents provides further clear evidence of the inconsistent attribution of ethnic names to slaves in the Americas. More specifically, slavemasters often substituted the name of a port of embarkation or middleman slave-trading state for the ethnic origins of individuals. At least seven individuals initially identified as *arará* or *mina* were soon reclassified as *aná,* a name which surely derived from the Ana.[42] Like several of their shipmates, María and Petrona were initially labelled as *arará* by their Spanish captors, but within a few months of their capture in Matina, were reclassified as of *casta aná.*[43] Years later, the two enslaved women offered an indispensable clue to the reassignment of African ethnic names in America. Asked their *castas* by

Spanish officials, both María and Petrona replied that their *casta* was called "*saná* in their language and in that of the Spaniards *lucumí.*"[44] María and Petrona's reply suggests that in Africa, they had not considered themselves part of any larger Yoruba (or *lucumí*) ethnicity, but had that identity applied to them by their captors in Diaspora.[45]

In time, for many enslaved Africans, the labels imposed by their masters mattered most. In a bill of sale drawn up on 25 May 1716, Antonio was described as belonging to the unidentified *casta dalá.*[46] Just two days later, a second bill of sale referred to Antonio's *casta* only as *negro,* but the name *dalá* remained part of his ascribed identity: the new document listed his name as Antonio Castadala.[47] In 1722, Antonio gave his own *casta* as *mina,* suggesting that by then, he was identified with the larger group.[48] But at least in later years, he was more commonly called after his first master, Antonio de la Riva. It was as Antonio de la Riva, *negro,* that he negotiated a contract with his master and mistress in 1737, and won his freedom in 1745.[49]

The findings of this paper support the view that the ethnic designations attributed by colonial masters to their African slaves cannot be taken at face value. At best, they may be accepted as evidence of broadly understood "culture areas" or "cultural zones" in West Africa.[50] Neither can knowledge of specific ports of embarkation, despite the potentially extraordinary value of that information, do more than suggest the provenances of enslaved Africans, even when combined with chronologically and geographically specific information on the supply of slaves within Africa. Colonial officials and masters showed a marked tendency to record slaves from small groups as belonging to larger *castas* with names more familiar to them. The methodological key to appreciating the significance of African-derived ethnicities for enslaved people—whether these corresponded to identities found in precolonial Africa, or ascribed only in the Americas—can be found nowhere else but in the words of the slaves themselves. Evidence from a small slaveholding colony such as Costa Rica can only contribute to a larger debate, but it can suggest the rewards to be gained by venturing beyond ships' manifests, bills of sale, or their equivalents to other documents such as those generated in criminal proceedings, where slaves identified themselves.

Notes

1. David Eltis, David Richardson, Stephen D. Behrendt, and Herbert S. Klein, *The Trans-Atlantic Slave Trade: A Database on CD-ROM* (Cambridge: Cambridge University Press, 1999; hereafter cited as *TSTD*).

2. Philip D. Morgan, "The Cultural Implications of the Atlantic Slave Trade: African Regional Origins, American Destinations and New World Developments," *Slavery and Abolition* 18, 1 (April 1997): 124.

3. John K. Thornton, *Africa and the Africans in the Making of the Atlantic World, 1400–1680,* 2nd ed. (Cambridge: Cambridge University Press, 1992), 192–97, quoting 192, 195, 197.

4. Georg Nørregård, "Forliset ved Nicaragua 1710," *Årbog 1948* (Helsingør, Denmark: Handels- og Søfartsmuseet på Kronborg), 70; John A. Holm, "The Creole English of Nicaragua's Miskitu Coast: Its Sociolinguistic History and a Comparative Study of Its Lexicon and Syntax" (Ph.D. thesis, University of London, 1978), 183. I have relied heavily on Holm's English summary of Nørregård's article in "Creole English," 182–86.

5. Nørregård, "Forliset ved Nicaragua," 71.

6. Ibid., 71, 72–73; Erich Lygaard to the Directors, Christiansborg, 19 August 1709, in *Danish Documents concerning the History of Ghana,* ed. and trans. Ole Justesen (forthcoming), Document V.20. I am especially grateful to Professor Justesen for allowing me to cite from his forthcoming volume.

7. Justesen, ed., *Danish Documents,* Documents V.20, V.23, V.25.

8. J. K. Fynn, *Asante and Its Neighbors, 1700–1807* (Evanston, Ill.: Northwestern University Press, 1971); Nørregård, *Danish Settlements in West Africa, 1658–1850,* trans. Sigurd Mammen (Boston: Boston University Press, 1966), 67–68; Commander Erich Lygaard to the Directors of the Danish West India and Guinea Company, Christiansborg, 3 May 1709, in *Danish Documents,* ed. Justesen, Document V.18; C. C. Reindorf, *History of the Gold Coast and Asante,* 2nd ed. (Accra: Ghana Universities Press, 1966), 68–69.

9. Robin Law, "Between the Sea and the Lagoons: The Interaction of Maritime and Inland Navigation on the Pre-Colonial Slave Coast," *Cahiers d'Études Africaines* 29, 2 (no. 114) (1989): 219, 229, 232; Robin Law, *The Slave Coast of West Africa, 1550–1759* (Oxford: Clarendon Press, 1991), 29, 150, 244, 249, 251; S. Wilson, "Aperçu historique sur les peuples et cultures dans le golfe du Bénin: Le cas des 'mina' d'Anécho," in *Peuples du golfe du Bénin: Aja-éwé (colloque de Cotonou),* ed. François de Medeiros (Paris: Karthala, 1984), 144–45; Kwame Yeboa Daaku, *Trade and Politics on the Gold Coast, 1600–1720: A Study of African Reaction to the European Trade* (Oxford: Clarendon Press, 1970), 154; Sandra E. Greene, "Cultural Zones in the Era of the Slave Trade: Exploring the Yoruba Connection with Anlo-Ewe," in *Identity in the Shadow of Slavery,* ed. Paul E. Lovejoy (London: Continuum, 2000), 92; Sandra A. Greene, *Gender, Ethnicity and Social Change on the Upper Slave Coast* (Portsmouth, N.H.: Heinemann, 1996), 20, 32.

10. Robert Cornevin, *Histoire du Togo* (Paris: Éditions Berger-Levrault, 1962), 57–59; William Bascom, *The Yoruba of Southwestern Nigeria* (New York: Holt, Rinehart, and Winston, 1969), 5; Biodun Adediran, "Yoruba Ethnic Groups or a Yoruba Ethnic Group? A Review of the Problem of Ethnic Identification," *África* (Centro do Estudos Africanos, Universidade de São Paulo) 7 (1984): 58.

11. Eltis et al., *TSTD.*

12. Law, *Slave Coast,* 184.

13. Ibid., 185, 186; Robin Law, *The Kingdom of Allada* (Leiden, Netherlands: Research School CNWS, School of Asian, African, and Amerindian Studies, 1997), 90, 101, 105.

14. Nørregård, "Forliset ved Nicaragua," 78–79.

15. Ibid., 81. Although the shipwrecked Danish sailors believed they had landed in Nicaragua—an error repeated by their modern chronicler, Georg Nørregård, in the name of

his article—two eighteenth-century maps in the British Museum show the site of "Pt. Carrett" and "Point Carata" to be at the site of modern Punta Cahuita, Limón Province, Costa Rica, a location confirmed by internal evidence in the Costa Rican documents. Holm, "Creole English," 185.

16. Nørregård, "Forliset ved Nicaragua," 79–83; Holm, "Creole English," 185–86.

17. Nørregård, "Forliset ved Nicaragua," 83–84.

18. Robert Hodgson, *Some Account of the Mosquito Territory: Contained in a Memoir, Written in 1757... Published from the Original Manuscript of the late Colonel Robert Hodgson, Formerly... Superintendant... of the Mosquito Shore...*, 2nd ed. (Edinburgh: W. Blackwood, 1822), quoted in Holm, "Creole English," 186.

19. Inventario de negros, Cartago, 14 April 1710, Archivo Nacional de Costa Rica (hereafter, ANCR), Sección Colonial Cartago (hereafter, C.) 187, fols. 12–13v; Avalúo de negros, Cartago, 23 April 1710, ANCR, C. 187, fols. 47–49; Auto de la entrega de 10 negros por Gaspar de Acosta Arévalo, Cartago, 2 May 1710, ANCR, C. 187, fols. 52–52v; Inventario de los negros y su depósito en Juan López de la Rea y Soto, Cartago, 2 May 1710, ANCR, C. 187, fols. 53–54v; Auto de noticia de 24 negros, Cartago, 22 March 1710, ANCR, C. 187, fol. 9; Declaración de Gaspar de Acosta Arévalo, Cartago, 16 April 1710, ANCR, C. 187, fols. 26–30; Declaración de Diego Oviedo, Cartago, 16 April 1710, ANCR, C. 187, fols. 30v–33v.

20. Nombramiento de Francisco de casta arará, esclavo del Cap. Francisco de la Madriz Linares, como intérprete, Cartago, 14 April 1710, ANCR, C. 187, fol. 17v.

21. Declaración del Cap. Antonio de Soto y Barahona, Cartago, 1 May 1710, ANCR, C. 187, fols. 75v–77v.

22. Inventario de negros, Cartago, 11 May 1710, ANCR, C. 187, fols. 97–100v.

23. Inventario de 16 negros y negras, Cartago, 11 June 1710, ANCR, C. 187, fols. 147–149.

24. Morgan, "Cultural Implications," 124.

25. Nørregård, *Danish Settlements,* 67; Erick Tilleman, *A Short and Simple Account of the Country Guinea and Its Nature (1697),* trans. and ed. Selena Axelrod Winsnes (Madison: African Studies Program, University of Wisconsin-Madison, 1994), 98.

26. Biodun Adediran, "Yoruba Ethnic Groups," 60; Robin Law, "Ethnicity and the Slave Trade: 'Lucumi' and 'Nago' as Ethnonyms in West Africa," *History in Africa* 24 (1997): 208, 212; Law, *Slave Coast,* 189–90.

27. Cesión de 5 negros y negras, Cartago, 8 January 1711, ANCR, Mortuales Coloniales de Cartago 774, fols. 82–84.

28. Cf. Michael A. Gomez on the alleged sensitivity of Latin American masters to the African ethnicities of their slaves as reflected in their increasing usage of *casta* nomenclature: "Clearly, the Spanish and Portuguese were learning rapidly. . . ." Gomez, "African Identity and Slavery in the Americas," *Radical History Review* 75 (1999): 116.

29. John K. Thornton argues for three "cultural zones" in West and West Central Africa, contending that Yoruba functioned as a lingua franca in the "Lower Guinea" region, in *Africa and Africans,* 2nd ed., 186, 188, 190. Sandra E. Greene refutes this assertion for the Upper Slave Coast in "Cultural Zones," 97, passim. The question of the mutual intelligibility of Gold Coast and Slave Coast languages is also touched upon in Daaku, *Trade and Politics,* 1–4; Law, *Slave Coast,* chapter 1; Stephanie Ellen Smallwood, "Salt-Water Slaves: African Enslavement, Migration, and Settlement in the Anglo-Atlantic World, 1660–1700" (Ph.D. diss., Duke University, 1999), 69, 125–26.

30. Declaración de Miguel Largo, Cartago, 4 September 1719, ANCR, C. 240, fol. 3; Auto para que don José Castellano solicite algún negro o negra que le entienda la lengua de Miguel Largo, Cartago, 3 January 1720, ANCR, C. 240, fol. 5v.

31. Declaración de la negra Lorenza y orden del gobernador que se ponga presa, Cartago, 6 August 1720, ANCR, C. 241, fol. 27.

32. Auto para que don José Castellano solicite algún negro o negra que le entienda la lengua de Miguel Largo, Cartago, 3 January 1720, ANCR, C. 240, fol. 5v.

33. Declaración de Miguel Largo, Cartago, 4 September 1719, ANCR, C. 240, fol. 3; Declaración del Gobernador don Lorenzo Antonio de la Granda y Balvín, Cartago, 23 June 1710, ANCR, C. 240, fol. 12.

34. Venta de esclava, Cartago, 3 September 1716, ANCR, Protocolos Coloniales de Cartago (hereafter, P.C.) 881, fols. 62–64v; Declaración de Antonia, negra esclava, Cartago, 12 September 1719, ANCR, C. 236, fol. 1v; Declaración de Antonia, negra esclava, Cartago, 22 June 1720, ANCR, C. 236, fol. 17.

35. See Robert Cornevin, *Histoire du Dahomey* (Paris: Éditions Berger-Levrault, 1962), chapter 5; Cornevin, *Histoire du Togo*, 59, 87.

36. Alonso de Sandoval, *Naturaleza, policia sagrada i profana, costumbres i ritos, disciplina i catechismo evangelico de todos Etiopes* (Seville: Francisco de Lira, 1627; reprinted as *De instauranda Aethiopium salute: El mundo de la esclavitud en América,* Bogotá: Empresa Nacional de Publicaciones, 1956), 94, 95–96. Robin Law and Paul E. Lovejoy have noted an absence of "Bariba" slaves in American documents between the sixteenth and mid-eighteenth centuries. Law and Lovejoy, "Borgu in the Atlantic Slave Trade," *African Economic History* 27 (1999): 74, 75.

37. For the early export of Borgu slaves by Oyo and Dahomey, see Robin Law, *The Oyo Empire, c. 1600–c. 1836: A West African Imperialism in the Era of the Atlantic Slave Trade* (Oxford: Clarendon Press, 1977), 226; Paul E. Lovejoy, *Caravans of Kola: The Hausa Kola Trade 1700–1900* (Zaria, Nigeria: Ahmadu Bello University Press Ltd., 1980), 34; Law and Lovejoy, "Borgu and the Atlantic Slave Trade," 74. Sandoval identified slaves of *casta barba* with the *lucumí* as early as 1627 (see previous note), and Law and Lovejoy have speculated that early Bariba slaves may have entered the Americas in small numbers, but been subsumed by record-keepers into the more numerous *lucumí.* Sandoval, *De instauranda Aethiopium,* 95; Law and Lovejoy, "Borgu in the Atlantic Slave Trade," 75.

38. Careo en el cual las negras María y Petrona identifica a María de casta aná como una de sus carabelas, Cartago, 5 October 1720, ANCR, C. 267, fol. 58v; ANCR, G. 185, fol. 45; ANCR, G. 188, fol. 34v; Cornevin, *Histoire du Togo,* 57–58; John Igue and Olabiyi Yai, "The Yoruba-Speaking Peoples of Dahomey and Togo," trans. Abiola Irele, *Yoruba* 1, 1 (1972), 4; Bascom, *Yoruba of Southwestern Nigeria,* 5; Adediran, "Yoruba Ethnic Groups," 58.

39. Declaración del Cap. Francisco de Bonilla, Cartago, 25 May 1720, ANCR, C. 232, fol. 19v; Declaración del Cap. Esteban de Zúñiga, Cartago, 25 May 1720, ANCR, C. 232, fol. 20; Declaración de Sebastián de Quirós, Cartago, 27 May 1720, ANCR, C. 232, fol. 20v; Careo en el cual las negras María y Petrona identifican a María Popo como una de sus carabelas, Cartago, 5 October 1720, ANCR, C. 267, fol. 59; don Nicolás de Ocampo Golfín afianza a la negra María Popo, Cartago, 25 February 1722, ANCR, C. 288, fol. 71; Declaración de María negra de casta popó, Valle de Barba, 12 November 1719, ANCR, G. 188, fol. 7v.

40. Declaración de Juana, negra de casta popo, Cartago, 9 September 1719, ANCR, C. 232, fol. 2. It has not been possible to identify Juana's father, who may have also have been identified as *popo.*

41. María's identification with the *aná* may have resulted from a deliberate deception. In a vain attempt to convince royal officials of his legal right to ownership of María, her master, Francisco de Ocampo Golfín, presented a document demonstrating that he had been ceded the slave María of *casta aná,* 20 years old in 1710. In fact, this document referred to another slave, as "María Popo" was 38 to 40 years old in 1719. Notificación al Sarg. Mr. Francisco de Ocampo Golfín que presente los instrumentos de su negra María Popó, y su respuesta, Valle de Barba, 23 May 1720, ANCR, G. 188. fol. 14v; Cesión del Gobernador don Lorenzo Antonio de Granda y Balvín al Sarg. Mr. don Francisco de Ocampo Golfín de María negra bozal de casta ana de 20 años, Cartago, 4 July 1710, ANCR, G. 188, fols. 15–15v; Declaración de María negra de casta popó que es de edad de 38 a 40 años, Valle de Barba, 12 November 1719, G. 188, fol. 7v.

42. Cornevin, *Histoire du Togo,* 57–58; Igue and Yai, "Yoruba-Speaking Peoples," 4; Bascom, *Yoruba of Southwestern Nigeria,* 5; Adediran, "Yoruba Ethnic Groups," 58.

43. Cesión de dos negras, Cartago, 14 July 1710, ANCR, G. 185, fols. 25–25v.

44. Declaración de Petrona, San Francisco de Tenorio, 17 September 1719, ANCR, G. 185, fol. 8; Declaración de María, San Francisco de Tenorio, 17 September 1719, ANCR, G. 185, fol. 6v. "*Saná*" appears to be a variant of *aná,* as the enslaved girls were described in a 1710 bill of sale (see previous note).

45. Cf. the dispute between Biodun Adediran and Robin Law in "Yoruba Ethnic Groups" and "Ethnicity and the Slave Trade."

46. Venta de esclavo, Cartago, 25 May 1716, ANCR, G. 187, fols. 30v–33; Auto sobre el esclavo Antonio Mina, Cartago, 30 July 1720, ANCR, G. 187, fol. 45.

47. Venta de esclavo, Cartago, 27 May 1716, ANCR, P.C. 878, fols. 77v–79v.

48. Declaración del esclavo Antonio de casta mina, Cartago, 7 November 1722, ANCR, G. 187, fol. 11.

49. Carta de libertad a favor de Antonio de la Riva, Cartago, 15 June 1745, ANCR, P.C. 933, fols. 54v–57.

50. Melville J. Herskovits, *The Myth of the Negro Past* (New York: Harper, 1941); Thornton, *Africa and Africans,* 2d ed., 186, 188.

9

AFRICA IN LOUISIANA: IN SEARCH OF "BAMBARA" AND CREOLE IDENTITIES IN LITERARY AND STATISTICAL SOURCES

Kevin Roberts

Scholarship on slave culture and ethnicities in the United States generally falls into one of two temporal categories: pre- and post-American Revolution. Those studies that emphasize the African-ness of the American slave population usually focus on the seventeenth and eighteenth centuries, before natural increase began to alter the cultural traditions of the enslaved population. Other studies, especially those that emphasize the creolization of enslaved Blacks, are usually centered in the nineteenth century, or at least after the American Revolution. In examining eighteenth- and nineteenth-century Louisiana during this transformative period of slave culture in America, one finds that the experience of slaves in Louisiana did mirror that of other bondspeople in the United States, though important geographic and ethnic diversity within the linear transformation from an "Africanized" to "creolized" slave population warrants close attention. Because of this diversity, the Louisiana example should remind scholars that even within the consensus explanation of how the culture of enslaved blacks in the United States evolved, significant complications particular to time and place exist. In short, I contend that scholars of enslavement must change our thinking and terminology: we must begin to speak of slave *cultures,* for that pluralized distinction applies not only to the vast variations of Afro-Creole cultures in the New World but even to a geopolitical entity as small as Louisiana.[1]

To outline how I see this approach working best, I have combined two types of diverse sources: slave narratives and slave-trade data. Marshaling the more traditional literary records used by historians of slave culture—the slave narratives—with the data sets used by scholars interested in the slave trade and African ethnicities, forms the documentary foundation of my study. Before the advent of David Eltis's *Trans-Atlantic Slave Trade* database and Gwendolyn Midlo Hall's *Afro-Louisiana History* database, scholars lacked evidence to examine how multiple African origins may have created multiple slave cultures in a single location. Pinpointing the origins and destinations of slaves that were imported by Louisiana slaveowners will allow historians to assess with greater precision how the lives, culture, and identities of Louisiana's enslaved population varied within the colony and state. Moreover, these new data sets, coupled with the well-used records of narratives, plantation documents, government sources, and travelers' accounts create an opportunity to assess how and why specific African ethnicities affected the slave cultures in Louisiana at specific times. Thus, before turning to the social and cultural aspects of Louisiana slaves, it is essential to first examine the ethnic composition of Louisiana's slave population.[2]

Slave imports to Louisiana began in 1719, when a shipment of 450 slaves from the Bight of Benin arrived in the fledgling colony. By 1731, Louisiana had imported 5,790 Africans. Unlike the origin of the first shipment of Africans, subsequent shipments from the French Company of the Indies originated in Senegambia. Of the Africans imported to Louisiana from 1719 to 1731, over half, 3,040, came from Senegambian slave-trading ports. The remainder consisted of 1,748 people, or one-third of the period's total, from the Bight of Benin, and 294, or less than 1 percent, from West Central Africa. During the remainder of the eighteenth century, slave shipments to Louisiana slowed as the Company of the West Indies, still drawing its supply of humans from Senegambia, found it more profitable to sell its slaves to the French Caribbean islands of Saint-Domingue, Martinique, and Guadeloupe. Thus, by 1743, when another shipment of slaves from Senegambia arrived in Louisiana, it was the first such voyage in twelve years.[3]

David Eltis's figures from 27,000 slave voyages illustrate the numerical superiority of slaves from Senegambia in Louisiana's enslaved population. Over the entire period of the slave trade to Louisiana, according to the voyages catalogued by Eltis and Richardson, just over 8,000 Africans were imported to the French colony directly from Africa. Of those, nearly 57 percent embarked from Senegambia, with the remainder originating from the Bight of Benin, West-Central Africa, and unspecified regions of Africa.[4] The Eltis figures create important questions regarding the ethnic composition of the Louisiana slave population. In particular, with such a large majority of Louisiana slaves originating from Senegambia, what were their ethnicities? Did the ethnic composition of slaves imported to Louisiana change over time? How did these slaves and the possible change in ethnic composition over time affect the development of slave cultures in Louisiana?

These issues, of course, are not new to historians of slavery. Gwendolyn Midlo Hall, in *Africans in Colonial Louisiana,* emphasizes that most, if not all, slave exports from Senegambia were Bambara, an ethnic group of the interior that was an important component of the Mande linguistic group. Arguing that "there is little doubt that the Bambara brought to Louisiana were truly ethnic Bambara," Hall focused her study on Bambara culture, portraying it as the most influential African group on Louisiana's Afro-Creole culture.[5]

That emphasis on the Bambara, however, has spurred debate between Hall and others about the reality of the Senegambians being "truly ethnic Bambara." That the region had sunk into incessant warfare, coupled with the typical murky and inexact records of the era, makes sorting out the dispute difficult. On one hand, historian Peter Caron rejects Hall's claim about the ethnic singularity of the Senegambian exports by raising two compelling problems with the assertion. First, Caron highlights the different meanings that the term "Bambara" had for the Africans themselves and the registrars in the colony. Second, he emphasizes that the Kingdom of Ségu, of which the Bambara were the dominant ethnic group, consolidated its power in 1721, thereby minimizing the supply of Bambara at the exact time Louisiana was receiving human cargo from the region.[6]

Historian Thomas Ingersoll adds a wrinkle to Caron's complication of the Hall argument when he focuses on her methodology in studying the Senegambians once they were in Louisiana. Ingersoll explains,

> While Hall does not limit her interest to the remote plantation region of Pointe Coupée, she focuses on it, a place that was far from the main concentration of slaves and masters in the New Orleans district. . . . Moreover, while the Bambaras may have been a distinctive and particularly rebellious group in the earliest period, they were merely one of many tiny minorities by the end of the colonial era, and they do not figure prominently in New Orleans records.[7]

As is often the case in such debates, each historian may be correct. When Peter Caron explains that "for Louisiana's Africans, 'Bambara' may not have referred to an ethnicity *per se* but instead to a group identification of another sort," he provides the conceptual framework within which the other historians' arguments fit. "Bambara" in its African usage referred to three categories of slaves: those found east of the Senegambia River, where the Kingdom of Ségu was and where ethnic Bambara lived; slave soldiers, no doubt the origin of the reputation slaves identified as Bambara in Louisiana had as being fierce and indignant; and non-Muslims. The term "Bambara," while fraught with complications as an ethnic identifier in Africa and Louisiana, actually became an important term in Louisiana, as it referred not only to those slaves who were, indeed, ethnic Bambara, but those who were identified as such and kept the designation. Even if Caron is correct that many non-Bambara slaves were simply identified as Bambara by their African captors, the reason for that designation contributed to the term "Bambara" in Louisiana being as ascendant an identity among all slaves, regardless of their ethnicity, as the ethnic group itself was in Africa during the 1720s and 1730s. The Islamic captors, barred from enslaving other Muslims, sold into enslavement either Hall's "truly ethnic Bambara" or peoples of nearby ethnic groups who, like the Bambara, refused to submit to the frequent jihads in the region. This practice by Islamic slave captors, seen by historians of Africa as creating so much difficulty with group identification, actually demonstrates a powerful cultural hegemony of the Bambara in Louisiana. Through their dual reputation as fierce warriors and holdouts against Islam, the Bambara who were enslaved created an identity—ironically, through the help of their African captors and French enslavers—that became strategically attractive even for slaves who had been misidentified. Moreover, with the common bond of being enslaved and of being non-Muslims, the Bambara and other Mande-speaking peoples in Louisiana had much more in common than not.[8]

The influence of the Bambara in Louisiana underwent two changes: one temporal and one geographic. Evidence from Hall's *Afro-Louisiana History* database shows the importance of the Bambara in Louisiana. By the first decade of the 1800s, however, the composition of the slave population in New Orleans had changed markedly. The influx of nearly 5,000 slaves from Saint-Domingue in 1803 and 1809 further diversified New Orleans' slave population, minimizing but not eradicating the influence of Bambara culture in the city and surrounding parishes. Thus, through imports that affected New Orleans more significantly, the slave population in western Louisiana remained more like its eighteenth-century predecessor than its New Orleans counterpart.[9]

The literary evidence bears out this distinction between regions and illustrates how the nature of Louisiana's Afro-Creole culture in the early nineteenth century remained similar to the snapshot historians have of it in the twentieth-century slave narratives. In the over one hundred interviews conducted of Louisiana ex-slaves during the 1930s there is a stark difference between the religious beliefs of slaves in the urban area and those in the rest of the state, a difference whose origins lie in the ethnic composition of the slave population in each region. In particular, the newly arrived Haitian slaves, most of whom were Fon, Ewe, and Yoruba, created an important core of voodoo practitioners in the city. Not surprisingly, therefore, New Orleans-area slaves all possessed knowledge of voodoo and the famous "voodoo queen" Marie Laveau, while two groups of slaves—those living outside the New Orleans area and those who were devoted to evangelical religions, especially the Baptist Church—may have heard of Laveau but, without exception, refused to believe in voodoo.[10]

N. H. Hobley, who had been enslaved on a plantation just south of New Orleans, not only knew of voodoo and Marie Laveau but claimed personal acquaintance with one of Laveau's associates. In spite of this knowledge, Hobley claimed a distance between the voodoo practices and his own beliefs. "I always attended the Congo Square functions," remembered Hobley. "I was too young to take any active part, but I learned everything. I do not practice voodooism—I never did—but no one knew more about it than I do." Harrison Camille, who had been enslaved in the Barataria region of Jefferson Parish, referred to these Congo Square functions as the "Hoe-Doe Creole Dance," and associated the dance directly with Laveau and her followers, describing them as "beating on barrels with sticks, yelling, and singing and dancing."[11]

The cultural diversity of the New Orleans slave population, illustrated by the intersection of West-Central African secular dance and the Fon-Ewe-Yoruba tradition of voodoo is apparent in Hobley's interview. The ex-slave remarked that New Orleans blacks danced the *bamboula,* a prominent Congolese dance form, in the square while practicing voodoo. "Divine healers," as Hobley called them, would dance with a sick person on their backs, and upon completion of the ritual, the person would be healed. As a microcosm of New Orleans Afro-Creole culture, the Congo Square rituals illustrated how multiple African cultural traditions had coalesced into a cultural form unique to New Orleans.[12]

Hobley's recollections also illustrate the importance of religious syncretism to the voodoo-practicing slaves and freedpeople of New Orleans. He explained that the Bible, in particular "the sixth and seventh books of Moses," were central to voodoo practices. Hobley's interviewer scoffed at the ex-slave's concoction of a new biblical book, but the significance of

Hobley's comment should not be missed by modern scholars. Although Moses is not a book of the Bible, Hobley could easily have been referring to the Book of Exodus, in which Moses's plight is the central story. Voodoo "divine healers" could have found much fodder for their practices in the sixth and seventh books of Exodus: not only does God turn Aaron's staff into a snake, but the first two plagues—water being turned into blood, a feat accomplished not only by God but by "Egyptian magicians," and the swarming of frogs, perhaps the single most common creature in voodoo potions—inundate Earth. Thus, whether Hobley was attempting to justify voodoo with the Bible, as the interviewer implied, or whether voodoo practitioners did really find inspiration in the extraordinary events of Exodus, Hobley, probably more involved in voodoo than he was willing to admit to his interviewer, demonstrates the importance of a variety of religious practices and beliefs to the unique New Orleans system of voodoo.[13]

One did not have to live far outside New Orleans to be outside the proximity of voodoo. Albert Patterson of Lasco Plantation in Plaquemines Parish knew of Marie Laveau, and knew of voodoo, but did not believe in its powers. Likewise, Gracie Stafford, who had been enslaved at Myrtle Grove Plantation in St. James Parish, offered an explanation that indicated the prevalence of status divisions within Louisiana's slave population according to one's practicing of voodoo. Stafford argued, "I was raised right and never did associate with common niggers like what they call the 'hoodoo' kind. In fact, I never heard of such things until I came to the city, and then I didn't until my husband got poisoned."[14]

Farther outside New Orleans, however, even if an ex-slave had heard of Marie Laveau, none of them believed in voodoo. While possible criticisms may be the verity of the slave in the face of an unknown and most often white interviewer, there is a clear distinction between the depth of knowledge of Laveau and voodoo by ex-slaves from the New Orleans area and those who were enslaved in other parts of the state. Interviewer Robert McKinney explained of Baton Rouge ex-slave Catherine Cornelius, "She has apparently led a quiet and sane life, and strange to say, not in the least bit superstitious, having no belief in voodoo, not even being familiar with the name of Marie Laveau."[15]

Further supporting the notion of the absence of voodoo practices among non-New Orleans slaves was that the practice of voodoo, at least in the Congo Square, was a public event for blacks and whites alike. Ex-slave Martin Dragney recollected, "I used to go out fishing in Lake Pontchartrain, opposite Spanish Fort, and I would see these voodoo people dance for the white people. They paid them money to dance the 'konk-konk' dance.

They were only half-dressed—they wore the breechcloth—and hollered and jumped about like they were crazy. And they had tambourines and drums and jawbones of jackasses."[16]

Slaves in north-central Louisiana rejected the Africanized rituals of voodoo and other similar practices. Enslaved on the Lester Plantation near Bunkie, Prince Haas, according to his interviewer, "does not believe in witchcraft or goodluck charms." While Haas may have been more typical of slaves in northern Louisiana, his counterparts to the south, where Catholicism predominated, retained religious practices akin to those of the Bambara. Verice Brown of St. James Parish appears to have held on to charm and amulet worship, a prominent feature of Bambara religion. In 1940 Brown told Louisiana Writers' Project interviewer Flossie McElwee: "I have got a good-luck bone I carry with me all [the] time. It is out of a black cat. You know how you get it? Well, just go to the forks of the road and build your fire. Put the pot on and put the black cat in there and boil him good. When all the meat come[s] off the bones, the lucky bone will float. Then take that with you for your luck. It will charm off evil too." Melinda, an ex-slave from the Baton Rouge area, told her interviewer that during enslavement she once used *gris-gris,* another Bambara tradition, on her mistress to prevent her from marrying a man from the North. Melinda's fear of the man was steeped in apparent slave beliefs' of the meanness of northerners and continental French, but that fear gave way to the success of her *gris-gris,* as her mistress instead married a Creole man from New Orleans.[17]

While some slaves integrated amulet worship into their masters' Catholicism, others rejected both practices for evangelical faiths. Elizabeth Hite remembered how fellow slaves on the Trinity Plantation, in spite of being christened Catholic by their French owner and receiving Catholic teachings from a French clergymen brought to Louisiana by their master, held Baptist meetings with a black preacher named Mingo. Attractive to Hite and her pseudo-Catholic, enslaved cohorts was the display of faith offered by their new religion. Hite remarked, "We didn't like to go to anybody brought from France because you could not do like you wanted to do. You could not shout and pray like you wanted to. That's what I call religion, prayin' and be[ing] free to shout. God says that you must shout if you want to be saved; that's in the Bible."[18]

One of Hite's fellow slaves was equally frustrated with Catholicism but expressed his anger more overtly. One afternoon Old Jim faked his death. As a growing group of would-be mourners gathered around Jim's would-be corpse, he rose from the ground, rushed into the house of his master, Pierre Landreaux, and claimed that he had died and gone to heaven. But once there, Jim explained to Landreaux, St. Peter ordered him back to life so that he could relay a message that Landreaux should free all of his slaves. Not surprisingly, Landreaux reacted not in understanding of St. Peter's message, but in serious threats to give Jim a real experience with the Pearly Gates.[19]

In addition to the prominence of amulet worship and *gris-gris* among slaves in western Louisiana, many in that area propagated animal tales, a significant feature of Bambara folklore. The French legend of the *loup-garou*, or werewolf, had been so etched in the minds of slave children that even during the 1930s interviews their fear of the animal was still present. Called a "gros lou-lou" by Francis Doby, an ex-slave in Opelousas, the *loup-garou* among the slave population appeared to have been an effective lesson in the constricted world of slaves' social lives: Doby remembered vividly the fear of the part-werewolf, part-man entering the quarters to eat the children who had misbehaved.[20]

Some African folklore was of course altered by slaves' surroundings in southern Louisiana. Folktales of the many cultures of the Mande linguistic group, especially those of the Bambara and Wolof, were remembered by many of the slaves interviewed by the Louisiana Writers' Project, and were recalled by late nineteenth-century Louisiana folklorist Alcee Fortier. The frequent tales of the rabbit—*Compaire Lapin* in Louisiana—were altered in the Acadiana region to include coons and crawfish.[21]

The folklore of *Compaire Lapin* and *Compaire Bouki,* the hyena, is perhaps the single most popular tale recounted by ex-slaves, as well as a central tale in the oral traditions of both the Bambara and Wolof, another Senegambian group important to Louisiana's slave population, but one whose members in Africa practiced Islam in greater numbers than the long holdouts to conversion within the Bambara group. The similarity between the Bambara form of these tales and their Louisiana Afro-Creole form demonstrates the linguistic influence Bambara had on slave communities in Louisiana. Interestingly, there may be a subtle but important religious distinction within the tale. That the *bouki* always gets outwitted by the rabbit not only maintains the traditional plot of the tales, but may, for Bambara and other non-Muslim slaves in Louisiana, been a strategy of indicating their greater influence over the slave community than their Senegambian nemeses, the Islamicized Wolof. Keeping the term *bouki* rather than assigning a Bambara or French etymon may have also brought Bambara and Afro-Creole slaves much satisfaction when they uttered the proverb, *bouki fait gombo, lapin mangé li,* or "hyena makes the gumbo; rabbit eats it."[22]

Throughout the eighteenth century, the Bambara ethnic identity—once ascendant in the interior of Senegambia itself—became, because of its overwhelming representation among the earliest slave shipments to Louisiana, the single most important African culture to Louisiana's creolized slave cultures. In New Orleans, where the ethnic fragmentation among the slave population was greater during both centuries than that of the slave population west and north of the city, Bambara culture, while still influential, meshed with Fon, Ewe, Yoruba, and Congolese cultures to create a slave culture that was distinct both for Louisiana and the South. By the nineteenth century, however, the slave cultures of Louisiana had become creolized, with distinct variations in each region of the state. The Afro-Creole cultures that emerged, while employing African cultural traditions, had long since abandoned specific references to Africa. Instead, their new identities rested in nineteenth-century religion and Creole culture.

Notes

1. Prominent examples of such studies are George Washington Cable, *The Creoles of Louisiana* (New York: Charles Scribner's, 1884); Thomas N. Ingersoll, *Mammon and Manon in Early New Orleans: The First Slave Society in the Deep South, 1718–1819* (Knoxville: University of Tennessee Press, 1999); and, to a lesser extent, Gwendlolyn Midlo Hall, *Africans in Colonial Louisiana: The Development of Afro-Creole Culture in the Eighteenth Century* (Baton Rouge: Louisiana State University Press, 1992).

2. David Eltis et al, *The Trans-Atlantic Slave Trade: A Database on CD-ROM* (Cambridge: Cambridge University Press, 1999); Gwendolyn Midlo Hall, *Databases for the Study of Afro-Louisiana History and Geneaology, 1699–1860* (Baton Rouge: Louisiana State University Press, 1999).

3. Hall, *Africans in Colonial Louisiana*, 31–35.

4. David Eltis, *Trans-Atlantic Slave Trade Database*. Search parameters used are "full time period" and "where slaves disembarked=Mississippi Delta. Also, it is important to note that the 8,000 figure does not represent the figures for all slave imports to Louisiana, but only those slaves imported directly from Africa. The total estimate is approximately 13,000. See Thomas Ingersoll, "The Slave Trade and the Ethnic Diversity of Louisiana's Slave Community," *Louisiana History* 37, 2 (1996): 152–53. Ingersoll convincingly disputes the 28,300 estimate in Philip D. Curtin, *The Atlantic Slave Trade: A Census* (Madison: University of Wisconsin Press, 1969), 82–83.

5. Hall, *Africans in Colonial Louisiana*, 42.

6. Ibid.; Peter Caron, "'Of a Nation Which the Others Do Not Understand': Bambara Slaves and African Ethnicity in Colonial Louisiana, 1718–1760," *Slavery and Abolition* 18, 1 (1997): 98–121; Richard Roberts, *Warriors, Merchants, and Slaves: The State and the Economy in the Middle Niger Valley, 1700–1914* (Stanford, Calif.: Stanford University Press, 1987), introd. and chap. 1.

7. Thomas N. Ingersoll, "The Slave Trade," 134.

8. Caron, "Of a Nation," 102, 107; Hall, *Africans in Colonial Louisiana,* chap. 2. For the similarities among the Mande linguistic group, see Michael Gomez, *Exchanging our Country Marks: The Transformation of African Identities in the Colonial and Antebellum South* (Chapel Hill: University of North Carolina Press, 1998), 38–39, 45–50.

9. Gwendolyn Midlo Hall, *Databases for the Study of Afro-Louisiana History.* Data from "Percent of African Origin By Decade" chart and "Percent of African Origin By District" chart. For influence of 1803 and 1809 Saint Domingue migrations, see Ingersoll, "The Slave Trade," 151–61.

10. For voodoo's history and development and in Louisiana, see Gomez, *Exchanging our Country Marks,* 55–56; Hall, *Africans in Colonial Louisiana,* 302; Robert Tallant, *Voodoo in New Orleans* (London: Cambridge University Press, 1962), 19–22; Lyle Saxon et al., *Gumbo Ya-Ya* (Cambridge: Cambridge University Press, 1945), 225.

11. N. H. Hobley narrative, Records of the Works Progress Administration Louisiana Writers' Project, Louisiana State Library, Baton Rouge (hereafter referred to as LWP-LSL).

12. Ibid.

13. Ibid.

14. Albert Patterson narrative, LWP-LSL; Gracie Stafford narrative, LWP-LSL.

15. Catherine Cornelius narrative, LWP-LSL.

16. Martin Dragney narrative, LWP-LSL.

17. Verice Brown narrative, LWP-LSL; Prince Haas narrative, LWP-LSL; Hall, *Africans in Colonial Louisiana,* 163.

18. Elizabeth Hite narrative, LWP-LSL; for the appeal of evangelical religions to Catholic slaves, see Randall M. Miller, "Slaves and Southern Catholicism," in *Masters and Slaves in the House of the Lord: Race and Religion in the American South, 1740–1870,* ed. John B. Boles (Lexington: University Press of Kentucky, 1988), 127–52.

19. Elizabeth Hite narrative, LWP-LSL.

20. Francis Doby narrative, LWP-LSL. For information on the south Louisiana version of the werewolf, or *loup garou,* tale, see Barry Jean Ancelet, *Cajun and Creole Folktales: The French Oral Tradition of South Louisiana* (New York: Garland Publishing, 1994), 159.

21. Francis Doby narrative, LWP-LSL; Alcee Fortier, *Louisiana Folktales* (Boston and New York: Houghton, Mifflin, and Company, 1895).

22. Proverb in Lafcadio Hearn, *Gombo Zhèrbes: A Little Dictionary of Creole Proverbs* (New York: W. H. Coleman, 1885).

PART III

Documentary Sources

10

SECTION INTRODUCTION
NEW APPROACHES TO
DOCUMENTARY SOURCES

Thomas Spear

Documentary sources are the *sine qua non* for historians, but few Africanists discuss them critically. This is partly because such sources are meager and we have been more intent on developing alternative sources and partly because they are largely seen as biased European accounts. This is ironic, given that we suffer from an overall lack of written sources, and it contrasts markedly with similar situations in classical, medieval, and East Asian history, where historians have developed sophisticated techniques to extract every possible detail from the few documents they have. But smarting from attacks that, without documentary evidence, Africa had no history, we looked elsewhere for sources to reconstruct that history while often dismissing what documentary sources there were as fatally flawed. There is only one journal that considers methodological issues, *History in Africa,* and it is only recently that critical editions of the *Periplus* and early European travel accounts have revealed the degree to which they were often based on hearsay, plagiarized from earlier accounts, and recycled through successive editions and translations. We thus need to take the written word both more seriously *and* more critically.

There are a number of different aspects in the critical examination of documentary sources. We must assess what types of document and perspectives have survived and which have not. We have to question a document's provenance, who produced it, when, and why. We need to ask how authentic a version is and how it may have changed through successive versions and editions since the original. We must carefully read what a document says, how it says it, and why. And we have to explore the historical context of the document, how that context informs the document, and what it reveals of the context.

Christian Jennings provides a classic example of close reading of accounts by early missionaries and travelers to question earlier interpretations of Maasai history. In doing so, he carefully establishes the provenance of the accounts by identifying who wrote them, their interests, and their linguistic abilities and experience. He establishes the identity and authenticity of their sources. And finally, he reads carefully for content, establishing the meaning of significant terms and their changes over time. In short, Jennings shows us just how much information can be gleaned from early European accounts, material that is otherwise unavailable.

Jennings also establishes a critical hierarchy among different versions of accounts, preferring those that were closest to the observations and events at hand. Krapf's extensive reports, for example, exist at seven different degrees of remove from the events he observed. First were the contemporary journal entries he wrote daily for himself, followed by the letters he sent periodically to his superiors at the Church Missionary Society in London, both of which can be found in the CMS archives. His letters were then edited and published in mission journals to edify the public and raise funds for the mission. Subsequently, Krapf synthesized much of his data in studies of local languages and societies published while he was still in the field. Still later, he reflected back over his journals, letters, and experiences to publish his memoirs in German, which were then abridged and translated into English. And finally, others subsequently quoted selectively from and reproduced his accounts. While many refer largely to his readily available abridged English memoirs, Jennings rightly refers to the unpublished journals and letters whenever he can.

The next two papers, by Kristin Mann and Meredith McKittrick, deal with issues of context as well as content. Both consider documentary sources—colonial court records and mission accounts—that many feel are especially subject to colonial bias and even invention, but the authors show how both sets of sources also reveal African interests and concerns together with wider socioeconomic and political forces.

Mann explores a series of court cases between a former slave and client and his patron, a wealthy Lagos trader. What is critical for Mann are not the immediate terms of the disputes over provision of goods and housing, but what these claims represented and how they were framed in the context of the violent social, political, and economic changes of the later nineteenth century. While the court was a colonial one and the judge, laws, and procedures British, Mann shows how it also reflected the local claims and conditions in which it operated in the tradition of British common law. In presenting their cases to the court, then, Africans inserted their own legal criteria and influenced the development of case law.

At the same time, the way that claimants and defendants argued their cases revealed much of the contemporary historical context, especially in the client's claims to a traditional patron-client relationship based on ex-changing his labor and political support for clothing, food, housing, provision of trade goods, and assistance in marrying and establishing himself. In response, his patron argued that their relation was purely an economic one based on receipt of wages for work performed and a detailed accounting of trade advances and receipts. Reflecting on these different claims, Mann concludes that the cases reveal the tensions inherent in a society undergoing transition from slavery and clientship to wage labor, personal relations to economic ones, and a moral economy to a capitalist one. The court records thus provide historical evidence in spite of themselves.

Similarly, McKittrick probes beneath the surface of missionary accounts of social and political violence in northern Namibia in the late nineteenth century. Often dismissed as evidence of missionaries' obsession with African savagery, she is able to show that Africans had a carefully calibrated morality of violence that normally tempered such violence, but the late nineteenth century was anything but normal. In the transition from the ivory trade to slave raiding and the disastrous impact of new diseases, political and moral control collapsed. In response, leaders sought to maintain their control of valuable resources and shore up their declining power bases through increased resort to witchcraft accusations and violence. Political violence was, thus, not innate in Ovambo societies, but a product of the economic and political conditions accompanying expanding European control in the later nineteenth century. And mission accounts, based on information gleaned from African informants, expressed African concerns with the increasing loss of political and moral control as much as they expressed missionary concerns. In McKittrick's words:

> We are left, then, to ask not whether these things happened, but to whom and what factors might shape the way such experiences were and are related. Like famine narratives, stories of insecurity in the face of royal power carry deeper messages about what people perceive as the normal or desirable state of society and how they feel that state is being violated.

Far from colonial inventions, then, mission accounts reflected both African and missionary concerns, both actual events and broader historical transformations, and both political and moral disputes among Africans generated by them.

As these papers make clear, the careful exploration and explication of documentary sources remain vital to our historical understanding, no matter who produced them and how and why they did so. Accounting for their production, the terms in which they were expressed, and the wider historical context in which they were recorded can tell us far more than simply the historical details they convey or the interests of their authors.

11

THEY CALLED THEMSELVES ILOIKOP: RETHINKING PASTORALIST HISTORY IN NINETEENTH-CENTURY EAST AFRICA

Christian Jennings

Scattered along the periphery of Maasailand are several smaller communities, who are historically related to the Maasai pastoralists, and whose inhabitants speak variations of the Maa language. These peripheral communities can be quite diverse, ranging from the compact Njemps fishing and farming community at Lake Baringo in Kenya, to the widely dispersed Parakuyo pastoralists of Tanzania. Although independent in name and ethnicity, they often are remembered as sharing a vague, overarching identity, and sometimes are called by the names "Iloikop," "Kwavi," or "Lumbwa." The consensus among scholars and Maasai themselves, for more than a century, has been that these peripheral communities are historically subgroups of an all-encompassing Maasai ethnicity and language dating back several hundred years. The purpose of the present essay is to challenge this "Maasai-centric" assumption, on the grounds that it is actually an inversion of the historical relationship between the groups in question: during the early nineteenth century, and probably for some time before, the pastoralists of the Rift Valley and its proximate savannas considered themselves to be Iloikop. The Maasai sections emerged from within this larger Iloikop family, and the idea of "being Maasai" itself is relatively new, perhaps developing as recently as the early nineteenth century.

The evidence for the thesis presented here is drawn primarily from the records left by the first three missionaries of the Church Missionary Society in East Africa: Johann Ludwig Krapf, Johannes Rebmann, and Jakob Erhardt. Their various journals, letters, and published articles, written during the 1840s and 1850s, are widely recognized as the earliest documentary evidence for Maasai and Iloikop history. But, as detailed later in the chapter, they have often been neglected in favor of later written or oral sources, perhaps because their views of Maasai and Iloikop history seem rather incongruous when compared to those of later writers, and even to those held by many twentieth-century Maasai themselves. The argument here is that despite the skepticism with which they have been met by later scholars, these early missionaries provided a coherent and convincing picture of Maasai and Iloikop pastoralists during the mid-nineteenth century. Given the credibility of their statements, then, the early missionary sources must be taken seriously by historians. Hopefully, the evidence presented here will provide a new appreciation for the dynamic changes that appear to have taken place in East Africa's not-so-distant past.

The Early Missionary Sources

Johann Ludwig Krapf was the first European to provide detailed written information about Iloikop or Maasai pastoralists. Krapf landed on the East African coast in December 1843. As soon as he left Mombasa and travelled to the mainland at Unyika in January 1844, he learned of the nearby "Okooafee," as well as their southern neighbors the "Quapee, who have abominable customs."[1] Within a year, Krapf had worked out that these two groups were in fact the same people. He soon adopted the name "Wakuafi" for them, and later learned that they referred to themselves by the name Iloikop.[2] Krapf gleaned the information that the Iloikop were "a very wild people" who consumed milk and meat, and who launched widespread cattle raids against neighboring peoples.[3] Krapf can also be credited with the earliest known written mention of Maasai, dating to February 1846, when he mentioned that "a tribe called Masai . . . celebrated as athletic archers" lived north of Ukaguru, beyond Chagga, adding that "circumcision is reported to be practiced among them even on the female sex."[4] Krapf learned that the Maasai language was "said to be that of the Wakuafi, of whom they are, in fact, only a division."[5] Krapf further learned that the Maasai had recently "fallen out with the Wakuafi and greatly contributed to their expulsion" from the plains near Chagga; the Maasai were now the most powerful group "strolling about in the plains" where the non-Maasai sections of Iloikop had been defeated.[6]

In June 1853 Krapf met an Iloikop slave living in the service of a Swahili master in Mombasa. The slave, whose Iloikop name was Lemasegnot, had spent most of his childhood with the Enganglima and Parakuyo sections of Iloikop, until he and his mother had been kidnapped and taken to the Pangani coast, where they were auctioned off as slaves. During his time in Mombasa, Lemasegnot had learned to speak fluent Kiswahili, and he had traveled as far as Barawa and Marka on the Somalian coast.[7] Lemasegnot's Muslim owner gave permission for him to reside with Krapf at the missionary's cottage in Rabai, outside of Mombasa. Krapf had become fascinated with the Iloikop language; Lemasegnot, in turn, took advantage of the opportunity to describe his life and homeland, often in striking detail. Krapf enthusiastically organized the information supplied by Lemasegnot, combined it with further information supplied by Swahili caravan traders, and published the results as *Vocabulary of the Engutuk Eloikob* in 1854. This document, like Krapf's writings on Iloikop and Maasai in general, would subsequently be met with tremendous skepticism by explorers, administrators, and historians alike. But the fact remains that Lemasegnot was a sound informant, indeed the best indigenous historical source until the appearance of Justin Lemenye nearly fifty years later.[8]

Similarly, the writings of Krapf's fellow missionary Jakob Erhardt often have been dismissed as misinformed, or as the result of hearsay from Swahili traders. But Erhardt also acquired most of his information directly from a native speaker, in this case a Maasai slave who had been captured in war by another section of Iloikop and sold to the coast. This informant's name was apparently never recorded, but his input, combined with that of the "Masai traders" (i.e., Swahili caravan leaders) interviewed by Erhardt at Tanga, provides a solid source with which to compare and contrast the information gathered by Krapf. Erhardt was particularly impressed by the fact that "Kikuafi" and "Kimasai" were identical languages, and by the thoroughness which which the Iloikop language had filtered even to the coastal areas of East Africa. "The Masai traders and my Masai," he noted, "have not the least difficulty in conversing with the Wakuafi slaves who are very numerous at Tanga."[9] Erhardt's *Vocabulary of the Enguduk Iloigob* of 1857, when compared with Krapf's earlier publication, completes a surprisingly well-rounded investigation into the Iloikop pastoralists, since each approached the subject from an opposite angle. That the information they collected agrees in its particulars to such a degree of consistency, as demonstrated below, is compelling reason to give credence to the comprehensive view of Iloikop society and history contained in their writings.

Johannes Rebmann, whose time of service in East Africa overlapped with that of Krapf and Erhardt, also left valuable records on Maasai and Iloikop. Rebmann made the first substantial journeys inland, travelling to Chagga in 1848 and again in 1849 under the guidance of Bana Kheri, who also guided Krapf to Usambara in 1848. Rebmann collected some useful information during his travels inland, but his closest and most dramatic experience with Maasai occurred during their large-scale attacks on Mombasa and its hinterland in 1855 and 1857 [see below]. Rebmann kept himself out of harm's way during the fighting; after all, as he wrote to the home office, "I need scarcely say that I do not consider it our duty to brave danger in which the great question is only about cattle."[10] But he nonetheless took great care to get as many eyewitness accounts as possible, checking them against each other for accuracy, and his information agrees with the account left by the explorer Richard Burton, who actually dashed off to Rabai with his companion John Speke to protect Rebmann before the three decided to retreat to Mombasa. In sum, then, the records left by Krapf, Erhardt, and Rebmann constitute a body of material that must be taken seriously by historians of East Africa.

The precise usage of the various names applied to Maasai and Iloikop pastoralists during the nineteenth century has been debated by scholars for more than a hundred years. A key factor in considering these terms is that they have been "in motion" since they were first put to paper; in other words, the first missionaries captured these terms at a particular point in their development, and later writers have considered them when they had evolved quite different meanings. But the meaning of the terms during the 1840s and 1850s appears clear-cut, based on the mutual agreement in their usage by Krapf and Erhardt. The basic scheme was as follows: Iloikop was the name by which the entire network of pastoralist communities, inclusive of Maasai and "Wakuafi," called themselves, and their language was called Enguduk Iloikop. Kwavi ("Wakuafi") was a Swahili term, probably derived from the word Iloikop, used at first to represent all Iloikop peoples, and later narrowed to represent only the non-Maasai sections of Iloikop. Likewise, the term Humba (or Lumbwa) was a Bantu word used by agriculturalists in the interior in reference to Iloikop pastoralists. The source of the term Maasai is as yet unconfirmed, but it may also be of Swahili origin; in any case it seems clear that the word came into widespread use not much earlier than the nineteenth century, and that in its early manifestation it referred specifically to an expansionist subgroup of Iloikop pastoralists.

Finally, the word Parakuyo referred to a powerful section of Iloikop who lived in the area near Usambara, but began to be used in the mid-nineteenth century by Maasai as a term of contempt, and was applied indiscriminately to any Iloikop peoples not yet under the sway of the Maasai.

For comparative purposes, the definition of terms provided by Krapf and Erhardt can be considered separately. Krapf first noted that the "Wakuafi" called themselves Iloikop in 1852.[11] In his *Vocabulary* a few years later, he speculated that Iloikop was an abbreviation of the word *engob* (land or country) combined with the article *loi*. The word Iloikop would then be defined, according to Krapf, as "those who are of, or in the country, to whom it belongs, the possessors of it, or those who have been there from the beginning, in short, aborigines."[12] Maasai and "Wakuafi" both referred to themselves as Iloikop, and Krapf believed that the names Kwavi (derived from the word Iloikop) and Maasai were given to their respective communities by the Swahili of the coast.[13] Further, the "Wakuafi" referred to the Maasai as Ilmangati (enemy), while the Maasai called the "Wakuafi" by the name Imbarawuio (Parakuyo).[14] Finally, Krapf noted that the "Wakuafi [were] called Wahumba in the language of Uniamesi," referring to the Bantu-speaking communities of present-day central and western Tanzania.[15]

Erhardt outlined an essentially identical set of distinctions between the various names for Iloikop peoples. On a map drawn in the 1850s, he labelled their country as "Iloigob (the land of the Masai and Wakuafi),"[16] and he agreed that both Maasai and "Wakuafi" referred to themselves as Iloikop, in reference to a mythical common ancestor. Each group, however, referred to the other as Ilmangati, meaning "any person of whom one has reason to be afraid . . . enemy."[17] In addition, the Maasai referred to themselves as Ilmaasai, specifically to distinguish themselves from the other Iloikop, who they contemptuously called Imbarawuio by adding a feminine form to the sectional name. Each group also referred to their common language as Enguduk Iloikop, the "mouth" (language) of the Iloikop.[18] It is particularly interesting to note that Erhardt came to his conclusions independently of Krapf, drawing on specifically Maasai rather than "Wakuafi" sources. Erhardt spent much of the year 1854 in consultation with the unnamed person he called simply "my Masai teacher," and noted in his journal that he "preferred [his] study of the most interesting enguduk iloigobani (language of the Masai) to any change."[19] Each missionary having come separately to strikingly similar conclusions, it made perfect sense for Krapf to list the Iloikop language in the index to his *Travels* as the overarching tongue encompassing both "Wakuafi" and Maasai dialects, as represented by their complementary published vocabularies.[20]

Iloikop Pastoralists and the Maasai Expansion

Perhaps the most important element of Iloikop society, as described in the early missionary sources, is that all Iloikop communities were fundamentally pastoralist in mode of subsistence. This contrasts starkly with later connotations of the word *loikop*, which would come to imply a connection with shameful agricultural labor. Krapf described the "Wakuafi" as specialized pastoralists, "following the course of grassy plains, where there are rivers, lakes and wells, without which nomadic tribes cannot exist."[21] The "Wakuafi" shared with their Maasai successors a disdain for farming. "They entertain such an aversion to agriculture," Krapf wrote, "that even Wakuafi slaves cannot be induced by the Suahili on the coast, to take the hoe and till the ground."[22] The Iloikop sections living near agriculturalists at Usambara and Kikuyu often traded for millet, corn, and bananas, but only women and children would eat them, not the *ilmuran* (warriors).[23] To maintain their pastoralist system, Iloikop (including Maasai) frequently launched cattle raids as far as Kamba, Galla, and the Tanga coast; Iloikop raiders used spears and shields, but their most feared weapons were throwing clubs, with which Iloikop ilmuran were deadly accurate from as far as seventy paces.[24]

The far-flung Iloikop communities considered Oldoinyo Eibor (Mount Kenya) to be their primeval home. They shared a common origin myth about a mysterious man named Neiterkob, who lived on the mountain. He was visited one day by a man named Enjemasi Enauner and his wife, who had travelled from their home near Oldoinyo Sambu. Neiterkob taught Enjemasi the ways of pastoralism, and impregnated his wife through magical means, then disappeared. Enjemasi returned home, and apparently the Iloikop community was said to have descended from his wife and Neiterkob. It is interesting in connection with pastoralist ecology that the name Enjemasi Enauner was said to refer to a pointed stick he carried with him, used to make "a hole or deepening in the ground wherever he touched it."[25] Krapf wrote that Iloikop continued to think of Oldoinyo Eibor as the home of their ancestors, and to make pilgrimages there to pray for rain, cattle, and health, calling on Neiterkob to provide intercession between themselves and Engai (God).[26]

Political power in the Iloikop communities was split between the influence of the elders and the *laibon*, who according to Krapf, "plans war or peace through divination."[27] Erhardt, who translated *laibon* as "king," wrote that their duties included rainmaking and spiritual protection for Iloikop warriors on raiding expeditions; if a *laibon* presided over three consecutive losses on expeditions, he would be killed and replaced.[28] Both Krapf and Rebmann reported in 1848 on the recent death of a "mighty king" of the "Wakuafi" named Embare Kisungo, who held sway along the banks of the Pangani River, and who wielded influence as part of a "powerful African triumvirate" that included Kimweri of Usambara and Rongua of Chagga.[29] Interestingly, while Kimweri and Rongua are still remembered as key political leaders of their era, the existence of Embare Kisungo has been entirely forgotten and might even be considered a fabrication by some later scholars. This unusual problem will be reconsidered later in the essay, but for the moment it is important to note that according to Krapf and Rebmann, it was common knowledge on the Swahili coast and in the Usambara Mountains that there had been a political figurehead for the Iloikop communities of the southeast, and that this person had recently died and left a political void in the region.

Krapf, Rebmann, and Erhardt recognized that Iloikop society was made up of various sectional groupings (which they called "tribes"), each named for the geographical area it inhabited. Maasai society today is still made up of these sections, called *iloshon*, and it has been well documented that their constitution can change dramatically over time; sections of both Iloikop and Maasai have been know to disappear entirely, or fall apart only to regroup at a later date. Further, it seems quite common for there to be sub- and super-sections which absorb, overlap, or exlude the other sectional levels over time. Rather than adhere to a strict definition of the sectional form of social organization, then, it seems best to heed Fosbrooke's explanation that "a section is in the first place a fortuitous grouping of individuals," constantly engaged in the twin processes of forming and dividing.[30] Tracing the formation of, and changes in, sectional organization over the course of the nineteenth century is one of the most useful ways to reconstruct Iloikop and Maasai history, and the earliest documentary evidence for sections comes from the missionary writings of the 1840s and 1850s. The sections of Iloikop mentioned as existing (or recently dispersed) at mid-century included: Parakuyo, Enganglima, Mao, Baringo, Ndigiriri, Tigerei, Laikipiak, Modoni, Kopekope, Burkineji (also known as Samburu), and the Maasai sections (who by this time had detached themselves to a considerable degree from the rest of the Iloikop sections).

Krapf and Rebmann agreed that the plains of Kaputei were the heartland and stronghold of the "primeval Wakuafi" sections;[31] positioned around this area were groupings of "Wakuafi" sections to the east-southeast and north, and Maasai sections to the southwest. Krapf wrote that the principal inhabitants of Kaputei in 1848 were the sections Enganglima, Kisongo, and Parakuyo.[32] Kisongo would eventually become the all-encompassing name of the vanguard Maasai sections, but it is unclear whether or not at this date the term still referred to a non-Maasai Iloikop section (possibly led by a certain Mbare Kisungo). The recently dispersed Enganglima section had inhabited the plains between Usambara, Teita, and Kamba, until it was attacked, seemingly from all sides, first by the Maasai and then by the Shambaa, Kamba, Mijikenda, Swahili, and Teita. The vacant area left by this disaster became known as the "Wakuafi wilderness," and will be discussed further below. Also in the southeast was the powerful Parakuyo section, which lived along the banks of the Pangani River, stubbornly refusing to give way under repeated attacks by Maasai.[33] The northern cluster of sections was less well known to the missionaries because it fell outside the areas of their travels, but Krapf visited close enough to the eastern side of Mount Kenya to acquire at least a sketchy knowledge from Kamba and Kikuyu traders. The sections in this northern area included the the Laikipiak, who would lead (and lose) a resurgence against the Maasai sections in the 1870s, and the Burkeneji (Samburu), who largely avoided conflict with Maasai because of their northern location, only to come into conflict with the equally expansionist Turkana. Krapf also mentions a "Wakuafi" section called Mao, who combined agriculture and pastoralism, and were friendly to visitors (apparently not the same as the "Mau" Dorobo hunters). Finally, the northern area included several little-known Iloikop sections: Baringo, Modoni, Tigerei, Ndigiriri, and Kopekope, who apparently lived in a marshy area between Lake Baringo and Samburu.[34] To the southwest of Kaputei were the Maasai sections, still in the process of acquiring territory. Krapf wrote that the Maasai stronghold stretched across the Serengeti plain near Kamritta and Ngoroini, and that Oldoinyo Sambu (near Monduli) was their most important center of activity.[35]

Although Iloikop were feared as cattle-raiders, they also maintained less violent relations with all of their neighbors. Two groups of neighbors actually lived in the midst of Iloikop pastoralists, in a somewhat subservient status: the Dorobo hunters, and the Konono blacksmiths. The Dorobo, also known by other names depending on their locale, were most likely the remnants of pre-Iloikop populations who occupied the savannas and forests of eastern Africa. The Dorobo living near the Iloikop and Shambaa center of Masinde in Usambara were called Ala, while those who hunted elephants deep in the forests of western Kenya were called Mau.[36] Krapf writes that the Dorobo made their living by supplying ivory to their neighbors, who then traded it to the passing caravans. The Konono blacksmiths made spears, swords, knives, and other implements for the Iloikop pastoralists, and Krapf believed that they also predated the Iloikop in East Africa. Both groups spoke Iloikop fluently, but also retained their own separate languages.[37] This relationship between pastoralists and smaller groups of hunters and blacksmiths was common throughout eastern Africa as far as Somalia, and would be maintained in turn by the Maasai sections after they had effectively conquered most of Iloikop-land.

Iloikop communities interacted closely with their agricultural neighbors in Kikuyu, Chagga, and Usambara, but they appear always to have been on the worst of terms with their neighbors, the semi-pastoral Kamba and the pastoral Oromo. Krapf was informed as early as 1845 that it was possible for farmers to "make friendship" with Iloikop pastoralists, and his later experiences supported that statement.[38] In 1853 Krapf was visited by a delegation of Kikuyu, who informed him that a section of "Wakuafi" was actually living in their territory and grazed their cattle freely on Kikuyu ground. One of the Kikuyu men struck up a fluent conversation in the Iloikop language with Krapf's teacher, Lemasegnot, who had been born near Oldoinyo Eibor (Mount Kenya); they found that they had a mutual acquaintance, an Iloikop "chief" who lived in the neighborhood of Kikuyu, and who Lemasegnot claimed as a relative.[39] In contrast, the missionaries only wrote of constant tension between the Iloikop and their cattle-owning neighbors. In eastern Kenya, in fact, the Mijikenda had developed an origin myth for these three mutually antagonistic groups: long ago, they had a common ancestor, a man with three sons. The first son, named Galla (another name for Oromo), had raided cattle from a nearby group. His two brothers, Mkuafi and Mkamba, had asked for a share in the prize, but Galla had refused. Mkuafi then robbed Galla, who turned around and plundered from Mkamba, and since then there had been only hatred between the descendants of the three.[40]

In contrast to the widespread and well-established Iloikop communities, the impression given by all of the missionaries in East Africa during the 1840s and 1850s is that the Maasai represented a new, rapidly expanding social entity which had originated from within Iloikop society and was now sweeping towards the coast with two interrelated goals: to capture all available cattle, and to put "empty" space between themselves and potential competitors. Krapf wrote in 1847 that the Maasai were "now the powerful tribes strolling about in the plains," and that they spoke the language of the Iloikop pastoralists, "of whom they are, in fact, only a division," although they had "fallen out" with the other Iloikop sections and defeated them.[41] The next year Krapf added that the Maasai occupied the area southwest of Chagga, and were "a nomadic pastoral people of wild habits," who had forcibly "cleared the road" to Chagga and Usambara by defeating their Iloikop relatives.[42] This view echoed that of Rebmann, who wrote that "the nomadic Masai [were] a tribe of Wakuafi," who lived in the plains south and southwest of Chagga.[43] Erhardt wrote that the Maasai inhabited the "plains beyond Arusa Kuba as far as a large lake . . . [they] are much subject to dearths, so that [they] are constantly on the move, following the rains or the courses of the rivers."[44] Erhardt frequently mentioned "the great King Sibeti," "the first king of the Masai," who treated passing caravans well, and who maintained a residence a short distance west of Mount Meru; he also noted that the young Maasai men "take their encampments in the forests about the settlement, carrying on warlike expeditions and watching their own."[45]

The missionaries agreed that the Maasai had developed a nearly unstoppable military system, which had been successful against both the neighboring communities in the interior and the Swahili caravans. In 1852, while visiting an outpost of Usambara governed by Kimweri, Krapf learned that a force of 800 Maasai warriors had passed through the nearby Karenge valley only a few days earlier, on their way to attack the Zigua in the plains near the Pangani River. Kimweri had given permission for this movement because he had been fighting the Zigua himself, and welcomed the additional pressure directed towards them.[46] In Mombasa, the next year, a trader recently returned from southern Usambara told Erhardt that the Maasai had been "very successful" in raiding not only the Zigua, but also the "Wakuafi" and Pare, attacking as far south as Masinde.[47] The Maasai were also particularly ferocious in dealing with Arab caravans from Zanzibar; according to Erhardt, one Zanzibari caravan was stopped in 1853 and forced to leave its goods rotting at Vuga, and the next year another was massacred entirely just west of Arusha.[48] But both missionaries recognized that the traders were often at fault, drawing Maasai anger because of their own thieving activities, and in one particular instance, because they had supplied muskets to an enemy group.[49] In spite of the amount of trading that took place, the hostility between Maasai and caravan traders was so intense that Rebmann's guides prayed for him as he prepared to travel inland, "may he not meet with an Emmessa."[50]

During the 1850s, the Maasai launched two major assaults into the area of Mombasa and its hinterlands, sweeping through the "Wakuafi wilderness" to attack Kamba, Mijikenda, Oromo, and even the suburbs of Mombasa itself. Maasai raiders had been seen along the Tsavo River in 1849, but their intent at that point had been to push through Kamba territory and raid the Oromo, rather than sweep down towards the coast.[51]

Six years later they returned, but it was evident to the missionary observers that the Maasai now had Mombasa and the Nyika country in their sights. Late in 1854 rumors began to spread along the coast that the Maasai were preparing to make "a great movement" for as yet unkown purposes. They had recently defeated Machame in Chagga, a massive advance of Maasai warriors had frightened a Swahili caravan into abandoning its journey, and the people of Usambara were said to be fleeing their plantations to hide in the mountains. The Maasai had crossed the Pangani River, their usual boundary, and in December 1854 they appeared in the "Wakuafi wilderness." A small party of Maasai interrogated some Duruma agriculturalists of the Nyika country, promising them that they only sought directions to Kamba and meant no harm. A Duruma youth provoked a fight, resulting in in several deaths; when news of this incident spread, a general panic ensued, and the missionaries fled to Mombasa. The intent of the Maasai was unknown, but rumors circulated that they desired to occupy the wilderness left vacant by the defeat of the Enganglima section of Iloikop. Rebmann felt that this had merely been a reconnaisance in preparation for a large-scale attack "by the time of the next rainy season . . . while now the scarcity of water, which is peculiar to this wilderness, makes it impossible."[52]

On 13 April 1855, Erhardt wrote in a letter to the home office that the news at Tanga recently warned of Maasai "all East of the Pangani . . . ready for overrunning all the Wanika tribes."[53] As it happened, on that same day a force of Maasai "in great numbers" attacked Duruma, setting villages aflame, killing men, and rounding up herds of cattle. Rebmann later wrote that the Teita were rumored to have guided the Maasai through the territory, setting the fires while the Maasai waited outside with their spears to catch the fleeing inhabitants. The Maasai warriors displayed "consummate boldness," feasting and dancing for two days at the site of their attack, taunting the Duruma survivors with requests that they take good care of their cattle so that the animals would be in good form when the Maasai returned for more. A few Mijikenda and Kamba mustered the courage to fight back, "but without even the effect of disturbing the great body in their mirth—a few skirmishers only thinking it worth their while to rise up and spear them."[54] Rebmann reported that a sense of resentment spread among the survivors because the government of Said Said had done nothing to help defend its nominal territory, a policy of inaction that could only have encouraged the victorious Maasai, who returned home in an unhurried manner.[55]

A second and more thorough attack on the coast was not long in coming. On 19 January 1857, Kamba families began to stream into Rabai, reporting smoke in the distance from "three divisions" of advancing Maasai. The people of Rabai, in turn, drove their cattle towards the coast, and the alarm spread quickly to Mombasa. The explorers Burton and Speke hurried to Rabai expecting a fight, but they and Rebmann soon retreated to Mombasa. The remaining Mijikenda at Rabai were attacked within days, the Maasai "just mowing them down as they found them in their way," and by 31 January the Maasai had reached the outskirts of Mombasa itself. "The terrible hordes of the Masai actually came down to the water's edge," Rebmann wrote, "even to the plantation of Abdullah Ben Bisallah . . . and even to Makuba (the ferrying place from the Continent to the island of Mombas)."[56] The people of Mombasa made a feeble attempt to resist, sending 150 Arab and Swahili "matchlock-men," who temporarily held off the onslaught;[57] but they ultimately gave way, losing several "principal men (among them the brother of the Governor himself)" in the effort, while communication between Mombasa and the mainland was cut off for a week.[58] The Maasai then turned their attention toward the Oromo in the north, but when they returned once more through Unyika "a small number of Arab soldiers from Mombas attempted again to attack them but with no success, nearly half their number being killed."[59]

Krapf, Rebmann, and Erhardt each travelled separately through a vast stretch of depopulated country in what is today eastern Kenya, known during the 1840s and 1850s as the "Wakuafi wilderness." This country had until recently been inhabited by Iloikop sections such as the Enganglima, who were nearly annihilated during the 1830s, suffering first from attacks by Maasai, and then a combined force of Mijikenda, Shambaa, and others. The "Wakuafi wilderness" centered on the area between Kilimanjaro, Usambara, and Teita, but also included lands north of Teita as far as the Tana River, and some areas south of the Pare Mountains in the Maasai Steppe that had not yet been occupied by the victorious Maasai.[60] Rebmann described the wilderness as "the ocean-like plain of the Wakuafi, at present wholly unoccupied by any human being, opened to the view even to a short distance from the seashore."[61] The only areas that remained inhabited were the isolated mountain masses that towered over the plains, such as the Teita Hills, and the oasis community of Taveta, lying in the shadow of Mount Kilimanjaro.[62] The desolate plains carried grim reminders of the recent past; Rebmann, for example, saw the skulls and bones of dead Iloikop scattered along the road between Teita and Chagga, and concluded that they had fallen in battle with the Maasai sections.[63]

The rapid depopulation of the "Wakuafi wilderness" brought about dramatic ecological changes in the area. The grass on the plains grew unimpeded, and thick brush and woods sprang up in patches, to the point that Rebmann actually described one area near Teita as a thick jungle.[64] The wildlife population shifted in favor of animals suited to dense woody vegetation: elephants preferred the tall grasses and uncrowded pools of water; rhinos hid themselves in the dense clusters of euphorbia trees; and buffalo grazed along the open ground near patches of acacia bush.[65] The human ecology of the area also changed, as neighboring people took advantage of the depopulation to expand their own communities. In the northern parts of the "Wakuafi wilderness," Kamba families moved westward into the former Iloikop-land around the Athi River, and the Oromo moved slowly out onto the Kikumbuliu plains.[66] In the south, the centralized political system of the Shimba actually dispersed, as the death of Muduahu, the ruler at Kwale, combined with the sudden absence of Iloikop in the area, allowed farmers to move down from the hills and onto isolated, lowland plantations.[67] The Swahili village of Gondsha sprang into existence as a way-point for traders after the Iloikop had been cleared from the Tanga hinterland, and travel along caravan routes from the coast to Teita and Chagga was generally considered much safer after the defeat of the Iloikop (although the Maasai sections would soon alter that perception).[68] One Swahili trader marveled that Rebmann, armed only with an umbrella, was now able to traverse an area that would have required 500 guns for protection only ten years earlier.[69]

As time passed, the name "Wakuafi" would gradually be disassociated from the wilderness, and the area would simply be known as *nyika* (desert). In 1873, missionary Charles New reported that the "lowland is fertile" in the Nyika, "but almost the whole of it is let to run wild," although Swahili settlement in the area was increasing "year by year."[70] The explorer Joseph Thomson, passing through in the early 1880s, described the Nyika of the plains surrounding Teita as overgrown with thorns and "gnarled trees," and was impressed by the manner in which the Nyika abruptly gave way to fine pasture-land as he crossed the Lumi River on the Nyika's western boundary.[71] Harry Johnston in 1884 described the Nyika as "a wilderness, but yet rather park-like . . . teem[ing] with game," but unoccupied by humans.[72] Krapf's prediction of 1848, that the "Wakuafi wilderness" would one day be "the land of the railroads," would be proven correct after the turn of the next century.[73] But the early missionary sources clearly indicate that during the mid-nineteenth century, the Nyika of eastern Kenya was remembered as a once-populated Iloikop territory, and that this land had been forcibly vacated under pressure from the expansionist Maasai sections.

Several major points regarding mid-nineteenth century Iloikop-land should be emphasized from our reading of Krapf, Rembann, and Erhardt. The most important for our purposes here is that both the Maasai and "Wakuafi" sections thought of themselves as Iloikop. All Iloikop communites were primarily pastoralist, and all of them probably supplemented their diet with agricultural produce acquired through trade with their neighbors. The Iloikop, and the Maasai after them, were linked in the regional trade networks that extracted ivory and slaves from the interior to the coast, and Iloikop communities often came into conflict with caravan traders. The Maasai sections of Iloikop began to expand rapidly sometime in the early 1800s, violently displacing the non-Maasai Iloikop sections such as Enganglima, and leaving behind vast uninhabited stretches of savanna. The Maasai military system was swift and far-reaching, and for a time at least, possessed an unmatched superiority in combat.

Later Interpretations of the Early Missionary Sources

Through the 1870s and early 1880s, missionaries and explorers who visited Maasailand generally agreed with the earlier views of Krapf, Rebmann, and Erhardt. Thomas Wakefield, stationed at Mombasa, wrote that the "poor Wakwavi . . . having long since been robbed of their cattle by the Masai, were compelled to turn their attention to agricultural pursuits," but also noted that "the Wakwavi of Ndara Serian" continued to raid Lumbwa (Kipsigis) for cattle.[74] Likewise in 1873, Charles New agreed with his predecessors that both Maasai and "Wakuavi" called themselves Orloikob, which he translated as "possessors of the soil," and that both groups were pastoralists.[75] James Last, stationed at Mamboia in central Tanzania during the early 1880s, concluded, as Krapf had done earlier, that "Humba" was an equivalent term for "Kwavi," and agreed with earlier observers that both the "Kwavi" and Maasai "live on ox flesh and milk, and neglect the cultivation of vegetable food."[76] The German explorer G. A. Fischer, who crossed Maasailand in 1882, found that "the Wa-kuavi, a pastoral and nomadic race like the Masai, formerly possessed the greatest part of the land inhabited by the Masai, but were gradually driven back by the latter . . . [and now] have settled and pursue agriculture."[77] Joseph Thomson, a Scotsman who advanced his own expedition directly on the heels of Fischer, made a subtle departure from previous observers, stating that the "Kwafi" were "one among many septs" of Maasai, rather than the opposite.[78] This inversion of the order laid out by Krapf and Rebmann would become the standard interpretation in years to come, perhaps influenced by the fact that the Maasai had indeed reduced the larger Iloikop society to mere scatterlings, and had subsumed earlier concepts of Iloikop identity within a new Maasai cultural system.

J. P. Farler, the archdeacon of Magila in Usambara, interviewed Swahili traders who had recently journeyed along the newly reopened routes from Pangani to the interior. Farler's informants led him to introduce a new distinction between the "Kwavi" and Maasai, one that would have been unthinkable to Krapf and his colleagues. The "Wakwafi," Farler wrote, "seem to be an agricultural branch of the Masai people, [who] are found scattered over four degrees," and who spoke a mere "dialectical variety" of the Maasai language.[79] This new interpretation led Farler to make several confused statements in the itinerary of caravan routes published by the Royal Geographical Society. For example, Farler believed that the "regular dynasty" and "settled government" of Mbatian at Kisongo (the very heart of Maasai society), was in fact an achievement of the agriculturalist "Wakwafi," who had "reached a much higher stage of civilisation" than their pastoralist Maasai relatives.[80] Thus, added to the inversion of social standing that somehow made "Kwavi" a mere subgroup of Maasai, there would now be a persistent notion that the "Kwavi" were essentially farmers, while their "pure" Maasai relatives were essentially cattle herders of the open plains.

Harry Johnston, a botanist and explorer who began his expedition to Kilimanjaro just as Joseph Thomson returned from his own, travelled along the Usambara chain to Kilimanjaro and back, meeting briefly with Parakuyo along the Pangani River, and with Maasai at Moshi. Johnston's popular book, published in 1886, reinforced the image of the agricultural "Kwavi" versus the pastoralist Maasai. After acknowledging that both Maasai and "Kwavi" referred to themselves as Iloikop, for example, Johnston went on to define the term as "people of the soil," and ventured that it was "more especially affected by the latter [i.e., "Kwavi"], as it implies a settled residence."[81] Johnston's interpretation of the Iloikop Wars imagined them as conflicts between pastoralists and agriculturalists, but his attempt to narrate their history was so vague as to be nearly unintelligible.[82] The precocious Johnston, who fancied himself an expert in any academic discipline, was perhaps the first to dismiss as useless the writings of the early missionaries. Of Erhardt and Krapf's *Vocabularies,* Johnston declared them of poor linguistic quality, and deemed inexplicably that "neither [Krapf nor Erhardt] seemed to be aware that they were studying the same language."[83] Johnston's casual, and mistaken, dismissal of Erhardt and Krapf, predated several later writers who would also neglect to give more than a superficial glance towards the early missionary sources.

By the turn of the century, then, a contradictory pattern had developed in writers' views of "Kwavi" and Maasai identity. On one hand, most missionaries and explorers who conducted detailed interviews and tried to learn the history of Iloikop and Maasai pastoralists found that their research confirmed the views of the early missionaries. Ludwig von Hohnel, for example, who accompanied Count Teleki on his 1887 journey to Lake Rudolf, learned at Njemps that "according to their own traditions, they [i.e., the "Wakwafi" of Njemps] too were once herdsmen leading a nomad life in nearly the same districts as the Masai of today," and that they had lost their cattle and been dispersed as a result of wars with the Maasai.[84] But on the other hand, the notion that the "Kwavi" were and always had been a farming subgroup of Maasai (most likely catalyzed by the apparent circumstance that most non-Maasai Iloikop sections had indeed been forced to take up farming by the 1880s), gained prominence quickly, and became entrenched as the standard interpretation of Maasai history.

Most of the colonial writers on Maasai and Iloikop adopted the agricultural-pastoralist distinction uncritically, although some gave it new twists. A. C. Hollis wrote in 1905 that there were two divisions of Maasai: the pastoralists, who called themselves Il-Maasae and lived in British territory, and the agriculturalists, who were called 'L-Oikop or Il-Lumbwa and lived in German East Africa.[85] Charles Eliot, in his introduction to the Hollis book, speculated that "the difference between the two is evidently not ancient," and it was "quite probable that there was a large agricultural settlement on the Uasin Gishu plateau from which the more adventurous warriors detached themselves."[86] On the German side of the border, colonial officer Meritz Merker speculated in 1910 that there had actually been three waves of "Maasai" pastoralist migrants into East Africa—the Asa (Dorobo), the "El kuafi," and the Maasai—each displacing the previous one and forcing it to give up pastoralism.[87] Merker's theory was interesting if sketchy, but he neglected it in order to devote more pages to the question of whether or not the Maasai were in fact the lost tribe of Israel. G. R. Sandford's 1919 paper on the history of the Maasai, written for the colonial record books, advanced the view that "the Masai tribe originally consisted of both pastoral and agricultural sections, of which the latter was almost annihilated by the former."[88] The 'L-Oikop were settled agriculturalists, Sandford wrote, while the nomadic Maasai pastoralists never practiced agriculture.

Henry Fosbrooke, who began work as a colonial administrator in Tanganyika's Masai District in 1935, published his account of Maasai history and society as a lengthy essay in the 1948 volume of *Tanganyika Notes and Records*. Fosbrooke had conducted interviews with Maasai in many parts of the country over the past decade, and felt that his information did not agree with that of his earlier colleagues. Fosbrooke's informants told him repeatedly that they shared a common pastoralist origin with the "Lumbwa," who they told him had only recently taken up agriculture. Further, these Maasai had specific traditions about when and how they had taken each of the areas they now inhabited from their previous pastoralist Iloikop occupants. Fosbrooke reviewed the literature on Maasai, and found much to agree with in Krapf and Thomson, especially their convictions that Maasai and "Kwavi" (or "Lumbwa") sections were essentially part of one broadly defined pastoralist community. He also dismissed the idea that there was a long-standing, traditional division between pastoralist and agriculturalist sections, and he rejected Eliot's suggestion that pastoralism had been a recent innovation in Maasailand.[89] Fosbrooke's oral and archaeological investigations match up quite well with the early missionary sources, and could be used to construct a chronology of Maasai expansion in the nineteenth century.

Alan Jacobs revived the debate over nineteenth-century Maasai and Iloikop with his 1965 doctoral thesis, combining his own research in oral history with selected contemporary written accounts. Jacobs concluded that not only were Maa-speaking peoples divided into "purely pastoral" Ilmaasai and "semi-pastoral" Iloikop sections, and that the Iloikop Wars were conflicts between these two groups, but that the "semi-pastoral" Iloikop were actually the "more militant" warriors of that era, while the Maasai did not even have a powerful military system.[90] As one might expect, Jacobs overlooked much of the Krapf-Rebmann-Erhardt material in order to reach his conclusions. Jacobs felt that these early missionaries had "failed to give an adequate picture" of nineteenth-century Maasailand, and opted instead to use the writings of Wakefield, and James Christie's *Cholera Epidemics,* which presents a second-hand view of Maasailand drawn from other sources, to provide an 1868 "baseline" from which to reconstruct Maasai history.[91] As an anthropologist, Jacobs also placed great emphasis on the oral interviews he conducted in Maasailand, and perhaps took too often at face value the Maasai version of events that had taken place a century earlier. Thus, the nineteenth-century Maasai are seen, in Jacobs' view, as provoked by the harrassment of the semi-pastoralists, until they eventually managed to fight back and rid themselves of the Iloikop threat. Yet Jacobs was still somewhat at a loss to explain the fact, as he readily admitted, that his Maasai informants still sometimes called themselves Iloikop, "in a boastful sense."[92]

John Berntsen, working in the late 1970s, focused his thesis on the history of the nineteenth-century expansion of the Maasai. Berntsen challenged some of Jacobs' conclusions, noting that the idea of a division between "pastoralist Maasai" and "agricultural Kwavi" dates back no earlier than the 1870s, when it was adopted by Farler and Johnston.[93] But Berntsen, too, was somewhat taken in by present-day Maasai ideas of identity and history. For example, Berntsen claimed that the word "Kwavi" did not derive from the word *iloikop,* which he translated as "murder." Berntsen felt that *iloikop* would have been a term used to refer contemptuously to a group other than one's own, rather than a term of self-identification; with this in mind, he dismissed the assertion made by Krapf, Erhardt, and others, that nineteenth-century Maasai and "Kwavi" pastoralists in fact called themselves Iloikop.[94] But Berntsen failed to recognize the possibility that the word *iloikop* had evolved new meanings and nuances during the past century, and further, did not explore the implications of his own admission that the word today is not a direct equivalent for murder, but rather also signifies bloodwealth, the social ramifications and consequences of violence, cultural prohibitions and prescriptions in the event of violence, and a general sense of "taboo." In other words, the word *iloikop* today has connotations of fighting that tears at the social fabric, not an unexpected development if in fact the non-Maasai Iloikop sections had been violently displaced by the expanding Maasai sections.

Richard Waller's thesis, written at nearly the same time, covered much of the same ground as Berntsen's, but arrived at some very different conclusions. First, Waller rejected the idea that Maasai and Iloikop were traditionally divided by their mode of subsistence into conflicting pastoralist and agriculturalist sections. Citing the Krapf-Rebmann-Erhardt material, Waller concluded that the Maasai and Iloikop sections had very similar, perhaps identical, subsistence practices during much of the nineteenth century. The Maasai may have idealized the idea of "pure" pastoralism, Waller wrote, but in day-to-day life they almost certainly supplemented their diet with just as much agricultural produce as the other Iloikop.[95] Further, he disagreed with the assertion that the Maasai sections were not highly militarized, noting that this viewpoint "ignores a great deal of contemporary evidence," and theorizing that the expansion of Maasai sections during the Iloikop Wars involved a high level of military coordination in order to successfully complete such massive cattle raids.[96] Waller recognized that the word *iloikop* probably did not always carry negative connotations, pointing out that both Krapf and Erhardt were firmly convinced that both Maasai and "Wakuafi" sections called themselves Iloikop; Waller also took seriously the fact that his Maasai informants were "emphatic" in declaring that they had once been the same as the Iloikop.[97]

Berntsen and Waller did much to restore an appreciation of the Krapf-Rebmann-Erhardt material, and to sort out many of the confused aspects of nineteenth-century Maasai and Iloikop history. Yet they both persisted in maintaining the inverted order of social groupings, in which the Iloikop are seen as a subgroup of an overarching "Ol Maa" family, rather than vice versa. "The Maasai community," as Waller wrote, "for part of the nineteenth century at least, also included the Iloikop . . . [who] remain shadowy figures . . . to be filled out by inferences rather than facts."[98] However, our reading of the early missionary sources indicates that the Maasai sections were originally but one part of a wider Iloikop community, a viewpoint that need not be inferred at all, since it is stated clearly and consistently by the early missionary observers. In the absence of any compelling reason to ignore the records left by Krapf, Rebmann, and Erhardt, any scholar who aims to gain an accurate understanding of the history of East African pastoralists must take these early missionary sources into account.

Notes

1. J. L. Krapf, journal entry, 4 January 1844, CA5/O16, Church Missionary Society [CMS].

2. Although Krapf and the other early missionaries noted that the proper term for these pastoralists was Iloikop, they continued to use the term Wakuafi in their correspondence and journals, most likely because it was the conventional term used on the coast. In this essay, we will use the term Iloikop in place of Wakuafi when discussing the early missionary sources, except for direct quotes, in the same way we substitute Oromo for Galla and Mijikenda for Wanyika. Note, however, that the meaning of "Wakuafi" appears to be quite different in the writings of later observers, invalidating the direct correlation between the terms when reading sources compiled after the early missionaries.

3. Krapf to Coates, 22 January 1845, CA5/O16, CMS.

4. Krapf to Coates, 25 February 1846, CA5/O16, CMS.

5. Krapf, journal entry, 11 October 1847, CA5/O16, CMS.

6. Krapf, journal entry, 11 October 1847, CA5/O16, CMS.

7. J. L. Krapf, *Vocabulary of the Engutuk Eloikob or of the Wakuafi-Nation in the Interior of Equatorial Africa* (Tubingen: Lud. Fried. Fues., 1854), 4–6, 11.

8. Krapf, journal entry, 30 August 1853, CA5/O16, CMS; Krapf, *Vocabulary*, 3–4, 25–26.

9. J. Erhardt to Venn, 27 October 1854, CA5/O16, CMS.

10. J. Rebmann to Venn, 18 April 1855, CA5/O24, CMS.

11. Krapf, journal entry, 18 March 1852, CA5/O16, CMS.

12. Krapf, *Vocabulary*, 6–7.

13. Krapf, journal entry, 30 August 1853, CA5/O16, CMS; Krapf, *Travels, Researches and Missionary Labors, during an Eighteen Years' Residence in Eastern Africa* (London: Trübner and Co., 1860), 358; Krapf, *Vocabulary,* 6–7.

14. Krapf, journal entry, 18 March 1852, CA5/O16, CMS; Krapf, *Travels,* 564.

15. Krapf, journal entry, 23 March 1852, CA5/O16, CMS.

16. J. Erhardt, "J. Erhardt's Memoire zur erläuterung der von ihm und J. Rebmann," *Petermann's Mittheilungen* (1856), 19–24, map.

17. J. Erhardt, *Vocabulary of the Enguduk Iloigob, as Spoken by the Masai-Tribes in East Africa* (Ludwigsburg: Ferdinand Riehm, 1857), 47–48; see also Erhardt, journal entry, 1 May 1854, CA5/O9, CMS.

18. Erhardt, *Vocabulary,* 18, 47–48, 57, 65.

19. Erhardt, journal entries, 1 May and 27 July 1854, CA5/O9, CMS.

20. Krapf, *Travels,* 563–64.

21. Krapf, *Vocabulary,* 9.

22. Ibid., 11.

23. Ibid., 12–13.

24. Krapf, journal entry, 1 March 1852, CA5/O16, CMS; Krapf, *Travels,* 359.

25. Krapf, *Vocabulary,* 8–9.

26. Ibid., 10; see also Krapf, *Travels,* 360; Krapf, journal entry, 30 August 1853, CA5/O16, CMS; Krapf to Venn, 10 January 1854, CA5/O16, CMS.

27. Krapf, *Vocabulary,* 13–14.

28. Erhardt, *Vocabulary,* 28.

29. Rebmann, journal entry, 12 May 1848, CA5/O24, CMS; Krapf, journal entry, 13 July 1848, CA5/O16, CMS.

30. H. A. Fosbrooke, "An Administrative Survey of the Masai Social System," *Tanganyika Notes and Records* 26 (December 1948): 9.

31. Rebmann, journal entry, 11 May 1848, CA5/O24, CMS; Krapf, journal entries, 12 September 1848 and 16 March 1852, CA5/O16, CMS; Krapf, *Travels,* 236, 360–61.

32. Krapf, journal entry, 12 September 1848, CA5/O16, CMS.

33. Krapf, *Vocabulary,* 4–5.

34. Krapf, journal entries, 30 November 1849 and 7 August 1851, CA5/O16, CMS; Krapf, *Vocabulary,* 30–31; for Kopekope, see Krapf, *Travels,* map after 554, and Joseph Thomson, *Through Masai Land* (London: Sampson Low, Marston, Searle, & Rivington, 1885): 369.

35. Krapf, *Vocabulary,* 9, 30.

36. Ibid., 28; Krapf, *Travels,* 399.

37. Ibid., 20–21; Krapf, *Travels,* 399.

38. Krapf, journal entry, 25 March 1845, CA5/O16, CMS.

39. Krapf, journal entry, 30 August 1853, CA5/O16, CMS.

40. Krapf, journal entry, 16 November 1848, CA5/O16, CMS; see also Krapf, *Travels,* 199; Richard Burton, *Zanzibar: City, Island, and Coast,* 2 vols. (London: Tinsley Brothers, 1872; reprint New York: Johnson Reprint Corporation, 1967), 2:63–64.

41. Krapf, journal entry, 11 October 1847, CA5/O16, CMS.

42. Krapf, journal entry, 20 July 1848, CA5/O16, CMS.

43. Rebmann, "Account of a Journey to Madshame," p. 12, CA5/O24, CMS.

44. Erhardt, journal entry, 1 May 1854, CA5/O9, CMS.

45. Erhardt, journal entries, 26 November 1853 and 1 May 1854, CA5/O9, CMS; Erhardt, "Memoire," 21.

46. Krapf, journal entry, 1 March 1852, CA5/O16, CMS.

47. Erhardt, journal entry, 8 November 1853, CA5/O9, CMS.

48. Erhardt, journal entries, 6 September 1853 and 28 July 1854, CA5/O9, CMS.

49. Erhardt, journal entry, 1 May 1854, CA5/O9, CMS; Krapf, journal entry, 27 March 1852, CA5/O16, CMS.

50. Rebmann, journal entry, 9 May 1848, CA5/O24, CMS.

51. Krapf, journal entries, 9 November 1849 and 14 November 1849, CA5/O16, CMS.

52. Rebmann to Venn, 15 January 1855, CA5/O24, CMS.

53. Erhardt to Venn, 13 April 1855, CA5/O9, CMS.

54. Rebmann to Venn, 18 April 1855, CA5/O24, CMS.

55. Rebmann to Venn, 18 April 1855, CA5/O24, CMS.

56. Rebmann to Venn, 23 March 1857, CA5/O24, CMS.

57. Burton, *Zanzibar,* 2:70–71.

58. Rebmann to Venn, 23 March 1857, CA5/O24, CMS.

59. Rebmann to Venn, 19 April 1858, CA5/O24, CMS.

60. Rebmann, "Rough Sketch of a Map," 22 September 1848, CA5/O24, CMS; Krapf, journal entry, 22 August 1851, CA5/O16, CMS.

61. Rebmann, journal entry, 13 May 1848, CA5/O24, CMS.

62. Rebmann, journal entries, 13 and 27 May 1848, CA5/O24, CMS.

63. Rebmann, "Account of a Journey to Madshame," 1849, p. 14, CA5/O24, CMS.

64. Krapf, *Travels,* 271; Rebmann, journal entry, 27 April 1848, CA5/O24, CMS.

65. Krapf, *Travels,* 271; Erhardt, journal entry, 12 August 1853, CA5/O9, CMS.

66. Krapf, journal entries, 16 and 22 November 1849, CA5/O16, CMS.

67. Krapf, journal entry, 13 July 1848, CA5/O16, CMS.

68. Krapf, journal entry, 19 July 1848, CA5/O16, CMS; Krapf to Secretaries, 27 October 1847, CA5/O24, CMS.

69. Rebmann, journal entry, 9 May 1848, CA5/O24, CMS.

70. Charles New, *Life, Wanderings, and Labours in Eastern Africa* (London: Hodder and Stoughton, 1873); 3rd ed. (London: Frank Cass & Co., 1971), 75–76.

71. Thomson, "Through the Masai Country to Victoria Nyanza," *Proceedings of the Royal Geographical Society* 6 (1884): 691–92, 698.

72. Harry Johnston, *The Kilimanjaro Expedition* (London: Kegan Paul, Trench, and Co., 1886; republished Farnborough, England: Gregg International Publishers Ltd., 1968), 65–66.

73. Krapf, journal entry, 14 July 1848, CA5/O16, CMS.

74. T. Wakefield, "Routes of Native Caravans from the Coast to the Interior of Eastern Africa," *Journal of the Royal Geographical Society* 40 (1870): 303, 306, 308.

75. New, *Life, Wanderings, and Labours,* 459, 469–70.

76. J. T. Last, "The Masai People and Country," *Proceedings of the Royal Geographical Society,* 4 (1882): 225.

77. G. A. Fischer, "Dr. Fischer's Journey in the Masai Country," *Proceedings of the Royal Geographical Society,* 6 (1884): 77.

78. Thomson, "Through the Masai Country," 692.

79. J. P. Farler, "Native Routes in East Africa from Pangani to the Masai Country and the Victoria Nyanza," *Proceedings of the Royal Geographical Society,* 4 (1882): 731.

80. Ibid., 731.

81. Johnston, *Kilimanjaro,* 313.

82. Ibid., 405–08.

83. Ibid., 449.

84. Ludwig von Hohnel, *Discovery of Lakes Rudolf and Stefanie*, 2 vols. (London: Longmans, Green and Co., 1894; new impression London: Frank Cass and Co., 1968), 2:2–3.

85. Hollis, *The Masai: Their Language and Folklore* (Oxford: Clarendon Press, 1905), iii, 260.

86. Ibid., xi.

87. M. Merker, *Die Masai by Merker (An English Translation)*, private circulation, n.d., 2.

88. G. R. Sandford, *An Administrative and Political History of the Masai Reserve* (London: Waterlow & Sons, 1919), 8.

89. Fosbrooke, "Administrative Survey," 1, 4–5.

90. Alan H. Jacobs, "The Traditional Political Organization of the Pastoral Masai," (D.Phil. thesis, Nuffield College, Oxford, July 1965), 2–3.

91. Ibid., 20–21, 37–38.

92. Ibid., 31.

93. John Lawrence Berntsen, "Pastoralism, Raiding, and Prophets: Maasailand in the Nineteenth Century," (Ph.D. diss., University of Wisconsin-Madison, 1979), 45–46.

94. Ibid., 47–48.

95. Richard Waller, "The Lords of East Africa: The Masai in the Mid-Nineteenth Century (c.1840–c.1885)," (Ph.D. thesis, Darwin College, Cambridge), June 1978, 25, 28, 137.

96. Ibid., 89–90.

97. Ibid., 138–39.

98. Ibid., 136–37.

12

INTERPRETING CASES, DISENTANGLING DISPUTES: COURT CASES AS A SOURCE FOR UNDERSTANDING PATRON-CLIENT RELATIONSHIPS IN EARLY COLONIAL LAGOS

Kristin Mann

On 17 February 1879, a Lagosian named Jose sued another named Jinadu Somade in the Supreme Court of the British Colony of Lagos to recover possession of a house and land and establish title to them. Two months later, Jinadu Somade sued a man named Seidu Ebite in the same court to recover a debt of £106.13.6. A month after that, three men, Oruoloye, Abuduranomi, and Amore, sued Jinadu Somade to recover possession of the land at issue in the first case.[1]

Max Gluckman taught us twenty-five years ago that in African societies, as elsewhere, overt legal conflict usually represents but a moment in an ongoing relationship among the participants.[2] The antecedents of the three interrelated cases referred to here stretched back to 1862, when the British allowed the former-Ọba Kosoko, whom they had deposed and driven into exile a decade before, to return to Lagos. A man named Seidu Ebite accompanied Kosoko home. The sources reveal little about Seidu's origins, but judging from his lack of kin in Lagos and subsequent experiences, he was probably a slave belonging to Kosoko or a member of Kosoko's entourage. On reaching the colony, Ebite left Kosoko, taking advantage no doubt of the weakening of owners' control over their slaves that immediately followed the British annexation.[3] Seidu Ebite and another man, Jinadu Akiola, probably also a former slave, lived and traded together as "partners" for about a year.

In early colonial Lagos, as in Nigeria today, persons obtained access to resources, opportunities, and assistance through different kinds of relationships with men and women richer, more powerful, and better connected than they.[4] By leaving Kosoko, Seidu Ebite undercut any claim to the help of the former Ọba or his close supporters. Evidently, Ebite and Jinadu Akiola found living and working on their own more difficult than they had expected, because at the end of their first year back in Lagos, they divided their profits and adopted the course of many other Lagos slaves who ran away from their owners. They constructed a patron-client relationship with a man, Jinadu Somade, whom they hoped would help and protect them, in return for labor and support.[5] The three cases referred to here grew out of conflict between Seidu Ebite and his patron Jinadu Somade.

Seidu Ebite may have chosen Jinadu Somade as his patron because Somade was not only a man of substance, but also a slave of Aṣogbon, a powerful chief and influential supporter of the reigning Ọba, Dosunmu. By constructing a patron-client relationship with Jinadu Somade, Seidu Ebite forged a path to Aṣogbon and through the chief to the Ọba himself.

Kosoko and Dosunmu's father and predecessor, Akitoye, had in the 1840s and 1850s led rival political factions in Lagos. Akitoye had himself reclaimed the throne after a period of exile by playing on British hostility toward Kosoko and helping to convince the local British consul and Royal Navy to depose Kosoko and install him as king.[6] After Akitoye's death, leadership of the Ọba's faction and hatred of Kosoko passed to Dosunmu, along with the crown of Lagos. Once confronted with protecting the integrity of his office and domain, however, Dosunmu's relationship with British representatives in the Bight of Benin deteriorated. Soon after the British annexation of Lagos in 1861, Acting Governor J. H. Glover wrote of Dosunmu,

> [he] is both a rogue and a fool. . . . I would venture with all respect to suggest . . . that Her Majesty's government impress upon him the fact that he was not a king of Lagos by his own right or might and that the same power that placed his father as king of Lagos and who at his father's death . . . made him king against the wish of his chiefs had the full right to unking him. . . .[7]

Kosoko's relationship with British officials improved, on the other hand, in part because he and many of his followers adapted readily to changes in trade and government that Britain was promoting.[8] Still, Dosunmu occupied the throne and Kosoko did not. By breaking with Kosoko and constructing a patron-client relationship with Jinadu Somade, Seidu Ebite had not only redefined his identity but also transferred his allegiance from the faction out of power to the one in power.

Patron-Client Relationships in the Political Economy of Nineteenth-Century Lagos

Yoruba-speaking peoples from the nearby mainland first settled the island of Lagos. Located at the confluence of an important network of waterborne trade routes, their town soon acquired commercial importance. The kingdom of Benin, to the east, established an outpost at Lagos in the sixteenth century and founded a new ruling dynasty, from which came the subsequent Ọbas. Families that descended, according to tradition, from the sons of the original Yoruba-speaking ruler retained ownership of the land on the island and nearby mainland. Religious, administrative, and military titles evolved, and many of them became hereditary within particular lineages.[9]

Around the turn of the nineteenth century, Lagos became an important port in the Atlantic slave trade. Lagosians did not capture most of the slaves exported from the town, but rather acquired them through trade at inland markets and transported them to the coast by canoe for sale to foreigners. Participation in the slave trade greatly enriched the Ọba, selected chiefs, and a few favored commoners and slaves. Members of this group used their increased incomes to amass large retinues of wives, children, clients, and slaves above all. During the era of the slave trade, slavery became a much more important means of organizing labor in the community than it had been before, although the labor of wives, children, and clients also remained important. The elite also invested heavily in canoes, guns, and gunpowder, which it employed along with slaves, clients, and kin, in lagoon warfare as well as trade. The vast households of the Ọba and leading chiefs required provisioning, and while Lagosians bought much of their food in the marketplace, big men and women also established farms worked by their dependants.[10]

The growing wealth and power of the Ọba and his supporters provoked conflict between them and certain Lagos chiefs over the distribution of political authority. Soon after this concluded to the Ọba's advantage in the late eighteenth century, there began a half-century of royal succession disputes, which culminated in the contest between Kosoko and Akitoye. These protracted political rivalries erupted periodically into civil war between claimants and their factions. The political support and military service of slaves and clients, as well as of kin and affines, shaped the balance of power in these contests.[11]

Different kinds of patron-client relationships existed in precolonial Lagos. With slavery, they provided a means of mobilizing non-family labor and support. In a community where access to opportunities and entrée into fundamental political and legal processes depended on representation by a well-connected member of the local political elite, all Lagosians but the Ọba and most powerful chiefs needed patrons. In return for interceding on behalf of clients, patrons demanded allegiance and support. Clients of this kind were known in Yoruba as *aláàgbàsọ,* which literally means one who has somebody to plead one's cause.[12] *Aláàgbàsọ* received limited material assistance from their patrons, and they had no rights to land or houses belonging to them. Although *aláàgbàsọ* contributed labor and gifts to their patrons on special occasions, such as the building of a house or staging of a funeral, they did not work for them on a regular basis.[13]

Non-kin commonly lived in and formed part of the households of prominent men and women. Persons from Lagos itself sometimes left their families and went to live with others because they or their kin believed that by doing so the individuals could acquire skills, knowledge, or contacts that would help them and their families. Residential clients of this type, known as *aláàbagbé,* were not regarded as "homeless and like dependent children." Although they could expect assistance from their patrons, they normally had limited rights in their benefactors' land, housing, and other material resources. Patrons, on the other hand, enjoyed clear rights to draw on the *aláàbagbé*'s skills, labor, and support when they were needed. *Aláàbagbé* also normally gave their patrons regular gifts from the fruits of their labor.

Strangers, who came to Lagos from elsewhere and had no kin in the town, commonly made a place for themselves there by constructing a different kind of patron-client relationship. Through an intermediary, they obtained an introduction to a wealthy and influential man or woman and asked to serve that person. If the big man or woman agreed, the client was supposed to receive clothing, food, housing, protection, and assistance as needed, in return for regular labor and support. "Homeless and like dependent children," clients of this kind, known locally as *asáforígẹ,* enjoyed rights to occupy their patrons' land and housing. *Asáforígẹ* were more commonly male than female, in part because women were in great demand as wives and concubines and thus enjoyed other means of entering households. Patrons often promised that if male *asáforíge* served them faithfully and well they would one day help the men marry and provide them the resources to begin working for themselves. A contemporary described as follows the relationship between patrons and male *asáforíge*, commonly called "boys" in English:

> The native law and custom with our boys in relation to us is for them to live with us in the house or compound and we feed them, clothe them, treat them as if they were our own family, but pay them no wages, as should they require money we dash them some. If they conduct themselves well, we get them wives and give them money to start for themselves. If they behave badly, we send them away without anything. In return for this, they do our work and go to market or where we wish them to go.[14]

Evidence internal to the court cases cited above indicates that Seidu Ebite constructed this type of relationship with Jinadu Somade.

After the British annexation, patron-client relationships took on new significance in Lagos. Slaves who wanted to leave their owners but could not flee the colony and did not have the resources to live on their own commonly obtained a place to live and limited physical and economic security by becoming *asáforíge* of patrons. Runaway slaves from the interior who reached the British colony also entered such relationships. The foreign slave trade from Lagos ended in the 1850s after the expulsion of Kosoko. It was replaced by the rapid growth of a new export trade first in palm oil and later in palm kernels. The value of the palm produce trade from the Bight of Benin quickly surpassed that of the slave trade. This burgeoning new commerce greatly increased the demand for labor in Lagos, because the commodities traded were bulky and had to be transported from the interior and stored and handled in Lagos prior to sale to exporters.[15] Moreover, factions remained a fact of political life in Lagos, ensuring the continued importance of commanding large numbers of followers.[16] The big and growing demand in Lagos for labor and political support, coupled with the existence in local culture of a type of patron-client relationship that enabled persons of wealth and power to harness the labor and support of freeborn dependants, provided slaves an alternative to remaining with their owners. Entrepreneurs who wanted to take advantage of new opportunities in the vegetable products trade found in patron-client relationships a means of mobilizing non-family labor at a time when slavery was slowly coming to an end and wage labor had not yet developed. Clientage absorbed many former slaves in Lagos.[17] The literal meaning of the term *asáforíge* captures the importance of this type of dependant in the expanding commercial economy of late-nineteenth century Lagos. The noun is constructed from the verb *ge*, which although no longer in current usage was once slang for porterage. The noun itself can be translated as "one who hurries to tote [loads] with the head."[18]

That many slaves chose to leave their owners and become *asáforíge* of patrons indicates where they thought they would be better off. Some acted, no doubt, on the basis of a careful assessment of the advantages and disadvantages of different kinds of labor relationships; others out of a hatred of slavery and/or their individual owners. But in leaving their owners to serve patrons, slaves were not gaining freedom. They were simply exchanging one relationship of subordination for another. Most *asáforíge* were little better off than many slaves. Indeed, they were in certain respects more vulnerable, because *asáforíge* normally had weaker rights to their patrons' resources than slaves did to their owners'.

Patron-client relationships of all kinds involved reciprocal exchanges in which both parties gave and received something. While norms existed that affected the obligations of different kinds of patrons and clients to one another, the precise responsibilities of each to the other were often contested and negotiated. Patrons and clients fought over exactly what they owed one another. Despite an element of reciprocity, patron-client relationships were unequal. Seeking to prove that he was not a client, a witness in a court case testified, "I was not a boy under Otibo. We lived as equals."[19] Over the long term, the transfer of resources and labor between patrons and clients generally favored patrons. As J. D. Y. Peel noted of the exchanges between chiefs and followers in Ilesha, "a certain portion of the resources won by the labor power . . . of . . . clients had to be retained . . . as a kind of capital for investment in the maintenance and extension of the [patron's] position."[20] While a degree of redistribution was necessary to retain the support of clients, patrons enriched themselves at the expense of their clients. The relationship between patrons and *asáforíge* was normally more unequal, however, that than between patrons and *aláàbàso* or *aláàbagbé*. *Asáforíge* could make claims on landed property and other family-owned resources that *aláàgbàso* and *aláàbagbé* normally could not. However, they also experienced much heavier demands for labor and enjoyed less autonomy.

In practice, the boundaries between slaves, *asáforíge*, *aláàbagbé*, and *aláàgbàso* were not always clear. Actors sometimes deliberately blurred identities. In most instances, it was preferable to be an *aláàgbàso* or *aláàbagbé* than a slave or *asáforíge*. If one was trying to sustain a claim to land or housing, however, there were advantages to being a slave or *asáforíge*. Moreover, relationships of dependence could change. Slaves and *asáforíge* could accumulate resources, establish households of their own, and become *aláàgbàse* of their owners or patrons. Oshodi Tapa, for example, began life in Lagos as a slave of Ọba Osinlokun. But he amassed great wealth and power and eventually made a transition from being an *aláàgbàse* of Osinlokun's son Kosoko to becoming his closest advisor, who enjoyed all the privileges of freebirth and was awarded a chieftaincy title.[21] Owners and patrons commonly benefited when slaves or clients built power bases of their own. This was the case because patrons could make claims on the dependants of their clients, just as owners could on those of their slaves.[22] Clients of all kinds sometimes became sufficiently wealthy and powerful that they threw off allegiance to their patrons. Chief Aṣogbon, for example, served for a time as the patron of a man named Taiwo Olowo. But in the 1880s, Taiwo asserted independence of Aṣogbon.[23] In addition, slaves and *asáforíge* were sometimes incorporated into the families of their owners or patrons by living permanently in their households and carrying out the obligations of kin.

Clients could have multiple patrons, although not all of them had the same importance or performed the same functions. Moreover, clients could transfer their allegiance along with their labor and support from one patron to another, if they believed that by doing so they would be better off. The intense competition that existed in Lagos for workers and political supporters ensured mobility. The fact that clients could move from one patron to another gave them a measure of choice and leverage. It served as a check on the patrons' demands, and it meant that they could not wholly ignore their responsibilities to their clients. Yet the variation among patrons was not great, and as a consequence the options open to *aláàbagbé* and *asáforíge* were limited. Furthermore, patrons often opposed clients who tried to switch their allegiance.

Law, Custom, and the Social Order

Important anthropological and historical research has explored the link in Africa between changes in law and in the wider social order.[24] These studies have shown that, contrary to the belief of early social scientists and colonial administrators, African law was not immutable tradition but a dynamic historical formation shaped by specific processes of economic, social, and political change. During the colonial period, for example, Africans and

Europeans acting out of beliefs and interests of their own used law as a weapon in conflicts over resources, labor, and authority. These contests often found their way into colonial courts, and they played out in other arenas as well, such as debates over legislation.[25] Their outcome shaped the colonial social order across the continent.

In the course of legal conflict, actors constructed moral arguments about the past. Research has shown that they often did so based not on the way things had been but on how they wanted them to be.[26] Contestants invoked custom—a particular representation of the way things had been before—partly because they understood that to render colonialism feasible both economically and politically, European administrators had committed themselves to ruling through indigenous authorities.[27] European officials believed that to uphold the power of local authorities in the face of the profound social and economic changes unleashed by colonialism, they needed to preserve traditional property and labor relationships, except when they were repugnant to "justice, equity, and good conscience." In the colonial context, invocations of custom served as powerful arguments supporting particular positions. Furthermore, as Chanock has shown, during the colonial period Africans often responded to change not by looking forward to a world of money, employment, and individualism, but by harkening backward to ideas and relationships they already knew. He concluded, "People grappled with the present not in terms of ideas about the future, about which they knew nothing, but in terms of ideas about the past, recast in the heat of present experiences."[28] In both instances, custom—the way identities, relationships, and institutions had been in the past—was contested and fought over. As some representations predominated and were enshrined first in legal precedent or colonial legislation and later in law codes, an African customary law was invented, which bore little relationship to indigenous precolonial law.[29]

Contributors to a useful anthology on the place of history and power in the study of law divide over the theoretical question of whether understanding of legal change should be rooted in investigation of social process or cultural meaning.[30] The theoretical debate manifested itself in different approaches to the study of law. Some authors adopted a cultural approach, examining discourse about rules and procedures; others favored an interactional approach, asking how individuals and groups use legal processes for their own ends. Still others advocated institutional research, which focuses on economic and political processes and treats actors as representatives of economic interests and laws as manifestations of ideological positions. The editors of the anthology conclude, "There seems to be no way to resolve these fundamentally different stances toward how 'objective' reality is constituted."[31]

A body of work by sociolinguistic and psychological anthropologists treats legal conflict as but one kind of a broader category of cultural activity, disentangling, in which people attempt to straighten out "tangled" relationships. Disentangling activities range from interpersonal gossip to village meetings, from courtroom encounters to ceremonial activities. On these occasions, actors seek solutions through talk and non-verbal communication to interpersonal conflicts and moral dilemmas. Research on disentangling shows that in the process, they pose and counterpose interpretations of events, contest identities and ideas, negotiate the premises on which they act, and create the realities in which they live. The talk during disentangling events is often avowedly moral and emotional. It enables us to glimpse persons as moral actors engaged in dialogue with significant others that shapes and reshapes identities and relationships, indeed culture itself. Watson-Gegeo and White demonstrate that whether the aim of disentangling is an authoritative statement on a contested issue or emotional rapprochement, the process requires constructing collective, and often contested, images of self and community through interaction with others.[32] One of the strengths of the disentangling approach is that it bridges the divide between studies of social process and cultural meaning, revealing how talk has the power to transform the course of conflicts, the meaning of individual and communal identities, the character of social relationships, and the shape of the social order.

Armed with insights from these two bodies of research, the remainder of this paper analyses the three cases involving Jinadu Somade and Seidu Ebite for what they reveal about the conflict between the two men. It focuses on the cultural logic behind the way events, identities, and relationships are represented in the arguments of each man. In the process, the analysis illuminates how the relationship between *asáforíge* and patrons was changing in the increasingly commercialized, monetized, and stratified world of late nineteenth-century Lagos. I have selected the cases not at random, but because they represent recurring themes in contests between *asáforíge* and patrons during the closing decades of the nineteenth century.

British colonial supreme courts were formal settings guided by bodies of law and rules of procedure that shaped not only what was communicated within them but also how it was communicated.[33] To be sure, participants in trials sometimes ignored or, perhaps more commonly, were ignorant of laws relevant to their cases. Moreover, they occasionally bent or broke rules of courtroom behavior and imposed their own stamp on proceedings.

In the end, court talk was shaped by both the dictates of the setting and the agency of individual actors. Yet legal ideas and courtroom procedures both established limits within which courtroom communication normally occurred. Therefore, analysis of the three cases investigated here must begin by situating them in the context of the court where they occurred. My interpretation of what was said in court moves back and forth between a close reading of the courtroom records and social and cultural information derived from extended research on the history of Lagos, a method advocated by both Sally Falk Moore in her work on Chagga customary law and Watson-Gegeo and White in their study of disentangling.[34] I bring data external to the texts to bear on an analysis of them.

The Courtroom Context

The Lagos Supreme Court was created in 1876, three years before it heard the cases examined here, to replace a number of earlier British courts. The Supreme Court was presided over by a British judge, and it was supposed to hear all criminal cases and civil ones involving claims of £25 or greater. Civil suits involving lesser claims went to a Magistrate's Court. The Treaty of Cession left the Ọba the right to settle disputes among his people, subject to appeal to British law. Officially recognized Native Courts did not exist in the town of Lagos, but the colonial government tolerated the intervention of the Ọba, chiefs, and elders in what it interpreted as civil conflicts.[35]

Records of the Lagos Supreme Court reveal that a surprisingly broad spectrum of the population brought cases to it. Although male, propertied, and western-educated Lagosians are over-represented among those initiating cases, poor, illiterate, and female Lagosians sometimes brought suits as well. To initiate a case, an individual needed to approach the Registrar of the Court, an office held from 1876 to 1899 by an influential educated African, John Augustus Otonba Payne.[36] Persons of low social status sometimes approached the registrar through more powerful patrons. Locally trained lawyers commenced representing clients in Lagos in the early 1860s, and after 1880, British-trained barristers began working regularly in the colony.[37] Wealthy or educated litigants often hired lawyers to represent them in court, but others usually appeared without legal counsel.

The court framed conflicts in terms that conformed to British law. When the person initiating the case was represented from the onset by legal counsel, the attorney may have formulated the claim and the relief sought to the registrar. But when Africans approached the registrar without counsel, I suspect that they often expressed their grievances in more open-ended language and the registrar then formulated the claim in terms that could be adjudicated in a British law court.

Once a case had been initiated, a date was set for its hearing. The court then served notice, through the sheriff, for the defendant to appear along with the plaintiff.[38] The old Supreme Court building no longer survives. It was located at Tinubu Square, in the heart of the new town, about a half-mile as the crow flies from the Ọba's palace, at the center of the indigenous community. To date, I have discovered neither photographs nor descriptions of the interior of the courtroom.

The court proceedings began when the court was called to order, all present in the courtroom rose, and the judge entered dressed in a British wig and robe. The clerk of the court named the plaintiff and defendant in the case and stated the claim as entered in the docket by the registrar. The judge then asked for the defendant's plea, which was always entered in the record as a response of but a few words. Next, the judge invited the plaintiff to state his case, which was done in narrative form, sometimes briefly and sometimes at great length. English was the language of the court, but African plaintiffs, defendants, and witnesses normally spoke in local languages, usually Yoruba but occasionally some other, except when western-educated. As the judges rarely spoke Yoruba, let alone other African languages, what litigants and witnesses said frequently had to be translated for them. A government interpreter performed the translation, and his control over language in courtroom must have given him great power. The judge created a written record of the case, in English, for use in appeals and to satisfy British notions of good government. The record was not a transcript, but rather it consisted of very detailed notes of what was said, sometimes including quotations. In short cases, the judge's record covered but a few paragraphs. In long ones, it stretched to many closely written foolscap pages.

When plaintiffs were represented by counsel, their lawyers undoubtedly coached them about what to say. When they were unrepresented, they structured their talk themselves or with the advise of kin, patrons, friends, or the African registrar or clerks of the court. If there were multiple plaintiffs, one among them usually spoke for the rest. The others were sometimes called upon to speak later in the trial. The judge could interrupt the plaintiff's statement with questions, which had to be answered. When the plaintiff had finished speaking, the defendant or his attorney was given an opportunity to ask questions. After these had been answered, witnesses for the plaintiff spoke, also in narrative form. The length of their testimony varied, and it too could be interrupted by questions from the judge. After each witness had finished, the defendant or his counsel was permitted to cross-question.

After the plaintiff's case had been stated, the judge occasionally ruled that insufficient evidence had been presented to warrant litigation, and the suit was dismissed. More commonly, however, the judge asked the defendant to present his case. Defendants spoke, also in narrative form, for varying lengths of time. As with the plaintiff, the judge could interject questions. When the defendant had finished, the plaintiff or plaintiff's lawyer could pose questions. Next, the defendant's witnesses spoke, and they too could be questioned by the judge and plaintiff or plaintiff's lawyer.

Cases were sometimes completed, with the judge rendering a decision, on the day they began. But trials often stretched over several days, and they were not uncommonly interrupted by breaks for one reason or another. Except when the judge ruled otherwise, the courtroom was open to the public.[39] Controversial cases attracted audiences, and the Lagos press covered trials it deemed newsworthy.

The Supreme Court was supposed to settle cases between "natives" according to "local law and custom," unless it violated the repugnancy clause.[40] When the judge was uncertain about the content of "native law," he called assessors to advise him.[41] The assessors were invariably older men, usually chiefs or traders, who the court believed could speak with authority about the issue at hand. As Chanock has noted, the privilege of advising colonial courts on the content of "custom" gave male elders power to shape customary law in their own interests.[42]

Interpreting the Cases

By 1879, Seidu Ebite had served Jinadu Somade for sixteen years. During the second of the three trials, Somade described the relationship between the two men as follows:

> I cared for [the defendant] and brought him anything he required. I fed and clothed him. I gave him no pay. It is not customary. I provided anything he wanted. I gave him a horse and a canoe. The horse died and I gave him another. . . . When the defendant married, I dashed him the expenses and bought a cloth for his wife and killed a bullock. I did not give him money, but I paid all the expenses. I never paid him wages, but if the defendant wanted money, if it was two bags I gave it him. I gave him plenty of things I

cannot name. There was no agreement. It was not customary when boys stay with a man who is [like their father] to make agreements. Wherever I sent him, he would go. The defendant could also send my children wherever he liked. He was in a place of confidence and trust.[43]

Somade referred to Ebite as his "canoeman," and witnesses for both sides also identified Ebite in that way. Ebite described his relationship with Somade saying simply, "The plaintiff sent me to market to trade for him as a boy."[44]

Ebite said during the second trial that the trouble between him and Jinadu Somade started when he pressed his patron to fulfill responsibilities to him. He argued that Somade had made much money from his trade. According to Ebite, Somade had promised to buy him land, give him a share of the profits, and put him in "a merchant's house to trade on his own account."[45] When Somade failed to keep these promises, Ebite refused to go to market for him again and threatened to summon him to colonial court for services rendered for so many years. Jinadu Akiola, Seidu Ebite's former partner, had also become an *asáforíge* of Jinadu Somade's. As a witness for Ebite, Akinola testified that he had left Somade several months before because "I worked for him and he never paid me. He promised me that if he got money he would buy a house for me and get me a wife. He did not do this."[46] Jinadu Somade apparently tried to placate Seidu Ebite by saying that trade was bad and he had no money. Ebite replied that Somade had "bought land and everything," and that he, Ebite, refused to "work more" for Somade until he was given his due.[47]

Seidu Ebite did not, in fact, summon Jinadu Somade before a colonial court, perhaps because he realized that he was unlikely to get what he wanted by doing so. Had Ebite laid his case before the Supreme Court, a British judge might have awarded him something for back wages. But Ebite's talk during the trials made clear that he did not want wages, the monetary equivalent of his labor. He wanted Somade to do what a good patron should: buy him land, give him a share of the profits, and help him go into business for himself. The Supreme Court did not enforce such customary obligations between big men and their boys. Ebite strove to become not a wage worker dependent for his livelihood on the sale of his labor, but a trader in his own right. In the end, Ebite pursued his grievance against Somade in a different manner.

In February 1879, a trader named Jose sued Jinadu Somade in the Supreme Court to recover possession of a house and land and establish title to them. Both men were represented by counsel, Jose by the European Allan McIver and Jinadu Somade by the locally-trained lawyer Charles

Foresythe. Jose argued that the land in question belonged to his deceased "father," Chief Wajoba, who during his life "gave it" to Seidu Ebite.[48] On questioning, the court established that Wajoba was in fact Jose's brother not his father. According to Jose, Ebite obtained the land during Wajoba's lifetime and built a house on it. Jose testified that the house belonged to Seidu Ebite, but that the land belonged to Wajoba and after his death devolved to his "relations." At the time of the trial, Jose said that Seidu Ebite was no longer living in the house, which was then occupied by Jinadu Somade's mother. "What I want to know," Jose asked the court, "is how it came into the hands of the defendant."[49]

On cross-examination, Jose testified that when he put this question to Seidu Ebite, he was told that in repairing the streets the government took the house of Jinadu Somade's mother. Seidu Ebite, at the time Jinadu Somade's boy, subsequently allowed the woman to stay in his house. When questioned by the court, Jose made the mistake of saying that he claimed the land for himself, his brother, and his sister, rather than for Wajoba's children. Called as a witness, Seidu Ebite told the court that Jinadu Somade had helped him build the house in order to store palm produce there and that the land "still belongs to Wajoba."[50] Ebite stated further that in Administrator Glover's time Jinadu Somade wanted to measure the property, commonly recognized as the first step in applying for a British crown grant to land. Crown grants were often interpreted as giving their holders rights of individual ownership in landed property and, if granted, would have transformed Somade's claim to the land. Seidu Ebite asserted that he had objected to the measurement and reported it to Jose, who insisted that any crown grant to the property would have to be in Wajoba's name. Cleverly, Ebite testified that the matter had been settled until recently, when Somade again called the surveyor to measure the plot, making it appear that Jose was bringing the suit simply to protect his family's rights to the land against encroachment by a man who was angry with Ebite. When asked why he did not live in the house, Seidu Ebite replied, "because I was the defendant's boy and if I had lived there alone, the defendant would have considered I was proud."[51]

The judge requested the advice of a number of assessors in the case: T. F. Cole, a Saro trader; Sunmanu Animaşaun, a Muslim trader; "Liemi," probably a misspelling of Layeni, a prosperous trader and former slave; and Odunbaku, whom I cannot identify. After hearing what they had to say, the judge dismissed the case on the grounds that the children of Wajoba, not Jose, were the proper plaintiffs.

Jose and Seidu Ebite had failed in their suit. What had Ebite tried to accomplish by it? He may have hoped that the threat of a lawsuit would convince Somade to live up to his obligations as a patron. If that was the case, his plan undoubtedly backfired, because the trial itself almost certainly so deeply alienated Somade that Ebite forfeited all hope of ever realizing what he believed his patron owed him. But Ebite may have had other motives. The relationship between Jose and Ebite before the case is unclear. If their story is to be believed, Ebite had once been some kind of a dependant of Wajoba, Jose's brother, from whom Ebite had obtained the land on which to build a house. By enlisting Jose's help in pleading his case, Ebite became the man's *aláàgbàsǫ,* if he had not been before. At the very moment that Ebite was ending an exacting patron-client relationship with Jinadu Somade, he was simultaneously, through the trial, constructing or consolidating another potentially less onerous one with Jose. In court, Jose attempted to secure title to the land on which stood the house occupied by Somade's mother. He argued that the house itself belonged to Ebite. Had Jose won the case, he might have allowed Ebite to live in the dwelling or provided him with a different house, redressing one of the man's grievances against Somade and bringing him a step closer to his apparent goal of economic independence. Furthermore, victory would have brought one clear triumph. It would have inconvenienced Somade's mother, who would surely have been ejected from her house, and it would have humiliated Somade himself. Lagos men placed a high premium on being able to take good care of their mothers, and had Somade's been turned out it would have reflected badly on him. At the same time, Ebite's strategy involved an element of risk. If Jose had won the case and put Ebite in the house, he might have proved every bit as demanding a patron as Somadę had been. As it happened, Jose failed in his suit, because the judge ruled that Wajoba's children, not his siblings, were entitled to the land.

Two months after the conclusion of the first case, Jinadu Somade responded by suing Seidu Ebite in the Supreme Court to recover a debt of £106.13.6, the value of goods Somade claimed to have sold Ebite. In this case, the two men contested not only whether Ebite was indebted to Jinadu Somade, but also the nature of the commercial relationship between them. Jinadu Somade, still represented by Charles Foresythe, began his testimony by trying to establish that Ebite was indebted to him. He submitted a passbook, A, of the kind that European merchants and some African traders used for recording transactions with customers who bought goods from them on credit. Somade claimed that his clerk had entered in the book the value of "all goods I gave the defendant to take to market," as well as of all produce that Ebite returned to pay for those goods.[52] Under such market-based arrangements, creditors traded on their own behalf. They realized any profit on the value of the produce returned over the cost of the goods taken, and they were responsible for any loss. Presumably, Passbook A showed a debt in Somade's favor, although the judge's notes did not say so explicitly. Next, Somade submitted his own passbook, B, from a German merchant, Mr. Escherick. This account showed, the plaintiff claimed, that he was indebted to Escherick for ninety heads of cowries. According to Jinadu Somade, Seidu Ebite had asked him "to buy" Ebite goods at Escherick's. Jinadu Somade said that he had told Ebite that he was indebted to the German for ninety heads of cowries and did not want to go to his shop until they were paid. Ebite purportedly offered to pay the debt, and when he did so, Somade claimed to have credited the amount in Passbook A. Somade said that he then took Ebite, along with Passbook B, to Escherick's and "recommended him to the agent with that passbook."[53] In this testimony, Somade presented himself as having stood surety for Ebite and enabled him to obtain goods on credit directly from the German merchant Escherick. Somade stated that he and the defendant had been together for sixteen years, but that the day he gave Ebite "Escherick's passbook was the last day he did business with me."[54] Presumably, Somade introduced the story about taking Ebite to Escherick's to show that in fact he had fulfilled his responsibility as a patron by helping his client establish an independent commercial relationship with a European merchant. Somade also signalled that he had pressed Ebite to repay the debt he owed Somade, only after his boy had left his service. Somade went on to argue that Ebite also owed him for eight palm oil casks, which Somade had given Ebite to use in trade and Ebite had never returned.

When it was Seidu Ebite's turn to speak, he denied any knowledge of Passbook A. He portrayed his commercial relationship with Jinadu Somade as the sort that normally existed between patrons and *asáforíge* or owners and trusted slaves. Ebite testified:

> The plaintiff sent me to market to trade for him as a boy. I received goods from the plaintiff who told me the price he got the goods for—what I sold them for I came and told him, and it was never entered in a book. If I took eight tons of salt which the plaintiff bought for £5 and I sold it for £8 of produce, I brought him the produce for £8.[55]

By this Ebite meant that he had not been trading on his own behalf, but as a representative of Jinadu Somade. He claimed that when his patron gave him goods to take to market, he neither kept any profit nor was liable for any loss. Ebite continued, "The plaintiff used to remunerate me by presents for my service. I never got into his debt."[56]

Ebite went on to argue that Jinadu Somade had given him the casks, a canoe, and Passbook B when he, Ebite, complained that his patron had not kept his promise to buy him land, give him a share of the profits, and help him set up on his own. Ebite said that the casks were old and that he had paid the cooper to repair them. Moreover, he claimed to have used the casks to bring oil from market for the plaintiff. Ebite implied that Somade had given him Passbook B to enable him to obtain trade goods at Escherick's on his own account, in an effort to retain Ebite's services as a boy. Ebite stated further that at about that time, he had begun getting goods "to go to market" for Fagbemi, another prosperous local trader, although he said nothing more about the terms of the new relationship. It was then, Ebite said, that Somade threatened to charge him for the empty casks, suggesting that his patron had done so to discourage him from trading with Fagbemi and retain control of his labor. Ebite concluded by remarking that after Somade gave him Escherick's "paper," the two men had no more transactions.[57]

Both men called witnesses whose testimony corroborated their stories. For reasons that are not clear, the court proceedings then ended abruptly. Ten months later, in February 1880, they resumed, only to be adjourned the same day to call from Little Popo, a town to the west, Jinadu Somade's clerk, who had allegedly kept Seidu Ebite's passbook. No further reference to the case appears in extant Supreme Court records, and it is likely that when the clerk never appeared it was not resumed.

How are we to understand the different representations of Jinadu Somade's and Seidu Ebite's identities and of the commercial relationship between them? On the face of it, the evidence favors Seidu Ebite. The trading relationship described by Ebite was more consistent with the patron-client relationship admitted by both men than was the contractual, monetized commercial relationship posited by Jinadu Somade. It is unlikely that a passbook recording debits and credits would have been kept if the patron-client relationship between the men was as Somade, himself, described it. In addition, a number of the statements made by Somade's witnesses are implausible, such as a remark that there was never any profit to enter in Passbook A for Ebite; that he lost money every single time he went to market.[58] Finally, the facts that the clerk, a key witness, never appeared for the plaintiff and that the case seems to have been allowed to drop prior to judgment suggest that Somade ultimately realized that he was not going to be able to sustain a case for indebtedness against Ebite in the British court.

But more important than who was telling the truth is what each side wanted to accomplish in this series of conflicts. After long service, Seidu

Ebite was attempting to redefine his relationship with Jinadu Somade by pressing him to fulfill what Seidu Ebite represented as the customary obligations of good patrons. Had Somade lived up to Ebite's expectations, Ebite would have been able to begin trading for himself, and, if he had been given land or a house, perhaps eventually to have established a household of his own. Both changes would have dramatically increased Ebite's autonomy and significantly reduced the demands that Somade could make on him for labor and support. When Somade refused Ebite's requests, Ebite enlisted Jose's help, and the two men commenced the first court case against Somade for the reasons that I have explained. Around the same time, Ebite also began exploring commercial and probably also other opportunities with another big man, Fagbemi.

Somade responded by seeking to monetize the commercial relationship between himself and Ebite. Drawing on the model of market-based trading relationships that then existed in the community, Somade ascribed a cash value to the goods and casks he had given Ebite for trade, as well as to the produce that Ebite had brought him in return. He attempted to prove by doing so that Ebite came up short. Somade apparently first tried this line of argument outside the colonial court, and when that failed, he hauled Ebite before the British authorities. Somade may have hoped, by charging Ebite with indebtedness, to frighten him off leaving his service and thereby to retain his labor. If that failed and Somade won his court case, he would at least receive a cash award that compensated him for the loss of his boy's labor and exacted a price from Ebite for challenging him. The charge of indebtedness had two more advantages. It implied that far from benefiting Somade, the overall exchange between the patron and client had really benefited Ebite. This strategy underscored Somade's generosity, as well as the dependence on him of his clients in general and Ebite in particular. Finally, it sent a message to other boys in Somade's service that they could neither desert nor challenge him with impunity. Somade did not attempt to recover the value of the food, clothes, horse, money, and bridewealth that he said he had given Ebite, because these were widely regarded as forms of support that good patrons owed their most trusted clients. And Somade was taking pains to show that he had in fact been a good patron.

In July 1879, another trader, Brimah Apatira, responded to efforts by three of his boys to redefine their relationship with him by ordering them to vacate a house that they occupied, which he said belonged to him. When they refused, he brought suit against them in the Supreme Court to recover possession of the house, establish title to it, and recover back rent. Apatira described his relationship with the men in terms very similar to those used by Jinadu Somade in discussing Seidu Ebite. But he went on to assert that the relationship between them was based on an exchange of labor for housing and was rooted in contract. He maintained that the men owed him rent, the monetary equivalent of their labor, for the period that they remained in his house but no longer worked to his satisfaction.[59] In the conflict between Jinadu Somade and Seidu Ebite, Somade tried to establish indebtedness and use credit as the instrument of control over Ebite. In the subsequent conflict between Brimah Apatira and his three boys, Apatira used ownership of land and a house occupied by his dependants as the mechanism of subordination. These two cases illustrate very well means that big men commonly employed in late nineteenth-century Lagos to discipline *asáforíge* and retain control of their labor and support.

If there was a wider purpose behind Somade's talk in court, there was behind Ebite's, as well. Ebite sought to show through what he said that Somade was not a trustworthy patron: after extracting sixteen years of loyal labor and service Somade had failed to help him set up on his own. Ebite had been one of Somade's senior boys, in charge of eight more junior ones. As Somade had said, he occupied a position "of confidence and trust" within his patron's household.[60] Somade had recently lost the service of at least one other boy, Jinadu Akiola, for failing to assist him satisfactorily. The trader must have been worried about the loyalty of his other *asáforíge*, as well as about his ability to attract and hold new clients. Disappointed in his aspirations and betrayed by the patron who should have been "like a father to him," Ebite struck a blow at Somade and perhaps stirred up the more junior boys in his service by broadcasting just what kind of patron Somade had been. While Somade and Apatira used the language of money and contract to pursue their grievances against their clients, the clients in both cases used the language of kinship in presenting their cases. Ebite and Apatira's boys likened patrons to fathers and clients to sons. They implied that the father-son relationship rested on an unbreakable moral bond, which could never be commoditized and given a cash equivalent.

Jinadu Somade and Seidu Ebite found themselves in court again in May 1879, about a month after the second case began, when Oruoloye, Abuduranami, and Amore, the children of Chief Wajoba, sued Somade to recover possession of the land at issue in the first case. The plaintiffs argued, much as Jose had before them, that their father had allowed Ebite to build a house on the property, but that the land belonged to them. The house, they said, was a matter between the defendant and Ebite. Somade countered that the land had belonged to him for fourteen years. He asserted that he bought a portion of it, asked Chief Wajoba for another portion, and obtained a third portion from a man named Adesina. Somade claimed that he built the house on the land, and that his boys, excluding Ebite, lived there until five years ago when he put his mother in the house. Somade argued that when he asked Ebite to pay him the money he owed, Ebite "set up a claim to the ground."[61] The plaintiffs, he concluded, are "friends" of Ebite's. The court then called Ebite, who repeated in shortened form the argument he had made in the first case: Wajoba had given him the land to build on; he and Jinadu Somade were trading together and built the house jointly; Somade's mother went to live in the property with Ebite's consent. The assessors, carried over from the first case and themselves important patrons, advised the judge that as Ebite had allowed Jinadu Somade to build on the land and as Somade had been in possession for the past fourteen years, they believed that Somade was justified in retaining possession of the land. The judge followed the advice of his assessors and ruled in Jinadu Somade's favor. Ebite had failed in his second effort to drive Somade's mother out of the house and strike a blow at his patron.

Conclusion

In the precolonial period, clients had doubtless sometimes struggled to renegotiate their relationships with their patrons to their own advantage. The fact of conflict between big men and their *asáforìgẹ* was not new in the 1870s. Political and legal changes in the colonial period, however, gave both big men and their boys new opportunities to try to redefine the relationship between them. The creation of colonial courts introduced new and alien authorities to whom patrons and clients could appeal for support in conflicts with one another. Locals did not necessarily know how British judges would respond to particular kinds of cases or lines of argument. Colonial law was complex and emerged slowly as the courts dealt with specific cases. Moreover, the courts did not always decide cases consistently. Lagosians used the courts to try out, through their talk, different means of transforming identities and relationships. They experimented in court with discourse to discover the boundaries of the new social order that Britain was imposing.

The Lagos Supreme Court provided an arena where locals could not only contest custom but also invoke ideas growing out of the commercialization and monetization of the local economy. Thus Brimah Apatira introduced into his arguments about his relationship with his boys notions of rent, contract, and monetary equivalents then developing in the community, and Seidu Ebite introduced ideas of credit, debt, and monetary equivalents. Talk in court about the substance of these and other identities and relationships helped give them form. Both by creating a venue where constituting talk could occur and by lending its weight to particular interpretations of identities and relationships, the Supreme Court played a role in shaping them.

Notes

1. *Jose v. Jinadu Somade*, 17 Feb. 1879, *Jinadu Somade v. Seidu Ebite*, 17 April 1879, and *Oruoloye, Abuduranomi, and Amore v. Jinadu Somade*, 13 May 1879, Vol. 2, pp. 97, 102, 110, Judges' Notebook in Civil Cases (hereafter JNCC), Lagos Supreme Court Records, High Court, Lagos State, Lagos, Nigeria.

2. Max Gluckman, Introduction, in *The Craft of Social Anthropology*, ed. A. L. Epstein (London: Tavistock, 1967), xvi. See also Sally Falk Moore, *Social Facts and Fabrications: "Customary" Law on Kilimanjaro, 1880–1980* (Cambridge: Cambridge University Press, 1986), 169.

3. Kristin Mann, "Owners, Slaves, and the Struggle for Labour in the Commercial Transition at Lagos," in *From Slave Trade to "Legitimate" Commerce: The Commercial Transition in Nineteenth-Century West Africa*, ed. Robin Law (Cambridge: Cambridge University Press, 1995), 144–71.

4. J. D. Y. Peel, *Ijeshas and Nigerians: The Incorporation of a Yoruba Kingdom, 1890s–1970s* (Cambridge: Cambridge University Press, 1983); Sara Berry, *Fathers Work for Their Sons: Accumulation, Mobility, and Class Formation in an Extended Yorùbá Community* (Berkeley: University of California Press, 1985); Richard A. Joseph, *Democracy and Prebendal Politics in Nigeria: The Rise and Fall of the Second Republic* (Cambridge: Cambridge University Press, 1987); Sandra T. Barnes, *Patrons and Power: Creating a Political Community in Metropolitan Lagos* (Bloomington: Indiana University Press, 1986).

5. Mann, "Owners, Slaves, and the Struggle," 159–66.

6. Sir Alan Burns, *History of Nigeria*, 8th ed. (London: George Allen and Unwin, 1972), 115–20; J. F. Ade Ajayi, "The British Occupation of Lagos, 1851–1861, a Critical Review," *Nigeria* 69 (1961): 96–105; Robert S. Smith, *The Lagos Consulate, 1851–1861* (Berkeley: University of California Press, 1979).

7. Glover to Newcastle, 10 Aug. 1863, CO 147/4, Colonial Office, Original Correspondence, Lagos Colony (hereafter CO 147), Public Record Office, Kew. See also Smith, *Lagos Consulate*, 66–133.

8. McCoskry to Russell, 4 Oct. 1861, 5 Dec. 1861, and 7 Jan. 1862, CO 147/2.

9. On the early history of Lagos see John B. Losi, *History of Lagos* (Lagos: Tika Tore Press, 1914); A. B. Aderibigbe, "Early History of Lagos to About 1850," in *The Development of an African City*, ed. A. B. Aderibigbe (Ikeja: Longman, 1975); Smith, *Lagos Consulate*, 1–17; Robin Law, "Trade and Politics behind the Slave Coast: The Lagoon Traffic and the Rise of Lagos, 1500–1800," *Journal of African History* 24 (1983): 321–48; B. A. Agiri

and Sandra Barnes, "Lagos before 1603," in *History of the Peoples of Lagos State,* ed. Ade Adefuye, Babatunde Agiri, and Jide Osuntokun (Ikeja: Lantern Books, 1987), 18–32.

10. Law, "Trade and Politics"; Ade Adefuye, "Ọba Akinsemoyin and the Emergence of Modern Lagos," in *History of the Peoples of Lagos State,* 33–46; and Kristin Mann, "The World the Slave Traders Made: Lagos, c. 1760–1850," in *Identifying Enslaved Africans: The "Nigerian" Hinterland and the African Diaspora,* ed. Paul E. Lovejoy, Proceedings of the UNESCO/SSHRCC Summer Institute, York University, Toronto, 14 July–1 August 1997, 182–254.

11. Robert S. Smith, "The Canoe in West African History," *Journal of African History* 11 (1970): 526–32; Robin Law, "The Career of Adele at Lagos and Badagry, c. 1807–1837," *Journal of the Historical Society of Nigeria* 9 (1978): 35–59; Smith, *Lagos Consulate,* 2–17; Adefuye, "Ọba Akinsemoyin"; Mann, "The World," 201–29.

12. R. C. Abraham, *Dictionary of Modern Yoruba* (London: University of London Press, 1958), 236.

13. Information about patron-client relationships in Lagos comes from interviews with A. L. A. Ojora, 5 Nov. 1984, S. B. A. Oluwa, 23 Jan. 1985, and A. W. A. Akibayo, 5 Feb. 1985, all of which were conducted in Lagos. I am also indebted to Sandra Barnes, for correspondence on this subject, 7 May 1991. For a brief published discussion of the subject see A. G. Hopkins, "A Report on the Yoruba, 1910," *Journal of the Historical Society of Nigeria,* 5 (1969): 77–78.

14. *Omotoso v. Seidu Owolu,* July 1881, JNCC, Vol. 3, p. 298.

15. C. W. Newbury, *The Western Slave Coast and its Rulers* (Oxford: Clarendon Press, 1961); A. G. Hopkins, *An Economic History of West Africa* (London: Longman, 1973), 130–46; Martin Lynn, *Commerce and Economic Change in West Africa: The Palm Oil Trade in the Nineteenth Century* (Cambridge: Cambridge University Press, 1997), 43, 65–68, 138–57; David Eltis and Lawrence C. Jennings, "Trade between Western Africa and the Atlantic World in the Pre-Colonial Era," *American Historical Review,* 93 (1988): 936–59.

16. Patrick D. Cole, *Modern and Traditional Elites in the Politics of Lagos, 1884–1938* (Cambridge: Cambridge University Press, 1975); Kristin Mann, "The Rise of Taiwo Olowo: Law, Accumulation, and Mobility in Early Colonial Lagos," in *Law in Colonial Africa,* ed. Kristin Mann and Richard Roberts (Portsmouth, N.H.: Heinemann, 1991), 98–99.

17. Mann, "Owners, Slaves, and the Struggle," 159–64.

18. Oyekan Owomoyela, Department of English, University of Nebraska, Lincoln, 12 April 2001.

19. *Chief Eletu Odibo v. Seidu Salako,* 29 June 1882, JNCC, Vol. 5, p. 11.

20. Peel, *Ijeshas,* 44.

21. Losi, *History,* 82–83; interviews in Lagos with Durojaiye Olajuwon Oshodi, 10 Jan. 1974, and Mobolaji Oshodi, 25 Feb. 1985. See also Sandra T. Barnes, "Ritual, Power, and Outside Knowledge," *Journal of Religion in Africa,* 20 (1990): 248–68.

22. For an interesting statement regarding the rights of owners in slaves owned by their slaves see *Alaka v. Alaka,* 23 Jan. 1904, *Nigeria Law Reports,* Vol. 1, pp. 55–56.

23. Mann, "Taiwo," 99.

24. Martin Chanock, *Law, Custom, and Social Order: The Colonial Experience in Malawi and Zambia* (Cambridge: Cambridge University Press, 1985); Moore, *Social Facts*; Kristin Mann and Richard Roberts, eds., *Law in Colonial Africa* (Portsmouth, N.H.: Heinemann, 1991).

25. Joan Vincent, "Contours of Change: Agrarian Law in Colonial Uganda, 1895–1962," in *History and Power in the Study of Law,* ed., June Starr and Jane Collier (Ithaca, N.Y.: Cornell University Press, 1989), 153–67.

26. Chanock, *Law, Custom*; Moore, *Social Facts*; Richard Roberts and Kristin Mann, Introduction, in *Law in Colonial Africa,* ed. Mann and Roberts, 3–58.

27. Sara Berry, *No Condition is Permanent* (Madison: University of Wisconsin Press, 1993), 22–42.

28. Chanock, *Law, Custom,* 22.

29. Ibid.; Moore, *Social Facts*; Roberts and Mann, Introduction.

30. June Starr and Jane Collier, eds., *History and Power in the Study of Law* (Ithaca, N.Y.: Cornell University Press, 1989).

31. Ibid., 21.

32. Karen Ann Watson-Gegeo and Geoffrey M. White, Introduction, in *Disentangling: Conflict Discourse in Pacific Societies,* ed. Karen Ann Watson-Gegeo and Geoffrey M. White (Stanford: Stanford University Press, 1990), 3–49.

33. Roberts and Mann, Introduction, 41.

34. Moore, *Social Facts,* 11–12; Watson-Gegeo and White, *Disentangling,* 3–4.

35. T. O. Elias, *The Nigerian Legal System* (London: Routledge and Kegan Paul, 1963), 67–93; Omoniyi Adewoye, *The Judicial System in Southern Nigeria, 1854–1954* (Atlantic Highlands, N.J.: Humanities Press, 1977), 18, 25–26, 45–52; Smith, *Lagos Consulate,* 140.

36. T. O. Elias, *Law in a Developing Society* (Benin City, Nigeria: Ethiope Publishing, 1973), 24–29.

37. Adewoye, *The Judicial System,* 108–10.

38. Elias, *Nigerian Legal System,* 76.

39. Supreme Court Ordinance, No. 4, 1876, Schedule I, Order 5, reprinted in George Stallard and Edward Harrison Richards, *Ordinances, Orders and Rules . . . in Force in the Colony of Lagos on December 31st, 1893* (London: Stevens and Sons, 1894), 18–135.

40. Supreme Court Ordinance, 1876, s. 19.

41. Ibid., s. 92.

42. Martin Chanock, "Making Customary Law: Men, Women, and Courts," in *African Women and the Law: Historical Perspectives,* ed. Margaret Jean Hay and Marcia Wright (Boston: Boston University Papers on Africa, 1982), 7:67.

43. *Jinadu Somade v. Seidu Ebite,* 102.

44. Ibid., 103.

45. Ibid., 104.

46. Ibid., 106.

47. Ibid., 104.

48. *Jose v. Jinadu Somade,* 97.

49. Ibid., 97.

50. Ibid., 99.

51. Ibid.

52. Ibid., 102.

53. *Jinadu Somade v. Seidu Ebite,* 102.

54. Ibid.

55. Ibid., 103.

56. Ibid.

57. Ibid., 104.

58. Ibid., 107.

59. *Eshubi, alias Brimah Apatira v. Oso, Opeluja, and Ogudula,* 14 July 1879, JNCC, Vol. 2, p. 129. For a fuller analysis of this case see Mann, "Owners, Slaves, and the Struggle," 160–64.

60. *Jinadu Somade v. Seidu Ebite,* 102.

61. *Oruloye, Abuduranami, and Amore v. Jinadu Somade,* 110.

13

CAPRICIOUS TYRANTS AND PERSECUTED SUBJECTS: READING BETWEEN THE LINES OF MISSIONARY RECORDS IN PRECOLONIAL NORTHERN NAMIBIA

Meredith McKittrick

On September 21, 1881, the Finnish Lutheran missionary Martti Rautanen reported in his diary that Sheya sha Namutenya, chief minister to Kambonde, king of Ondonga in modern-day northern Namibia, had died of a chronic abdominal illness. He continued, "Some eight days before his death a man was accused of witchcraft and killed. A woman was supposed to undergo the same fate, but she still had time to flee." Nearly three weeks later Rautanen wrote, "Yet another man, Uusiku ua Nepaya, an owner of a large homestead, was shot dead on account of Sheya while he slept. O! Cruelty without measure!"[1]

Decades later, an Ndonga man training to become a pastor wrote of the same time period:

> I don't know my father. My father was killed when I was three years old. He was killed by king Kambonde Nehoya. The king himself did not kill my father, but the man who killed my father was sent by the king. It was a process of raiding. My father and I were sitting by the fire in the morning, warming our bodies, when the people from the king's house came to our house. I don't know the story; I tell it according to what I was told. My father was also one of King Kambonde's *omalenga* [advisers]. When the killers came to our house, they pretended to be peaceful. I was sitting in my father's lap when the gunmen killed my father.[2]

219

By far the richest written documentation on the nineteenth-century history of much of Africa was produced as a result of mission endeavors. The Ovambo communities of northern Namibia and southern Angola, of which Ondonga was one, are no exception. The archival sources left by the Finns who dominated the Ovambo mission field include diaries, annual reports, correspondence, several published ethnographies, collections of proverbs and photographs, and a massive body of ethnographic fieldnotes from the 1930s, some written by literate, Christian Ovambo and the rest transcribed by a missionary who interviewed older Ovambo men in the local language. Also within these archives are records written by Ovambo, primarily male seminary students writing in the 1930s and 1940s about their lives and stories their parents told them.

Regardless of authorship, mission records from Ovambo communities in the late nineteenth and early twentieth centuries portray a population traumatized by the random violence of kings and aristocrats. Terror was described as a feature of everyday life and the source of massive insecurity and instability. Missionaries wrote of women accused of witchcraft because they had rejected the sexual advances of powerful men, of property and people seized on the flimsiest of pretenses so kings could buy alcohol and firearms, of executions and bodily mutilations. The Finnish Mission Society's archives are hardly unique in this sense; similar tales emerge from the nineteenth-century records of missions around sub-Saharan Africa.

Such accounts echo a bit too closely for most scholars' comfort colonial stereotypes of savage Africa. And historians—particularly those not interested in religious change—have grown increasingly skeptical of nineteenth-century European sources. They argue that mission and explorers' reports of violence and instability were propaganda meant to legitimate both evangelization and imperialism.[3] Outside of historical studies of Christianity and Christianization, therefore, the recent tendency has been to read mission records as texts more revealing of European attitudes than African realities. The statements of missionaries themselves certainly encourage such a reading. As a German Lutheran missionary (who later became a colonial official in South West Africa) wrote in his published 1911 account after describing how a suspected witch was tortured and executed:

> The above is yet another illustration of the much-praised "idyll of the heathen," which so many "experts" on the African peoples refer to even today in their attempts to discredit missionaries as disrupters and destroyers of this idyll. In Uukwanyama [a kingdom north of Ondonga and the base of his mission], numerous people accused of being *ovalodi* [witches] are murdered in the above manner every day.[4]

Again, this passage is remarkable only for its ordinariness; it could have been written by missionaries of any nationality in virtually any part of the continent.

The skepticism which greets missionary sources is perhaps an understandable reaction to the credulousness with which they have been and sometimes still are treated. From Roland Oliver, who wrote of the "missionary invasion" of East Africa, yet faithfully treated evangelists' most horrific accounts of African violence as representative of the place and time, to Marcia Wright, who argued that narratives missionaries collected from slaves and refugee women were representative of a much larger population, many academic histories have viewed the writings of missionaries—and those of explorers, missionaries' pioneering counterparts—as virtually unmediated representations of reality.[5]

In recent years, those who have used mission sources as evidence of more than European attitudes have typically straddled this division. They have recognized that Europeans had reason to exaggerate the degree of insecurity in African societies, yet at the same time have used European records to argue that the late nineteenth century *was* a particularly insecure time across much of the continent.[6] There is a real tension in much of this work, relying as it does so heavily on sources whose credibility it simultaneously challenges.

The different genres contained within mission archives share a common origin in that their production was initiated by missionaries. But missionaries did not produce mission records by themselves. In this sense, the creation of mission archives has much in common with the creation of Christian communities within Africa. It has become a truism in mission studies that Christianity in Africa was spread not so much by missionaries as by African evangelists, who acted as mediators (or "translators," as some would have it) between an imported religion and a local context. A whole host of motives are attributed to these evangelists, but it is no longer considered acceptable to see them as brainwashed and riddled with false consciousness. And yet scholars have proved reluctant to recognize the process in reverse: that information about African societies was frequently collected by Africans—not always the same people who were disseminating Christian ideas—and fed back to the missionaries. The emphasis has rather been on what happened next: missionaries selecting and shaping this information into accounts which either justified their cause (and sometimes the cause of would-be imperialists as well) or coincided with their own understanding of African societies.

Yet mission records, while not representing "reality" per se, are nonetheless products of both a European *and* an African context—and they thus provide a valuable window into African societies in the earliest years of mission endeavors. The value of this cannot be overstated. Missionaries frequently preceded colonial officials, and their records are often our first substantial body of written material for sub-Saharan societies; indeed, often their records contain more substance than later colonial records, since missionaries usually had better command of local languages and interacted with a wider variety of Africans than colonial administrators.

Missionaries did not, however, witness everything they reported. They had informants with motives and agendas of their own. Perhaps those informants realized that missionaries were interested in certain kinds of tales, but they nonetheless made decisions about what to tell and how to portray it. The context in which all stories were produced left a great deal of room in the shaping of the details. And unraveling those processes of shaping and selection, made many times over by many different informants, can tell us a great deal indeed about nineteenth-century African societies.

Carolyn Hamilton, in her discussion of the production of images about the Zulu king Shaka, notes that scholars who argue that historical images of Africa are simply the products of early European explorers and colonials acting unilaterally assume "that nineteenth-century Africans were without an intellectual history of their own and that they were unable, or at least failed, to produce history in the service of complex ideological objectives worthy of comparison with their European neighbors. . . ." She then notes that some of the most horrific stories of Shaka's abuses originated among Zulu dissidents.[7] The same problems plague the treatment of nineteenth-century missionary sources. Historians have focused on the agendas of Europeans rather than investigating the agendas of those Africans who provided Europeans with information.

Early African converts to Christianity were subordinate partners in the mission enterprise. It could thus be argued that to some extent converts told missionaries what the latter wanted to hear. This would imply a process of selection dominated by Europeans even when information was transmitted from Africans to missionaries. However, it is important to realize that not all, or even most, missionary informants were converts or people who intended to convert. Finnish and German Lutheran missionaries in northern Namibia carefully cultivated friendships and alliances with a variety of people, from kings, headmen, and other prominent citizens to their immediate neighbors. Their sources of information cut across lines of religious, political, and economic affiliation. While anyone seeking favor with missionaries would have hoped to please them, and therefore taken into account what would most interest missionaries, this is not tantamount to claiming that Africans played no independent role in the production of these stories. The type of violence they recount, the alleged perpetrators, and the supposed causes of the violence all originated within local understandings of morality and just and unjust uses and abuses of power. As such, they provide insight into debates that took place within African communities in the nineteenth century—debates which otherwise are obscured from view—and can be read as a form of local intellectual history.

Portraying an Insecure World

Finnish Lutheran missionaries arrived in northern Namibia and southern Angola in 1870 (they eventually left their few bases in southern Angola) and baptized their first local converts in 1883. They were joined briefly by German Lutherans from the 1890s to 1915, when South Africa took the territory from Germany and expelled German missionaries. While other mission societies—particularly the Oblates of Mary Immaculate and the Anglican Church—later established stations in the area, Finnish Lutherans were always the largest presence by far, and most Ovambo today are Lutheran.

The sources left by these early missionaries are rife with vivid descriptions of violence. In 1896, Martti Rautanen wrote in his diary of an aristocrat who accused three of his wives of bewitching him; two were killed and one had her eyes cut out and her fingers amputated instead—the latter punishment, according to Rautanen, was a perversion of custom: she had managed to grasp the leg of the king, thereby guaranteeing her immunity from execution. In another case, an Ndonga man reportedly had his hands and upper lips cut off at the order of the local headman, while a missionary published a photograph of a woman whose ears had been amputated.[8] In some cases, people summoned to appear before the court were said to have committed suicide instead.[9]

By another missionary estimate, the king of a relatively small community to the west had more than 40 people killed as witches in 1910. In 1915, a woman who had been accused years earlier of bewitching the king's mother and had fled the kingdom dared to return for a visit and was strangled—even though the king's mother was then in good health. Missionaries said she had been framed by a diviner for refusing to surrender a young female dependent to an aristocrat's demands for sexual services.[10]

Other sources echo these accounts. Proverbs and riddles collected by missionaries detail perceived corruption among the palace elite, who sent courtiers to rob and kill unsuspecting and innocent people. The brief autobiographies of some early converts—all men in ordination classes—contain some of these themes as well. The man whose father was killed by the king's men as he warmed himself before a fire one morning spent his childhood fleeing repeatedly with his mother from kingdom to kingdom due to accusations or impending raids from the palace.[11] Another recounted his youthful obsession with amulets and other magical devices designed to protect him equally from witchcraft and from the plundering expeditions of the king's men.[12]

These narratives are different from the life stories used by Marcia Wright. Like hers, they were not intended for publication in Europe; they are in handwritten notebooks in the Finnish Mission Archives. Their primary purpose seems to have been to prompt reflection among those aspiring to the pastorate. Filipus Uusiku, whose father was murdered, opens his narrative thus: "This booklet is asking me to talk about how I spent my pagan days, how I became a Christian, and how I spent my Christian days. I am asked by the head of the mission to talk about myself. I am happy to do that." Unlike Wright's stories, however, these stories do not end with the authors finding safety and refuge at mission stations; most of the men place their initial exposure to Christianity near the beginning of their stories, portraying a constant movement between mission station and "pagan" village, between the straight and narrow road of Christian living and "reversion" into heathenism—along with forays into labor migration, service at the palace, and so forth. The end point of most of these stories is the moment at which they are writing for their ordination classes. These are still stories of the ultimate triumph of Christianity, but they do not so clearly delineate boundaries between an insecure, pagan world and a secure, Christian one.

Another important difference rests in the authors' social standing. While the narrators in Wright's stories were women and people who had been marginalized through enslavement, the male authors of these stories, that first group of Ovambo pastors, descended largely from the elite and had not been slaves. Their parents and uncles were of royal birth or were royal advisers; they grew up among their relatives; they were, by and large, children of the more important and economically prosperous people in society.

If these stories are accurate depictions of the level of insecurity in the lives of the relatively privileged in Ovambo communities, what were the lives of the poor and enslaved like? And how representative are these mission accounts of violence and what, exactly, do they represent? As a way of beginning to answer these questions, it is worth examining two additional missionary quotes. The German missionary Tönjes, after mocking those who romanticized "idyllic" Africa, then proceeds:

In former times, I was told, this superstition was not as widespread as it is today. The chiefs are largely to blame, since they still have the power to decide whether or not a person accused of being an *omulodi* [witch] is to be killed. However, each time they grant permission, they receive one head of large stock, and for this reason they will not withhold their approval.[13]

Albin Savola, a colleague of Martti Rautanen in Ondonga, recounted in a published account a time when King Kambonde tested a diviner's skill: The diviner drew stripes in the dust, and the king was to associate with each stripe a person who might be a witch—"and usually they are very wealthy." The king secretly "named" a stripe after his mother and the diviner pointed to that stripe—thereby inadvertently accusing the king's mother of witchcraft. "Kambonde became very angry, and drove the witch [diviner] out. To save his life, the witch had to escape to another kingdom. During his escape, he went to complain about his misery even to the person writing these lines."[14]

In both of these passages, something seldom transparent is revealed: the process by which missionaries learned about events and relationships in the society around them. Tönjes' use of the passive tense obscures the identity of his own informant(s), while Savola makes it clear that he heard this story secondhand from someone who felt aggrieved at a loss of status. Particularly in diaries, missionaries often mentioned their sources of information, recounting the visits of local villagers, people seeking missionary intervention with the palace or some sort of material aid, and a variety of headmen and other elites who came to share coffee, pipes, dinner, and conversation on a regular basis. It is here, then, that we should turn our gaze if we want to understand the origins of the stories missionaries told. What relationship do stories of violence and witchcraft have not just to missionaries' own world and their evolving view of Africans but to local ideas about violence and power?

Moralities of Violence

From the time of their arrival in Ovamboland, missionaries peppered their correspondence, reports, and diaries with examples of the power of some people to kill or harm others. Missionaries sometimes noted, with little interest, forms of violence they knew from home: husbands' violence toward wives; violence between two drunken men; violence emerging out of romantic triangles or legal disputes. They dwelled longer on forms of violence, especially killing, which seemed novel to them. Children born to uninitiated girls were killed at birth because they were believed to threaten the lives of their relatives and the king. Twins born to royal families were supposedly killed for the same reason (although this did not always happen). Ceremonial war leaders captured by those they attacked were killed to render the aggressors harmless. Oral traditions recounted other stories never recorded by eyewitnesses: of uninitiated pregnant girls themselves being killed, of their lovers being killed, of ritualized cannibalism during warfare and human sacrifices to make rain and bury kings, and of cruel kings being assassinated by their subjects.

All of these forms of violence are still remembered in oral tradition. They posit a morality of violence, centered on the well-being of the community, whose parameters could shift in different contexts. Those whose death could save the lives of many could justly be killed; thus the murder of Ombalantu king Kampaku, probably in the early nineteenth century, is represented within Ombalantu as justifiable because he caused famine, killed his advisers, and far exceeded his legitimate powers. Strangers—such as warriors—whose open, physical aggression threatened the community, also could be killed. Yet more threatening than warriors or cruel kings were those who caused harm in ways not visible, through their behavior and actions or through their simple existence. The very invisibility of this chain of harm, via unseen forces or spirits, rendered people uniquely vulnerable, and those who threatened others in this way forfeited their humanity. Thus, for example, children of uninitiated girls—and often the girls themselves— were seen as something other than human, and their lives were rendered less valuable, their deaths less troubling.

But it was another type of violence that most captured the European imagination: punishment for witchcraft. In the late nineteenth century, it appears repeatedly in written accounts and garners the most editorial commentary of any form of violence.[15] People were tortured and killed for bewitching headmen, wealthy people, royal wives, royal advisers, and the king himself; often more than one person was held responsible for a single instance of misfortune. A person who stood to gain from a death was more likely to be accused than an impartial bystander; thus the wealthy often found themselves targeted. Missionaries also were accused of witchcraft: in 1885, Catholic missionaries recently arrived to southern Angola were among those executed following the death of the Kwanyama king.

The persecution of witches is remembered in oral tradition, but with a significant difference. The kings who are remembered as diligently pursuing witches ruled long ago. In these stories, witches are among the people who caused harm to the society at large by invisible means, and a king who killed witches was usually portrayed as one who strengthened the kingdom, protected his or her subjects, and guarded the community's health. In this context the killing of witches was comparable to other examples of sanctioned murder in the society.

By situating justified witchcraft persecution in the distant past, these oral traditions essentially argue for a distinction between early kings who hunted witches to protect their subjects and the massive witchcraft accusations of the late nineteenth and early twentieth centuries. Many of the kings who ruled in the decades immediately before colonial conquest[16] were recalled in early traditions as greedy robbers; even those viewed sympathetically were said to have been unable to stop others in the society from killing and plundering with abandon. Ovambo informants told missionaries witch-hunting had become more common in recent years; but their traditions hint at a difference that is also implicit in European accounts. These later accusations were almost always prompted by the sickness or death of a wealthy person. People believed the wealthy were more likely objects of the jealousy and greed which motivated witches, but the wealthy also had the means to pay diviners high fees to hunt witches—and by the late nineteenth century they did so only to benefit themselves, rather than the larger society. The years of rinderpest, when poor people's cattle died but elite herds were vaccinated by missionaries, yielded astonishingly few recorded witchcraft accusations; the same is true of the Great Famine of 1914–16, when thousands died but the elite were rarely among them.

The link between witch-hunting and wealth in the latter half of the nineteenth century speaks to a society which was rapidly stratifying in the context of a long-distance trade in horses, guns, alcohol, and other commodities. Kings controlled this trade and raided their neighbors to obtain the resources to purchase such goods; they also lavishly rewarded the elites who led the raids. This process escalated in the mid-1870s and 1880s. Ivory supplies vanished rapidly before the onslaught of firearms and horses, forcing rulers to extract cattle and slaves from others to pay traders. The need for these resources expanded steadily as these same rulers became more dependent on imported commodities to maintain and expand their power. Indeed, it is difficult to separate the frequency with which Ovambo rulers terrorized their subjects from their involvement in long-distance trade. When Martti Rautanen recorded the belated execution of a man accused of Sheya's death he did so in the passive tense, thereby obscuring the identity of the perpetrator. But just three days earlier, Rautanen noted the arrival of a Portuguese trader who sold large quantities of brandy to King Kambonde.[17]

Over the next few years, frequently only hours or a day separated the naming and execution of witches and the sale of slaves to Portuguese traders in exchange for alcohol. This was due partly to the erratic behavior that accompanied royals' drunken binges after the traders visited, but the connections were more complicated than this.

In the mid-1880s and beyond, the accounts of violence in missionary and explorers' writings begin to change. The quantity of recorded internal violence rose sharply as kings—and increasingly, their ever more autonomous advisers and relatives—initiated raids against their own subjects, justified on the grounds of treason, usually in the form of bewitchment. Accusing wealthy people of witchcraft and killing them or selling them into slavery was a quick way to seize a quantity of property, and it is striking how often the accused were elites rather than the poorer members of society. But the poor also were accused on a regular basis, and it seems likely that the heightened pursuit of witches was due in part to the kinds of catastrophes that were affecting the region—a variety of ills that had no indigenous explanation because they were new. Long-distance trade was part of a process of incorporation into not just the world economy but also the world disease environment. Bovine pleuropneumonia (lung sickness), rinderpest, and human afflictions such as syphilis, tuberculosis, and alcoholism and its related physical devastations were introduced to or became more common in Ovambo societies at this time. Many of these diseases affected the wealthy disproportionately—because they had the largest herds, because they could afford alcohol, and because they could demand sexual access to more women. In 1886, when the Ndonga king's brother-in-law had syphilis, robbery, murder, and flight were rampant.[18] Over the years, alcohol abuse led to early, seemingly sudden deaths among many important men, including several kings. Many places saw a series of short reigns and a string of monarchs and important headmen dying in their early twenties. Each incident precipitated the persecution of witches.

Compounding the insecurity of the elite was the increasing tendency of the population to resist the predations of rulers. People moved en masse between kingdoms or left the settled area altogether and formed small, well-defended communities in formerly vacant lands.[19] Others joined the church, hoping to gain security through the missionaries. The amount of scheming and autonomy among people close to the court increased dramatically, so that kings heard accusations of disloyalty, true or otherwise, on a daily basis. The decentralizing tendencies which existed alongside kingship meant that the power to command death lay in the hands of more people than just the king: royal relatives were notorious for pronouncing the death penalty, and diviners had considerable power over who was labeled a witch. The result was an extended series of accusations not just within the palace but among a whole network of royal households scattered across the community, so that through the 1880s and 1890s missionaries reported executions at least monthly; many more doubtless took place outside their purview.

In the face of both popular discontent and centrifugal forces, kings insisted upon their legitimacy by claiming ever greater rights to inflict violence on their own subjects. Their competitors—advisers, headmen, and members of their own family—laid claims to power in the same way. Raiding expanded dramatically, and the misfortunes which sparked witch hunts among royals became increasingly trivial; in one case, an injury to the king's horse was supposedly sufficient to justify the execution of a wealthy man.[20] Not just death, but also bodily mutilation to the living which often resulted in death, demonstrated royal power over people's lives. So did a growing refusal on the part of royals to recognize other people's power: the case of the diviner who was exposed as a sham by King Kambonde is but one example. Another is the refusal of kings after the 1880s to accede to demands made by their subjects, usually female, who claimed to have communicated with God (a form of prophesy which apparently had carried great legitimacy and served as a check on royal powers in the past). After an Ndonga king threatened to kill a young woman who told him God had ordered him to stop killing his subjects, Missionary Savola noted with pleasure this new royal refusal to believe such claims and willingness to punish those who made them. He gave the mission credit for undermining such beliefs, without placing them in a larger context of struggles between royal claims to power and the claims made by ritualists and others. Yet this is almost certainly how those who related the stories would have understood them.[21]

Violence and insecurity were not limited to the large eastern kingdoms with the greatest exposure to traders; even those areas with more limited access to European commodities were affected. Missionaries had a much more sporadic presence in the smaller western communities, but oral histories amply attest to insecurity there as well. A woman born in Uukolonkadhi was captured by raiders from Uukwambi, together with her mother and sisters. She was sent to a royal household while the others were sold to Portuguese traders; she never saw them again. One informant's father was captured in a raid on his small noncentralized community and given to the Ngandjera king's son as a slave. In the east, a young girl witnessed the beating death of a man accused of stealing food while another lost her father to armed robbers. Across the region, informants moved with their families when famine forced them to rely on the goodwill of distant relatives or were sent to live elsewhere when parents died or were killed.[22]

The elite were no less mobile. Several informants were children of important men who fled to neighboring kingdoms when they were accused of disloyalty and witchcraft, and Kwaluudhi oral traditions in the west claim that one late nineteenth-century king cut off his subjects' limbs, lips, tongues, ears, and breasts as punishment—an interesting, if more dramatic, counterpart to the stories missionaries told about eastern monarchs.[23]

The life stories of people born between the 1870s and 1915 are filled with enslavement, expulsion, flight, deprivation, and assassination. While security is of course a Christian trope, and while one might expect to find it in conversion narratives, it is nonetheless a trope that resonates with local perceptions of the past, and people insist that those attached to the missions were only marginally more secure.[24] While some missionary tales were undoubtedly exaggerated, it would be a stretch to argue that missionaries simply invented all the stories they reported. These were not born of whole cloth, but rather were created by a variety of people over time. On the whole, oral tradition and the limited written accounts by Ovambo support them.

The myriad stories of everyday and exceptional cruelties reached a fever pitch and moved outside the realm of royalty during the Great Famine of 1914–16. Missionaries and oral tradition recount mothers casting away or killing their children, legal complaints lodged on the flimsiest of pretexts in order to seize another's assets, marriage and families crumbling, neighbors and kin stealing from each other, and instances of cannibalism and other atrocities. In a region which held, at least in theory, that refugees could not be rejected—that is, that those suffering from want could not be turned away and that, concomitantly, that people were wealth—no one's position was safe. In Ombalantu, a society famed for embracing refugees and one which drew much of its ritual power and authority from neighboring Ombandja, residents supposedly denied food to 300 Mbandja refugees, including members of the royal family, imprisoning them and leaving them to starve, one by one.

Narratives of the famine show with particular clarity the way in which stories of the wrongful death of innocent people could symbolize a general sense of disintegration. Famine traditions of death and killing contrast with traditions that portrayed the death of problematic people—illegitimate children, witches—as necessary to protect others. Whether the stories of the famine are symbolic narratives or actual events, their power in memory and insistence in being retold across time and space flows from their ability to speak more broadly about the linkages between unjust killing and social disaster. The tales of the Great Famine are a form of social critique that defines what it means to be and to act human. During the famine, it is said, the starving were cast out to die like animals in the wild; the survivors became animals in other ways. People slept outside (being too weak to build huts), wore no clothes (having consumed their skins and bartered away their ornaments), and ate grass and other food more commonly consumed by creatures of the wild. They hoarded food from each other and ate alone; family relationships and friendships broke down. In the process, everyone lost a degree of their humanity.

Political Legitimacy and the Control of Violence

The Great Famine; the narratives it encompasses; and the ideas about life, death, and humanity embedded in those narratives suggest indigenous conceptions of the morality of death and the meaning of humanness. The tenacity of famine stories told across time parallels that of narratives of political killing that were repeated across time but also across space, extending from one household to another and finally reaching the ears of the missionaries.

Another clue to the motives of missionary informants can be found in the ways that human killing was treated within Ovambo belief systems and practice. It was never a matter to be taken lightly. A soldier who killed another in war committed a justifiable killing that earned him riches and a local reputation for bravery. But he also returned home polluted and making sounds like a canine predator. He had to undergo a series of ritual cleansings before he was permitted to rejoin human society and to sleep again in a house. Until that time, he ate alone and slept alone outside, as a wild creature might.[25] The murder of Kampaku, king of Ombalantu, has been remembered and retold for nearly two centuries, while detailed stories of contemporaneous kings in neighboring societies have long since been forgotten. The basic elements of the story have remained constant for at least 125 years; they revolve around justifying the murder as necessary to save the population from destruction. The need for such justifications is perhaps best understood in light of how neighboring populations regarded the Mbalantu in the late nineteenth century—"with horror," European travelers said, because they had committed regicide.[26]

Tremendous energy went into recognizing even those who were executed. In 1892, a missionary traveling between kingdoms watched as his companions paused by a heap of dirt and branches, each taking a branch, spitting on it, and laying it with the others. It was, they told him, the grave of a woman who had been executed; if they did not stop and recognize this event, her spirit would take its revenge on them.[27] Like the story of Kampaku, the insistence that those whose lives were taken by the king be remembered challenged royal claims to unrestricted powers over life and death. Such a challenge was more subtle than the acts of flight so common at the time, but it was perhaps also more potent by virtue of being woven into the fabric of the community, rather than demanding a break with that community. This was not a marginalized view of a discontented few; it was a tension inherent in political centralization which kings did not have the power to erase.

The treatment of a soldier who killed another in battle and of the graves of those killed by kings reflected a doubt that killing could ever be unproblematic, even if it was justified. It also insisted that murder was not simply a secular act, but also a sacred one with implications far beyond the visible, human world—not in the Christian sense of accountability in the next life, but in the sense that the secular and sacred aspects of life were intertwined in the here and now, rather than proceeding one after the other. This belief is hardly surprising, considering that the necessity of killing was itself often rooted in this same connectedness of the visible and invisible worlds.

What is often missing from mission and colonial readings of these accounts is a possibility that the trajectory of violence—and with it, conceptions of who had power over life and death—was changing in the late nineteenth century. The idea that one person had the power to kill another was never unconditionally accepted and was always troubling to people in the region. The death of a person, whether at the hands of a witch, by the power of a gun, or as a means to protect others, demanded elaborate ritualized responses even when deemed morally acceptable. Not everyone had an equal right to life, but there was nonetheless an ambiguity present in the idea that some could be killed. Indeed, to some extent tensions over who controlled life and death offered missionaries their first entrée into society. People came to missionaries when their own lives were at stake, or when they were troubled by what they saw happening around them. These people saw in missionaries a possible remedy to new configurations of power that they saw as problematic and, it is unlikely that missionaries discouraged informants from stating their grievances. At the same time, missionaries realized that while powerful men and women were unlikely converts, their goodwill was vital to mission work. And the many conversations between missionaries and kings or aristocrats gave the latter ample opportunity to tell stories that made their own power seem uncontested and well established.

Thus narratives demonstrating the "cheapness" of human life were prompted partly by uneasiness and discord over the expanding powers of some to take life. But while missionaries sometimes asserted that the scale of violence, if not the type of violence, was changing in the late nineteenth century, most Europeans did not conclude from this that something was amiss in the political landscape of Ovambo societies. Instead of historicizing the violence of the region, they drew upon a wide range of stereotypes about African "despots" in circulation by the mid-nineteenth century. They could only conclude that people had no rights under the indigenous legal system—thereby leaving them free to impose their own conceptions of rights, but also leaving them puzzled at people's constant resistance to European "protection."

Conclusion

Missionary records do not represent unmediated, objective "reality" any more than any historical document does. But the baggage they carry is considerably weightier than the preconceived notions of missionaries, and to read them simply through the lens of missionary agendas is to gravely oversimplify them—and to discredit them as sources of local history. Rather, missionary records were also shaped by the agendas of Africans who interacted with missionaries—which is to say a whole lot of people, ranging from kings to slaves and orphans.

In late nineteenth-century Ovambo communities, struggles over political centralization described in oral tradition intersected with two new forces: a raiding economy grounded in trade of cattle and humans for guns, horses, alcohol, and other consumer goods; and incorporation into a global disease environment which ravaged cattle herds and the families of the elite in particular. The result of the former was increased warfare, both external and civil, and expanded potential for mortality within war. The result of the latter was a search for causes and solutions that sparked waves of witch-hunting and witchcraft accusations. The result of both was insecurity and dislocation.

As elsewhere, oral traditions and early Ovambo autobiographies tend to mirror these accounts of violence to some degree, as do missionary diaries not intended for public consumption. Those aspects of missionary records that offer descriptions of African societies beyond the doings of missionaries and their converts represent far more than mission propaganda. To reject their claims out of hand because missionaries had an interest in publicly portraying African societies in as negative a light as possible and because they describe extraordinarily high levels of violence assumes certain things about African societies and African-mission interaction which remain unproven. It assumes, for example, that African societies *could not* have experienced the levels of violence described by missionaries, and that mission perceptions of African societies emerged in a void, divorced from anything happening around them.

Contrary to what missionaries thought, violence in Ovambo societies was neither a long-standing state of affairs nor simply the result of trade in European commodities. Kings and other aristocrats used violence to claim and demonstrate contested powers, and subjects recounted—and perhaps exaggerated—accounts of such violence as a way of challenging royal actions. Dissidents found a sympathetic audience in missionaries. Thus these accounts of violence reveal African perceptions and debates as well as European perceptions and debates.

In many parts of Africa, mission records are the earliest and most detailed written documents, and they are almost always the first documents written by Europeans who understood local African languages. Yet they remain underutilized except by historians focusing on mission history. This chapter has examined how these accounts of unrestrained violence can be read to reveal broader socio-political and intellectual histories. It has argued that missionaries were not just inventing or exaggerating events in nineteenth-century Ovambo communities and that the motives of Africans who were missionaries' sources for such stories have been disregarded.

Notes

1. National Archives of Finland (NAF), Helsinki, Martti Rautanen Diaries (MRD), 21 September 1881 and 10 October 1881.

2. NAF, Finnish Mission Society Archives (FMSA), Ha 2, life story of Filipus Uusiku. Translation by Fanuel Shingenge.

3. Such concerns are most clearly laid out in Julian Cobbing, "The Mfecane as Alibi: Thoughts on Dithakong and Mbolompo," *Journal of African History* 29 (1988): 487–519, and the ensuing debate about Cobbing's thesis, well represented in Carolyn Hamilton, ed., *The Mfecane Aftermath: Reconstructive Debates in Southern African History* (Johannesburg: Witwatersrand University Press, 1995). While this debate deals primarily with the accounts

of two non-evangelist explorers, the general skepticism toward nineteenth-century European accounts has also affected scholars' views of mission accounts—perhaps even more so, since these are frequently more abundant.

4. Hermann Tönjes, *Ovamboland: Country, People, Mission* (1911; reprint, Windhoek: Namibia Scientific Society 1996), 196.

5. Roland Oliver, *The Missionary Factor in East Africa* (1952; reprint, London: Longmans 1965); Marcia Wright, *Strategies of Slaves and Women* (New York: L. Barber Press, 1993) argues that the life stories of converts, despite being requested and transcribed by missionaries, are in fact reflections of unmediated "reality."

6. Just a few examples are Wright, *Strategies of Slaves and Women*; Steven Feierman, *Peasant Intellectuals* (Madison: University of Wisconsin Press 1990), especially chap. 4; Elizabeth Schmidt, *Peasants, Traders and Wives* (Portsmouth, N.H.: Heinemann, 1992), chap. 1; Patricia Hayes, "A History of the Ovambo, c. 1880–1930" (Ph.D. diss., Cambridge University, 1992). See also Robin Law, ed., *From Slave Trade to "Legitimate" Commerce: The Commercial Transition in Nineteenth-Century West Africa* (Cambridge: Cambridge University Press, 1995), whose essays deal with a "crisis of adaptation" to the abolition of the slave trade, and Mary Smith, *Baba of Karo* (New Haven: Yale University Press, 1981), especially part 1.

7. Hamilton, "'The Character and Objects of Chaka,'" in *Mfecane Aftermath*, ed. Hamilton, 185, 187.

8. Archiv der Vereinten Evangelischen Mission, Wuppertal (AVEM), Rhenish Mission Society (RMS), 1905 Annual Report, 240; Karl Angebauer, *Ovambo: Funfzehn Jahre unter Kaffern, Buschleuten und Bezirksamtmännern* (Berlin: A. Scherl 1927), photo preceding 161.

9. AVEM, RMS March 1892 report, 69.

10. NAF, FMSA, MRD June 16, 1915.

11. NAF, FMSA, Ha 2, autobiography of Filipus Uusiku.

12. NAF, FMSA, Ha 2, autobiography of Sakeus Iihuhua.

13. Tönjes, *Ovamboland*, 196.

14. Savola, *Ambomaa ja sen Kansa* (Helsinki: Suomen Lähetysseura, 1924), 186–87, translation by Niina Valtanen.

15. Like other Europeans, Finns would hardly have been strangers to notions of charges of and execution for witchcraft, since such procedures had been common in their country in the 16th-18th centuries.

16. South African forces formally set up a colonial administration in Ovamboland in 1915, while Portuguese forces conquered the northern kingdoms in the early 1910s. Though officially claimed by Germany and Angola from an earlier date, there was no effective colonial rule in the area until 1910.

17. NAF, MRD 7 October 1881. Although Portuguese traders were plying kings with alcohol and frequently buying slaves in return, Rautenen accepted a gift from this trader and offered one in return without commenting on any moral qualms he may have felt at his complicity in the trader's presence.

18. Gordon, "William Chapman Diaries," 140; NAF, MRD, 22 August, 1886.

19. P. Möller, *Journey in Africa Through Angola, Ovampoland and Damaraland* (Cape Town: C. Struik 1974), 95.

20. Savola, *Ambomaa*, 187.

21. Savola, *Ambomaa*, 170.

22. Stories of the lives of informants and their parents in the late precolonial period are detailed in Meredith McKittrick, *To Dwell Secure: Generation, Christianity and Colonialism in Ovamboland, Northern Namibia* (Portsmouth: Heinemann, 2002).

23. Viktor Lebzelter, *Eingeborenenkulturen in Südwest- und Südafrika* (Leipzig: W. Hiersemann 1934), 195; C. H. L. Hahn, *Native Tribes of South West Africa* (Cape Town: Cape Times 1928), 9; Oiva Shivute, interview by Fanuel Shingenge, Uukwandongo, Ongandjera, June 1996.

24. To be sure, all of them became members of the church. But this is not particularly revealing since virtually everyone in Ovamboland has converted. In months spent interviewing elderly people throughout Ovamboland, I met one man who had not been baptized and he was currently taking baptism classes.

25. Helsinki University Library, Emil Liljeblad Collection, mf 3, "Ontoni"; mf 26, "Ontoni."

26. P. Serton, ed., *The Narrative and Journal of Gerald McKiernan in South West Africa, 1874–1879* (Cape Town: The Van Riebeeck Society, 1954), 107; Archives of the Finnish Mission Society (Helsinki), K. Himanen, "Ehistori lj'Ombalantu," 9

27. AVEM, RMS, March 1892 report, 70.

PART IV

Oral Tradition

14

SECTION INTRODUCTION ORAL TRADITION: CLASSIC QUESTIONS, NEW ANSWERS

Dennis D. Cordell

Oral tradition, apart from being a source and resource for research on the African past, has a long history of its own in the historiography of the continent. The conventional narrative would hold that when faced with a dearth of written documentation representing "African points of view," the elders of African historical studies, like the ancestors of the Dogon, turned to the Word. Indeed this search for an "authentic" African history led the author to The University of Wisconsin in the 1970s, the decade after Wisconsin professor Jan Vansina published his classic *Oral Tradition: A Study in Historical Methodology.*[1] Similar efforts in Africa around the same time led African historians to collect and publish compendia of oral traditions, which, it was hoped, would provide a counterpoint to written documents—archives, memoirs, and ethnographical studies—associated with and tainted by European colonialism. Volumes such as B. A. Ogot's *A History of the Southern Luo*[2] indeed shed much new light on the history of African societies. Space does not permit an essay here on the historiography of oral tradition in African studies; nor is this an appropriate place for such an undertaking.[3] It is important to say, however, that the four chapters on oral tradition that make up this part of the collection are both descended from, and worthy of, the ancestral studies that preceded them.

The four chapters of this section fall into two pairs, each of which examines a related set of topics. The first pair, by Jan Jansen and Constanze Weise, focus on West Africa. They demonstrate in surprisingly concrete ways how historians and other social scientists may arrive at valid understandings of precolonial history through the careful analyses of oral traditions written down in the relatively recent past, contemporary narratives, ritual and performance, artifacts, and sites of memory. While being ever attentive to the questions of context and situation raised by postmodern and post-colonial studies over the last decade or so, they insist on, and show, that empirical knowledge of the African past may be derived from close analysis of oral texts and cultural forms associated with them.

In his provocative essay entitled "Narratives on Pilgrimages to Mecca: Beauty versus History in Mande Oral Tradition," Jan Jansen reviews several prominent scholars in the American tradition of Mande ethnography, suggesting that their work displays "obscuring tendencies" in the historical analysis of oral narratives. Jansen argues that many Mande scholars have relied on exotic—if not intuitive and somewhat mystical—interpretations of such traditions. He emphasizes that "'suggestive similarities' or an analogy are not evidence," calling instead for strict empirical historical interpretations based on evidence internal and external to the narratives.

Jansen locates his critique in an analysis of the corpus of stories about Nfa Jigin, a Mande trickster character. Nfa Jigin purportedly went on pilgrimage to Mecca, returning with ritual objects most often associated with classical African religions and rituals. It is also said that Nfa Jigin made the journey to the east to seek forgiveness for having sexual relations with his father's youngest wife—a tale which Jansen maintains is not so much an episode of incest, but of lust and sex. Unlike Sunjata, who, Jansen observes, dominates Mande history (and historiography), Nfa Jigin is not widely discussed, probably because no one claims descent from him. However, he is tied to the origins of the Komo initiation society, which affords him some notoriety among the Mande.

According to the author, canonical interpretations usually link Nfa Jigin stories with Sunjata, rather loosely concluding that they probably date from the medieval era and simply illustrate the syncretism of Islamic and local religious traditions. Dominant scholarship in the field suggests that a more precise analysis is impossible. In this regard, Jansen cites David Conrad who has concluded that the Nfa Jigin texts are "virtually worthless as sources of information about the historical deeds of Mansa Musa."

Jansen disagrees with this approach to the Nja Jigin narratives and the larger school of interpretation that it represents. He believes that evidence both internal and external to these traditions provides a basis for more concrete judgments about their veracity and their place in the corpus of Mande narratives. In so doing, the author suggests that scholars may, and should, treat this material as they treat other sources—indeed as they are accustomed to treating written and material sources about the past. This belief demystifies African "oral traditions," because it subjects them to the same kind of scrutiny that is permitted of other historical sources. At the same time, it elevates them to their rightful place in the ranks of evidence that scholars use to write history.

Jansen offers a concrete analysis of the Nfa Jigin narratives to prove his point. Unlike many Mande scholars who have worked in the more Islamized zones of central and western Mali, Jansen collected narratives and background information on Nfa Jigin in the Sobara region southwest of Bamako, near the Guinea border. Islam and cash crop production have not "completely penetrated" this area. The Komo initiation society remains viable, and Ciwara masks are still widely performed. Jansen observes that altars and sacred places—Pierre Nora's "*lieux de mémoire*"—are "still all around."[4] Without stealing Jansen's thunder—which resonates more profoundly in his own words—he [Jansen] demonstrates in a convincing fashion that the Nfa Jigin narratives, as well as the Komo society, probably date from the nineteenth century. Both were Mande responses to the challenge of Islam and the new commercial culture associated with it—the Nfa Jigin stories drawing on the larger trickster tradition in Mande culture, and the Komo society representing a ritualization of older cultural themes, or an "invention of tradition" in the face of Islamization.

What does Jansen teach us about oral tradition? He suggests that such narratives are not "the product of an additive patchwork," which simply layers newer material over older, static elements. Oral traditions are, rather, the embodiment of an ongoing process whereby new influences and concepts are assimilated in ways that hide and even obliterate previous versions. Nonetheless, valid empirical analysis is possible, and Jansen concludes on a positive (and positivist) note:

> Historians of Mande cultures must learn to appreciate and to accept the impressive production of historical narratives in Mande and to propose hypotheses without neglecting systematic study of external evidence. . . . History is an empirical search for external truths . . . and speculation does not please Clio, the historians' muse.

Constanze Weise picks up on these themes in her essay, "Kingship and the Mediators of the Past: Oral Tradition and Ritual Performance in

Nupeland, Nigeria." Oral traditions among the Nupe report that Tsoede, "the cultural hero . . . of [the] Nupe," founded the Nupe kingdom and the Edegi dynasty. F. Nadel, the most famous ethnographer of the Nupe, reports this version of events virtually without commentary in books and articles based on oral traditions collected in 1934, and the contemporary Nigerian scholars Obayemi and Idrees support his interpretation. Two score years later, however, Michael Mason rejected the Tsoede tradition as a creation of colonial officials "force-feeding" a random list of names made up by members of the Nupe elite who were primarily concerned with protecting their positions following the British conquest in the late nineteenth century.[5] Following a detailed, multidimensional analysis, Weise offers the following hypothesis:

> The enthronement rituals of the Nupe kings have the potential to demonstrate not only that Tsoede is not an invention of the twentieth century, but also that the institution of kingship is rooted in a precolonial and pre-Islamic religious complex.

The remainder of the chapter first sets the context for what Weise calls "the preservation of tradition in Nupeland" through a summary of the history of the Nupe over the past two centuries—eras of succession disputes and civil war in the early nineteenth century, later conquest and rule by the Muslim Fulbe from the north, a return to Nupe control following conquest by the British, and division of the Nupe state into two kingdoms under colonial rule. The author then offers a three-fold proof of her hypothesis—of oral traditions; of enthronement rituals, and associated sacred places and artifacts among the Nupe; and of ritual performances, and related "*lieux de mémoire*" and objects connected to initiation into the pre-Islamic Ndakogboya cult.

Weise's examination of oral tradition is classic—drawing on pioneer works such as Jan Vansina's *Oral Tradition as History*, and David Henige's *The Chronology of Oral Tradition* and *Oral Historiography*. She asks if an "institutional means of recording history" existed among the Nupe, and, marshalling the evidence in a convincing way, arrives at an affirmative answer.

The analysis of enthronement rituals, places, and objects confronts in a very straightforward way the challenge of showing that aspects of classical Nupe religion survived the Islamization of Nupeland over the last two centuries. Weise goes so far as to suggest that Nupe rulers may have been "nominal Muslims" even before the Fulbe conquest. Nonetheless, she also identifies a variety of classical Nupe institutions that demonstrate the important role that the cultural hero Tsoede played in Nupe historical memory: a chief priest called "Ndazhigi" associated with Tsoede, a figure referred to as "Ndeji" who ruled during interregna between rulers, and a shrine house named the "Tsoedemba" or "House of Tsoede" located in the center of town. The compound still exists and custodians of the shrine still live there, "keeping," in the words of an informant, "'the memory of the place alive.'" Weise also identifies objects such as iron canoes and chains linked to Tsoede that were—and, in some cases, still are—required for enthronement ceremonies.

The final part of Weise's proof is perhaps the most original. Hypothesizing that "pre-Islamic" forms of kingship rituals might be better preserved outside the now-Islamized Nupe court, the author explored the Ndakogboya cult centers found throughout Nupeland, looking for evidence of links with the Tsoede traditions. These centers are the last enclaves of classical Nupe religion. Informants in a variety of the Ndakogboya centers recalled that Tsoede traditions were associated with the establishment of central kingship among the Nupe. Masquerades performed by cult members for their communities are said to have come with Tsoede in an iron canoe from Idah, a precolonial state to the southwest linked with the foundation of the Nupe state. Ndakogboya initiates learn the story of Tsoede— who is present in the form of a chain, which is, in turn, associated with enthronement rituals. Finally, prayers said during the Ndakogboya initiation link the cult with Tsoede, with Nupe ancestors, and with Soko, the classical Nupe high god.

Weise concludes that Ndakogboya worshipers remain the custodians of Nupe classical religion; that the kingship system was, and remains, linked to the cult centers; and that knowledge of Tsoede has been retained in oral tradition and ritual despite the advent of Islam. Her argument resembles that of Jansen in some ways. Both re-legitimize the use of oral tradition for historical inquiry. Impressionistic and mystifying analyses of oral traditions are not likely to lead to convincing historical conclusions. However, research that situates analysis of oral traditions in empirical investigations of institutions, objects, places, and performance may well yield viable and valuable historical understandings. Weise firmly believes that the "longstanding link between Nupe religion institutions and their function in legitimizing Nupe kingship can still be discerned today through careful analysis." Rituals and oral traditions can (and should) be analyzed by the historian.

The third and fourth chapters, by James Giblin and Jamie Monson, respectively, raise quite different, but vitally important, questions about narrative forms and levels of oral inquiry. In his essay on the collection of oral traditions about Maji Maji in Ngombe district of Tanzania, Giblin is not so much concerned about the "loss" of the past as he is worried about the ways that formal history de-centers and de-values local narrative practices that make the past meaningful to local people. Also writing on Tanzania, Monson describes her efforts to understand how peoples' lives changed with the construction of the TAZARA railroad after independence. Her essay explores how the choice of narrative genres encourages or discourages informants to speak about the past.

Inspired in part by the work of Elizabeth Tonkin on narration, "articulation," and "disarticulateness,"[6] James Giblin's chapter, "Passages in a Struggle over the Past: Stories of Maji Maji in Njombe, Tanzania," calls for a reassessment of the history and historiography of the Maji Maji revolt of 1905–7. His overarching concern is that academic historians are often, and probably quite unwittingly so, not so much involved in conservation of the past as in its alienation. Armed with diploma-sanctioned knowledge and formal research "instruments" (interview schedules, questionnaires, censuses, and the like), Giblin suggests that the image historians project in the field, as well as the methods they use, may serve to deprive local people of the ability to speak articulately about their pasts. Rather than locating Maji Maji and Njombe history at the level of the colonial or nationalist state, most local people, Giblin submits, understand and recount events in the local contexts that they know about and that matter to them most. They situate their accounts in narratives about family, clan, and village—microhistories which are neither privileged by the dominant historiographies created by the state nor validated by academic historians with institutional credentials and access to official archives.

Giblin illustrates his argument by reviewing interpretations and events linked to Maji Maji in Njombe district in southern Tanzania, supplementing this received historiography and history with new narratives that he collected in the course of recent fieldwork in Njombe. The author first recounts how, in the wake of the German defeat in World War I, the new British overlords and the local chiefs that they appointed retold the past. The British imposed indirect rule, declaring that they had "reinstated traditional forms of tribal authority" that had prevailed before Maji Maji. In Njombe, this policy translated into the consolidation of the power and influence of the Mkongwa clan. Said to have laid seige to a mission in Yakobi during Maji Maji, the Mkongwa cultivated a belligerent image. The British dealt with this potential challenge to their authority by naming the Mkongwa chiefs and incorporating them into the colonial administration.

The local traditions about chiefly authority that Giblin collected in Njombe tell a somewhat different story—a story on another level. According to them, not only was the area of Mkongwa rule much more circumscribed than the conventional narrative would have it, but the "chiefly" clan did not even enjoy the status of *primus inter pares*—they were but one clan among several. Moreover, these traditions assert, the attack on the mission during Maji Maji was more the outgrowth of the fancy of Mkongwa chief Mbeyela's son for the wife of the German missonary than Mkongwa solidarity with the Maji Maji uprising.

Why were these dissenting voices not heard? Giblin hypothesizes that although the Mkongwa chiefly narrative elevated the status of one clan, it also served to create unity: "many Bena concluded [that] accepting a chiefly master narrative of the past was small price to pay for tribal cohesion." The chapter goes on to suggest that the same fate befell local narratives when the chiefly narrative gave way to a nationalist appropriation of Maji Maji in the 1950s, 1960s, and 1970s. Giblin leaves detailed exploration of this example of alienation of the past to Thaddeus Sunseri,[7] but concludes, nonetheless, that these nationalist histories represented themselves as a superior form of knowledge to which common villagers lacked access.

The latter half of the chapter drives home Giblin's point by a detailed illustration of how local narratives resituate two events usually related to Maji Maji in alternative contexts of family, kinship, and marriage. The first is the tale of the attack on the German mission mentioned earlier. Local people refer to the episode as the "War of Korosani," the name they assigned to the German missionary Paul Gröschel, and emphatically deny that it was part of "Hongo Hongo" (the local terminology for Maji Maji). Their version of events is a family narrative. In Giblin's words, "not only does the family genre make the past meaningful, but it also allows anyone with experience of family and married life to speak about it with authority." The second tale concerns the death of Mkwawa, a local leader who fought against the Germans in the 1890s. In colonial accounts, Mkwawa is said have died alone at his own hand. However, a local informant in Njombe whose mother was present when Mkwawa died, tells another story. According to her, Mkwawa was surrounded by family. The children were sent off to eat, and while they were gone he purportedly committed suicide. The rest of the narrative describes burial arrangements fitting for the head of a family—it identifies Mkwawa as kin and places him and his death in a broader social context. He is claimed and acclaimed by local people.

This detailed analysis of local "village genres" of historical narrative, as well as the ways that they are excluded from formal histories and historiography associated with power, lead Giblin to conclude that villagers establish an identity grounded in alienation from power. He urges those of us who collect, analyze, and legitimize oral traditions to remember that:

> This is the complex situation that we academic historians enter when we undertake research in landscapes such as Njombe. The sites of commemoration can be found quickly. It takes us much longer to understand the social processes and competing genres which are both continually threatening to alienate the past and continually resisting its alienation.

Jamie Monson's essay, "*Maisha*: Life History and the History of Livelihood along the TAZARA Railway in Tanzania," like that of Giblin, is a study in the recovery of voices alienated by the formality and scale of academic history. Monson set out to record how the "ordinary," or local train changed the lives of people who lived in formerly isolated regions along its route in southern Tanzania. Despite what seemed to be a straightforward topic, Monson found that when she sat with ordinary people, the formality of her interview schedule with its broad focus on "the role of TAZARA in their lives and communities," made people "uncomfortable, confused, eventually silent." Confronted with a topic so distant from everyday concerns, Monson observes that the rural families she worked with—farmers, traders, fishers and herders—did not perceive themselves in relation to the railway in this way, even though it was a central resource in their daily lives."

Monson's silent sources eventually spoke. Her resolution of this problem, like Giblin's, was, in part, inspired by Tonkin. For Tonkin, Monson writes, "memory and its reconstruction are narrated within genres," which join the storyteller and the audience. Both parties must understand and value the genre. When that happens, "narrators become articulate." As it happened, a local informant—in this case a market woman—helped Monson identify the narrative genre that produced articulation, and in so doing, revealed how TAZARA had indeed changed peoples' lives. Monson calls the genre *maisha*, an emic narrative style that refers to "life circumstances," "livelihood," and "life cycles." Whereas questions meant to elicit *historia* in Swahili—formal, large-scale narratives of political and economic change—silenced her informants, inquiries about *maisha* brought forth an avalanche of words. Engaged now with her informants, Monson collected personal narratives, not complete life histories, but what she, after Geiger,[8] refers to as "directed" or "modified" life history interviews. The nature of these interviews reveals the degree to which Monson succeeded in finding a genre that was both understood and valued by the women and men who told her their stories:

[T]he interests of the researcher influence both the questions that are asked and the locution of the narrator. Thus even though I had abandoned my structured survey questionnaire, the conversations I had with those who shared their lives with me were focused largely on the time period of TAZARA and on the Kilombero valley geographic region.

Following this theoretical and methodological introduction, Monson demonstrates through concrete narratives how stories of *maisha* illustrate—often in dramatic ways—the impact of the TAZARA railroad on the lives of people in the Kilombero valley. For Mama Robi, for example, *maisha,* in this case life circumstances, "found her single with small children to care for after her husband's death." Faced with the challenge of making a living, she eventually received help from her maternal uncle who introduced her to associates and advanced her goods that enabled her to "get a start in trading." In this case, *maisha,* in the form of "life cycle" or the participation of elders of the preceding generation, launched her on a new career. *Maisha,* or her new livelihood as a trader, eventually led her to take the TAZARA regularly to distant villages where she bought foodstuffs that she shipped back to the town for sale.

The collection of other stories of *maisha*—from both women and men, from farmers and traders and fisherpeople and others, and from several locales along the railroad—ultimately merged into a larger picture of how TAZARA had changed the lives of many people who lived along its itinerary. Monson concludes that the railroad brought new opportunities because it enabled people to develop livelihood strategies that incorporated new dimensions of mobility, flexibility, and diversification. These conclusions are, of course, important in themselves, and the *maisha* stories of Monson's essay illustrate them quite concretely and very convincingly. For purposes of this introduction, however, what is striking about this essay is Monson's own tale of how she and her informants became articulate—a result of the advice of Tonkin, the example of a marketwoman, and a historian who truly heard what people told her. For without words there can be no oral tradition.

Notes

1. Jan M. Vansina, *Oral Tradition: A Study in Historical Methodology* (Madison: Uniersity of Wisconsin Press, 1965). An earlier edition of this work appeared in French. See Jan M. Vansina, *De la tradition orale: Essai de méthode historique* (Tervuren: Musée Royal de l'Afrique centrale, 1961). Vansina published a completely rewritten text on the topic twenty years later: *Oral Tradition as History* (Madison: University of Wisconsin Press, 1985).

2. B. A. Ogot, *A History of the Southern Luo* (Nairobi: East African Publishing House, 1967)

3. A brief bibliography may, nonetheless, be helpful to readers who wish to place the essays included here in their larger historiographical context. Apart from the titles cited above, see Daniel F. McCall, "The Heritage of the Ears," in *AFRICA in Time Perspective: A Discussion of Historical Reconstruction from Unwritten Sources,* ed. Daniel F. McCall (Boston: Boston University Press, 1964), 3—61; Jan Vansina, "The Use of Oral Tradition in African Culture History," in *Reconstructing African Culture History,* ed. Creighton Gabel and Norman R. Bennett (Boston: Boston University Press, 1967), 55–82; David Henige, *The Chronology of Oral Tradition* (Oxford: Oxford University Press, 1974); Joseph C. Miller, ed., *The African Past Speaks: Essays on Oral Tradition and History* (Kent and New York: Dawson and Archon, 1980); David Henige, *Oral Historiography* (London: Longman, 1982); "Part II: The Historiography of Oral Discourse," in *African Historiographies: What History for Which Africa?* ed. Bogumil Jewsiewicki and David Newbury (Beverly Hills, Calif.: Sage, 1986), 49–110; Karin Barber and P. F. de Moraes Farias, eds., *Discourse and Its Disguises: The Interpretation of African Oral Texts* (Birmingham: Centre of West African Studies, University of Birmingham, 1989); Elizabeth Tonkin, *Narrating Our Pasts: The Social Construction of Oral History* (Cambridge: Cambridge University Press, 1992); Luise White, Stephan F. Meischer, and David William Cohen, eds., *African Words, African Voices: Critical Practices in Oral History* (Bloomington: Indiana University Press, 2001).

4. Pierre Nora, ed., *Les Lieux de mémoire,* 7 vols. (Paris: Gallimard, 1984–93).

5. Michael Mason, "The Tsoede Myth and the Nupe Kinglists: More Political Propaganda?" *History in Africa* 1, 2 (1975): 101–11.

6. Tonkin, *Narrating Our Pasts.*

7. Thaddeus Sunseri, "Statist Narratives and Maji Maji Ellipses," *The International Journal of African Historical Studies* 33, 3 (2000): 567–84.

8. Susan Geiger, *TANU Women: Gender and Culture in the Making of Tanganyikan Nationalism, 1955–1965* (Portsmouth, N.H.: Heineman, 1997), 15–17.

15

NARRATIVES ON PILGRIMAGES TO MECCA: BEAUTY VERSUS HISTORY IN MANDE ORAL TRADITION

Jan Jansen

The *aesthetic fallacy* selects beautiful facts, or facts that can be built into a beautiful story, rather than facts that are functional to the empirical problem at hand. It consists in an attempt to organize an empirical enquiry upon aesthetic criteria of significance, or conversely in an attempt to create an *objet d'art* by an empirical method. To do so is to confuse two different kinds of knowledge and truth. To the truth of art, external reality is irrelevant. Art creates its own reality, within which truth and the perfection of beauty is the infinite refinement of itself. History is very different. It is an empirical search for external truths, and for the best, most complete, and most profound external truths, in a maximal corresponding relationship with the absolute reality of the past events. Any attempt to conduct that search according to aesthetic standards of significance (most commonly in an attempt to tell a beautiful story) is either to abandon empiricism or to contradict it.
—D. H. Fischer, *Historians' Fallacies,* 87

Introduction: Mande Historical Imagination and Academic Historical Research[1,2]

The figure of Nfa Jigin is featured in Mande[3] oral traditions that relate the origin of the secret Komo initiation society to a pilgrimage to Mecca. In recent decades the time depth and the interpretation of Nfa Jigin traditions has been subject of systematic analysis, for instance by Sarah Brett-Smith and David Conrad, authors who have also published texts of new variants of the narrative. This article is a methodological exercise to investigate the external validity of their interpretations of Nfa Jigin narratives, and—as a consequence—the personage of Nfa Jigin "himself." The interpretation of Nfa Jigin is an important issue in both West African historical imagination and academic historical research, since it is being *suggested* that—although authors emphasize at the same time that nineteenth- and twentieth-century additions, changes, and deletions continue to occur in the Nfa Jigin narratives—these narratives might represent the fusion of a core of information that is pre-fourteenth century with a set of post-1324 A.D. islamized tales.[4] The date 1324 refers to the visit of Mansa Musa—the king of the Mali empire who was on pilgrimage—to Cairo, an event which has been reported in some fourteenth and fifteenth-century Arab sources (and probably the seventeenth-century Tarikh al-Fattash).

The Nfa Jigin narrative is one of the few issues that have been discussed in a debate on Mande societies in precolonial times (circa before 1850). For the period before 1850 there hardly are any sources, and most of the area where Nfa Jigin stories have been transmitted—roughly the area covered by present-day Mali and Guinea—was occupied by colonial powers only in the second half of the nineteenth century. Therefore, the argumentation and method become of great importance when a relationship with a medieval source is proposed.

Older anthropologists labeled Nfa Jigin as "a fictive personality . . . created by the Malinke";[5] no particular period was attributed to Nfa Jigin by the scholars of the colonial era. By linking the Nfa Jigin narrative to Islam and to traditions about Sunjata, the legendary founder of the Mali empire, new pathways as well as a new time frame for Mande history have been explored in the last decades of the twentieth century. The difficulties David Conrad faced in this attempt, he expresses as follows:

> Thus, any historian addressing thirteenth-century Mali must either accept the severe limitations of the external written sources and say very little indeed about that period, or face the difficulties involved in supplementing these with references to the oral sources.[6]

Citing Moraes Farias, Conrad continues by "warning against nourishing an illusion instead of contributing to knowledge of the subject."[7] Recently, he summarized the interpretation of Nfa Jigin texts as follows:

Taken by themselves and at face value, the individual oral texts are virtually worthless as sources of information about the historical deeds of Mansa Musa, something that is unusually clear in this case because the oral traditions can be checked against the relatively substantial external accounts.[8] . . . The Fajigi legend endured because it was an entertaining story about a heroic quest that Mande audiences could appreciate, and in the process it also became an expression of accommodation between religious practices and Islam.[9]

Thus, a connection between Nfa Jigin and Mansa Musa is presupposed, and the endurance is explained not by the importance of the content (a pilgrimage by a pious king), but by the changed function, i.e., the need to announce "the legitimate origin of various autochthonous ritual institutions" as well as the format of "an entertaining story."[10]

In this article I aim to elaborate methodological arguments to judge how and to what extent the "difficulties" mentioned by Conrad have been overcome, and to what extent a connection between Nfa Jigin and Mansa Musa is methodologically justified.

I will observe the tendency, by authors who write on Nfa Jigin and the origin of the Komo, to avoid non-sensational or nonaesthetic explanations. I explain this tendency by referring to the fallacy of narration mentioned above: the aesthetic fallacy. Fischer's quote provides me with the analytical tools and terms that I will use to question the external validity for the historic dimensions of Nfa Jigin as they have been proposed. I elaborate the idea that those who wrote on Nfa Jigin tacitly seem to have "forgotten" to pay attention to rules for external validity. Here I define validity to measure to what extent the data prove what the researcher aims to prove. A difference must be made between internal and external validity. External validity is related to "generalizability"; to what extent the data can be trusted when analyzed in relation to a wider set of data—a routine exercise in philological research. Validity should not be confused with reliability, which is related to replicability. I consider all the narratives on Nfa Jigin as they have been collected and published as reliable data. The focus on internal validity meant in practice that the authors' focus was only on research data regarding Nfa Jigin and the Komo; analysis of the Nfa Jigin narrative in relation to other oral literary products that were collected in the same area during the same period was not undertaken.

Lack of attention to external validity has a narrowing effect on the discussion of precolonial Mande, because it overlooks or underestimates the dynamics of oral tradition and Mande society. This phenomenon I consider to be an omnipresent danger in research on history in and of

Africa—often the local historical imagination is presented as an in-depth study of the local history—and therefore I chose to address to this topic in this volume on methods and sources.

Is elegance proof? This is the title of Jan Vansina's 1983 article in the journal *History in Africa*. At the time, Vansina directed his critique against structuralism. Nowadays structuralism has almost completely disappeared from academia, and the question posed by Vansina seems also to have disappeared from the historians' research agenda. This last aspect is unfortunate, since in recent decades narrativist and literary models for the writing of history have come to the fore and flourish—sometimes presented as "new epistemologies" for historical research—thus turning the question of elegance, a category connected to aesthetics, once again into a central issue in the historian's craft. Hence, I place "beauty" versus "history," since in my epistemology elegance is not proof.

I plan to support my critique on lack of external validity by sketching, on the basis of my own fieldwork data, an alternative interpretation of Nfa Jigin narratives that better meets the scientific prerequisite to maximize the external body of evidence and to maximize corresponding relationships between the available sources (cf. Fischer supra). Most of my ethnographic data for this analysis have been collected during six months of fieldwork conducted among the Kante blacksmiths in the village of Farabako, in the Sobara region (Mande hills) southwest of Bamako, near the Guinean frontier. The Sobara region has, compared to the adjacent area along the borders of the river Niger, a thin population density and an "undeveloped" infrastructure and economy. Islam has not yet fully penetrated the area, but is clearly present is local discourses on correct behavior. Komo societies are numerous, and altars (*boliw*) are omnipresent. I heard stories about Nfa Jigin several times, plus other narratives that I had not heard during previous research along the banks of the river Niger. This inspired me to work on the Nfa Jigin narratives.

A Historiographic Contextualization of the Nfa Jigin Stories

Mande history has been dominated by Sunjata and his helpers, in Mande historical imagination as well as in academic research.[11] Sunjata and his helpers are the alleged ancestors of the present-day Mande peoples, they are at the origin of the system of patronymics ("family names"). These ancestors are often publicly celebrated in griots' performances. Next to Sunjata and his helpers, other heroes exist, and these are even sometimes incorporated in the 'discourse' on Sunjata.[12] However, these heroes are either of local/regional historical importance, or relatively marginal in Mande historical imagination as well as not incorporated in griots' performances. Nfa Jigin is a hero of this last mentioned category.

I seek to explain the marginality of heroes like Nfa Jigin by the fact that they are not celebrated as ancestors of particular groups; no one claims descent from them. I see no reason, in contrast to many others, to attribute the marginal position of Nfa Jigin in Mande historical imagination to an alleged taboo on talking about Nfa Jigin, and as alleged evidence that Nfa Jigin actually would be crucial in Mande culture. I draw this conviction from my own fieldwork experiences. Indeed, several times someone who told about Nfa Jigin of the Komo society suddenly stopped or was ordered to stop, but this happened also during previous research on Sunjata or on Mande village foundation stories. Such sudden stops I seek to explain as (power) games between informants or between informant and researcher, and I do not consider them to be produced by an alleged secret character of the narrative.

Nfa Jigin is said to have visited Mecca, where he begot important sacred objects that—in most versions of the narrative—happened to fall in the river (often the Niger) where they transformed into living beings, such as the *tigin*, a subspecies of the catfish. As an example of Nfa Jigin's life and deeds, I will present the version that Bala Kante[13] told me:

One day, Nfa Jigin left for Mecca. He returned with hundred magical poisons (*kòròtè*), with hundred *kolo*. He returned to Mecca once more. The sin for which he had departed had not yet been forgiven. He left for Mecca, because the fourth wife of his father had hidden herself to spend the night with him.[14] Nfa Jigin had not recognized her. The next morning she transformed herself and took her former [real] shape. When Nfa Jigin arrived in Mecca this sin was not at all forgiven. That is the reason why your father's wife is bad; you must never sleep with her. Don't sleep with your father's wife.

He has been liberated after seven years; they let Nfa Jigin go. He had studied, he studied much; Nfa Jigin is at the origin of maraboutism [koranic scholarship —J. J.]. He returned from Mecca with the Koran. It was Sorijan Kante, the ancestor of the blacksmiths, who left to meet him and to carry his sac made of skin. When they arrived at the middle of the river, a ritual object (*basi*) fell and it transformed into a fish which, when it is touched with a stick, trembles [by sending out an electric shock wave], and the shock goes to your brain. This fish took the name of "electric fish" (*tigin*). When they continued their trip, another object fell and took the name of *manògò* [another sort of catfish —J. J.]; it has two body parts to swim with. If you are hurt by one of these, the effect is equal to a magical poison, although it must be treated in a different way. Another one fell and became a *kònkòn* (*synodontis*). It is quite small, but when you touch it, you must treat it with a *kolo* amulet. Well, another object fell in the water and became the *sumè* (*arius gigas*) whose "touch" is equal to a snake bite. To cure it, you must make use of the medicine to cure a *kòròtè*.

Nfa Jigin's objects, brought from his travels, feature as *basiw* (ritual objects, often translated as "amulet" or "fetish") and *boliw* ("altars") in the Komo secret initiation society; Komo masks are said to represent or to be connected to an object that was once brought from Mecca by Nfa Jigin.

I have two problems regarding interpretations of Nfa Jigin narratives, both related to issues of external validity in historical research. The first is related to the interpretation of Nfa Jigin's name and and Nfa Jigin as a historical personality, and the second is the absence of a deliberate search to contextualize the Nfa Jigin stories as broadly as possible within the framework of Mande oral tradition, thus "maximizing corresponding relationships between the available sources."

Nfa Jigin: Name and Historical Personality

The first syllable of Nfa Jigin's name consists of two parts: *fa* = father, *n* = my. *Nfa* (which is pronounced as "mfa") may be translated as "my father," but it is also a common way of addressing a male person respectfully. A Guinean school teacher explained to me, in Jelibakoro, in November 1992: "This is our way of saying 'vous' in Maninka."[15] This second translation, *Nfa* as "mister," has never been mentioned in literature. This should be done, even when informants do not do so.

Jigi or *jigin* (the "n" is hardly pronounced)[16] can be translated in various ways. Indeed, it is a word used for "hope," "trustworthy," and "descent."[17] However, it has more meanings. As a verb it means "to descend" (in a very broad way) or "to give birth to." Moreover, it is a Malinke man's name.[18] Thus, Nfa Jigin may be translated "magnificently" as Father Hope, but also "simply" as Mister Jigin.[19] These different translations certainly make different impacts on readers and evoke different readings. Methodologically, ignoring the less "aesthetically attractive" "Mister Jigin" cannot be justified, even if informants do so, but yet this is systematically done in the academic literature, which thus follows in this case Mande historical imagination.

Whatever the meaning of Nfa Jigin, it is problematic to derive a historical or cultural meaning from semantic interpretation, since Mande peoples love word games. For instance, John Johnson once observed men discussing the deeper meaning of "koka kola / coca cola."[20] An open eye and ear for the word games Mande people enjoy would have resulted in including less aesthetic interpretations of Nfa Jigin than currently is the case.

Nfa Jigin's name is also a point of historical debate: a point of discussion is whether he was inspired by a "historical" figure. Nfa Jigin is often called "Makantaajigi" (or variable combinations of "Makan'" [which can be translated as "Mecca"] and "Jigin"). Then, the name means "Jigi who went to Mecca."[21] This name has been used to suggest that Nfa Jigin echoes (a follower of) Mansa Musa, the king of the Mali empire who made a pilgrimage to Mecca according to medieval Arab sources and (probably) the seventeenth-century *Tarikh al-Fattash*. I object to this: analogy is not evidence.

After having connected Nfa Jigin to the historical Mansa Musa, the question is asked whether Nfa Jigin was contemporary of Sunjata.[22] Brett-Smith and Conrad thus implicitly accept Sunjata to be a historical figure, although this idea (taught in primary schools and generally accepted) has been constructed in the late nineteenth and early twentieth centuries by ethnographers who read Sunjata's name in Ibn Battuta and Ibn Khaldun; in these sources Sunjata is mentioned as the ancestor, several generations earlier, of the fourteenth-century kings. For me, this is no reason to consider him to be a historical figure who lived in the thirteenth century.[23] I consider Sunjata to be the central figure in an organizational model: in present-day oral tradition Sunjata is (still) told to be seven to ten generations ago, following well-known and almost universal schemes of storytelling.

What is even more striking is that in this line of thinking, oral traditions on Sunjata or those related to Sunjata are related to the thirteenth century, thus denying how oral traditions usually develop, transform, and change during processes of transmission. The suggestion that a narrative cycle on Sunjata came into existence shortly after the Middle Ages[24] or even before the Mali empire[25] or transformed much in form and content in the eighteenth or nineteenth century, should certainly be taken into account.[26] Since Sunjata is the hegemonic framework of Mande imagination of medieval history, it is logical that other stories about heroes are connected to Sunjata in order to increase the prestige and historical importance of these heroes. Some people might say that I take a "hardliner's stance" regarding the historicity of Sunjata, but I maintain that this is not a matter of "belief": it cannot be accepted when one applies generally accepted methodological criteria for historical research.

Exploring Nfa Jigin as related to the Middle Ages and to Sunjata thus denies certain possible changes in Sunjata traditions as well as the possibility that Sunjata traditions have been incorporating other traditions in the long run. Therefore, I consider this to be a case of the static fallacy:

> The *static fallacy* broadly consists in any attempt to conceptualize a dynamic problem in static terms. This form of error represents an intermediate stage of historical consciousness, in which *change is perceived merely as the emergence of a nonchanging entity* [my emphasis —J. J.]. [27]

Thus, a discourse with alleged deep history is created by adding probabilities to each other. A variable is presented as a fact, and the leading idea becomes: "If it has not been rejected, why not then shouldn't it be true?" Aesthetic standards of significance (see Fischer, supra) then have taken grip on the researcher, and his topic of research has become an *objet d'art*. [28]

By mentioning Mansa Musa, the perspective has been changed, following the image that is supported by the Malians and Guineans themselves. It is commonly accepted by historians that, in order to study the past, the point of departure should be the present, and not the reverse. [29] Thus, it is not allowed, on the basis of a "wishful reading" of a fourteenth-century text (using analogy as evidence), to suggest an age-old "core" in the oral tradition, in particular since external evidence gives reason to accept a more recent period for the rise as well as the creation of the Nfa Jigin story (see infra). Of course, oral tradition sometimes accumulates, but this is not a given; most of the time it changes into forms in which previous versions are difficult or even impossible to trace. Oral tradition should not be analyzed as the product of an additive patchwork. Fischer could categorize the approach I criticize here either as a fallacy that combines two fallacies of factual verification, i.e., the fallacy of the prevalent proof (Malians love to hear Nfa Jigin is Mansa Musa) and the fallacy of the possible proof. [30]

In Search of Corresponding Narratives: Patarapa and Mamadi Bitiki

In this section I present two narratives that have several similarities with and connections to the Nfa Jigin narrative, and which have been classified as of relatively recent origin. Thus, I explore the external validity of interpretations of Nfa Jigin by incorporating material that is comparable or corresponding, both in form and content. Although in one case—Patarapa— the name of the stories' antagonists has a clear historical origin, the events they relate are not historical. I will argue that these stories offer a more convincing framework of external relationships to interpret Nfa Jigin stories than the interpretations that are usually given. Both of the two narratives deal with the complex position of knowledge—which is conceived as something imported from outside—in Mande society, and both refer to late nineteenth- and early twentieth-century experiences, the period when Islam penetrated Mande cultures and colonial powers introduced new technologies: the narrative of Federeba/Patarapa, the "ancestor of the Whites," and the narrative of Mamadi Bitiki, the "first African owner of a retail shop."

Federeba (in Brett-Smith's recording) has some renown in Mande literature. It is generally accepted that his figure has its origin with Faidherbe, the French governor of the West African colonies in the mid-nineteenth century. Faidherbe was open, in his own way, to Islam, which he used as an instrument to get a grip on the colonies. For instance, Robinson writes:

> Faidherbe also inaugurated the practice of the "sponsored" pilgrimage to Mecca for selected friends of the colonial regime—a way of demonstrating the consideration for the Islamic faith. He made sure that these achievements, and the exploratory missions that he commissioned, were widely publicized. [31]

This "open attitude" may explain why his name is being connected to a pilgrimage to Mecca, although Faidherbe is portrayed in oral traditions as the inventor of new technologies: in present-day Mande oral tradition he is the unflattering hero connected to the invention of the bicycle, a reference to both steel and mobility. These inventions are located in Mecca. I will give the version I collected in 1999.[32] This version has some unique features (Faidherbe as a false imam for a period of thirty years as well as the philosophy of wage labor), but is still comparable to the other versions hitherto collected, which often establish a relationship between Faidherbe and Cheikh Umar Tal, the leader of a nineteenth-century jihad:[33]

> I told him [me —J. J.] that he [Patarapa —J. J.] was his ancestor (*mòkè*). He replied that he did not know him. His ancestor is Patarapa. He was imam in Mecca for a period of thirty years. After these thirty years Cheikh Umar Tal departed for a pilgrimage to Mecca. In those times pilgrimages were by foot. When he arrived there, he stayed with his host. At sunrise (*fijiri*), Cheikh Umar Tal did not go to the mosque to pray.

In the morning, people asked him, according to the law (*sariya*), why he had not gone to the mosque to pray. He replied that the person behind whom they pray had not become a Muslim and that he refused to pray standing behind him. The inhabitants of Mecca consulted the law. (They decided that) if he had not spoken the truth, Cheikh Umar Tal would be decapitated the next morning. But if it was true, Patarapa, the ancestor of the White, would be decapitated. So it went.

The next morning, when people were called for the morning prayers, Cheikh Umar Tal went to the mosque, and the ancestor of the White fled. Ha! The Koran descended, "Lanyini" descended, "Tuwerata" descended, "Jaburu" descended, plus another Koran to complete the Five Korans. The ancestor of the White ran away with them. It is said that they contain the divine proposals about how to deal with iron; and the secret names of God are in the Lanyini.[34]

In the morning, when people were called for prayer, Patarapa was not seen. The second call (*kannya*) took place, he was not seen. At the third call, Cheikh Umar Tal rose to his feet and walked in front of the people to pray, to lead their prayers. After the prayers, people said that it was he who had spoken the truth.

Regarding the pursuit of him . . . , an old lady happened to give Patarapa some advice; if he did not flee, the man who was to arrive would reveal his secret (*gundo kòròbò*). If this person could seize him, he [Patarapa] would be killed. He was pursued, he was chased. Being chased, he looked behind and saw a horseman right behind himself. He happened to be close to the horseman. He quickly grasped a branch of a tree, cut it on both sides and joined these sides, did this again and made a bicycle from it.

After he did that, he was not seen again. His first destination was Chad, where he stayed for a while. He left Chad to go tp France, which is called Paris. All the clans (*bonda*) of the White descend from him, Patarapa. This law was established (*jèn?*) between him and the Blacks (*farafinnu*). He acquired this book [*sèbèn*, also "amulet" —J. J.], but if the Blacks had had it, they [the Whites] would never have colonized us.

The secrets they [the Whites] keep,[35] we were getting to know them. However, what they got, we did not get. What we got, is that of the prayer. Putting God's name in an affair. Ah! With the exception of the Christians, there are many Whites who don't pray. But they are afraid of everything that doesn't please God, [for everything] which is without respect. Because, when a White takes you to a job, after you have finished the work, before you relax, he gives you your salary. Such a practice we don't have. We command suddenly people to work for us and do so for one or two years without paying him a salary. Such a situation [of paying a salary —J. J.] doesn't exist there. They don't pray, but they are more afraid of everything concerning God than we are. That is, in short, the case of their ancestor. So! Now you first turn off your radio [cassette recorder —J. J.]; then I will tell you one more story (*tariku*) later.

It is clear that the main topics and antagonists in this story (invention of the bicycle, use of steel [railway!], introduction of wage labor, technological knowledge from books, Faidherbe and Umar Tal) suggest an origin after 1850, at least post-Industrial Revolution. Islamic ideas, such as pilgrimages to Mecca, may be of older origin (although pilgrimages to Mecca became more common in West Africa in the nineteenth century), but these fit well in the Mande story theme of knowledge imported from outside. The formative period of this narrative will be the nineteenth century.

A nineteenth-century origin (or a later one) can also be attributed to the narrative of Mamadi Bitiki, whose name literally means "Mohammed Shop" (*bitiki* = boutique). Mamadi Bitiki is a popular song that praises either all the fine goods in Mamadi's shop[36] or Mamadi's destiny to loose all the richness he once had. Kaba gives as the following text for this song:

> On l'avait surnommé Mamadi Bitiki
> Ou 'Mamadi Maison'
> Grâce à sa maison
> Unique au pays.
> Et même les génies
> Des savanes et forêts
> Surpris et stupéfaits
> Devant la célébrité
> Qu'il s'était forgé,
> Scandaient son nom
> A l'unisson:
> "Mamadi Bitiki,
> Notre meilleur ami." [37]

Narratives about Mamadi Bitiki are, however, rare. The narrative about Mamadi Bitiki that I recorded in Farabako is the first text of this theme ever published, as far as I know. The narrative clearly is about the miracle of retail trade, the knowledge how to acquire money:[38] You just sit down and at the same time you bathe in luxury that attracts women. Physical labor is absent is the story. Part of the narrative is about the bush spirits that multiply your money.

Mamadi Bitiki has, like Patarapa and Nfa Jigin, Islamic dimensions, thus reflecting social changes in the nineteenth and twentieth centuries. Mamadi nowadays is the most current man's name in Mande, and it is derived from Mohammed. Moreover, many of old shopowners in Mande have been connected to Islam. Conversion to Islam is a prerequisite for successful commerce; the two are inseparably related. Money, however, is a secret that cannot be explained by Islam; in the Mamadi Bitiki narrative a white man establishes the shop, puts Mamadi Bitiki in it, and then leaves.

Mande culture has always gone through deep changes, not only recently. Islam, money, time, and import products are all issues that ask for an explanation, but at the same time have an explanatory power; Islam as such is a source of knowledge, and it can locally be used as an explanation of a practice.[39]

Narratives like the one about Patarapa or Mamadi Bitiki can be interpreted as dealing with "modernity" and privileged knowledge, and "knowledge-from-outside" is a Mande narrative model that is able to represent modernity, because it can incorporate the histories of Islam and colonialism, trade and books. Pilgrimages to Mecca are a logical category in a Mande etiological legend, since in Mande historical imagination—as well as elswhere in sub-Saharan Africa—power (rulers and founders) always come from elsewhere, and knowledge is acquired outside someone's society.[40]

Faidherbe's stay in Mecca has no historical base; the widespread popularity of Patarapa-(and Umar Tal)-in-Mecca stories demonstrates that the pilgrimage to Mecca is a popular narrative model to explain the world-as-it-is. Authors who write on Nfa Jigin do not deny the "modern" layers in the narrative, as we saw, but they suggest an old core by not pointing to corresponding or comparable narratives, thus not deliberately attempting to demonstrate the external validity for their interpretation. In this article I suggest that this is not done, because that would de-veil the alleged beauty of the Nfa Jigin narrative and would emphasize the historian's impossibility, on *methodological* criteria, to connect Nfa Jigin to medieval events. Criteria for external validity give only reason to place Nfa Jigin in the nineteenth century, since corresponding data exist (Patarapa and Mamadi Bitiki).

Historians therefore can and must analyze Nfa Jigin narratives only as nineteenth- and twentieth-century narratives. Oral tradition has to be understood with a processual model that analyzes oral tradition as a product, at any given moment, of an ongoing process of assimilation of the new and loss of some older elements; the fact that "accumulation" sometimes may take place should not be used as a *deus ex machina* to suppose huge time depths to oral traditions. The twentieth-century production of etiological legends with the theme "knowledge-from-outside"—and therefore comparable to Nfa Jigin's—is overwhelming. Thus, the suggestion to relate Nfa Jigin to a thirteenth-century Sunjata or fourteenth-century Mansa Musa or "traditional" Mande is untenable.[41] Corresponding external evidence justifies seeing Nfa Jigin as a nineteenth-century narrative, and oral tradition has to be studied from the presence (see note 29).

Moreover, data that can offer a counterweight to falsify this interpretation are almost absent; data on the Komo are of relatively recent origin,[42] and therefore the Komo as we have learned to know it can be understood as a nineteenth- or twentieth-century institution.

Some Concluding Remarks

Although I agree with Tauxier's point of view that Nfa Jigin was a "legendary figure," my methodological critique as well as my search for external validity are—as far as I know—new. I argued those who published on Nfa Jigin in the last decades of the twentieth century ascribe to this figure historical dimensions by focusing too much on internal evidence: research is limited to data from many versions of the Nfa Jigin narrative. External evidence (regarding both form and content of other, from a narrative point of view, corresponding Mande oral traditions) has often not systematically been investigated. As examples of possible sources to determine the external validity of the Nfa Jigin narrative, I proposed the well-known narrative of Patarapa/Faidherbe and the seldom recorded narrative on Mamadi Bitiki.

I described how, by evoking an analogy with some references to African pilgrim kings from medieval Arab manuscripts, a historical time frame that connects Nfa Jigin to the Middle Ages is suggested by analogy, not evidence. Even when the speculative character of such a historical reconstruction is mentioned, many authors yet feel tempted to elaborate on this speculation, which is confusing to the reader. In this process of elaborating on the speculation, traditions on Sunjata are used to prove the time depth, although there is no evidence to believe that these traditions are medieval. That would be the "static fallacy." Hence, it is clear that I see no possibility to "supplement" the medieval written sources "with references to the oral sources" (Conrad, supra), without loosening the rules for historical research. The Nfa Jigin narrative is, I propose, one among the many Mande narratives that explain "modern" life by "knowledge-from-outside." Reading them as accounts of pilgrimages can be challenged by rules for validity: these sources do not prove what the authors aim to prove.

The beauty of the argument seems to be the justification for the lack of evidence to connect Nfa Jigin with medieval Mansa Mussa. Moreover, it impeded alternative hypotheses. I explained this by referring to the aesthetical fallacy.[43] Nfa Jigin has been portrayed as a human without any reason, and his name has been translated, in my opinion, uncritically, following local historical imagination. Mande etiological legends of nineteenth- and twentieth-century origin, such as Faidherbe/Patarapa and Mamadi Bitiki, provide external evidence for the idea that Nfa Jigin stories can be read as etiological legends of a relatively recent origin that are based on often used narrative models. Some scholars seem to believe that, when more traditions are collected, the historical depth of Nfa Jigin will better come to the fore. I hold a contrary point of view: the more we collect, the more we shall realize that Nfa Jigin should be analyzed only as something of relatively recent origin. Historians of Mande cultures must learn to appreciate and to accept the impressive production of historical narratives in Mande and to propose hypotheses without neglecting systematic study of external evidence. Thus, I disagree with Conrad (supra), who claims that the Nfa Jigi legend "endured because it was an entertaining story"; this demonstrates his personal literary appreciation of the narrative, but does not elaborate on its function as an etiological legend, since this would emphasize the fact that the narrative has a contemporary function in society that can be compared to other traditions (Patarapa and Mamadi Bitiki in this case) and this becomes a questionable source of reference to the Middle Ages.

Indeed, it is elegant and aesthetically attractive to evoke a great past for Mande by referring to a limited selection of sources without judging them one for one by philological standards, thus emphasizing to what extent they confirm each other internally. Some people may even be of the opinion that this is a sound epistemology for the (post)modern historian. To me, however, it is too speculative: history is an empirical search for external truths (cf. Fischer, supra) and speculation does not please Clio, the historians' muse.

Notes

1. Research in the period 1999–2002 has been financed by the Royal Netherlands Academy of Arts and Sciences KNAW. Previous research projects, all in Mali in the period 1991–98, were on the "griots" of Kela ("cercle" of Kangaba) and on village foundation stories in the *arrondissements* of Narena and Siby, geographically located between Kangaba and Farabako.

2. This article is a strongly revised version of the paper presented at the "Pathways to Africa's Past" conference. The article must be read as a methodological attempt to bring forward an alternative analysis of a well-known Mande narrative. This analysis elaborates on the consequences of hitherto not explicitly stated methodological procedures. I express my

gratitude to Sarah Brett-Smith and David Conrad—who know that I admire their field-work and share their fascination for Mande oral tradition—because of their willingness to discuss previous versions of this article with me, although they are the authors to whom I direct in particular my critique. Both these authors see serious shortcomings in my analysis and both of them have announced that they will comment on my point of view in future publications. I am also grateful to Peter Mark, Wouter van Beek, Saskia Brand, Akare John Aden, and Geert Mommersteeg for comments on earlier versions of this paper, and to Barbara Flemming and Pekka Masonen for an interesting discussion on medieval royal pilgrimages to Mecca.

3. Belcher describes Mande in the following way: "The Manden (or Mande) is a space, in some way perhaps a time, and for many, an idea. The space is roughly defined by the headwaters of the Niger and its affluents and lies in western Mali and eastern Guinea; it is occupied by the Malinke, for whom it is a symbolic heartland from which the more widespread branches of their people have departed [or claim to have departed —J. J.] at various times to take on different names (Mandinka, Dyula, Konyaka, and others). As a time, the Manden looks back to its period of unification and glory under the emperor Sunjata. . . . To speak of the Manden is, of necessity, to evoke the time and space of Sunjata's rule: thus, the Manden is also an idea spread across Africa" (Stephen P. Belcher, *Epic Traditions of Africa* [Bloomington and Indianapolis: Indiana University Press, 1999], 89). The region where I have done all my fieldwork is often called the "Mande heartland."

4. This was the way it was worded by Sarah Brett Smith (letter, May 2, 2001). In 1992, David Conrad was more convinced: "The collective pilgrim figure [Nfa Jigin —J. J.] is based on, or at least largely influenced by, Mansa Musa, the Malian emperor who made the pilgrimage to Mecca in 1324" (David C. Conrad, "Searching for History in the Sunjata Epic: the Case of Fakoli," *History in Africa* 19 [1992]: 152). In 2001, Conrad wrote: "It seems safe to say that this pilgrimage was similarly important for Mansa Musa's subjects back in Mali, and in fact it seems possible that it could have given rise to the legend of Fajigi. . . ." (David C. Conrad, "Pilgrim Fajigi and Basiw from Mecca: Islam and Traditional Religion in the Former French Sudan," in *Bamana Art of Existence in Mali,* ed. J.-P. Colleyn [New York: Museum for African Art, 2001], 25–33).

5. Tauxier in Sarah Brett-Smith, *The Artfulness of M'Fa Jigi—An Interview with Nyamaton Diara* (Madison: African Studies Program, University of Wisconsin at Madison, 1996), 4.

6. Conrad, "Searching for History," 147.

7. Ibid., 148.

8. [Note added by J. J.] Whether the external accounts are substantial might be a matter of taste. However, it should be noted that all the authors discussed here (including myself) accept the "fact" that a rich African king really visited Cairo in the fourteenth century. It might be doubted whether a muslim king was allowed to go on pilgrimage. B. Flemming, emerita Prof. of Turkish at Leiden, informed me (e-mail, May 16, 2001) that there is no tradition of pilgrimage to Mecca by Ottoman reigning Sultans. Rather, there is a tradition of making lavish endowments to the Holy Places. She referred to Hannes Moehring, "Mekkawahlfahrten orientalischer und afrikanischer Herscher im Mittelalter," *Oriens* 34 (1994): 314–29 (which I have not read). Pekka Masonen replied to me (e-mail, June 18, 2001), when I asked him about pilgrimages and Al-Maqrizi's text on Mansa Musa in particular: "Al-Maqrizi's text lists several rulers (not only West African) who made pilgrimage to Mecca. Besides the monarchs of Mali, the rulers of Bornu, for instance visited Mecca.

Mansa Musa was not the first Malian monarch who went to Mecca. Before him, Mansa Qu and Mansa Sakura performed the pilgrimage. For the Malian royal pilgrims, al-Maqrizi is not an original source. He largely repeats al-Umari and Ibn Khaldun and some other fourteenth-century Egyptian eyewitnesses." See also Pekka Masonen, *The Negroland Revisited— Discovery and Invention of the Sudanese Middle Ages* (Helsinki: Finnish Academy of Science and Letters, 2000), chaps. 4 and 5.

9. Conrad, "Pilgrim Fajigi."

10. Conrad, "Pilgrim Fajigi."

11. For an impression of the hegemony of Sunjata in Mande history, see Ralph A. Austen, ed., *In Search of Sunjata—The Mande Oral Epic as History, Literature and Performance* (Bloomington and Indianapolis: Indiana University Press, 1999); for a sociohistorical explanation of this hegemony, see Stephen P. D. Bulman, "A School for Epic? The 'École William Ponty' and the Evolution of the Sunjata Epic," paper for the conference "Emergent Epics" (Leiden, 21–22 May 2001).

12. This, in my impression, is done often by poorly informed storytellers, who— confronted with a hero they do not know—take a safe escape route by referring to the main frame of historical imagination, which is the Sunjata epic. An example of this is the way the famous storyteller Wa Kamissoko—who published several books with Y. T. Cissé, and who is from a village fifty kilometers from Narena—incorporated Narena's founding hero Nankoman into the Sunjata epic, although this hero is in Narena the protagonist of an narrative cycle that does not refer to Sunjata (see Seydou Camara and Jan Jansen, eds., *La geste de Nankoman—Textes sur la fondation de Narena* [Leiden: Research School CNWS publishers, 1999]). See also Conrad ("Searching for History") on the way Fakoli and Nfa Jigin "travel" between the Mecca narrative and the Sunjata epic.

13. Bala Kante (born 1926) from Farabako was enthusiastic about my work, and in 1999 he often came voluntarily to me to "talk about the past." He was a unique person. In total, I recorded him for more than six hours. When I met him in March 2000, Bala had become ill, and he was not so talkative anymore. A selection of recordings with Bala Kante is scheduled to be published in a Maninka-French text edition in 2003. The translation I present here is based on a transcription and French translation by Muntaga Jarra (DNAFLA, Bamako).

14. Authors tend to relate Nfa Jigin stories to incest and sex—Nyamaton's account (in Brett-Smith, *Artfulness*), for instance, has many references to sexuality. It is often said that Nfa Jigin sinned, because he slept with his mother, thus making of him an African Oedipus. In Bala Kante's version, given the terms he uses, the intercourse between Nfa Jigin and his father's wife has—practically—nothing to do with ("biological") incest. Maninka have a polygamous marriage system. Men marry one to three wives, but some rich men marry a fourth wife. The marriage of a fourth wife always generates a lot of discussion. This fourth wife is (very) young and very beautiful—I can assure you from the few I ever met. She usually is quite younger than the husband's oldest son(s), and therefore the (classificatory) son is a sexually attractive partner to his (classificatory) mother. Muntaga Jarra translated "fourth wife" with "young spouse," which explains already local tensions related to this phenomenon; thus, in Bala's interpretation, this theme is about lust and sex, not about incest.

15. "Vous" can also be produced in Maninka by addressing someone with *kòrò* or *n kòrò* ("elder" or "my elder"), or *n ba* ("my mother") to women.

16. Charles Bailleul, *Dictionnaire Bambara Français* Bamako: Donniya, 1996) gives *jigi* as "hope," and *jigin* as "to descend." In my area of fieldwork, people clearly pronounced the second "n" in Nfa Jigin.

17. Mentioned in Brett-Smith, *Artfulness,* and in Paulo F. de Moraes Farias, "Pilgrimages to 'Pagan' Mecca in Mandenka Stories of Origin Reported from Mali and Guinea-Conakry," in *Discourse and Its Disguises—The Interpretation of African Oral Texts,* ed. Karin Barber and Paulo F. de Moraes Farias (Birmingham: University of Birmingham, Centre of West African Studies, 1989), 162.

18. The name "Jigin" features often in Mande stories: "Jigifagajigi" (*faga* = to kill) is mentioned in the Traore praise song as a king killed by Tiramagan Traore (cf. Jan Jansen, Esger Duintjer, and Boubacar Tamboura, eds., *L'Epopée de Sunjara, d'après Lansine Diabate de Kela* (Leiden: Research School CNWS publishers, 1995). I suggest that Jigifagajigi and Jigimakanjigi (which features as "Jigin from Mekka" in Nfa Jigin stories) are the same figure, who happened to become pronounced differently because of the context. Cissé's comparaison of Jigin with a sacred ram (cf. Moraes Farias "Pilgrimages," 163–64) is interesting, but equally speculative.

19. For the moment, I don't see a relationship with the term *mansa jigin,* the "local" term for the Sunjata epic in the region of Kela. *Mansa* = king, and the term *mansa jigin* is explained as "the event the kings come together" or "the dispute of the kings" or (most acceptable to me) "the genealogy of the kings" (cf. also Bailleul, *Dictionnaire,* 162 and 270). The term for the Nfa Jigin story—*nfa jigin* as a general genealogical account of the deeds of the ancestor(s)—might have become the name of the story's antagonist, but this is mere speculation.

20. Conference, "Transcript of the Sunjata Epic Conference" (Chicago, 13–15 November 1991).

21. I agree with reading "Makantaajigin" as "Jigin who went to Mecca." However, one should not always translate "Makan" into Mecca (I disagree here with Brett-Smith, *Artfulness,* 40); Magan/Makan is a word that features in many names of Mande kings and heroes. It probably is an old word for ruler, of Soninke origin (see Viacheslav Misiugin and Valentin F. Vydrin, "Some Archaic Elements in the Manden Epic Tradition: The 'Sunjata Epic' Case," *Saint Petersburg Journal of African Studies* 2 [1993]: 105), but certainly is a Maninka man's name.

22. See Brett-Smith, *Artfulness,* 3: "M'Fa Jigi and Early Mande History." Brett-Smith applies an argument similar to the one applied to Nfa Jigin and also to Jitumu Bala and the origin of sand divination.

23. See Ralph A. Austen and Jan Jansen, "History, Oral Transmission and Structure in Ibn Khaldun's Chronology of Mali Rulers," *History in Africa* 23 (1996): 17–28.

24. Ralph A. Austen, "The Historical Transformation of Genres: Sunjata as Panegyric, Folktale, Epic and Novel" in *In Search of Sunjata—The Mande Oral Epic as History, Literature and Performance,* ed. Ralph A. Austen (Bloomington and Indianapolis: Indiana University Press, 1999), 69–87.

25. Jan Jansen, "Masking Sunjata—A Hermeneutical Critique," *History in Africa* 27 (2000): 131–41.

26. I disagree here with Conrad, who wrote: "Evidence from all available oral sources indicates that the major characters of the Sunjata epic can be composites of any number of mythological, legendary, and historical figures from virtual any period prior to the sixteenth century." (Conrad, "Searching for History," 149). In my opinion, this general statement is self-evident, with the exception of the "prior to the sixteenth century," which cannot be proven, due to lack of sources.

27. D. H. Fischer, *Historians' Fallacies—Towards a Logic of Historical Thought* (New York: Harper Pereenial, 1970), 153–54.

28. Here, I might pay not enough attention to Moraes Farias ("Piligrimages"), who proposed seeing similarities between Nfa Jigin's trip and the initiation to the Komo society. Moraes Farias avoids in this article a historical claim in for the time depth of the Nfa Jigin narrative, but does not seem to have had the intention of searching the methodological debate which I seek in this article.

29. Cf. Yves Person, "Nyaani Mansa Mamadu et la fin de l'empire du Mali," in *Le Sol, la parole et l'écrit: 2000 ans de l'histoire africaine: mélanges en hommage à Raymond Mauny* (Paris: Société française d'histoire d'outre-mer, 1981), 630; Person seems to hint at researchers such as Niane, who embellished West African history by mixing twentieth-century oral tradition with medieval written sources.

30. Fischer, *Historians' Fallacies,* 51–53.

31. David Robinson, *Paths of Accomodation—Muslim Societies and French Colonial Authorities in Senegal and Mauritania, 1880–1920* (Athens, Oxford: Ohio University Press/James Currey, 2000), 80.

32. Told by Modibo Keita (born circa 1957) from the village of Farabako (arrondissement de Siby) on August 25, 1999. Modibo is a devote Muslim who does not drink alcohol and who is not practicing sand divination. He was surprised that I had not heard the story before. This recording was the first recording/interview Modibo Keita ever did. Hence the introduction to the other people in his room and the deliberate end. For my translation, I heavily lean on the transcription and translation into French by Ouana Faran Camara (DNAFLA, Bamako).

33. For El Haji Umar, see David Robinson, *The Holy War of Umar Tal* (Oxford: Oxford University Press, 1985) and John H. Hanson, *Migration, "Jihad," and Muslim Authority in West Africa—The Futanke Colonies in Karta* (Bloomington and Indianapolis: Indiana University Press, 1996).

34. The part about the five korans is difficult to translate. I am grateful to Geert Mommersteeg (see also his "Allah's Words as Amulet" *Etnofoor* 3, 1 [1990]: 63–76) for comments that improved the translation that Ouna Faran Camara had made for me. Mommersteeg told me that the theme of Five Holy Books is well known in Islamic magical traditions; it represents the idea that the Bible has hidden knowledge that has never arrived into Islam. "Lanyini" (in Camara's transcription) is the verb "to investigate" in Bailleul, *Dictionnaire,* but must be pronounced as a word derived from "injil," the Arab word for the Bible. "Tuwereta" is the Torah. "Jaburu" is the Book of Psalms. The fifth book is the book of the secrets of the West. I also had difficulties in understanding Camara's translation of the divine proposal on iron, but hearing the story, Boubacar Tamboura, a friend of mine with whom I translated the Sunjata epic (Jansen et al., *L'Epopée*), interpreted it as a reference to the use of steel in the construction of buildings and railways. The Farabako blacksmiths often expressed to me their admiration for trains and railways, and this supports Tamboura's interpretation.

35. For a fine article on the alleged secrets of the white people, see Molly D. Roth, "The 'Secret' in Malian Historical Consciousness: Re-narrating the West," *Mande Studies* 2 (2000): 41–54. Mommersteeg suggested also a book by H. Turner, titled *The Secrets of the West.* I have not been able to locate this book.

36. For a recording of this song by the griots from Kela: *Bonya/Respect—Griot Music from Mali II* (Leiden: PAN Records, CD 2059, 1997).

37. Mamadi Kaba, *Anthologie de chants mandingues* (Paris: L'Harmattan, 1995). In a note Kaba adds: "Aux premières heures du régime colonial, un riche marchand fut le pre-

mier à se construire une maison en dur. On l'a surnommé 'Mamadi Bitiki' ou 'Mamadi en maison dur.' On lui dédia ce morceau qui fut fredonné partout. Mais malheureusement, Mamadi Bitiki par un revers de fortune, devint très pauvre et se mit à vendre du bois de chauffe. Quand il surprit une riche cliente fredonnant cette chanson, il lui déclina son identité et son passé en concluant que ce qui compte pour tout homme, ce n'est pas le départ, mais l'arrivée, c'est-à-dire la fin. Le mot bitiki est une déformation de boutique qui désigne la maison en dur. Ce morceau est un diagba." Ibid., 8 describes a "diagba" as a popular dance with jembe music.

38. On June 18, 2002, I presented a paper on the Mamadi Bitiki narrative (recorded in 1999 with Bala Kante from Farabako) at the 5th International Conference on Mande Studies (held in Leiden, The Netherlands, June 17–21).

39. See, for instance, Clemens Zobel, "Les génies du Kòma: Identités locales, logiques religieuses et enjeux socio-politiques dans les monts Manding du Mali," *Cahiers d'Études africaines* 144 (1996): 625–58.

40. See, for instance Jan Jansen, "The Younger Brother and the Stranger-in Search of a Status Discourse for Mande," *Cahiers d'Études africaines* 144 (1996): 659–88.

41. I disagree here with Conrad, who says that these stories "viewed in isolation seem more relevant to the history of Mande oral art than to the thirteenth century" ("Searching for History," 161). Here Conrad delimits his body of evidence to the Sunjata corpus (cf. the title of Conrad "Searching for History"); if he had incorporated a wider range of products of "oral art," these sources would have come "out of the isolation" and should be interpreted as meaningful in a nineteenth- or twentieth-century context.

42. The first reference to a Komo ceremony stems from 1881, as far as I know (Vallière's account in Joseph S. Gallieni, *Voyage au Soudan français (Haut-Niger et pays de Segou), 1879–1881, par le Commandant Gallieni* (Paris: La Hachette, 1885). Thus, corresponding ethnographic data for a possible earlier date of the Nfa Jigin narrative is also absent.

43. Brett-Smith's choice to present Nfa Jigin as the "prototypical artist" (in *Artfulness)* embodies, in my opinion, the aesthetic fallacy by making him an artist.

16

KINGSHIP AND THE MEDIATORS OF THE PAST: ORAL TRADITION AND RITUAL PERFORMANCE IN NUPELAND, NIGERIA[1]

Constanze Weise

Introduction

According to oral tradition, the precolonial centralised Nupe Kingdom and the Edegi dynasty were founded by the culture hero Tsoede or Edegi.[2] This legitimating tradition provides support for both the kingship system and its rulers up to the present day. It is therefore not surprising that most existing Nupe king lists also begin with Tsoede.[3] Scholars like Ade Obayemi and Aliyu Idrees have found the Tsoede legend to be a valid source for the reconstruction of the precolonial Nupe History.[4] However, Michael Mason has argued that Tsoede is an invention of the twentieth century.[5]

Before the nineteenth century, the Nupe kingdom belonged to the most important military powers in the Niger-Benue confluence area.[6] Its spheres of political influence reached far into the territory of Bussa in the northwest, the regions of the Kamuku, Gbayi, and Kamberi in the north, and the Yoruba subgroups of the Igbomina, Yagba, Owe, and Oworo on the west bank of the river Niger.[7] By the time of Etsu Mohammad's death in 1805, the moment when the kingdom began its decline, the influence of the Nupe Empire had extended beyond Nupeland into the northeast of the Old Oyo kingdom of the Yoruba people.[8]

Although the Nupe people have experienced many transformations during the last two hundred years—such as the fall of the Nupe kingdom by 1805, the impact of Muslim Fulbe rulers during the nineteenth century, the British colonial power by the end of that century, and finally the modern Nigerian state in the post-colonial period—its system of kingship has survived into the present with the two Edegi successor dynasties at Pategi and Zugurma. The complex traditions concerning the origins of the Nupe Kingdom that have collected around the mythical hero Tsoede and subsequent history are preserved by the Nupe kings themselves, as well as by royal officials. Until recently these accounts were supplemented by non-Islamic ceremonies and rituals recalling and reenacting the past, such as the installation of the Nupe kings. Although these rituals have since been abandoned in favour of Islamic rituals, their performative plots and speeches are preserved by those officials who were involved in their performance, namely the king-makers and the traditional priests.

While historical events in the nineteenth century and the beginning of the twentieth century in Nupeland are analysed in the historical studies of Mason and Idrees, the pre-nineteenth-century era is discussed only as the introduction to their main themes.[9] However, Obayemi pays more attention to this time period in his various articles on the peoples of the Niger-Benue confluence area.[10] One of the reasons that the pre-nineteenth-century history of the Nupe people has been so neglected may be the fact that for this period we have to rely entirely on nonwritten sources, of which oral tradition is probably the most important, as other sources have so far been ignored.

This chapter argues that the historical circumstances in which the Tsoede legend has been preserved suggest that it is not an invention of the twentieth century and again emphasises the hypothesis of its historical value for the reconstruction of the pre-nineteenth-century history of Nupeland. The concern of the present author is also to show that the Tsoede legend was and is still part of the ideology of Nupe kingship as rooted in the precolonial, non-Islamic religious complex of Nupe society. While each of the above-mentioned views contains important insights, the imprint of ritual on the Tsoede tradition has largely been overlooked, while the importance of rites connected to Tsoede, the mythical ancestor, for historical analysis has not been examined. I shall therefore try to shed light on the installation rites of the Nupe kings as the core of the royal ritual and show their relationship with the Tsoede legend. I shall also demonstrate that Tsoede belongs to a non-Islamic religious complex of the Nupe society by examining the structures of the ritual practices associated with the Ndakogboya or Gunnu cult, which are still attached to the mythical ancestor.

The Circumstances of the Preservation of Tradition in Nupeland

The Tsoede legend, the different royal rituals, and the Nupe king lists owe their preservation to a particular set of historical circumstances. By the beginning of the nineteenth century, the precolonial Nupe kingdom had begun its decline. According to Idrees, the main cause of its downfall was the political instability that resulted from a series of succession disputes among the ruling Edegi dynasty after the death of Etsu Mohammed in 1805. This friction culminated in the splitting of the Edegi dynasty into the Gwagbazhi and Yissazhi factions.[11] The political weakness of the Nupe state was exploited by the Fulbe under the leadership of Malam Dendo, who intervened in Nupeland and eliminated the dynasty.[12] Although their power had effectively been eclipsed, the two factions of the Edegi dynasty tried to regain some measure of political independence and waged wars of resistance against the alien rulers between 1833 and 1897.[13] During these wars the Gwagbazhi faction suffered considerably more casualties than the Yissazhi. The resulting numerical advantage eventually benefited the Yissazhi, whose members held on to many royal traditions and institutions at Gbara, their last residence before the exodus to Patigi.[14] Towards the end of the nineteenth century, an opportunity to regenerate the Edegi dynasty was created by the British conquest of Bida, which had become the capital of the Fulbe rulers by 1857.[15] Both factions supported the British conquest of Bida and, as a reward for their assistance, both groups won spheres of political influence under British overlordship.[16] In effect, freedom from Fulbe domination did not result in independence for either the Gwagbazhi or the Yissazhi: the latter established an Emirate at Patigi in 1898, while the former founded a district around Zugurma that was absorbed into the Fulani Emirate of Kontagora in 1906.[17]

Oral evidence from traditional titleholders at the royal court in Patigi, whose parents were witnesses to the exodus, confirms the movement of the Yissazhi faction and of many of its supporters to this new base.[18] Idrees classified the migration into four waves. First came the shadow Etsu Nupe at Gbara, Idrisu Gana, followed by his children and members of the royal family. Next came a group of royal and nonroyal, civil and military Nupe nobility. Among the people making up the second wave was also the

Ndazhigi, the traditional chief priest of the royal shrine to Tsoedemba. Finally, Nupe and non-Nupe runaway slaves, as well as the inhabitants of several settlements that had given their allegiance to the Yissazhi, moved into the area and founded settlements around Patigi. According to eyewitness accounts, as soon as the Patigi Emirate was established, these various newly arrived groups began functioning in offices that were current in pre-Fulani times.

The reestablishment of the revived socio-political instititutions provided the foundations on which the regenerated factions of the dynasty developed at Patigi and Zugurma.[19] The Yissazhi were apparently more successful than the Gwagbazhi in reestablishing Nupe kingship and the associated rituals because they benefited from the Emirate that the British had created for them. The Gwagbazhi had been so much absorbed in the Fulbe Emirate of Kontagora that it was very difficult for them to establish their own political identity.

The Tsoede Legend and the Foundation of the Nupe Kingdom

Both successor dynasties, the Yissazhi at Patigi as well as the Gwagbazhi at Zugurma, claim descent from the mythical ancestor Tsoede, who is said to have founded the precolonial Nupe kingdom and established the Edegi ruling dynasty. Accounts of this tradition of origin are also known as the Tsoede legend, which provides a justification for the bases of Nupe kingship. The most elaborate version of the Tsoede legend was recorded by Nadel in 1934. His informant was the Nupe king of Patigi, Etsu Umaru Ibn Muazu (1931–66).[20] Although this is not the first record of this tradition of origin, it is probably the best known. An earlier version had been collected from an important traditional Nupe titleholder, the Lille of Mokwa,[21] by Leo Frobenius during his fourth DIAFE expedition to Nigeria and northern Cameroon in 1910–12.[22]

The legend recorded by Nadel runs as follows:

> The earliest history of Nupe centres round the figure of Tsoede or Edegi, the cultural hero and mythical founder of Nupe kingdom. . . . At this time, the tradition runs, there was no kingdom of Nupe, only small chieftainships which, among the Beni, were united in a confederacy under the chief of Nku, a village near the confluence of Niger and Kaduna. At that time the Nupe people were tributary to the Atta (king) of Gara, at Eda (Idah), far

down the Niger. The tribute was paid in slaves, and every family head had annually to contribute one male member of his house. These slaves, as tradition has it, were always sister's sons. It so happened that the son of the Atta Gara came hunting to Nku in Nupe country. Here he met the daughter of the chief of Nku, a young widow, fell in love with her, and lived with her for some time. When the death of his father recalled him to his country, to succeed to the throne of the Gara, this woman was pregnant. He left her a charm and a ring to give to their child when it was born. This child was Tsoede. Then the old chief of Nku died, his son became chief, and when Tsoede was 30 years of age the new chief sent him, as his sister's son, as slave to Eda. The Atta Gara recognised his son in the new slave by the charm and ring which he was wearing, and kept him near his person, treating him almost like his legitimate sons. Tsoede stayed for thirty years at his father's court. Once the king fell victim to a mysterious illness which nobody could cure. . . . Thus, when the Atta felt his death coming, he advised his son to flee, and to return to his own country, the rule of which he bestowed on him as a parting gift. He assisted him in his flight, he gave him riches of all kinds, and bestowed on him various insignia of kingship: a bronze canoe "as only kings have," manned with twelve Nupe slaves; the bronze kakati, the long trumpets which are still the insignia of kings in the whole of Northern Nigeria; state drums hung with brass bells; and the heavy iron chains and fetters which, endowed with strong magic, have become the emblems of the king's judicial power, and are known today as *egba Tsoede,* Chain of Tsoede. . . . Tsoede than went to Nupeko . . , killed the chief, and made himself the chief of the place. He conquered Nku, the town of his maternal uncle, made himself the ruler of all Beni . . . , and assumed the title *Etsu,* king. He made the twelve man who had accompanied him from Eda the chiefs of the twelve towns of Beni and bestowed on them the sacred insignia of chieftainship, brass bangles and magic chains. . . . Tsoede carried out big and victorious wars against many tribes and kingdoms, conquering in the south the countries of Yagbam Bunu, Kakanda, as far as Akoko, and in the north the countries of Ebe, Kamberi, and Kamuku. . . .[23]

The above Tsoede legend points first of all to the possibility that Nupeland might once have been tributary to the king of the Igala, the Attah of Idah, because, up to the middle of the nineteenth century, all the riverine polities up and down the Niger and Benue, including the Ebira kingdoms of Opanda and Igu with the Kakanda, acknowledged the Attah of Idah as their overlord and paid him tribute.[24] A probably late reflection of this could still be observed some years before Nadel's arrival in Nupeland, when the Attah of Idah visited Bida and insisted on being given a higher seat than the Emir of Bida, basing his claim on the remembered historical fact of ancient Nupe vassalship to Idah.[25] Although it is not clear which time horizon the reference to Igala overlordship reflects, there is a general agreement that the legend may contain historical evidence for the former political relationship between the Igala and the Nupe.[26]

Secondly, as observed by Obayemi, the narrative provided in the Tsoede legend, that Tsoede killed his maternal uncle in his maternal home at Nupeko before declaring himself Etsu,[27] might be an indication of the military conquest of Nupeland by Tsoede and the establishment of a new order of political centralisation.[28] This hypothesis is supported by Idrees, who sees in Tsoede the representation of a revolutionary introduction of a new political order that overwhelmed the Bini confederacy.[29]

However, Mason interprets the Tsoede legend entirely differently. For him it is simply an invention of the twentieth century, and he argues strongly against any value the legend might have for the historical reconstruction of the Nupe past before the nineteenth century:

> "Tsoede" was born in the early twentieth century (as "Edegi," "Choedi," or "Tsoede") and was properly christened with the appearance of his name in *A Black Byzantium* in 1942. The myth, or "mythical charter" as Nadel called it, had almost no substance before he and his colonial predecessors began to force-feed it. It was linked to modern history by a chain of names that apparently were forged in the minds of one or more of the Bida ruling class in the late nineteenth century. Neither "Tsoede" nor his successors before the mid-eighteenth century are demonstrably historical figures. Thus we can fruitfully discuss Nupe history without mentioning them, for the real basis for a reconstruction of the Nupe past comes from sources independent of those created by colonial officials and colonial anthropologists.[30]

The question that arises here is whether or not the Tsoede legend could indeed reflect historical events that led to the foundation of Nupe kingship. Strong evidence against Mason's argument that Tsoede may have been invented during the twentieth century comes from an account of the traveller Clapperton, which was published in 1829 and is probably the earliest written evidence for the Tsoede legend:

> He (Tsoede as Thoodyar) first conquered the territory of Beni (Bini), from the river called Bakoo (Gbako) to that which is named Kaduna. . . . He thence embarked on the river Kowara, and subdued the people on its bank, called Abagha (?), after which he conquered the country of Abbi (Ebe) (in which we now are) and that of Kambari (Kamberi) in conjunction with the Prince of Yaouri (Yauri).[31]

In certain other oral accounts, it is assumed that Tsoede died at Gbagede in the Kamberi territory on a military expedition, where in the village of Gwagede a grave and some relics, including a shrine, are still identified today with Tsoede.[32] Obayemi argues that this oral tradition and the Tsoede legend might be indications of an initial territorial expansion of the Nupe kingdom northwards.[33]

Unfortunately we still lack precise time indications for the pre-nineteenth-century history of Nupeland. Here archaeological research, especially at the settlements along the rivers Niger and Kaduna and the places which served as the residences of the Nupe kings at various times, like Nupeko, Gbara, or Jima, might provide some chronological clues.[34] Until now the pre-nineenth-century chronology of the Nupe kingdom has relied only on the Nupe king list, of which several versions exist, and some synchronisms in external sources. In contrasting the different versions of the king list, only one synchronism can be established in the *Kano Chronicle,* the chronicle of the Hausa kingdom of Kano. Here, the ruler Etsu Nupe Jibrilu is mentioned as the first Nupe king, who introduced shields to Kano during the time of Sarkin Kano Kumbari (1731–43).[35] While the Patigi list indicates that Etsu Jibrilu reigned between 1733 and 1746, the Zugurma list gives the dates 1719–32.[36]

While Obayemi uses the existing Nupe king lists to support the thesis that "the legend and the king lists are rooted in the actual experience of an African people,"[37] Mason argues that both the Tsoede legend and the king lists, especially those that were recorded during the colonial period, are a "colonial version of the Nupe history."[38] According to him the king lists have become the "twin offspring of the mating of the colonial administration and the Nupe ruling class" and have served for the legitimation of Nupe rule for the two Edegi succession dynasties.[39]

The different versions of the Nupe king list can be classified into at least two groups: those that were recorded outside the Edegi ruling family, and those that were transmitted by the two successor dynasties. The king list collected by the second British Resident at Bida, H. S. Goldsmith, had been recorded from the Alkali and Limam of Bida, Umaru, in 1902.[40] Although Umaru was a great scholar of his time and had even provided the account of Nupe history published in *Labarun Hausawa da Maƙwabtansu,* he did not belong to the Nupe royal family but was related to the Fulbe conquerors.[41] One colonial officer, Rochfort-Rae, obtained information from the Alkali at Shonga, while the missionary Samuel Crowther collected notes on king names in 1857 at Jebba but did not identify his informants.[42] Frobenius was given a king list by the Lille of Mokwa in 1911.[43]

The lists associated with the ruling houses of Patigi and Zugurma seem to be far more precise than those of the above-mentioned group.[44] According to the Etsu Zugurma, the Zugurma king list was first written down during the time of Etsu Majiya (1804–56) in Arabic and was translated into Hausa. The Patigi list is said to have been written by a Mallam at Bida in Arabic and brought to Patigi by Etsu Idrisi Gana in 1898. It has been used since then by the Patigi rulers, and new kings were always added to it.[45]

According to Mason, the recorded king lists and oral traditions are not particularly well preserved, "as might have been the case had there been in Nupe an institutional means of recording history."[46] However, Mason did not investigate the transmission of the Nupe king lists or the Tsoede legend, and nor did Nadel. Nor did he make inquiries into the context in which the Tsoede tradition was narrated. Therefore, instead of discussing the different versions of the Nupe king lists, I shall focus interest on how the king lists and the *Tsoede* legend were transmitted and by whom.[47]

Although it is not possible to extrapolate from the present back into the past, we may obtain some clues as to how Nupe history and culture might have been transmitted at the Nupe royal court. According to the present Etsu Nupe Patigi, the Nupe kings were traditionally taught from several sources, including their fathers, important titleholders like the Ndeji (the chief king-maker), and members of the Royal Council.[48] The Patigi king lists were always recited by court musicians on certain occasions. These were the enthronement ceremony of a new king, the two Islamic festivals, īd al-fiṭr and īd al-kabīr, and the marriage of the king's daughters. Above all, the musicians played every Thursday night in front of the Etsu's palace, and the bards would praise the king's ancestral fathers up to the present king, including when the king was not in town. According to the Etsu Patigi the knowledge and history of the kingdom was passed on from the king to his sons, but was also often recalled by certain important titleholders who were close to the king.[49]

As the chief king-maker, the Ndeji is especially considered to be the bearer of this knowledge. It is he who will advise the king after the installation and who will rule the country during the interregnum to prevent chaos until the appointment of a new king. When a new king comes to the throne, he will be provided with knowledge about his forefathers.[50]

The strong association between the Nupe king list, in which Tsoede is always mentioned as the first king, and the Tsoede legend is evident. What is also very interesting in this context is the fact that the court historian of the royal court at Zugurma started to recite parts of the Tsoede tradition of origin when he was narrating the history and the Zugurma king list of the Nupe kings.[51] Therefore it may be of interest to examine the enthronement rituals of the Nupe kings. Although Nadel recorded the Tsoede tradition during his very short stay at Patigi, he did not ask about the royal rituals.[52] These rituals have the potential to demonstrate not only that Tsoede is not an invention of the twentieth century, but also that the institution of kingship is rooted in a precolonial and pre-Islamic religious complex.

The Installation Rites of the Nupe Kings

The succession dispute which had been responsible for the schism in the Nupe kingdom and the factionalisation of the Edegi dynasty at the beginning of the nineteenth century had led to both factions limiting the succession to the descendants of their progenitors. The Gwagbazhi were able to make succession an exclusive preserve of the descendants of Etsu Majiya,[53] while the Yissazhi limited succession to the descendants of Etsu Jimada and beyond that to the descendants and brothers of Etsu Idrisu Gana (1898–1900).[54] Both factions reconstituted the institution of the king-makers on the basis of the old Nupe principle of government. However, it took until the reign of Etsu Usuman Tsado (1923–31) for this institution to start functioning in Patigi.[55] No member of the Royal Council was appointed to the king-makers' group to counter their bias. The king-makers were chaired by the Ndeji, the head of the Enagitsu, the Civil Council.[56] The Islamic institution of the Alkali was integrated into the king-maker's group to provide legal advice after the kingdom at Patigi had been newly established.[57]

According to most of the Nupe king lists, the Nupe kings had already been converted to Islam before the nineteenth century. The Nupe king Etsu Jibril, who is also mentioned in the *Kano Chronicle,* is even described in it as the first Muslim ruler.[58] Nevertheless the installation rituals of the Nupe kings were perhaps less influenced by Islam in pre-Fulani times, as they were based on the non-Islamic ideology of kingship. Although the kings may have converted to Islam earlier than the majority of the Nupe population in central Nupeland, which experienced the strong impact of Islamisation during the Fulbe domination of the nineteenth century,[59] oral sources claim that it was only when the Yissazhi arrived in Patigi that Islam became generally accepted in this area.[60] The first ruler after the advent of this dynastic branch, Etsu Idrisu Gana (1898–1900), personally recruited Islamic scholars to preach permanently in the Patigi Emirate and sent his children to Islamic schools.[61]

While the Tsoede legend did serve, and still serves today, as an expression of royal ideology in both dynastic branches of the former Edegi dynasty, only the Yissazhi continued to commemorate Tsoede's founding of the Nupe kingship at the installation of a new king. The Gwagbazhi dynastic branch at Zugurma had been absorbed immediately into the Fulbe Emirate of Kontagora and adapted its installation ceremonies to Islamic practice. While at Zugurma, the Etsu and his councillors could only demonstrate the symbolic paraphernalia of kingship, the king-makers and older councillors at Patigi remembered the performance of the royal installation ceremonies and the role played by the Ndazhigi, the traditional chief priest of the Tsoede shrine at Patigi, Tsoedemba, in choosing the new king.[62] Only much later, at the end of the twentieth century, was this role taken over by the chief Imam of Patigi.[63]

The priest of Tsoedemba, whose title was Ndazhigi, also sometimes called Swagannuwon, and his family migrated together with the dynastic branch of the Yissazhi from the old residence of Gbara to Patigi at the end of the nineteenth century.[64] The oldest chief king-maker of Patigi and the head of the Enakun or Military Council and present member of the king-makers group, Tsadza, could still remember the role this institution played in the succession to the throne and the kingdom. As they state, up until the 1940s the shrine Tsoedemba had been in the centre of the town and its priest Ndazhigi, who was in charge of the shrine, served the Patigi kings directly. The shrine contained an iron canoe with the iron chain of Tsoede, which served as object of worship.[65] Whenever a king died, the Ndeji ruled for the period of the interregnum, which usually lasted not more than seven days.[66] The Ndazhigi, who was quickly informed of the ruler's demise, immediately conducted certain sacrifices on the chain of Tsoede. Once the new king had been appointed a message was sent to the shrine, and the priest conferred with the oracle and offered additional sacrifices on the chain. Only if the sacrifices were accepted and the oracle agreed with the choice of candidate could the new king be installed.[67]

During the installation, the new king was handed specific regalia by the Ndeji. Some of these items were accepted as having been brought by Tsoede from Idah to Nupeland in his canoe and may have been maintained by the Yissazhi during the devastating period of the nineteenth century and finally brought to Patigi by them. Among the most important items of paraphernalia were the *efin Tsoede,* the Tsoede bangles made from brass, which the Etsu had to wear until he died.[68]

Some of the regalia of the former Edegi dynasty were lost during the resistance wars of the nineteenth century. The famous royal drums, as the most effective paraphernalia of office, were seized by the Fulbe authorities and are now in the possession of the Fulani Emir of Bida. They had been used exclusively by the Edegi dynasty during special ceremonies and in military campaigns in the pre-Fulani era.[69] Others, such as the bronze ring presented to Etsu Idrisu Gana in 1898 by the Royal Niger Company, were incorporated by the Yissazhi into the staff of office of Patigi as a mark of its independence from Fulbe domination.[70]

According to the Tsadza, the installation ceremonies ended with the king's investiture on the throne. But before the investiture was complete, the king and the senior members of the Royal Council had to offer sacrifices to Tsoede. The prayer that the Tsadza could remember the Ndazhigi saying was:

> In the name of Soko[71]
> Whatever calamity is present now
> May Soko not let it prevail
> may the Almighty God remove it from our land
> Be there present disease
> Be there something in the town
> Be it that something afflicts the Etsu
> In the name of the king
> I should remove it
> May it be so
>
> Sòkó
> Eyan na dando gbâní na
> Sókò à lugwa yan wŭncìn dan bo ma
> Tsóci u lá wun kpe u ya kînmi yi bo
> Ráshè danbo o
> Eyan dan zhì o
> Eyan de etsu o
> Etsu ci lá yà mi na
> Mi ci à lá kjábo na
> Nyan wŭncìn gà fé

The Tsadza concluded:

> After they had said all what they wanted in prayer to the god Soko through Tsoede, then the Ndazhigi spread the blood of the animal and the corn-flour paste on the chain of Tsoede that was inside the canoe three times. All items used for the sacrifice had to be provided by the king.[72]

The last time these ceremonies were performed was at the investiture of King Etsu Umaru Ibn Muazu (1931–66). It was also he who gave Nadel the most elaborate account of the Tsoede legend. According to the present Etsu Patigi, the British took away the chain of Tsoede in the 1940s for "repairs" but never returned it.[73]

Some parts of the enthronement ceremony may have changed since then, because the most important symbol of power was missing. The installation rituals, however, were remembered by the oldest king-maker and the custodians of Tsoedemba, the latter of whom still live in the compound where the shrine was retained to keep the "memory of the place" alive.[74] The Tsadza, who belongs to the custodian family of Patigi, still bears the clan name Tsoedemba as part of his family name.[75]

Even though, compared to the 1940s, the enthronement rituals in Patigi have changed in such a way that Islam dominates them completely today, they still make reference to Tsoede. The Ndeji presents the traditional regalia and other staff of office to the king after the turbanning and the recitation of Islamic prayers by the Chief Imam.[76] Also, after the investiture, the king becomes part of the king list and takes his place in the royal genealogy that starts with Tsoede. From then on, the reigning king embodies the royal ancestor; as the present Etsu Nupe Patigi declares: "I am Tsoede."[77]

While the Yissazhi were able to retain a few insignia of office in their possession at Gbara and take them to Patigi, the Gwagbazhi were not so keen to maintain royal traditions. By the time they had been reestablished at Zugurma by the colonial administration, the Etsu Zugurma had to be content with just a few paraphernalia of office. His reduction to the status of a district head under the Emir of Kontagora even prevented elaborate paraphernalia from being re-created.[78] Nevertheless, after I asked him about the chain of Tsoede, the Etsu Zugurma showed it to me, explaining that it had been kept in a separate room since his father's and grandfather's time. Unfortunately he could not tell me what its purpose had been, but he was aware of its symbolic value and of the Tsoede legend associated with it.[79]

Even though the two Nupe kings base their legitimation on their descent from Tsoede, it is not clear what the royal ancestor represents. Deciphering who Tsoede was and his current significance remains a task for the future. Nevertheless, it is apparent that he represents a continuity of religious attitudes and practices of the pre-colonial past. Possibly, as Nadel has already stated, in pre-Fulani times the Nupe kings were semi-sacred rulers who owned the sacred power over the land and the people they ruled, and occupied a central position in the cosmic order of the Nupe universe.[80]

The Tsoede legend tells the story of the royal ancestor who arrives in Nupeland and makes a pact with the already established chiefs of the Bini confederation by giving them part of the sacred chain he had brought along with him in the boat. When Nadel conducted his field research, some villages along the river Niger between Jebba in the north and Egga in the south had owned the iron chain of Tsoede. They were called the *ledu* villages and were associated with prison and execution. Here the chain was considered a sacred effigy that protected the village from sickness and gave fertility to woman. According to Nadel here the chain was also called *ti zana,* the head of Dzana.[81] One legend tells how Tsoede inaugurated the chain by beheading his own maternal uncle, Dzana, placing the head and the chain together on the wooden tray as a permanent symbol of his power over life and death. From that day on the chain became a symbol of execution, and the villages that possessed it were those that performed executions: they were the king's hangman and were also known as *tete-cigbeci,* executioner–medicine-man. This term was also later changed to *Dogari*[82] *nya Tsoede,* or "Tsoede's policeman."[83]

During my fieldwork in 2000, in most of the villages along the river Niger I visited, that owned the chain of Tsoede, I observed a dual rulership of the political head, the *zhitsú,* and the religious head, the *zhigi.* Only at certain annual ceremonies the political head also performed priestly functions for local shrines to safeguard the welfare of the village and the fertility of the land. Apart from this exceptions, customarily the *zhitsu* caused the *zhigi* to perform the rituals. These villages belong to the network of the Ndakogboya/Gunnu cult that is spread all over central Nupeland and whose members still perform traditional rituals, despite having since become nominal Muslims. The question to be raised here might also be whether any relationship existed between the Ndakogboya cult and the Nupe kingdom, given that both institutions seem to be linked through the Tsoede legend and the symbolic chain.

Tsoede's Role in the Ndakogboya Cult Centres

Today the Ndakogboya[84] centres are associated with the last enclaves of the Nupe religion, whose origins may predate the introduction of Islam into Nupeland.[85] Although none of the informants I interviewed during my visits to these centres could recall the Tsoede tradition of origin completely, members of this secret society[86] trace the origin of the cult back to the time the central kingdom was established. In some versions of the legend, like that recorded by Frobenius at Mokwa in 1911, even the Ndakogboya masks are said to have come from Idah together with Tsoede in the bronze canoe.[87] Today most cult members remain firm in this belief. Each centre keeps an iron chain that Tsoede is said to have brought to Nupeland as an object of worship. The effigy is referred to as Tsoede and is used to contact Soko, the high and thunder god.[88] Especially during the annual Gunnu festival, which is celebrated in the Ndakogboya centres, the chain of Tsoede is used during the ritual initiating new cult members.

The medicine that will be used in the Ndakogboya centres throughout the year is produced during this seven days lasting festival. It is usually celebrated in the dry season after the harvest and performed to ask the god Soko to renew the fertility of the land, to safeguard the welfare of the village and the king, as well as to honour the ancestors.[89] While Gunnu is connected with herbal knowledge and the wisdom of medicine (*cigbe*), the Ndakogboya cult is also associated with the notion of a secret society. Most of the cult leaders are also addressed as "Ndace," head of the hunters. Some of them still perform this function.[90]

The Gunnu festival is usually the occasion when new members are initiated into the Ndakogboya cult.[91] Only initiated members are allowed to dance wearing the Ndakogboya masks. These masks consist of a long tube that in the past was colored white but today more usually is made from a coloured cotton cloth.[92] When Nadel was carrying out his field research, the masks were also known as *gunnuku* all over Nupeland, a name they still have as synonym in some centers. The term *gunnuku* may have been more popular in precolonial time than now because the neighboring Yoruba also call the Ndakogboya masks *igunnu*.[93] The Ndakogboya masks symbolize the collective authority of the dead and the association between former members of the community and the land. It is considered extremely dangerous to come too close to a mask during a performance. The masks are therefore always accompanied by men holding sticks to keep the crowd away. The cult is dominated by men, although women take part in it as singers or dancers. A masked performance consists of different elements: dancing, acrobatics or demonstrations by magicians performing sensational actions like swallowing fire or cutting themselves with a knife without getting hurt. The different dances of the masks are framed by songs and drumming. The songs which accompany the dancing are invocations to the god Soko, praise songs, proverbs, traditional wisdom and prayers.

Although the Nupe are aware that the dancer inside the mask is one of them, nobody knows his identity. The masked dancer speaks in a shrill, stylized voice that is associated with the ancestors. The audience feels the power it represents, which is potentially dangerous if wrongly treated, but if worshipped correctly will help the community by protecting it from communal impurities. Often the leader of the women, the *Sagi* or *Lelu,* dances opposite the masks. Traditionally the *Sagi* or *Lelu* was considered to be the most powerful "witch" in the village, whose secret knowledge could be used to benefit the community when turned into an organ of village administration. She was and still is seen as somebody who has the power to check and control the subversive activities of the other "witches."[94]

The initiation[95] usually lasts seven days, during which the novice will be given the secrets and knowledge of the cult and taught the procedures of the ceremony, the ways of manipulating the mask, the special dance steps and drum rhythms, and the story of Tsoede.[96] Tsoede, the ancestor, is present during the initiation in the form of a chain. Before the initiation starts the priest must conduct divination to confer with the Eba oracle as to whether the suggested candidate will be accepted.[97] If the oracle agrees, the young male applicant can bring the gifts for the sacrifice, which consist of a male cock, a black billy goat, different herbs, seven white kola nuts, palm wine, cowry shells, and certain other items. On the first day of the initiation, the chain of the ancestor Tsoede is used as an object of worship on which the blood of the cock and guinea-flower paste is spread. The prayer said during an initiation that I observed in Kusogi Doko was as follows:

> All right, Tsoede heel of the world
> Standing by our grandfathers
> Father Maajin of Awanko[98]
> You who planted the bamboo
> And bamboo began to fruit
> We, we have decided
> We want to say prayers
> By the tradition of our grandfathers
> As well as of our great-grandfathers
> The earthworm has no hoe
> When it breaks the ground with its mouth
> All right, the work we want to do
> By the tradition of our grandfathers
> Oh! Soko, whoever we initiated into it
> May Soko not allow him to sabotage us
> Whenever he sabotages us
> Both the mask and the spirit of the death, you know it yourself
> Both the mask and the spirit of the death should lead us
> In what we shall do
> All right Tsoede heel of the world
> Whoever plans evil

To come and meet us
Right on his way
May Soko fell him down for a disgrace
If he falls, he should not rise up again.

Tò, Tsoèdè bòkùn yìzhè
Gí bo yà ndákó yizhì
'Bá Màájin Awankó
Wo na dzò èba
Èba ci è sun bánkórò na
Yi, yi á nínya lá
Yi gàn yi à bà àdúwa
Etí dandan ndákó yi bo
Bè nya èyà yizhì nyi
Ègo de dùgbà à
Na wun è lá misun lo kîn na
Tò, etun na yi gàn yi à lo etí
Àláda nya ndákó yi bo na
Sòkó, zà na yi gá lá danbo na
Sòkó à lugwa u gí àmána yi ma
U gá bé á àmána yi gí
Kúti bè Kuci,wotsó wo kpe
Kútí bè Kuci u shì yi dzò
Nya na yi gà jin na
Tò, Tsoèdè bòkùn yìzhè
'Zà nínya 'gùn lá
Ci gn 'bà yi wun è bé o na
Dàngàn yèkó o
Sòkó à wun nìkîn nyá 'gbàci
U gá à nì, wun à na ma

The chain of Tsoede is present on the first day as the mediator of the god Soko, and also on the seventh day, the last day of the initiation. This last day also starts with certain rituals. The goat will be slaughtered, roasted, and eaten by the leaders of the cult and the initiate. Its liver must be eaten raw. The chain is placed in the middle of the shrine, which is here called Kutimba, while different rituals are conducted over it by the chief priest. A ritual drink is shared among the leaders of the cult who take part in the initiation ritual. The drink is passed from the priest to the other cult members in the hierarchy of their importance. The novice drinks last. Afterwards the priest sacrifices the rest of the drink over the chain. The drink is a mixture of different herbs and palm wine. After the sacrifices have been made, the priest communicates with the ancestors, who, according to Nupe belief, live in the ghost land of Mani Mankera.[99] If they have accepted the novice, and after the leading members of the cult and the initiate have greeted the ancestors in another shrine outside the village, the initiate is allowed to take part in the mask performance. Before he does this he puts certain medicines on his body as a defence against evil forces. Then the mask appears in the crowd while the drummers accompany it dancing and sing special songs.[100]

Although the importance of the Ndakogboya for the kingship and the possible connection between the two institutions is still difficult to interpret from the sources, they seem to have fulfilled a police function within the king's spheres of political interest throughout Nupeland in precolonial times. Some oral traditions qualify the Ndakogboya as the *kuti* or "magic" of the kings.[101] The first Etsu Patigi, Idrisu Gana, established a good relationship with the Ndakogboya cult centres of the area immediately after arriving in Patigi to obtain their assistance in cases of communal impurities.[102] They also performed at least once throughout the year at Patigi.[103]

The Fulbe also called the priest of Kusogi in Cekpan and his sons, in those days the strongest Ndakogboya lodge in all Nupeland, to the new capital of Bida to work for them. They established a new lodge between Doko and Bida, which was named Kusogi in memory of their old home. Under Masaba's reign in Bida (1860–73) the first novices were trained in the center and founded other lodges in the Bida Emirate.[104] Although the Fulbe were interested in the economic revenues of the cult, having the support of a police instrument like the Ndakogboya also contributed to the consolidation of their power.[105]

The prohibition of the cult by the colonial administration of Nupe Province in 1921 led to the disappearance of the different cult centres as a policing instrument in public, especially within Bida Emirate. This prohibition did not affect the Emirates of Patigi and Lafiagi, which belonged to Ilorin Province.[106] When Nadel conducted his field research he learnt that the Nupe people in Nupe Province "spoke with envy of their cousins in Patigi who had kept their Ndakogboya and hence preserved the sure protection against witchcraft."[107] Despite the prohibition through the colonial officials, the Ndakogboya were still thought of as being an instrument of execution and were considered the policemen of Tsoede and the Nupe kings.[108] Even today, older Nupe still speak with great respect and fear of the Ndakogboya priests and their power to judge evil and good and to punish the "witches" and "wizards" who had "polluted" the community.

And while its masks have become merely objects of cultural displays on the stage, radio, and television, the priests and initiates affiliated with the still active Ndakogboya cult aim to preserve and transmit knowledge and pass on traditions to the declining numbers of new members.[109]

In one of the prayers during the initiation into the cult, the priest of Kusogi Doko said:[110]

> By the time we were opportuned
> When we were disarming the witches and wizards
> The Etsu gave us the knife
> Which stood like a symbol
> This knife we sharpened it
> What the Etsus have given to our forefathers is that
> We have the permission to punish
> Anybody that is wicked
> Any wicked person who is warned or asked to stop but refused
> They will come and inform us
> But from the owners of the land to Zhitsu, from Zhitsu to Etsu Nyankpa, from Etsu Nyankpa to Hakimi, from there to Ndeji
> Immediately they will go to the Etsu
> Ndakogboya masquerade is the lord of witches and wizards
> But now that the situation has come
> Under the control of changes, we have paused our actions
> That is why the evil persons (witches and wizards) have the chance to operate freely now
> Because there are some people now
> Claiming to be traditional medicine practitioners[111]
> They can't prevent them from operating
> Because it is now the council that is frightening them
> But at the period of our forefathers we were able to stop them
> Anybody who is reckless will be eliminated
> That power was with our forefathers
> As it is still with us now
>
> Lókàci na yi yí kafa de re na
> Na yi fée ku 'gà na
> Etsu ci lá èbi yà yi
> Na a fé èrí yà yi na
> Èbi gá á zhè wuka yanka
> Nya na Etsuzhì lá yà dákó yizhì na
> Yi de kafa fée zún zà
> Zà na gá è jin'gùn na
> Zà na (zhì) è jin gùn, a gàn u lá lugwa u gǎn wun à lugwa à na

A jin à bé tá yà yi
Àmâ dàngàn bà zà kînzhì o, dàngàn bà Zhìtsu o lo bà Etsu Nyankpa.
Dàngàn bà Etsu Nyankpa o lo bà Hákìmi. Dàgàn bàgá o lo bà Ndèjì
Edagá o a da bà Etsu
Ezà wŭncìn ndákógbòyá tsá yi Tsóci a yi o
Àmâ, dàngàn na lókàci bé dà bé nyi
Nyá zàmánzhì na, yi á cínta
Tò, wun gá è lá 'zà dèdèzhì ci è de kafa gbâní o
Ebó ezà na zhì fi bo gbâni na
A ci gàn a è jin cigbè nyá gargajiya na
A kàn gwa a wò à
Ebóna Ùkúma tsá è be 'yé fi a gáncin o
Àmâ, lókàci na ndákó yizhì lotun na, yi á kàn 'gwa
'Bóna zà na gá sò kpyarya kángá na, yi gà wuntsó lá kyábo
Yíkúnci wŭncìn dan 'gwa dákó yizhì o
Kemina u dan gwa yi bo na

Whatever may be possible to conclude from the historical memory maintained by the priests of the different cult centers, in performing their policing duties they were responsible for maintaining the law, because violating the law could mean violating the sacred authority of the king and might upset the balance of the universal power.[112] After all, the most highly protected of all Nupe were the Nupe kings, because they embodied the royal ancestor Tsoede, the mediator with the high God Soko. In this role they were the centre of the Nupe universe, mediating between the sacred and the profane worlds, and maintaining a balance between power and law.

Following Nadel's interpretation, we might conclude that in the beginning only the Nupe king was entitled to act through the *ledu* organisation, which was probably later associated with the Gunnu or Ndakogboya cult. The geographical, historical, and symbolic facts reflected in the Tsoede tradition account for the connection with the river area. What appears, in the context of the Tsoede legend, to be the path of the ancestor king of Nupe was like the "Kings Highway," a vital artery of the political and economic organism over which the king extended his sacred authority.[113]

Conclusion

Despite the strong presence of Islam in Nupe society today and at the royal court of the kings of Patigi and Zugurma, this long-standing link between Nupe religious institutions and their function in legitimising Nupe kingship can still be discerned through careful analysis. Tsoede, represented by an iron chain, was the mediator of the god Soko in the royal shrine to Tsoedemba at Patigi until the 1940s, and is still seen as such in the Ndakogboya cult centres today. The Nupe kings are believed to be descended from Tsoede and still define themselves as the embodiment of this great mythical ancestor. Before the impact of the Muslim Fulbe on Nupeland, the Nupe kings probably had divine authority over the people and land they ruled. The sacred iron chain of Tsoede, which has been maintained in many villages throughout Nupeland, may be considered as a symbolic relict of a precolonial past when its ownership guaranteed the affiliation with the Nupe kingship and its religio-political organisation. This may be reflected also in the Tsoede tradition of origin according to which the culture hero makes a pact with the chiefs of the Bini confederation by handing them over part of the iron chain after his arrival in Nupeland.

From the time of transformation, which can be traced back to the beginning of the nineteenth century, up to the present, the Ndakogboya cult centres have remained important loci for the performance of non-Islamic rituals, as well as initiation into this secret society. Priests and initiates affiliated with the active Ndakogboya cult preserve and transmit this traditional knowledge and pass it on to the always-shrinking number of new initiates.[114] Yet despite having been relegated to the margins of contemporary Nupe society, Ndakogboya worshippers remain the custodians of the traditional Nupe religion and worldview.

The kingship system, on the other hand, remains at the centre of Nupe life and retains a strong sense of knowledge from a past linked to the traditional Nupe religion through oral traditions maintained by the kings, court musicians and bards, and important titleholders. The very core of royal rites, the enthronement of a new king—at least among the dynastic group of the Yissazhi—remained attached to the traditional religion long after the establishment of the Nupe Emirate at Patigi and the complete acceptance of Islam as the religion of the kings.

Despite all the transformations that have taken place in Nupeland during the last two hundred years, the institution of kingship still holds the key to understanding the pre-nineteenth-century Nupe history and culture. The chronology of precolonial Nupe history is currently based on the existing king lists and a few synchronisms in external sources, but future archaeological work in the area, as well as comparative and historical linguistic research on the Nupe language, would be useful in understanding the long-term cultural historical sequence in Nupeland, especially regarding political, social, and possibly also religious and ideological transformations that were associated with Tsoede. In a broader context, systematic knowledge of pre-nineteenth-century Nupeland would also contribute to the assessment of historical transformations within the Niger-Benue confluence area and of the social, political, and economic relationships with neighboring peoples.

Notes

1. This article is based on research for my doctoral dissertation. I would like to thank the Graduiertenkolleg "Religion and Normativität" of the Ruprecht-Karls University of Heidelberg for two years of affiliation and the Deutsche Forschungsgemeinschaft for a two-year dissertation scholarship, as well as the Peter Dornier Stiftung for financially supporting my fieldwork. I am also grateful to Dr. Akinwumi Ogundiran, Dr. Richard Kuba and Gregorio McDonald for comments on and criticisms of the manuscript. In Nigeria I would like to thank Dr. Idrees of Abuja University, who introduced me to Nupeland, its people, and their history; Mr. Mohammed Ndanusa, Principal of the Government Day Secondary School at Edozhigi and his family at Bida, who hosted me generously, made their house my own, and supported me always during my field research. I would also like to thank my research assistants, J. B. Adams and Dauda Abdulrahman. And I should not forget to mention my main informant, Maji Dodo from Kusogi near Doko, who gave me an insight in the Ndakogboya cult, although he kept its "secrets" to himself; and the support I received from the Etsu Nupe Patigi, the Etsu Nupe Zugurma and the Emir of Bida. I am also grateful to Dr. Blench, who gave me access to the yet unpublished manuscript of Nadel's field notes, which he is preparing for publication: S. Nadel, *Nupe Field Notebooks,* 15.11.1935–19.11.1936, ed. R. Blench (in prep.).

2. According to Nupe folk etymology the name Tsoede is derived from Etsu Ede or "tsu Ede," i.e., king Ede. Therefore the culture hero is said to be known as Edegi: S. F. Nadel, "The King's Hangmen: A Judicial Organization in Central Africa," *Man* (ed. the Royal Anthropological Institute of Great Britain and Ireland, London) 35, no. 143 (1935): 129 n. 1.

3. Obayemi gives in the appendix an overview of all existing king lists and their source. A. Obayemi, "Concerning Tsoede, Etsuzhi and Nupe History before 1800 A.D." (Seminar Paper, Department of History, ABU Zaria, 28/10/1978), appendix.

4. Obayemi, "Concerning Tsoede"; A. A. Idrees, *Political Change and Continuity in Nupeland: Decline and Regeneration of the Edegi Ruling Dynasty of Nupeland 1805–1945* (Ibadan: Caltop Publications, 1998), 10–14.

5. M. Mason, "The Tsoede Myth and the Nupe Kinglists: More Political Propaganda?" *History in Africa: A Journal of Method* (African Studies Association) (1975): 2, 109.

6. A. Obayemi, "States and Peoples of the Niger-Benue Confluence Area," in *Groundwork of Nigerian History,* ed. O. Ikeme (Ibadan: Heinemann, 1984), 159.

7. Obayemi mentions that the traditions of the Igbomina and Ibolo reflect numerous encounters with the Tapa, the name given to the Nupe by the Yoruba, and it is not uncommon to find two or more lineages among the Igbomina and Ibolo preserving memories of their Tapa ancestry in their *oriki* (praise songs) and lineage rituals. Obayemi points

here to an unpublished B. A. dissertation. A. Obayemi, "States and Peoples of the Niger-Benue Confluence Area," 158 n. 78.

8. Idrees, *Political Change and Continuity in Nupeland,* 14.

9. Ibid.; M. Mason, *Foundations of the Bida Kingdom* (Zaria: Ahmadu Bello University Press, 1979).

10. A. Obayemi, "The Yoruba and Edo-Speaking Peoples and their Neighbours before 1600," in *History of West Africa,* 3rd ed., ed. J. F. A. Ajayi and M. Crowder (New York: Longman, 1985), 255–323; Obayemi, "Concerning Tsoede"; Obayemi, "States and Peoples of the Niger-Benue Confluence Area," 144–64; A. Obayemi, "History, Culture, Yoruba and Northern Factors," in *Studies in Yoruba History and Culture: Essays in Honour of Professor S. O. Biobaku,* ed. G. O. Olusanya (Ibadan: University Press, 1983), 72–88.

11. According to Idrees, the subjects and partisans of the rival Etsuzhi were identified by adapted names: those loyal to Etsu Majiya were known as Gwagbazhi, which means "weak in the hand." This term was used in a derogatory fashion, ostensibly referring to the ineligibility of Majiya to occupy the throne. Those who were the partisans of Jimada were referred to as the Yissazhi, which means the descendants and supporters of Etsu Muazu Yissa, Jimada's grandfather; Idrees, *Political Change and Continuity in Nupeland,* 22.

12. Malam Dendo was first used as a nickname for Mallam Muhammad Bangana, a professional herbalist and spiritual leader. It is derived from the Nupe phrase "*Dan yan dondon,*" meaning "the man on whose shoulders hang all sorts of bags containing herbs." Bagana is a little village about twenty kilometres southwest of Birnin Kebbi. Another name given to him was "Manko," great scholar. Cf. A. Bida and P. G. Harries, "Notes on Nupe," National Archives Kaduna, *NAK SNP 17/25355,* in Idrees, *Political Change and Continuity in Nupeland,* 34.

13. Idrees, *Political Change and Continuity in Nupeland,* 40–72.

14. Ibid., 66–67, 142.

15. Ibid., 58.

16. Ibid., 81.

17. Ibid., 82, 133, 141.

18. Idrees mentions Mal. Ndamarufa Patigi, *Shaaba* Abubakar Patigi, Alhaji Mamudu Koro and Alhaji Jimada *Nakorji* Patigi as his informants. Idrees, *Political Change and Continuity in Nupeland,* 82–88, esp. nn 51, 55, 58, 60.

19. Ibid., 84, 141.

20 S. Nadel, *A Black Byzantium: The Kingdom of Nupe in Nigeria* (London: Oxford University Press, 1942), 73 n 1.; other earlier versions are reflected in H. Clapperton, *Journal of a Second Expedition into the Interior of Africa from the Bight of Benin to Soccatoo and the Journal of Richard Lander from Kano to the Sea Coast* (London: Murray, 1829), 339; S. A. Crowther and J. Taylor, *The Gospel on the Banks of the Niger* (London: Church Missionary House, 1859), 117, 170, 210; H. S. Goldsmith, " Nupe History," in *Northern Nigeria: Historical Notes on Certain Emirates and Tribes,* ed. J. A. Burdon (London: Gregg International Publishers, 1909; reprint, 1972).

21. L. Frobenius, *Und Afrika sprach . . . : Wissenschaftlich erweiterte Ausgabe des Berichts über den Verlauf der dritten Reiseperiode der Deutschen Inner-Afrikanischen Forschungsexpedition in den Jahren 1910 bis 1912,* vol. 2, *An der Schwelle des verehrungswürdigen Byzanz* (Berlin-Charlottenburg: Vita, Deutsches Verlagshaus, 1912–13), 274. Within the Nupe hierarchy of administration the Lilles were next to the king.

22. Frobenius, *Und Afrika sprach,* 274, 373–79; L. Frobenius, *The Voice of Africa,* vol. 2, Being an Account of the German Inner African Exploration Expedition in the Years

1910–1912 (Benjamin Blom, Inc. Bronx: New York and London, 1913; reprint, 1968). Most of what Frobenius collected on Nupe culture appeared in L. Frobenius, *Volkserzählungen und Volksdichtungen aus dem Zentral-Sudan* (Jena: Eugen Diedrich, 1924; and L. Frobenius, *Dichten und Denken im Sudan,* (Jena: Eugen Diedrich, 1925); it never received the same attention as *Voice of Africa,* because it was published only in German. On the value of Frobenius' research to the West African historian, see also J. M. Ita, "Frobenius in West African History," *Journal of African History* 13, 4 (1972): 673–88.

23. The complete version of this tradition of origin can be found in Nadel, *A Black Byzantium,* 72–75.

24. Obayemi, "Concerning Tsoede," 15–16; A. Obayemi, "Kakanda: A People, a History, an Identity," *Journal of the Historical Society of Nigeria* 9, no. 3 (1978): 1–21; See also E. V. Rochfort-Rae, "Certain Notes Collected from Various Native Authorities (1921)," National Archives Kaduna, *NAK BIDDIV 375.*

25. Nadel, *A Black Byzantium,* 75.

26. Idrees, *Political Change and Continuity in Nupeland,* 11.

27. Nadel, *A Black Byzantium,* 74.

28. Obayemi, "Concerning Tsoede," 16.

29. Idrees, *Political Change and Continuity in Nupeland,* 11.

30. Mason, "The Tsoede Myth and the Nupe Kinglists," 109.

31. Clapperton, *Journal of a Second Expedition,* 33, Appendix No. 8.

32. The Tsoede relics and the tomb have been declared to be a Nigerian National Monument; cf. also the mention of the village as Gwagede with regard to Tsoede in A. Adamu, *A Hausa Government in Decline: Yawuri in the 19th Century* (M.A. thesis, Ahmadu Bello University Zaria, 1968). The village is called Yangulugi in E. G. M. Dupigny, *Gazetteer of Nupe Province* (London: Frank Cass, 1920; reprint, 1972), 7.

33. Obayemi, "States and Peoples of the Niger-Benue Confluence Area," 137.

34. Cf. ibid., 157. Although some excavations were carried out all around Nupeland, there are no comparable archaeological data from within Nupeland. Obayemi, "Concerning Tsoede," 8.

35. Anonymous, "ta'rīkh arbāb Kanū"; H. R. Palmer, "The Kano Chronicle, Translated with an Introduction," *Journal of the Royal Anthropological Institute* (1908): 58–98; H. R. Palmer, *Sudanese Memoirs: Being Mainly Translations of a Number of Arabic Manuscripts Relating to the Central and Western Sudan* (Lagos, 1928; reprint, 1967); R. M. East, ed. and trans., "Littafin tarihin Kano," in *Labarun Hausawa da Maƙwabtansu, Littafi na biyu,* (Zaria: Northern Nigerian Publishing Company, 1933; reprint, 1979), 3–57. Although the Kano Chronicle mentions a Sarkin Nupe during the reign of King Dauda (1421–31) and King Yakubu (1452–63), unfortunately it does not give a name for this king or kings.

36. Unpublished manuscripts of the king lists of the ruling houses of Patigi and Zugurma which were given to me by the two kings of each branch.

37. Obayemi, "Concerning Tsoede," 16.

38. Mason, "The Tsoede Myth and the Nupe Kinglists," 103.

39. Ibid., 108.

40. Mason suspects Umaru, the Alkali of Bida, as Goldsmith's informant, who provided him with the king lists, Mason, "The Tsoede Myth and the Nupe Kinglists 103; cf. Goldsmith, "Nupe History," 51.

41. East, ed., "Labarin tarihin Kano," 50.

42. Mason, "The Tsoede Myth and the Nupe Kinglists," 103; Obayemi, "Concerning Tsoede," 19 n 13.

43. Frobenius, *Und Afrika sprach*, 274; 373–79.

44. The king list of the Zugurma kings drawn up by Mamuda Daja is written in Hausa and according to oral tradition is based on an older Arabic manuscript composed during the time of Etsu Majiya (1804–56).

45. List of Patigi Dynasty. This king list is identical up to the 24th ruler (apart from some spelling differences) with that published by K. V. Elphinstone, *Gazetteer of Ilorin Province* (London: Frank Cass, 1921; reprint, 1972), 43–44. The last four entries have been added by the Patigi kings since the publication appeared.

46. Mason, "The Tsoede Myth and the Nupe Kinglists," 103.

47. The reader should be directed to Obayemi's discussion of the different versions of the Nupe king lists in his manuscript: Obayemi, "Concerning Tsoede."

48. Interview with Alhaji Ibrahim Chatta Umar, the present Etsu Nupe Patigi, Patigi 6/29/2000.

49. Oral evidence, Alhaji Ibrahim Chatta Umar, Etsu Nupe Patigi, Patigi 6/29/2000.

50. Weise, Fieldnotes, Patigi, 6/30/2000. The titleholders will keep their office also after the enthronement of a new king.

51. Oral evidence, Alhaji Kolo Saati, Benu of Zugurma, 9/7/2000.

52. Nadel did not stay very long time at Patigi and did not establish a good relationship to the king of Patigi. In the introduction to his monography *A Black Byzantium* he states: "and once I spent two weeks in Patigi (a quite uninteresting visit by the way) because there the last descendants of the old dynasty of Nupe kings hold court," Nadel, *A Black Byzantium*, ix; It should also be noted that the subtitle of his monograph *A Black Byznantium: The Kingdom of Nupe in Nigeria* is misleading, since the book describes the kingship institution and the throne succession rituals of the Fulbe Emirs at Bida and not of the Nupe kings of the two successor dynasties at Patigi and Zugurma, 94–95.

53. Idrees' assumption is based on the oral evidence of Mall. Baba Zubairu of Ibbi; cf. Idrees, *Political Change and Continuity in Nupeland*, 141.

54. Oral evidence, Alhaji Nakorji Jimada and Shaaba Abubakar Patigi, in Idrees, *Political Change and Continuity in Nupeland*, 144. For the political history and the history of the succession disputes, see ibid., 18–23.

55. On the basis of the oral evidence given by Shaaba Abubakar, a younger brother of Etsu Muasu: Ibid., 46.

56. Ibid., 146. The title of "Ndeji" is given to certain families and is held by a very old senior person. The Ndeji is appointed by the king but does not keep the office until he dies. Therefore I was able to interview a former Ndeji who had retired from the office because of his age and health problems. The Ndeji also has certain relics, such as a staff of office, which had been used during war time. Weise, Field notes, Patigi, 7/1/2000.

57. A. A. Idrees, *The Emergence of Patigi Emirate: Establishment and Consolidation* (Kano: B. A. History Department, Bayero University, 1982), 56–58.

58. Anonymous, "ta'rīkh arbāb Kanū"; Palmer, "The Kano Chronicle," 58–98; Palmer, *Sudanese Memoirs*; East, "Littafin tarihin Kano."

59. S. Abubakar, "Political Evolution or Revolution? The Ccase of 'Kin Nupe' before the Aadvent of Colonial Rule," in *Evolution of Political Culture in Nigeria*, Proceedings of a National Seminar organised by the Kaduna State Council for Arts and Culture, ed. J. F. Ajayi and B. Ikara (Ibadan: University Press Limited and Kaduna State Councils for Arts and Culture, 1985), 70–74. According to the census of 1921 by the administration of the Northern Provinces, Nupe province had already 194,404 Muslims but still a population of 167,009 so-called animists. Cf. C. K. Meek, *The Northern Tribes of Nigeria. An Ethno-*

graphical Account of the Northern Provinces of Nigeria together with the a Report on the 1921 Decennial Census (London, 1925; reprint, Oxford: Frank Cass, 1971), 2:246

60. Oral evidence, Mall. Mohammed Patigimin, in Idrees, *Political Change and Continuity in Nupeland,* 141; S. F. Idrees, "Islam in Patigi Emirate," (unpublished NCE Long Essay, College of Education, Ilorin, 1983), 42.

61. Idrees, *Political Change and Continuity in Nupeland,* 141; S. F. Idrees, "Islam in Patigi Emirate," 42.

62. Another title given to him was Swagannuwon; Idrees, *Political Change and Continuity in Nupeland,* 152.

63. Inteview with Alhaji Adamu Jiya, Wambai of Patigi and oldest king-maker in town (95 years old), Patigi 6/30/2000. According to him, it was under the present Etsu Nupe Patigi that the chief Imam was inaugurated.

64. Idrees, *Political Change and Continuity in Nupeland,* 83–84.

65. Oral evidence from Alhaji Adamu Jiya, Patigi 6/30/2000, and Umaru Tsoedemba, *Tsadza* of Patigi, Patigi 6/29/2000.

66. Alhaji Adamu Jiya, Patigi 6/30/2000.

67. Oral evidence from Alhaji Adamu Jiya, Patigi 6/30/2000; and Umaru Tsoedemba, Patigi 6/29/2000; cf. Idrees, *Political Change and Continuity in Nupeland,* 147.

68. Oral evidence, Alhaji Adamu Jiya, 6/30/2000; the bangle does not exist anymore.

69. Idrees, *Political Change and Continuity in Nupeland,* 142.

70. National Archives Kaduna, Nigeria, *NAK ILOPROF 5/1,* The Royal Niger Company treaty with the Etsu of Patigi. Cf. Idrees, *Political Change and Continuity in Nupeland,* 142.

71. I am grateful to Dr. Ahmadu Ndanusa Kawu for his assistance with the transcription and the translation of the Nupe texts in this chapter.

72. Oral evidence from Umaru Tsoedemba, Patigi 6/29/2000.

73. When Nadel visited Patigi in 1936, the chain was still at Patigi. According to Nadel's field notebook from 9/16/36, the day he met the Ndeji of Patigi and discussed several issues on the politics, the organisation, and the law at Patigi with him, in particular the Etsu's position, he learnt of the existence of two sacred chains: one used as Chain of Ordeal (referred to as egban Tsoede, or just Tsoede) and at the same time general magic; and a second chain as Chain of Punishment (referred to as Ti zana). But he was not allowed to see these chains and told by the Ndeji: "zunma Etsu za ndoro de yiko u wu egban Tsoede a" [Other than the Etsu no man has authority to explain about the chain of Tsoede].

74. Oral evidence from Mmadu Alhassan Shiagi, Patigi 7/1/2000 (80 years old). He was born in this compound and still lives there.

75. Oral evidence from Umaru Tsoedemba, Patigi 6/29/2000.

76. Oral evidence Alhaji Ibrahim Chatta Umar, Etsu Nupe Patigi, Patigi 6/29/2000.

77. Oral evidence Alhaji Ibrahim Chatta Umar, Patigi 6/29/2000. It should be noted that the majority of the Nupe population throughout Nupeland still recognises the king of Patigi as their traditional ruler.

78. Idrees, *Political Change and Continuity in Nupeland,* 143.

79. Interview with Usman Isah, Etsu Nupe Zugurma; 9/7/2000.

80. Nadel, *A Black Byzantium,* 88.

81. See note 74.

82. In Hausaland the *dògarì* are known as the king's bodyguard. This Hausa loan word may have entered the Nupe vocabulary in the nineteenth century and may have been introduced by the Fulbe rulers who came through Hausaland into the Nupe country.

83. Nadel, "The King's Hangmen," 130; Oral evidence, Etsu Nupe Patigi, 6/29/2000.

84. According to Nadel, Ndakogboya consists of the word *ndako* (= grandfather) and *gboya,* which contains the recognisable root *gbo,* implying "to be large" in a physical sense.

85. Obayemi, "The Yoruba and Edo-Speaking Peoples and their Neighbours," 295. Some of the former Ndakogboya cult centres no longer perform the rituals, although their memory is still kept alive in the oral history. Recently the very famous Ndakogboya logde at Kusogi in Cekpan in Kwara State stopped the performance of the rituals because the members had converted to Islam and considered the rituals as purely pagan. In Tankpafu, another once famous Ndakogboya logde in Kwara state, the village head even prohibited the performance of the rituals because of their pagan character. Weise, Fieldnotes, 7/1/2000.

86. Nadel qualified the cult as a secret society, although he admitted that "the Ndakogboya represent something between the organisation of a kinship group in which a secret knowledge and practice is vested and a 'society' proper, a voluntary association that is, of which (theoretically) everybody can become a member. Yet like the 'real' secret societies the Ndakogboya is secret only in so far as its inner organisation and its esoteric proceedings are concerned. The society as such is well known and even recognised officially." S. F. Nadel, "Witchcraft and Anti-Witchcraft in Nupe Society," *Africa* (Journal of the International African Institute, London) 8, 3 (1935): 435.

87. Frobenius, *Und Afrika sprach,* 376–78. See also S. F. Nadel, *Nupe Religion* (1954; reprint, London: Schocken Books, 1970).

88. Recording during the initiation ritual into the Ndakogboya secret society at Kusogi, 15/5/2000.

89. S. F. Nadel, "Gunnu: A Fertility Cult of the Nupe in Northern Nigeria," *Journal of the Royal Anthropological Institute* 47 (1937): 95; Nadel supposed that the Ndakogboya cult may have merged with the main ritual of Nupe, the Gunnu, because he could still find places where Gunnu priests worked but where the Ndakogboya masks were not known.

90. Oral evidence from Maji Dodo, Kusogi near Doko 5/6/2000.

91. All heads of the different Ndakogboya centres confirmed that initiations take only place during the Gunnu festival. Interviews with the head of the Ndakogboya cult at Kusogi Doko 5/15/2000; at Lade 7/1/2000; at Gbado 6/29/2000, 6/30/2000.

92. During the time of Frobenius' (1911) and Nadel's (1934; 1935–36) field research, they used only white cotton. I found both forms during my own field research in 2000.

93. Nadel, *Nupe Religion,* 189; cf. interview with the *Alagba* of Ejigbo, 6/126/2000.

94. Cf. Weise, Field notes from Gbado, 6/29/2000, 6/30/2000; Nadel, *A Black Byzantium,* 147–49.

95. The initiation rituals will be described in detail in my forthcoming doctoral dissertation.

96. Nadel, *Nupe Religion,* 194. The following descriptions are based on my own observations in Kusogi Doko. The heads of other Ndakogboya cult centres confirmed the existence of similar rituals and their performance.

97. On the Eba divination see Nadel, *Nupe Religion,* 38–67.

98. Majin of Awanko is said to have founded the Ndakogboya logde at Kusogi Doki. He came from Kusogi in Cekpan and named the new established lodge after his own place of origin.

99. Recordings at Kusogi 5/6/2000, 5/15/2000; Lade 7/1/2000; Mani Mankera is mentioned during the initiation and in songs which accompany the mask, whose spirit may come from there when it enters the mask. It has the connotation of the underworld / other world.

100. The initiation ritual is performed with only slight variations all over Nupeland wherever the Ndakogboya cult is still active. Interviews at Kusogi 15/5/2000; at Lade 1/7/2000, at Gbado 6/29/2000, 6/30/2000.

101. Nadel, *Nupe Religion,* 191–92; Similarly the Nupe word *kuti* has the meaning of spiritual activity and the rite in which that activity is actualised.

102. Ibid., 193 n 1

103. Nadel, "Witchcraft and Anti-Witchcraft in Nupe Society," 442.

104. Nadel, *Nupe Religion,* 193.

105. From that time the head of the cult centre at Kusogi near Doko has been appointed by the Emir of Bida, although he is designated by the old head before his death. The title is kept within the lineage.

106. Nadel, "Witchcraft and Anti-Witchcraft in Nupe Society," 442.

107 Nadel, *Nupe Religion,* 200.

108. Nadel, "The King's Hangmen," 130; oral evidence, Etsu Nupe Patigi, 6/29/2000.

109. Interview with the heads of some still active Ndakogboya centres: Maji Dodo at Kusogi near Doko, Kusogi 5/15/2000; with the Ndace of Lade 7/1/2000, and the Lille of Gbado 6/29/2000, 6/30/2000.

110. Recordings at Kusogi 5/6/2000, 15/5/2000.

111. Here the reference is made to the so-called *Bocis*. These are Marabouts who practise divination and work as medicine men, but in the name of Islam.

112. Nadel notes here that the Ndakogboya never practiced their rituals in the capital of the kingdom. The purpose was apparently to avoid this secret society from causing social and economic disorganization in the town where the kings resided. He writes: "The *ndákógbòyá* supported, as it is, by the political authority, is to be a weapon which may turn against him and endanger his own interest," Nadel, "Witchcraft and Anti-Witchcraft in Nupe Society," 441–42.

113. Nadel, "The King's Hangmen," 131.

114. Interview with the heads of some still active Ndakogboya centres: Maji Dodo at Kusogi near Doko 5/15/2000; with the Ndace of Lade 7/1/2000, and the Lille of Gbado 6/29/2000, 6/30/2000.

17

PASSAGES IN A STRUGGLE OVER THE PAST: STORIES OF MAJI MAJI IN NJOMBE, TANZANIA

James Giblin

Introduction

Tanzania's Southern Highlands are rich in sites of commemoration. Burial grounds and places of ancestor veneration evoke the histories of clans and the succession of generations. Churches and sites of abandoned mission stations recall the generations of the early twentieth century who embraced the Christian faith. Other sites memorialize wars, including the campaigns that pitted the famous Hehe leader Mkwawa against the Germans, and also the Maji Maji conflict of 1905–7. Among the areas where sites of these sorts are found is Njombe, one of the districts in the Iringa Region portion of the Southern Highlands. At the oldest Christian mission in Njombe, Kidugala, visitors to its well-known school and seminary are reminded that its church stood at the heart of the compound where African Christians and German Lutheran missionaries took refuge against the rebels in 1905. Far to the east, at the village of Lupembe, churchgoers emerge from Sunday services to stroll around the still-standing house where the missionary Christian Schumann offered refuge to his congregation in 1905. Should they pause to examine the rusting cannon barrel in the courtyard, they may notice that it is stamped "1904," the date of its casting.

At Utengule, visitors must scale a very steep hill should they wish to view a monument erected with the aid of the Historical Association of Tanzania in 1986. For their effort they are rewarded with an inscription informing them that they stand on the site of a mass execution committed by the Germans in the aftermath of Maji Maji. At Yakobi Village, by contrast, visitors need stroll no more than a few dozen yards around the parish church to find several memorials. One is the grave of a German medical officer killed at the height of Maji Maji in early 1906. Another marks the one hundredth anniversary of the founding of the Yakobi parish in 1898. A third is the house now occupied by the Lutheran pastor of Yakobi. This very house played a key role in the best-remembered incident of the Maji Maji period in Njombe. For in it, Yakobi's Christians, who included the German pastor, Paul Gröschel, Gröschel's wife, and numerous local converts, anxiously awaited attack for several days in September 1905. Besieged by a neighboring chief, Mbeyela Mkongwa, they fired upon their attackers from the safety of the house, repelled them, and fled to the safety of Pastor Schumann's compound at Lupembe.

For several years I have been studying the history of Njombe. In the course of this work, I have become increasingly concerned about the role played by the historian in a place so rich in markers, memorials, and memories of the past. In such a landscape the academic historian cannot claim to be preserving a past that is threatened with extinction. To the contrary, the past is proliferating. In recent years new memorials have been erected not only at Utengule, Yakobi, and Kidugala in Njombe, but elsewhere in the Southern Highlands as well. Within the last couple of years, for example, a member of parliament sponsored the erection of a new memorial to mark the remote location where Mkwawa took his own life to avoid capture by German pursuers in 1898. Clearly the people of the Southern Highlands do not need academic historians to preserve their history.

My experience in Njombe has led me to feel that we academic historians engage as much in the alienation of the past as in its conservation. My thinking has been led in this direction by the work of the anthropologist Elizabeth Tonkin. Tonkin has argued that the ability to be articulate is socially constructed. Individuals achieve it, she suggests, when they are able to express their knowledge in genres with which they and their audiences share familiarity. She also contends, conversely, that disarticulateness is equally a social construction, for it appears when people are forced to speak in genres with which they are not familiar.[1]

I believe that we unwittingly force people into situations that deprive them of their ability to speak articulately about the past. We do this in part by presenting ourselves as experts who possess special knowledge gained from reading archival and other sources which most people cannot access, and from our claims that our comparative and theoretical perspectives give us special insight. Moreover, our interests and obsessions often lead us to ask questions that, besides making little sense to people who do not share our academic background, are framed by terms and assumptions that are unfamiliar to non-scholars. The effect of such questions, I believe, is to make the people whom we meet in the villages feel that, in our view, knowing the past means commanding esoteric knowledge which is available only in schools and universities. Our questions implicitly claim that we possess a better, more sophisticated way of speaking about the past. For this reason they alienate villagers from their past, for they imply that they lack the ability to speak meaningfully about it. Another way of explaining this problem is to say that our questions have this alienating effect because they demand that villagers speak in genres—particularly the genre of "interview"—whose rules and conventions they do not know.

Merely presenting ourselves as "historians" who wish to study "history" already puts the past on ground that is alien to most rural men and women. It makes us appear to be seeking specialized knowledge that they cannot command. The obvious reason why most people feel unable to speak with confidence about this arcane thing called "history" is that it is *taught and learned in school.* For if there is one lesson that most rural Tanzanians learn very well in school, it is that they cannot master the forms of knowledge taught there. Had scholastic success spared them this painful lesson, after all, they would have left the villages to seek jobs in the city and would no longer be found in the countryside.

So it seems to me that as we practice the academic discipline of history, we alienate rural Tanzanians (and perhaps villagers elsewhere in rural Africa as well) from their own past. While I cannot offer a solution to this problem, I do believe that historians can begin to grapple with it by becoming more aware that we have plunged ourselves, perhaps unknowingly, into a struggle over the past that began long before we appeared on the scene. This is a struggle over who will control the past, and who will suffer alienation from it. Once we recognize the existence of this ongoing struggle, we see at least two key problems. The first is that people become alienated from knowledge of their own past through a historical process. Like other processes that unfold through time, it can be reconstructed, and indeed must be reconstructed if we are to gain a better grasp over our own role in this struggle for control of the past. The second problem involves resistance to alienation from the past. Rural people resist losing control over their past, I believe, and do so by relying upon familiar forms of talk which allow them to speak about the past with articulateness and confidence.

The purpose of the following pages is to sketch out some dimensions of this struggle in Njombe. During the twentieth century, much of the struggle there hinged on the conflict which historians know as the "Maji Maji Rebellion," but which villagers know by other names. Indeed, the very concept of "Maji Maji Rebellion" can be regarded as a crucial instrument of alienation. This paper also examines an instance of rural resistance to alienation of the past. Here again, this instance involves memories of the struggle that historians have constructed as the anti-colonial uprising called "Maji Maji," but which some villagers in Njombe understand in quite different terms.

Alienating the "Maji Maji" Past: Chiefs and Nationalists

In the mid-1920s, the British colonial administration, having assumed responsibility for Tanganyika as a League of Nations Mandate after the First World War, tried to impose firmer control over its rural societies by instituting a system of administration called Indirect Rule. Throughout the territory, British officials appointed chiefs. Their intention was to appoint men who had inherited traditional claims to political authority over their tribes.[2] Identifying chiefly lineages and traditional authorities proved to be both difficult and very contentious, however, and many appointees found that their legitimacy was quickly challenged. Recently, Thaddeus Sunseri has argued, in a fascinating study of the forces that shape historical interpretation, that British authorities tried to uphold the legitimacy of their chiefly appointees by retelling the story of Maji Maji, the calamity that had occurred only two decades earlier. In so doing, argues Sunseri, they emphasized that it had shattered traditional forms of tribal authority. This retelling allowed British officials to argue that in instituting Indirect Rule they were righting a wrong, for they were returning legitimate traditional authority to power and restoring the integrity of tribal cultures. This was but one example, argues Sunseri, of the way in which, over the seven decades that followed Maji Maji, it would be recast in various "statist narratives" whose purpose in each case was to justify state authority.[3]

Meanwhile, Maji Maji was also being recast into a narrative which supported chiefly authority in Njombe, where Indirect Rule brought to power the Mkongwa clan. The Mkongwa claim to authority over Ubena (Indirect Rule divided Njombe District into three tribal units, Ubena,

Upangwa, and Ukinga) was weak. Precolonial evidence suggests that their authority had been quite localized. It was Maji Maji, however, that inflated their reputation among Europeans. For after Mbeyela Mkongwa and his sons led the attack on the Yakobi mission in 1905, the Germans regarded them not merely as local leaders, but as the primary instigators of rebellion in the entire Bena tribe. British officials of the 1920s were strongly influenced by this view. They believed that the Mkongwa had been the most important leaders in precolonial Ubena, and felt that the bellicosity that they had showed during Maji Maji would more likely be restrained if the clan were incorporated into tribal administration. In this way the Mkongwa gained control not only of the paramountcy of Ubena, but also of several subchiefships as well as local offices during the late 1920s and 1930s.

During these years, Mkongwa officeholders retold history in order to legitimize the extension of their authority throughout Ubena.[4] They did this partly by appropriating clan histories that grounded the claims of clans to particular tracts of land by showing that they had traditionally venerated their ancestors in these clan territories. The Mkongwa chiefs asserted authority over Nyumbanitu, a site of ancestor veneration that was renowned not only throughout Ubena, but also in much of the Southern Highlands. They did so by claiming their clan had long venerated their ancestors in that location. By claiming control of the best-known shrine, they asserted the primacy of their clan. They also tried to counter what many villagers understood to have been the precolonial situation—that Mkongwa power had been confined in those days to a small area—by telling stories about Mbeyela Mkongwa's efforts to travel the length and breadth of Ubena in an effort to build unity among all the Bena.

Mkongwa office holders appropriated Maji Maji by telling stories that placed Mbeyela Mkongwa and his sons at the center of the conflict. They cast their clan as having played a crucial role in winning over the Bena tribe to the side of the rebels. In the context of Indirect Rule, such stories served several purposes. They demonstrated antipathy to the Germans, with whom their British superiors had only recently been locked in a world war whose campaigns had twice spilled into Njombe. They also kept alive a sense of their muted capacity for belligerence. Most importantly, however, stories of Maji Maji could be used to show that the Mkongwa had long possessed influence over the entire tribe. Such stories were particularly important in the early years of Indirect Rule, for there was much opposition in Ubena to Mkongwa paramountcy, just as there were many challenges to the legitimacy of appointed chiefs throughout Tanganyika. Stories that emphasized the hold of Mkongwa influence over the entire tribe were intended to persuade the British that they should dismiss doubts about the legitimacy of the Mkongwa, and remain confident that they had chosen for chiefship a clan that could be expected to run tribal affairs efficiently.

While stories that suggested that the Mkongwa had led the entire Bena tribe into Maji Maji served the political interests of these officeholders, it would be too simple to say that they engaged in a cynical fabrication of history. Their use of the past was no more cynical than was the use that would be made of it in a later generation by the nationalists. Not only did they believe, no less than the nationalists, that their understanding of the past was true, but they also believed—like the nationalists—that their interpretation of the past served the general good as well as their own personal interests. For just as the nationalists believed that histories of Maji Maji fighters transcending precolonial tribal divisions demonstrated African capacity for self-rule, so too colonial chiefs believed that finding antecedents for Bena tribal unity was a vitally important use of the past. From early in the period of Indirect Rule, chiefs recognized that tribes that were united and possessed of a strong self-identity were more likely to succeed in having their concerns and grievances taken seriously by the colonial administration. The Mkongwa generation who served as chiefs after the Second World War came to adulthood convinced that Ubena would escape its impoverishing reliance on labor migration only if the Bena stood united as a tribe, allowing their chiefs to press the colonial government for economic development.

The manner in which the Mkongwa clan developed their understanding of Maji Maji was no more calculated and conspiratorial, moreover, than was the way in which other groups and generations acquire their knowledge of the past. Because sources of knowledge about the Maji Maji period were varied, members of the chiefly families were continually reevaluating their understanding in light of the new stories, details, and knowledge that they gathered. The generation who were too young to have remembered Maji Maji probably learned about it initially at the knees of parents, grandparents and other family members who had witnessed the horrors of 1905–7. New and different ways of learning about Maji Maji emerged later, however. After the British established a school for the sons of chiefs at Malangali (just outside Njombe in present-day Mufindi District) in the late 1920s, for example, Mkongwa boys learned about Maji Maji in new ways. At Malangali they learned not only in the classroom, but also outside class, when they listened to stories told by members of the school staff who had seen the fighting. One of the teachers at Malangali was the sole survivor of an engagement in northern Njombe during Maji Maji. "We first saw this

Mnyakyusa [teacher] when we registered for school in 1928," said Maynard Pangamahuti, a grandson of Mbeyela Mkongwa. "He had been chosen to teach sons of chiefs. We got this history from him. He said he was the only one fortunate enough to survive."[5] The boys who traveled to Malangali from homes in central and southern Njombe also learned about Maji Maji as they crossed a landscape which still bore the signs of war. Many of the schoolboys were drawn to the site south of the modern town of Njombe where Albert Wiehe, the German medical officer whose grave is at Yakobi, was ambushed and killed in 1906. In later life, these boys would claim that in the 1920s the battlefield remained littered with human skulls. "The skulls were like so many pots," recalled Maynard Pangamahuti. "They'd been burned by fire, and all the bones had also been burned, but the skulls could still be seen." The battle had occurred on the banks of the Hagafilo River, and afterwards the place became known, said Franz Mwalongo, another of the boys walking to Malangali, as "Nyikamtwe," or "the river which flowed with skulls." "I hear that the stream ran with blood," said Mwalongo. "We saw many skulls there."[6]

As was the case in many Bena families, younger members of the chiefly families probably heard fresh eyewitness accounts of Maji Maji when their homes were visited by women relatives who had been taken captive during the war. For several decades after Maji Maji, women who had been captured by local allies of the Germans and marched off to be married into new homes in Iringa, Usangu, and other parts of the Southern Highlands returned to Njombe to renew ties with their natal families. Surely such visits provided new occasions for storytelling about the fearful events of 1905–7, and generated new accounts that tested established understandings of the period.

The point in saying that the chiefly clan constructed its understanding of the past out of multiple sources of knowledge is not to deny that their interpretation was shaped by political self-interest. Rather, the point is to come closer to the intellectual process through which the chiefs constructed their accounts of the past. If stories of the past were to be even partially effective in legitimizing the political claims of clan (or any other group or class), they had to be constructed so as to be capable of incorporating fresh knowledge as it appeared. They could not be persuasive in legitimizing authority if their fundamental credibility were to be cast into doubt each time fresh knowledge surfaced. Like other creators of accounts about the past, Mkongwa storytellers who composed open-ended accounts of this kind understood themselves not to be fabricating stories of the past, but rather to be generating true knowledge of the past by testing old stories against new accounts each time they discovered fresh knowledge. Yet, their reason for judging an account to be a truthful telling of the past lay outside their knowledge of history. It derived primarily from their political conviction that the general good required chiefs to exercise authority and commoners to obey their chiefs.

Despite their openness to multiple sources of knowledge and their desire to create an understanding of the past that would serve the general good, the accounts of Mkongwa chiefs were a powerful form of alienation of the past. Indeed, the lesson in this example is that people do not have to set out deliberately to distort and falsify the past in order to cause its alienation. It may be alienated by people who intend to tell the truth about the past, and who possess means of persuading others either to assent to the superiority of their account, or at least to desist from challenging it. The Mkongwa chiefs enjoyed both the discursive means of persuading some of their subjects to accept the truth of their interpretation, and the political means of quashing the dissidence of those who were not easily persuaded. One source of their persuasiveness was that, while they were like Bena commoners in that they drew their understanding of the past from multiple sources, the Mkongwa could claim command of a source which everyone else lacked. This was the insiders' knowledge that came from their membership in the family of Mbeyela Mkongwa and his sons, the foes of the Yakobi Christians. Their children and grandchildren were presumed to have privileged access to family histories of the war, and for that reason were assumed to know more than commoners about how decisions had been made and why events had unfolded as they had.

Yet, this was only once reason why Mkongwa stories silenced competing narratives, including those told by the many villagers who had been enemies of the Mkongwa during Maji Maji and who remained opponents of the Mkongwa chiefs under Indirect Rule. The chiefs silenced other narratives partly because they possessed means of quashing dissidence, and partly because politically thoughtful people sometimes subordinated telling the truth about the past to more pressing political concerns. Like their chiefs, and indeed like many Tanganyikans elsewhere, many residents of Ubena thought that improvement in their condition would come about only when they had achieved a strong sense of tribal identity and unity. From their perspective, accepting a chiefly master narrative of the past was a small price to pay for tribal cohesion.

Storytelling about the Maji Maji period was shaped primarily by the issue of chiefly legitimacy from the mid-1920s through the late 1950s. At that time, however, it began to be influenced by a new current of change.

This was the emergence of nationalism and the growing popularity of the Tanganyika African National Union. Because Thaddeus Sunseri has offered a compelling account of how nationalism appropriated Maji Maji and shaped a new "statist narrative" around it, it is not necessary to cover the same ground here.[7] It need only be said that many of the same factors involved in chiefly appropriation of Maji Maji came into play once again. During the campaign of the late 1950s for independence, Julius Nyerere and other TANU leaders made use of Maji Maji in encouraging Tanganyikans to think that they could achieve unity. Narratives of Maji Maji become more important to nationalism after independence, however. During the 1960s and 1970s, they served as a usable past that could inspire collective rural mobilization, initially to defeat the enemies of "poverty, ignorance, and disease," and later to resettle the rural population in *ujamaa* villages. Once again, knowledge of the past was transmitted in a variety of ways, although now primary schools and party political education were very important. Once again, people asked themselves whether they should decide not to question interpretations which, even if they did not convey the truth of the past as they understood it, upheld values and ideas which promised to bring improvement. And once again, the tellers of nationalist history claimed access to privileged forms of knowledge about the past that common villagers lacked. Like the earlier chiefly narratives, nationalist accounts presented villagers with a dilemma. Either they must remain mute and inarticulate before these superior forms of knowledge, or they must make their own genres means of resisting these alienating narratives.

The War of "Korosani" and a Genre of Village Storytelling

Among villagers in Njombe one sees a strong tendency to place the past in a genre of talk about family, kinship and marriage. In this genre they speak with immense confidence about the past, because it allows them to ground their stories in many unspoken assumptions and understandings about family life which they share with their audience, and also because they bring their own experience of family and married life to their reconstructions of this context. This is a genre, moreover, in which the past serves an important purpose. It makes stories of the past into occasions for judging the behavior and character of individuals. More broadly, it provides a context for talking about the nature of relations between generations and genders. I first began to become aware of this genre when I heard a story about the death of the famous Hehe leader, Mkwawa, from an elderly woman named Mama Kapwani, who lived in the town of Makambako.

Mkwawa became famous for destroying an invading German force near Iringa in 1891. He was forced into hiding when the Germans invaded for a second time in 1894, and thereafter fought a guerrilla campaign until his death in 1898. The Germans portrayed Mkwawa as having been a lonely fugitive during the last stage of his life. By the time of his death, they said, his formerly large following had dwindled to a single loyalist. They insisted that villagers turned against him and informed his pursuers of his movements. To prevent his capture, the isolated Mkwawa finally took his own life in a remote bush clearing, according to the German officer who found his body, after killing his lone companion. Other German officers painted a similar picture. Whereas "the mere mention of his name had once made people throughout the heart of Africa tremble," wrote one of them, Mkwawa perished when, "as a lonely fugitive deep in the bush [he] turned his last cartridge on himself." Images of a solitary Mkwawa are also found in scholarly accounts.[8]

Mama Kapwani used the context of family, however, to create an account that was both moving and astonishingly different. Mkwawa was the *mjomba* [mother's brother] of Mama Kapwani's mother. From her mother, Mama Kapwani learned not only about the death of her mother's uncle, but about an earlier encounter between her mother and the great warrior. "She had just learned to walk," said Mama Kapwani of her mother,

> and [the women of Mkwawa's household] had gone to fetch water. They were hurrying her, "Let's go, let's go." And then suddenly he appeared, and lifted her out of the water [where apparently she had strayed unnoticed] saying, "What are you doing, letting her walk on her own." So he picked her up, but she didn't want to be held.

And that is how, by niece and her daughter, Mkwawa would be remembered: in the failing light he is bending, gently admonishing the women, now lifting the tiny girl. And she, oblivious to his awesome reputation, struggles to be free of his grasp. One imagines that Mkwawa was emerging from a daytime hiding place as dusk descended and the women were hurrying to their cooking.

By 1898, Mama Kapwani's mother was old enough to remember the end of Mkwawa's life. By then the net drawn round him by the Germans was fast closing. Almost a century later, Mama Kapwani would masterfully tell the story from the fascinated and bewildered perspective of a child from whom the affairs of adults were hidden. "On the day that my mother's uncle [Mkwawa] took his own life," related Mama Kapwani, he said, "Bring me milk," so they brought him milk and meat, and when he had drunk the milk he began to cry and cry. Everyone was looking at how he was saying "My mother." "What is he crying about," wondered my mother, for she was still thinking in a childish way. After some time he said, "My children, I am leaving you . . . you there [addressing an adult or older child], look after them." Then he ordered others to fetch firewood and make a fire, but they had no idea what he wanted to cook. Then he said, "Give the children milk," and so they drank the milk and ate meat. All the while he was crying and crying, but they had no idea what was happening. Well, after a short time he stood and went out, they saw him but they had no idea, and then they heard a sharp "Te!" They were startled, but went on with their games.

Soon they saw people running here and there, for he had already killed himself . . . then they saw large men carrying him, and there was a crowd milling, but they still had no idea what was happening. The next morning they peeked into his bathing chamber, but there was no one there. Everyone had left and gathered at the burial ground, and they began asking one of their sisters what had happened. "Where is uncle?" they asked. She said, "Those men took him." "Those men, where did they send him? We want to go too."

"I hear that day [the children] were herded around like goats," said Mama Kapwani. "It was my mother herself who told us all this."[9]

In German accounts, Mkwawa is betrayed by former supporters and deserted by all but one of his followers, whom he kills. In Mama Kapwani's version, however, he is surrounded to the end by family. Mama Kapwani's story restores to Mkwawa a dimension denied by the German accounts. She describes him as a benevolent family head. The contrast with the German account is heightened by her description of arrangements for his burial. Whereas the Germans made a trophy of his head, in Mama Kapwani's version the family maintains strict propriety in burial arrangements, making sure that young children see nothing. She placed Mkwawa in a context, family, where individuals reveal both their goodness and weakness. By restoring him to this context, she could bring out his full humanity, not just the ferocity and desperation that were caricatured by the Germans. Her preference for placing individuals in the context of marital and kinship relations, where their character and behavior could be judged, is shared by many storytellers of her generation.

Villager storytellers such as Mama Kapwani also use the context of family in speaking about Maji Maji. Knowledge of the 1905–7 conflict came to commoner villagers in many ways, just as it did to the chiefly clans. In the 1990s, only a few villagers could claim to have witnessed Maji

Maji as children. One of them was Mzee Mgaiwa of Lupembe, who had
been a boy of perhaps eight or ten years during Maji Maji. He remembered
that, "we had to flee while we were farming maize. When those monsters
[the Maji Maji rebels] appeared, we ran with my mother." Most of the
elderly were too young to remember terrified flight, but had been told by
mothers and grandmothers about the wartime dramas of their early childhood. Tulalumba Kawogo of Matowo knew that, "We ran, they tied me
with a sheep-hide rope [because her elders feared that her movements would
reveal their hiding place], that's what they told me, but we survived."[10]
They had also learned about their parents' wartime escapes. Leknard and
Ferdinand Matola knew that their parents survived a "war among local
people" by hiding for three days in a grain bin. When they emerged from
the granary, they too ran.[11] Children often learned about the horrors of war
in stories intended to caution them against mischief. From her grandmother,
Mama Kapwani learned what happened when parents fleeing from warriors became frightened that the cries of babies would betray them. "A little
child like that one," she said, pointing to a three-year-old playing nearby,
"they would just stuff her into *makorongo* [erosion rills]. Her own mother
might do this." A more comforting story explained that whole families
found refuge in the trunks of baobab trees. Mothers cooked there while
fathers stood watch outside. When the enemy came near, parents held their
children close, "without saying anything, because if they made a single
sound it would be all over."[12]

Many children heard these tales. "They were told by our parents,"
explained Lupumuko Lugalla. "In 1921, when I was eleven and had just
started school, these stories were all over."[13] No doubt many stories were
intended to explain war's disturbing aftermath, for it left many troubling
sights, particularly the mutilated. Lutengano Nganilevanu of Mtwango remembered seeing a neighbor who liked to sit naked while tending his cattle,
exposing a horrible wound suffered when an arrow was extracted from his
side. "Better if the arrow passes all the way through you," said Lutengano,
"because if it had to be pulled out it wounded terribly."[14] "I myself," recalled Lupumuko Lugalla,

> saw one women who had been stabbed with a spear. I saw how they had
> taken a sewn gourd and placed her intestines in the gourd, then they sewed
> it up, and she was fine. I saw this myself when I was a boy of fourteen. I
> asked about this and they said, "She was killed." Well, what had happened is
> that she had appeared to die, falling [after being stabbed] while the Maji
> Maji people from Songea were chasing everyone away. After regaining con-
> sciousness she crawled into a stream. . . . In the evening [her friends] came,

and she cried out, "It's me, I'm here in the water." So they took her home and cared for her.

Children also found disturbing the circumstances of unwounded neighbors and relatives. One villager learned that many women, "were known as *mgalule* [Kibena, captive] because at the time of Maji Maji they took many captives." "We were told," she said to a younger relative in 1994, now confiding knowledge which could no longer cause anyone shame, "that Andowise, the wife of Futwe, was an *mgalule*." Another woman, she explained, "named Judith, was an *mgalule* . . . that's how it was with them at that time. Even my grandmother," she added, divulging a deep secret, "was from Upangwa. She was taken captive and brought here where she was married by my grandfather." As late as the 1950s, children met long-lost mothers and *shangazi* [fathers' sisters] who, after having been taken as captives to other parts of the Southern Highlands, sometimes returned to Njombe to visit their relatives.[15]

These means of memory and transmission provide storytellers with material that they embed in the context of family and marriage. Some villagers use this context in describing the famous attack by Mbeyela Mkongwa on the Yakobi mission in 1905. The attack was part of a rapid sequence of events that occurred just as word of Maji Maji was reaching Njombe in September 1905. In a matter of days following the arrival from Songea of news of an anti-German rising, Mbeyela's forces killed a party of colonial tax-collectors before turning on the mission.[16] These circumstances would seem to suggest that Mbeyela Mkongwa was indeed rebelling against the Germans. And yet, village storytellers speak of the Yakobi attack as if it had nothing to do with "Hongo Hongo," as Maji Maji is known in Njombe. They know the attack as the "War of Korosani," because the Bena who lived near Yakobi called Paul Gröschel, the German missionary at Yakobi, "Korosani." Indeed, when in 1968 a University of Dar es Salaam student collected accounts of the attack on Yakobi, he was told not that it was part of an anti-European movement, but that it occurred because,[17]

> Mbeyela's son, Mpangire, wanted to marry Mwangasama, the wife of "Kolosani," for the very reason that Mpangire had great desire for brown [i.e., light-complexioned] women and he hoped that by marrying her she could bear him a brown son who could inherit his title afterwards. Some say that it was Mbeyela himself who wanted to marry Mwangasama.

In the 1990s village elders explained the "Korosani War" in the same way:[18]

The cause of this war was a woman. It was not a war involving a whole tribe, but instead was entirely local. . . . It was not a national war [*vita ya kitaifa*], unlike the "Hongo Hongo" which was national . . . and tribe against tribe... instead it happened only right here when a few people decided to fight with one man.

Accounts of the "Korosani War" often link the fighting to the folly of men's sexual desire. In one version, the object of Mbeyela Mkongwa's affection was not "Korosani's" wife, but his daughter-in-law.[19] In another account the aggressors were two of Mbeyela's sons, though their motives remained the same. A grandson of Mbeyela Mkongwa explained that despite Mbeyela Mkongwa's warnings against war with Europeans, his sons Mpangile and Ngozingozi were determined to take the European women.

Accounts that attribute the attack to men's desire link warfare with a fiercely debated dimension of family and marriage. Once the incident is situated in this context, history becomes intensely meaningful. No woman could have heard the story of the "Korosani War" without being struck by what it must have meant for Mbeyela's wives, particularly if they also heard that after Mbeyela Mkongwa perished along with his sons Ngozingozi and Mpangile in Maji Maji, Mbeyela's wives were enslaved. It could not have failed to make them ponder the impulsiveness and inconstancy of men, and the insecurity of married women.

Not only does the family genre make the past meaningful, but it also allows anyone with experience of family and married life to speak about it with authority. It also resists appropriation by both chiefly and nationalist authority. We can see this by comparing different accounts of Mbeyela Mkongwa and the attack on Yakobi. One of those accounts was told by his grandson, the former paramount of Ubena, Joseph Mbeyela. None of Mbeyela Mkongwa's descendents worked more energetically to burnish his historical reputation than did Joseph Mbeyela, who assumed his grandfather's name when he became Paramount in 1949. As nationalism became popular in the 1950s, Joseph Mbeyela, acting cautiously to avoid offending the British, portrayed Mbeyela Mkongwa as a unifier who opposed German colonialism. When Julius Nyerere sought to win Joseph Mbeyela's support for the nationalist movement, apparently he too spoke of Mbeyela Mkongwa as a proto-nationalist. According to Joseph Mbeyela, during his first public appearance in Njombe in 1955, Nyerere reminded his audience that they should, "remember what [the clan of Mbeyela] had accomplished . . . it was they who brought Maji Maji."[20]

This is the backdrop against which villagers attributed the attack on Yakobi to Mbeyela Mkongwa's character flaws, and denied that the "Korosani War" was part of Maji Maji.[21] They would not allow history to be alienated and reinterpreted for the benefit of either chiefs or nationalists. Explicit opposition to chiefly appropriation of their history emerged in conversation among elders. They flatly rejected the nationalist interpretation of the "Korosani War" given by Joseph Mbeyela. Told that their former paramount had said that Mbeyela Mkongwa wished to drive away the Europeans, they disagreed strongly. He attacked the Yakobi mission, they said, simply to seize the missionary's wife. They could not accept a version of history that described the chiefs as proto-nationalists.

In their stories of Maji Maji and the "war of Korosani," villagers resist attempts not only by chiefs, but also by nationalists, to appropriate their past. For while many villagers supported TANU in its opposition to the colonial chiefs, they could not accept a version of the past which spoke of a tribe united in opposition to colonialism, even if it was told by nationalists. Nationalists as well as chiefs sought to derive legitimacy from such an account, but villagers were willing to acknowledge the legitimacy of neither group. For not only had they suffered at the hands of oppressive chiefs during the colonial period, but villagers were alienated from nationalist government soon after independence. The government's imposition of bureaucratic controls over crop marketing and its restriction of village political autonomy in the 1960s, followed by its resettlement of many farmers into *ujamaa* villages in the early 1970s, stirred deep resentment against government.

Using the command of the past that they drew from their preferred genre of stories about family, storytellers resisted alienation of the past by nationalists as well as chiefs. They used this same genre to preserve what they believed to be a truer image of their past, an image of powerlessness and vulnerability before not only the Germans, but also before local chiefs such as Mbeyela Mkongwa.

This is the complex situation that we academic historians enter when we undertake research in landscapes such as Njombe. The sites of commemoration can be found quickly. It takes us much longer to understand the social processes and competing genres which are both continually threatening to alienate the past and continually resisting its alienation. Yet, if we fail to see that these social and political complexities shape understandings of the past, we risk alienating it unintentionally, as did colonial chiefs and nationalists.

Notes

1. Elizabeth Tonkin, *Narrating Our Pasts: The Social Construction of Oral History* (Cambridge: Cambridge University Press, 1992).

2. Throughout this chapter I refer frequently to "tribes" and "tribal" forms of identity. In so doing, I think of "tribe" as a form of identity that gained its modern shape in the course of interaction between rural societies and the colonial state. I also think of it as a kind of identity that coexists alongside other identities. This form of identity, which was based upon shared language and ethnicity, was the foundation of rural administrative ideology and practice in the British period. People who shared such identities were called "tribes" by British colonial administrators, and are still called "tribes" by English-speaking Tanzanians. While rural communities of the colonial period would have rarely used the English world "tribe," they attached great importance to what modern Tanzanian speakers of English call "tribes": that is, identities based upon the sharing of language and the bundle of cultural ideas and practices that we call ethnicity. In the region discussed in this paper, few people, either during the colonial period or afterwards, would have denied the fundamental importance of the identities which the British called "tribal." Where they diverged from the thinking of British administrators, and where they disagreed among themselves, was in their manner of defining the significance of "tribal" identity in relation to other identities. In particular, they disagreed about the political significance of "tribe." This chapter describes one arena of discourse in which the political salience of that form of identity was contested.

3. Thaddeus Sunseri, "Statist Narratives and Maji Maji Ellipses," *International Journal of African Historical Studies* 33, 3 (2000): 567–84.

4. The following paragraphs are based primarily upon conversations with Maynard Pangamahuti, Utengule, November 15, 1997; Mwalimu Franz C. Mwalongo, Uwemba, November 10, 1997; and Chief Joseph Pangamahuti Mbeyella II, Mdandu, June 29, 1994.

5. Maynard Pangamahuti, Utengule, November 15, 1997.

6. Maynard Pangamahuti, Utengule, November 15, 1997; and Mwalimu Franz C. Mwalongo, Uwemba, November 10, 1997.

7. Sunseri, "Statist Narratives and Majimaji Ellipses."

8. Feldwebel Merkl, "Bericht über den Tod des Sultans Quawa," *Deutsches Kolonialblatt* (1898), 645–46; Ernst Nigmann, *Die Wahehe: Ihre Geschichte, Kult-, Rechts-, Kriegs- und Jagd-Gebräuche* (Berlin: Ernst Siegfried Mittler, 1908), 19. Similar accounts are found in Magdalene von Prince, *Eine deutsche Frau im Innern Deutsch-Ostafrikas* (Berlin: Ernst Siegfried Mittler und Sohn, 1908), 179–83; Heinrich Fonck, *Deutsch-Ost-Afrika: Eine Schilderung deutscher Tropen nach 10 Wanderjahren* (Berlin: Doffische Buchhandlung Verlag, 1910), 28–29; Alison Redmayne, "Mkwawa and the Hehe Wars," *Journal of African History* 9, 3 (1968): 423; and Edgar V. Winans, "The Head of the King: Museums and the Path of Resistance," *Comparative Studies in Society and History* 36 (1994): 221–41.

9. Mama Kapwani, Makambako, May 18, 1992.

10. Tulalumba Kawogo, Matowo, July 5, 1994.

11. Leknard Matola and Ferdinand Jacob Matola, Luponde, November 13, 1997.

12. Mama Kapwani, Makambako, May 18, 1992.

13. Lupumuko Pandisha (Ero P.) Lugalla, Dar es Salaam, August 20, 1997.

14. Lutengano Nganilevanu, Mtwango, June 28, 1994.

15. Mtwa Phillip (Mlangali) to District Commissioner (Njombe), December 7, 1950, Tanzania National Archives 178/D.1/3.

16. John Iliffe, *A Modern History of Tanganyika* (Cambridge: Cambridge University Press, 1979), 189.

17. University of Dar es Salaam, Majimaji Research Project, 1968: Collected Papers, J. M. Makwetta, "Majimaji in Ubena," Paper no. 4/68/1/1.

18. Michael Asangile Mkongwa and Samligo Josephina Mapugila, Igominyi, July 9, 1994.

19. Mwalimu Franz C. Mwalongo, Uwemba, November 10, 1997.

20. Chief Joseph Pangamahuti Mbeyella II, Mdandu, June 29, 1994. A written account of Nyerere's speech of November 30, 1955 at Njombe makes no mention, however, of any reference to Maji Maji: *Twende Pamoja* (Njombe), no. 13 (February 1956): 2.

21. Some former chiefs also take this position because they feel antipathy towards nationalism, the movement that deposed them. They side with the Europeans, and reject any account of their ancestors as enemies of Europeans. For example, Maynard Pangamahuti, Utengule, November 15, 1997.

18

MAISHA: LIFE HISTORY AND THE HISTORY OF LIVELIHOOD ALONG THE TAZARA RAILWAY IN TANZANIA

Jamie Monson

Introduction

In the spring of 2000, I began to carry out field research on the rural history of the TAZARA railway in southern Tanzania. My goal was to learn how the railway had affected the lives of the people who lived along the railway corridor, particularly in those areas of southern Tanzania that had been isolated and without transportation before TAZARA was built. My focus was on the "ordinary train"—the train that stops at every small station along the railway, and serves as a lifeline for small-scale trade and economic development in the region. I wanted to use the "ordinary" train (rather than the "express" train) as a starting point for my investigation of TAZARA's impact on everyday life.

I found that there were very few records or other written documents that could tell me much about the ordinary train or about everyday economic activity in the small stations and their surrounding villages. Most of the focus of TAZARA administrative records was on larger-scale international trade between Zambia and the port of Dar es Salaam. Data on local traffic was aggregated in ways that made it difficult to learn much about local use of the railway and its relationship to local development.

My research strategy, therefore, was twofold. I began to develop a database of parcel receipts, the documents that are generated each time a passenger takes a small load of goods on the train. At the same time, I began to interview local traders, farmers, fishermen, livestock herders, wood-cutters, and others about their economic activities and how they had changed since the arrival of TAZARA. I had developed a simple, unstructured inter-view questionnaire that I hoped would get people talking about the role of TAZARA in their lives and communities. After my first set of interviews, however, I began to doubt whether this approach was going to help me to learn very much. My questionnaire about the railway had the opposite effect of what I had hoped. Rather than stimulating talk, my questions seemed to make people uncomfortable, confused, and eventually silent. Fortunately, early on in my research I began an interview with a market woman that evolved into a discussion of her life story. From that conversa-tion onwards, I began to rely increasingly on life history narratives in order to learn about changes in the lives of people who lived and worked along the corridor of the ordinary train.

When I asked people to tell me about their own lives, rather than about their relationship with the railway, they became articulate. In James Giblin's forthcoming book, he reflects on the way fieldwork can lead to silences and also to narrative openings. He writes that the rural elders he spoke with in Njombe District felt excluded from forms of knowledge that they associated with political authority or western science. Because they did not feel that they possessed the specialized knowledge required to talk about such things as *historia,* or formal history, they were reluctant to answer his questions. When he lis-tened to elders speaking in family settings, however, Giblin found that they often spoke openly and animatedly about the past. Drawing on Elizabeth Tonkin's work on the social construction of oral history, Giblin's book illus-trates the way articulateness in Njombe was socially created.[1]

In Tonkin's analysis, memory and its reconstruction are narrated within genres, which connect the teller of the story and the audience through a set of mutually understood codes and expectations. When both the genre and the context of narration are understood and valued by teller and audience, narrators become articulate. Tonkin argues that an interview is one form of oral genre, in which there is a social relationship between tellers and listen-ers. This relationship involves differences of power, perception, and expec-tation. The interview setting itself creates a social context in which narra-tors may not feel comfortable speaking, or may feel that they lack authority over the subject at hand. When researchers fail to understand this, they may miss the fact that a teller who is inarticulate during an interview will "have command of other genres in which they would speak differently." She suggests that researchers tap into this expertise of the narrator, rather than insisting on conformity to the interview genre.[2]

Like James Giblin, I found that my initial interviews in the Kilombero valley resulted in closed rather than open-ended conversations about the past. My interview agenda was influenced by social science research on demography and development that had already been conducted along the railway line. My questions were therefore based on assumptions about cause and effect that were not shared by the rural farmers and traders that I worked with. I had presumed that there would be a discernible and discrete relationship between people's lives and the railway, and that people could be expected to report upon this in response to my questions. Yet the people I interviewed did not perceive themselves in relation to the railway in this way, even though it was a central resource in their daily lives.

My interview experience changed when I began to talk with people about their own life histories. In subtle ways, this also caused my project focus to shift. People who had found little to say to me when I asked them formal questions about TAZARA became articulate when talking about their own life experiences. As their stories unfolded, I learned about the contexts of life, livelihood,and life cycles that they expressed using the Kiswahili word *maisha*.[3] My own concept of "life" in life history narrative expanded to include the many meanings *maisha* held for the men and women I interviewed. In turn, I realized that TAZARA's role in the everyday lives of ordinary people did not necessarily take the form of measurable "outcomes" that could be correlated with specific policies or actions. Rather, the railway's importance was more nuanced, as reflected in people's stories of enhanced physical, social and economic mobility.[4]

The idea that personal narratives can reveal important truths about social and economic life is certainly not new. Life histories have been central to the work of many Africanist historians, most notably in research on women's history over the past two decades.[5] And long before this scholarly work, missionaries in East Africa were collecting autobiographical narratives for evangelical and other purposes. One missionary in particular, Elise Kootz-Kretschmer, recognized that autobiographies contained important information about local history, culture, and knowledge.[6] She wrote:

> In these stories we were surprised by the wealth of valuable information that we found, not only about the individual but also about local customs and practices. Thus we had discovered the path through which we could gain an even deeper understanding of the life of the people.[7]

Kootz-Kretschmer collected these autobiographical narratives for both missionary and ethnographic purposes. Their value to historians for understanding local experience of the nineteenth century has continued to be appreciated; as Marcia Wright notes, "autobiographical narratives by the survivors of these times evoke the period as no other kind of source can."[8]

The personal narratives I collected during my research on the TAZARA railway were not true "life histories," of the genre represented by Kootz-Kretschmer's work, in that they were not elicited in order to represent the narrator's life as a whole.[9] Rather, I recorded life stories as part of a larger research project, in order to increase my understanding of a particular topic. This topic was known to the people I interviewed, and therefore to a large degree the topic shaped the chronological and substantive focus of our exchanges. This method is closer to what Susan Geiger calls "modified" or "directed" life history interviews, in which the interests of the researcher influence both the questions that are asked and the locution of the narrator. Thus, even though I had abandoned my structured survey questionnaire, the conversations I had with those who shared their stories with me were focused largely on the time period of TAZARA and on the Kilombero valley geographic region.[10]

Histories of Livelihood

The first person to share her life history with me was a woman market trader named Mama Robi.[11] The richness of her narrative and her attention to chronological details caught my attention and drew me towards the genre of life history interviews. Mama Robi began her story by explaining why she had decided to move from her ancestral family home in Mbeya to the town of Ifakara. Mama Robi said that she moved to Ifakara "because of life" (*kwa sababu ya maisha*). Mama Robi had been married to a man who was in the Tanzanian army, stationed at Musoma, where they had lived together. She moved to Ifakara after his death—she did not want to re-marry, she told me, because she wanted to raise her children by herself.

In Mama Robi's telling, she moved to Ifakara because of life—*maisha*—meaning here the life circumstances that found her single with small children to care for after her husband's death. She went on to tell me that her *mjomba*, or maternal uncle, helped her to get a start in trading. Her *mjomba* lived in Ifakara, and had connections in the marketplace. He introduced her to influential wholesalers who gave Mama Robi goods on loan that she then sold retail, returning the price of the goods to the wholesaler and keeping a small profit for herself. In this section of her narrative Mama Robi makes reference to the importance of life cycles—the way older relatives or patrons support younger generations. This theme was common to many of the life history interviews.

Once she had been assisted by her *mjomba*, Mama Robi began to work on her own. The lengthiest section of her life story is a chronicle of her livelihood—the third meaning of *maisha* in the life history narratives. Several of the men and women I interviewed remembered the evolution of their livelihoods, which they also referred to as *maisha*, with careful attention to detail. Mama Robi's livelihood chronicle begins after her uncle got her started in retail trade. When she had saved enough money, she stopped buying from wholesale traders in Ifakara and began traveling to Mbeya herself, where she bought maize by the gunny sack and transported it on TAZARA. It had taken her three years to get to the point where she was trading wholesale goods. She traveled as far as Sumbawanga and Songea, searching for low-priced maize, beans, and millet. Outside of Mbeya, she bought directly from farmers whenever she could. When she returned to Ifakara, she sold her goods to other women traders who were involved in retail trade in the marketplace. After she had saved enough capital through trading, she bought a small plot of land in Ifakara and put up a thatched house of six rooms. She then began to farm, growing rice during the rainy season. She is now relatively self-sufficient in food. She continues to save and has opened a savings bank account at the Micro Finance Bank in Ifakara.

Mama Robi's narrative, like the other oral life history narratives I heard in Ifakara, used the term *maisha* to express these three components of life: life circumstance; life cycle; and livelihood. Mama Robi first described the life circumstances that led her to move to Ifakara on her own. She then described the assistance she received from her maternal uncle, representing the intergenerational obligations that accompany changes in life cycles. The bulk of her story dealt with the details of her pursuit of livelihood, from retail trading to wholesale trading to rice farming. After listening to Mama Robi, I began to speak with other people about their own autobiographies. I found that these themes of *maisha* wove through all of them.

Amadeus Mushi is a young man from Kilimanjaro region. He moved to Ifakara at the age of nineteen, he said, "*kutafuta maisha*"—to seek life.[12] For a young man in Kilimanjaro region in the mid-1990s, there were few economic opportunities. Like many of his fellow youth, Amadeus had completed primary school to Standard 7 but was unable to go on to the secondary level. He saw retail trading as a possible source of livelihood, but without a large amount of capital, he found it was difficult to get started.

An older male relative hired Amadeus to come to Ifakara to help him in his retail shop on the town's main street. Once Amadeus had established his own contacts and saved enough money, after about two years, he decided to move out on his own. His first independent enterprise was as a *machinga*—one of the young itinerant peddlers who sell everything from *sufurias* (aluminum cooking pots) to sunglasses from the back of a bicycle or from a gunny sack spread on the ground outside small town marketplaces.[13] Two years as a *machinga* earned him enough to rent a stall in the marketplace, where he sold *dagaa,* small dried fish. He soon hired his own assistant, a younger relative whom he sent to Morogoro to purchase *dagaa* and bring it to Ifakara for sale. He has since expanded his business to include beans, which he purchases in Mbeya and transports by TAZARA. He also takes the train to Dar es Salaam occasionally to buy consumer goods such as plastic dishes. He has planted a small rice farm where he tills with a tractor and harvests using hired laborers.

Amadeus feels that his livelihood has improved from year to year, as he has grown from sales clerk to *machinga* to market trader and rice farmer. Soon, he hopes, he will be able to save enough capital so that he can open his own shop in town. "Once I can start my own shop," he says, "then just like the man who brought me here, I will go to Kilimanjaro and get someone to come and work for me here, just like that man did for me." He has not yet married, but hopes to build a house in Ifakara and then to start a family.

The life story told by Amadeus started out with the statement that he came to Ifakara "to seek life"—*kutafuta maisha.* He began his story by detailing the life circumstances that faced him as a young man leaving primary school in the 1990s. During this difficult period of structural adjustment policies and other economic stresses, Amadeus found it was difficult to support himself in northern Tanzania. His life circumstances were challenging, but they were ultimately relieved by the intervention of a relative. The theme of life cycles is the strongest thread in Amadeus' story. He mentioned the role played by his older relative in several places in his narrative. He stressed that his first intention after achieving success—defined as opening his own shop on Ifakara's main street—would be to return to the north to find a young man that he in turn could mentor.

The theme of livelihood was strong in Amadeus' narrative, but not as detailed as in some other life histories. One trader in particular recalled very specific details of the history of his livelihood. Brown Mwasongwe began providing for himself at the age of 18, when he went to work in a cement factory in Mbeya.[14] He found cement work to be grueling and unhealthy, so he quit working there after a short time. He then worked as an *askari* (watchman) for three months before deciding to become a trader.

Brown's sister, meanwhile, had moved to Ifakara with her husband, who worked for the police force. The sister became pregnant and gave birth. Brown's mother traveled by train from Mbeya to Ifakara to stay with the young mother for four days. After talking things over, the mother took 250 Tanzanian shillings from the sister back with her to Mbeya to give to Brown, so that he could begin trading Irish potatoes. This was not a gift, he said, but an *ushirika,* a cooperative venture. After some time, his sister left Ifakara with her husband, and asked Brown to return her share of the business he had started with her. With his own share he has been able to continue trading on his own.

Brown Mwasonge's first business transaction was in the year 1983, some seventeen years prior to my interview with him. Brown's precise recall of the details of trading—from the amounts paid for goods to their destinations—was noteworthy. His life history narrative was in large part a history of these successive transactions. After receiving the initial capital of 250/= from his sister, Brown bought Irish potatoes in Mbeya and brought them to Ifakara by train. When he had sold the potatoes, he returned to Mbeya to buy more. Soon, he branched out from potatoes to cabbage. He traded both cabbage and potatoes for a while, until he saved enough to buy *ulezi* (millet). When he sold the *ulezi,* he had even more money, around 600 Tanzanian shillings. During the time that he was doing this trading in Ifakara he was still living at the home of his sister and her husband in their police quarters.

Once he had accumulated 600 shillings to spend, Brown got together with some other traders from Mbeya to buy beans. They decided to go to Kidodi to get the beans, and brought them back to Ifakara. He made enough money this time that his sister asked him to find his own place to stay. He continued to trade and establish himself independent of his sister and her husband. Brown now buys a number of goods from Mbeya, including millet, maize, beans, and potatoes. He sells them wholesale in the market at Ifakara. In 1993 he decided to begin farming, and now has a rice farm. He rents his own home, and hopes in the future to be able to buy a house plot and build a home for his family. Brown says that he is doing very well with his business in Ifakara, much better than he could do if he had stayed in Mbeya. Before coming to Ifakara, he says, "I didn't know what there was to do in life (*maisha*); after coming here I saw a lot of things, and learned a new way."

Brown remembered very specific details of the items he traded and their costs going back over a period of seventeen years. He remembered the livelihood choices he made before beginning to trade, and recalls the exact life circumstances that started his trading career—his sister's marriage and pregnancy; his own mother's visit to the new mother; and the trip to Mbeya to purchase Irish potatoes. Brown's story, like that of Amadeus, followed a similar pattern. Both of these young men started with difficult life circumstances and followed a trajectory of betterment. For others, particularly older persons, life circumstances went up and down in cycles, and they consequently told life history narratives of crisis and recovery. Lazaro Mbilinyi, a farmer originally from a village in Iringa, told a story that followed this pattern.

When Lazaro was a young man, his desire to have "more from life" led him to quit his job as a tobacco harvester for a Greek farmer in Iringa.[15] He decided to train as a carpenter and took up that trade for a short time. When his boss failed to pay him for his work, he left carpentry and became a self-employed tailor. Tailoring was a good enterprise for him, he remembers, and he was able to build himself a shop and take care of his wife and small child. His prosperity did not last long, however. While he was out of town one day, thieves broke into his shop and took everything he owned, including his sewing machine and his stock of fabric and clothing. He was left with only the empty shop.

Without any capital, Lazaro had few options. Like Brown and Mama Robi, he decided to move to Ifakara to become a trader. He had a friend who was a teacher near Ifakara, and this friend helped him to get a start in trading fish. After trading fish for two years, Lazaro began to trade in maize. Three years later he had earned enough to begin trading in charcoal. He traded charcoal for two years, and was then able to open a small shop in Ifakara. He now owns and operates the shop, but has not been able to develop his business further because of pressures from extended family members.

Once Lazaro became moderately successful in his trading business, his family members began to look to him for assistance when their own life circumstances became difficult. Lazaro has been caring for the five children of a sister who recently disappeared, along with children of other relatives who have been sent to stay with him. To support this growing family of dependents, Lazaro has been growing rice on a nearby farm. He has been redirecting the profits from his trading business into farming, and hopes to save enough to hire a tractor to farm a new plot of land he has just acquired outside of town. Farming makes sense for him economically now that he has so many dependents, he says. He can use their labor in the fields, and his harvest provides food for the large family.

These four narratives—of Mama Robi, Brown, Amadeus, and Lazaro—are examples of the kinds of stories I heard in the Kilombero valley as I interviewed people about their lives. There are many similar stories that could be included here. For example, there is the *daladala* (minibus taxi) driver from Dar es Salaam who had pinned his dreams on becoming wealthy in the urban transportation sector. When a government official accused him of forging his driving license, he had to give up that work and find a new livelihood. He decided to join his sister as a rice trader between Dar es Salaam and Mngeta, where I interviewed him. Other young people from Dar es Salaam purchased used clothing (*mitumba*) in the city and brought it by rail to sell at lively rural village auctions on Sunday afternoons. The concept of *maisha* as both life circumstance and as livelihood was present in each of these narratives as people recollected what they considered to be important events or processes in their pasts. These events often included a person's birth, education, marriage, work, moves, illnesses, and death. They spoke of life circumstances, largely outside of their control, that impacted them and their family members.

As they spoke of life's circumstances, people also talked about life cycles and how they affected their livelihood choices. Older people often described their experience of both good and bad times, and how they survived and moved on. Younger and older generations relied on one another for assistance during times of hardship, when help could take the form of financial contributions, housing, insider knowledge or trading contacts. In the marketplace, mothers and daughters frequently traded together. A young woman trader in Mngeta remembers moving there from Mbeya as a young girl, when her own mother was single and had taken up vegetable trading as her livelihood. Now the daughter is following the same path, trading in the market and raising her children without a husband as her mother did before her. The grandmother, meanwhile, has retired from the marketplace and spends her days cultivating her rice farm. She helps her daughter with child care when she must travel to Mbeya to the produce markets.

The people I spoke with talked at length and in great detail about their livelihoods. Traders described how they progressed from retail to wholesale market trading, and how they later diversified into farming and shopkeeping. There was a progression in the status of trade goods from retail to wholesale, and from millet to beans to charcoal. Those who had started out as wage workers or craftsmen were able to turn to trade when their livelihood collapsed, and to supplement this work with rice farming. These narratives helped me to understand the role played by the TAZARA railway in the everyday lives of the people living in the Kilombero valley. The people I spoke with did not make explicit connections between their life experiences and the presence of TAZARA. They did not tell me directly how the train had changed their lives, nor how it had affected the communities in which they lived and worked. Yet the train was a strong presence in the background of each of these stories.

The TAZARA Railway

The TAZARA railway provided the means through which people were able to respond to adversity, to take advantage of opportunity, and to diversify their livelihood. The train provided people living in a formerly inaccessible area with new mobility—they could undertake both long- and short-term moves, whether relocating to a new place of settlement or transporting trade goods from station to station. The train also maintained connections for people with extended kinship ties. Thus people could be mobile—moving long distances at times—yet retain their ties to the people and places that were important to them.

a. Mobility

The railway made it possible for people and their families to migrate and resettle in new areas.[16] During the time of TAZARA's construction, from 1970 to 1974, thousands of workers had come into the Kilombero valley as laborers.[17] Many of these workers stayed on, either as TAZARA employees or in other occupations including trade and agriculture. Some were joined by their families, while others married locally. As these communities grew, traders moved to the area that operated at both the wholesale and retail level. Farmers from the surrounding highlands of Mbeya and Iringa also began to move into the Kilombero valley. In the 1980s, fertile farmland was becoming increasingly scarce in those districts. At the same time, the liberalization of the economy and cutbacks in government farm subsidies made it difficult for highland farmers to profit from maize production.[18] Many of these farmers relocated into the valley, where rice farming could be done without expensive inputs, and some profit could still be made in agriculture. Thus in the past two decades, families have moved into the railway corridor for long-term settlement as laborers, traders, and farmers.

For others, the railway has facilitated short-term moves for the purposes of trading. Mama Robi provides a good example of this use of the railway. She typically traveled by train from Ifakara to Mbeya, where she stayed until she had amassed enough trade goods to bring back with her to the market. This kind of short-term mobility has been especially important for young people on the margins of the formal economy. The young men known as *wamachinga,* who traded in the small towns along the railway line often began their journeys at Mang'ula or Ifakara. They purchased shop goods there—pots, plasticware, sunglasses—then boarded the train with their parcels and bicycles. They traveled out to small stations like Chita, where there are few shopkeepers, and remained in the rural areas until they had sold their wares. They then packed up their bicycles and returned again by train to their starting points. Sellers of *mitumba* (used clothing) came into small stations to set up shop for a month or two until their supplies were gone, after which they returned to Dar es Salaam to obtain another consignment. Frequently, those who started out with short-term moves eventually settled more permanently in the valley. Amadeus is one example of a young man who worked as a *machinga* for a time before moving on to more stable forms of trade and acquiring a farm.

Trade itself has depended upon the mobility provided by the railway—for both goods and passengers. Most often, traders traveled from the place of sale (a market town like Ifakara or Makambako) to the source of the goods they traded. Once they had purchased their goods, a process that might take an extended period, they returned home with them. They commonly carried their items as accompanied baggage or "parcels" on TAZARA, or grouped together to rent a *behewa* (goods wagon). Thus, for example, Mama Robi traveled to Mbeya for millet and to Sumbawanga for maize, while Brown went to Kidodi for beans and Lazaro to Mikumi for charcoal. Products from the valley were purchased in similar ways—market sellers from the cities came to the Kilombero valley to purchase rice and fish directly from their producers. Only rarely would a fish trader from Mngeta travel to Dar es Salaam with a load of fish to sell. It was more common for the city traders to come to him.

Mobility was not only important for trade and economic activity. It was also important for social, cultural, and medical reasons. Funerals, births, weddings—these events normally required the presence of family members and close friends. The railway made it possible for people to attend ceremonial and cultural occasions even though they lived some distance away. Similarly, the railway made it easier for family and friends to help one another during times of hardship. When Lazaro's tailoring business collapsed in Iringa, he used the train to visit his friend, who was a teacher near Ifakara. This friend helped Lazaro to start a new life as a market trader. The train made it easier to send children to stay with relatives in town, as Lazaro found with his growing houseful of dependent nieces and nephews. These forms of mutual aid were not dependent on the train—they took place before TAZARA's construction and did not always involve communities located along the railway line. In many stories I heard, however, the train facilitated contact and mutual assistance between families and friends.

Mobility was important for health—for the obvious reason that it helped the sick and injured to get to hospitals more easily—but also because it connected family members who depended on one another for support. In Tanzania, relatives are responsible for providing food and care for family members who have been hospitalized. TAZARA has made it easier for relatives to visit the hospital in Ifakara as well as other clinics. The railway has also made a big impact on the treatment of leprosy in southern Tanzania, because the disease can now be treated on an outpatient basis. Young children who formerly would have been taken away from their families to live in the leprosy home in Ifakara can now come by train to the clinic to get their medication, and then go home again.[19] In these and other ways, the railway has made it easier for individuals and families to seek and benefit from health care.

b. Diversification

The detailed livelihood chronicles that people shared with me had a common theme. Each of the people I interviewed had changed his or her livelihood strategy multiple times. Some moved from one occupation to another, while others stayed within the same occupation but changed the products they were trading or the location of trade. This pattern of livelihood change has been called "serial diversification" by Pekka Seppala and is one of the most significant economic strategies of the people living in the TAZARA railway corridor.[20] It is clear from the life histories I collected that the railway has played an important role in facilitating serial diversification. The potential for diversification within the local economies along the railway line is in turn one of the most important factors in migration and resettlement to the rail corridor.

Pekka Seppala's recent book on Lindi district shows how rural populations use income diversification as a livelihood strategy. Seppala argues that diversification is not only a means for risk aversion, as is often observed in African settings, but can also be a strategy for accumulation. The major path to wealth in Lindi district, he found, was more than hard work and technical know-how. It was the ability to make timely conversions from one resource or occupation to another, in response to the "imperfections, discontinuities and fluctuations that are characteristic of the rural economy."[21] In order to make these conversions, rural actors needed to be able to move laterally (i.e., from one product to another); sectorally (i.e., from one occupation to another); and geographically. An individual or household could carry out more than one activity at the same time, or (more commonly) move in sequence from one form of livelihood to another. Most of the life histories I collected fall into this category.

The chronicles of livelihood that people shared with me all described some form of serial diversification, and show that it took place on a number of levels. The clarity of recall with which people described their economic transitions—along with the social networks and other assets that facilitated them—illustrates their importance in rural economic life. Within the trade sector, people moved from one level of exchange to another. For example, market traders like Mama Robi shifted from retail to wholesale trade, while young entrepreneurs like Amadeus moved from itinerant peddling as *wamachinga* to retail trade in the covered market.

TAZARA played a large role in these transitions. Mama Robi was able to shift more easily from retail to wholesale trading because the railway linked both of these kinds of markets. When she began trading, the wholesalers that sold her sacks of millet in Ifakara brought their produce by rail from regional markets in Mbeya. When Mama Robi was ready to move into wholesale millet trading, she also used this rail link to travel between Ifakara and Mbeya. The train gave her easy access to a variety of additional wholesale markets between Ifakara and Mbeya, and between Ifakara and Dar es Salaam. At key junctions where road and rail traffic converged, such as Makambako, Mama Robi was able to tap into even wider trade networks. TAZARA thus facilitated her transition from retail to wholesale.

Diversification among different products was also made easier by TAZARA. The railway passes through several ecosystems located at different altitudes, resulting in substantial local specialization in crop production along the rail line. Railway stations are known for the particular products they export: Ifakara exports the most dried fish and rice; Mngeta has the best bananas; and Mlimba is the source of popular sweet oranges from Masagati. Because these varied products are available along the same line of transport, traders can shift from one product to another in response to external pressures or personal circumstances. Crop specialization along the railway line also has a cultural component. Individual stations have attracted migrants from different regions, which impacts not only what is produced and sold, but also what is consumed. Mngeta produces more bananas in part because of its ecological suitability, but also because numerous Nyakyusa speaking migrants from Mbeya have settled there who specialize in banana cultivation. The market for meat has grown dramatically in Ifakara with the influx of migrants from Ubena and Uhehe, thus herders, cattle traders and butchers have congregated there.

While TAZARA has for the most part facilitated livelihood diversification along the railway corridor, it has had a limiting effect on trade in some circumstances. This has happened, for example, when the railway management has favored large-scale traders over smaller entrepreneurs, as was the case last summer when I was conducting research. The railway had a chronic shortage of goods wagons (*behewa*) for shipping, and there were frequently long delays in shipment of produce between Mbeya and Dar es Salaam. This was especially problematic for those who trade in perishable goods such as bananas and dried fish, which must be consumed soon after harvest. Trains originating in Mbeya would be full by the time they reached the stations in the Kilombero valley, where goods would accumulate on the platforms waiting for a wagon. Large-scale rice traders from Dar es Salaam, particularly the companies Mohammed Enterprises and Fida Hussein, were given preferential access to railway wagons. This made it more difficult for smaller traders to transport their goods and, therefore, to compete.

Differentiation between large- and small-scale traders was most noticeable at stations where both were competing for grain and for transport at the same time. The relationship between large-scale and smaller-scale rice traders still needs to be looked at more carefully with regard to diversification. Small-scale traders depend upon the railway in order to maximize their diversity strategies. They are vulnerable to TAZARA officials' willingness to make goods wagons available to them. Farmers, meanwhile, may also diversify their trading partners when they seek markets for their rice crop. Seasonal differences in volume and pricing make it profitable for Fida Hussein to come into the railway corridor to purchase rice in some seasons, but not in others. Farmers may sell some of their rice after harvest to one of these large companies, but will continue to rely on small-scale traders to exchange smaller quantities of grain post-harvest. In order to maintain relationships with a variety of traders and markets, farmers may diversify their trading partners from season to season. The relationships between farmers, traders, TAZARA. and state marketing policies are complex and connected to local economic and political authority. Marketing diversification in this context may also be read as resistance, for example when produce is diverted from one marketing system to another. This issue requires further study.

The people who told me their life histories used serial diversification as a strategy for economic survival and accumulation. Many of them also described intersectoral diversification, most commonly as a combination of rice farming with another economic activity. Because TAZARA passes through the fertile floodplain of the Kilombero river, where there is still good land available for rice farming, many of the people I interviewed combined their economic activities with agriculture. They called agriculture their economic foundation, or *msingi*, and invested in rice farming as soon as they were able to accumulate enough capital to obtain a plot, labor, and access to a tractor (if they were prosperous). Farming could be the foundation of family subsistence, absorbing labor and providing food for the table, as the narrative of Lazaro Mbilinyi demonstrates. In other cases, rice farming proved so lucrative that it became the capital basis for other enterprises. A medical entrepreneur who moved from Dar es Salaam to Mang'ula in 1998 used his income from rice farming to establish and to expand his small neighborhood clinic. As one observer commented, "rice built his hospital."[22]

Conclusion

Mobility, flexibility, and diversification—all three of these three livelihood strategies were revealed through the personal narratives I listened to along the TAZARA railway corridor. Personal narratives showed me the contexts in which people lived their lives, and helped me to see TAZARA within these contexts rather than merely as a variable that has created measurable outcomes. The complexity of the individual life experiences that people shared with me has caused me to move my inquiry away from the impact or effect of the railway and towards the larger processes that the railway is a part of. These processes—movements of people and goods, flexibility in responses to life circumstances, diversification of livelihood—did not depend solely upon the presence of the railway. Yet to a large degree, the railway facilitated them and shaped their direction.

The significance of these processes was revealed to me through the stories that people told me about their lives. Each of the four narrators I have mentioned here spoke of *maisha* as they talked about their personal history. Mama Robi came to Ifakara "because of life," and Amadeus "in search of life." Brown "didn't know what there was to do in life" as a young man, and Lazaro sought "more from life." The way people spoke of life in these narratives—*maisha*—had multiple meanings. One way of understanding *maisha* was as the story itself, as the narrative recollection of the events and circumstances of one's own past. Another way of thinking about *maisha* was in terms of life cycles—described as relationships between generations, or as cycles of crisis and recovery. Lastly, people spoke of *maisha* as livelihood. As people talked with me about their lives, I became attentive to the larger patterns and contexts that existed in the TAZARA corridor.

I learned from their detailed and extended livelihood chronicles that serial diversification was one of the most important strategies they had for averting risk, surviving adversity and accumulating wealth. They told me that their survival and success depended upon their ability to shift labor and resources from one activity to another. They did not make direct connections between the presence of the railway and their livelihood histories. It was clear from their testimony, however, that the railway has facilitated their mobility and has made the railway corridor an attractive destination for migrants.

Notes

1. See Giblin's article in this volume; Elzabeth Tonkin, *Narrating our Pasts: The Social Construction of Oral History* (Cambridge: Cambridge University Press, 1992), 1–9.

2. Ibid., 54.

3. James Giblin found similar use of the term *maisha* in the stories told by elders in Njombe; see his article in this volume.

4. Pekka Seppala's "case study" approach to economic activities in the informal sector is similar to mine. Seppala also collected livelihood histories from several individuals, in Lindi District. See Pekka Seppala, *Diversification and Accumulation in Rural Tanzania* (Uppsala, Sweden: Nordiska Afrikainstitutet, 1998); and also Pekka Seppala, "The Informal Sector in Lindi District," in *The Making of a Periphery: Economic Development and Cultural Encounters in Southern Tanzania,* ed. P. Seppala and Bertha Koda (Upsala: Nordic Africa Institute, 1998), 233–64.

5. These scholars include Claire Robertson, Susan Geiger, Peg Strobel, Marcia Wright, and Heidi Gengenbach.

6. Elise Kootz-Kretschmer was a Moravian missionary and ethnographer stationed in Mbeya district, where she began collecting women's life stories in the 1890s. The testimonies Kootz-Kretschmer recorded were evangelical biographies, intended to be read at funerals to illustrate the spiritual progress of the departed during her lifetime. Marcia Wright, *Strategies of Slaves and Women: Life-Stories from East/Central Africa* (New York: Lilian Barber Press, 1993), 23.

7. Elise Kootz-Kretschmer, *Die Safwa, ein ostafrikanischer Volkstamm, in seinem Leben und Denken* (Berlin: D. Reimer, 1926–29), 1:8 (my own translation). See also Wright, *Strategies of Slaves and Women,* 23–24 for a description of Kootz-Kretschmer's work.

8. Wright, *Strategies of Slaves and Women,* 23.

9. A classic anthropological definition of a life history is contained in Lewis L. Langness, *The Life History in Anthropological Science* (New York: Rinehart and Winston, 1965), 4–5.

10. Susan Geiger, *TANU Women: Gender and Culture in the Making of Tanganyikan Nationalism, 1955–1965* (Portsmouth, N.H.: Heinemann, 1997)., 15–17.

11. Interview with Mama Robi, Ifakara, May 2000.

12. Interview with Amadeus Mushi, Ifakara, July 2000.

13. *Wamachinga* are small-scale traders, normally young men, who buy items from larger traders and then peddle them in towns. The *wamachinga* in Dar es Salaam are said to be of southeastern origins and have made an impact on the national political scene. In the Ifakara area, *wamachinga* denotes the livelihood of small-scale itinerant trading rather than ethnic or geographic origin. See Nestor Luanda and Eginald Mihanjo, "The South-East Economic Backwater and the Urban Floating Wamachinga," in *The Making of a Periphery: Economic Development and Cultural Encounters in Southern Tanzania,* ed. Pekka Seppala and Bertha Koda (Uppsala: Nordic Africa Institute, 1998), 222–32, for information about *wamachinga* in Dar es Salaam and Lindi.

14. Interview with Brown Mwasonge, Ifakara, May 2000.

15. Interview with Lazaro Mbilinyi, Ifakara, June 2000.

16. A good survey of migration and demographic change in the region between Ifakara and Kidatu is R. P. Mayombo, "Economic Structural Changes and Population Migration in Kilombero Valley," (Master's thesis, University of Dar es Salaam, 1990).

17. Ibid.; George T. Yu, *China's Africa Policy: A Study of Tanzania* (New York: Praeger, 1975).

18. Giblin, see chapter in this volume.

19. Interview with Sister Maria Paula, Nazareth Leprosy Center, Ifakara, 2001..

20. Seppala, *Diversification and Accumulation in Rural Tanzania.*

21. Ibid., 27.

22. Conversation with a bystander, Mang'ula clinic, July 2000.

PART V

Innovative Sources and Methods

19

SECTIONAL INTRODUCTION
INNOVATIVE SOURCES AND METHODS

David Henige

As a latecomer to the historiographical enterprise, African history has been in a position less to reinvent the wheel than to take advantage of sets of wheels already in place. True, at first the new enterprise tended to concentrate on using existing written sources and newly mined oral ones, and the results of archeology. Still, the promise of more was always there, as exhibited in an early work, Daniel McCall's *Africa in Time Perspective* (New York: Oxford University Press, 1969), which had separate chapters devoted to a number of other approaches which were then in their infancy, even outside African studies. In the ebb and flow of the past forty years, various sources and various approaches have come and, in some cases, gone as well. The papers in this section each treat sources that might not in the normal course of things be regarded as historical sources, except by those willing to regard all evidence *from* the past as evidence *for* the past as well. Given the paucity of source materials, Africanists can hardly afford to think otherwise.

In her paper, Cynthia Brantley treats colonial reports on nutrition as such an opportunity. To do so she must first argue against those who would reflexively treat such evidence as "tainted by the ignorance, arrogance, and racism of their producers." To what degree this point of view is common is hard to say. Certainly examples are not hard to find, but Brantley rightly points out that there is no pressing reason to regard this evidence any differently than, say, oral data, which has certainly done very well in accruing credibility. Brantley's source of choice is the 1939 Nyasaland Nutrition Study, the very title of which is enough to put off the unsuspecting. For various reasons these data remained unpublished, so Brantley's paper represents a case of bringing new data into the public domain. Better yet, there appear to have been both an official and a minority report, allowing the modern scholar to study two differing, yet equally primary, perspectives. Needless to say, this is hardly very often the case, at least for these kinds of material, which usually appear in anodyne and impenetrable officialese. (Some might disagree with Brantley, though, in her contention that there is a "presumption that all colonial data [are] in colonial archives and that projects undertaken exist at least in some sort of report." If only!)

The nutrition study concerned only three villages, although each inhabited different ecological niches, but the study covered a full agricultural cycle. The reports on the study differed. One was "scientific," that is, it measured—in this case the size of plots, kinds of crops grown, expenditure of labor, and resulting yield. The other was "anthropological" and looked at behavior and organization as crucial variables behind agricultural productivity. Both reports had points of view that might—or might not—have affected the findings. That of Dr. Benjamin Platt judged that productivity was adversely affected by "lack of organization and initiative," as well as lack of foresight, while Margaret Read attributed it to the inefficiencies—as she saw it—of matriliny. Thus neither report can escape at least the imputation of *parti pris*.

It is just this fact—two reports instead of one, resulting in two points of view about causes, if not effects—that makes Brantley's study suggestive beyond its original ambit of three villages. That is, we have every right to assume provisionally that even the most bland reports from the past—and hardly just colonial Africa—mask divisions, debates, and disagreements that preceded their creation. In short, they, like oral data, were often the results of small group dynamics in action, but unfortunately not in view.

If nutrition sounds unappetizing, what of electricity? Catherine Coquery-Vidrovitch thinks there is more to the study of how electricity was wielded than meets the casual eye, and that social history can be discerned from its study. In fact, although Coquery-Vidrovitch does not stress the point particularly, electricity, whether in Africa or not, can serve as a useful microcosm of how control of desirable goods and services implies control of a great deal more, especially in a context where rewards are not necessarily related either to need or to performance.

Electricity was slow in reaching rural Africa, even urban Africa, and its pattern of spread almost certainly reflected the colonial authorities' needs and goals almost exclusively. Thus, for the French, Algeria alone was deemed worthy to receive more raw materials for producing electricity than all of sub-Saharan Africa. Of course, proximity helped, but the pretense that Algeria was an extension of metropolitan France helped as much. Ironically, Africa suffered precisely because of the lack of local sources for these raw materials during the colonial period. On the other hand, Africa, especially southern Africa, had certain sources of hydroelectricity that helped to compensate. Once independence was established, the situation improved. Foreign governments were willing, even eager, to underwrite the costs of such things as dams and petroleum reserves and, at first anyway, production was at a level high enough to provide higher levels of service at lower costs—a set of circumstances that was not allowed to continue.

At first glance, generating electricity and Ghanaian high life seem reciprocally far removed. Steven Salm shows at least one interface when he discusses the results of his study of the "Bukom Boys" in Accra. Embracing the high life experience, the youth generation of the time sought sanctuary from the postwar milieu of depression and the angst of the freedom movement there, even if they had to create the ambiance themselves. This coalesced in the 1950s and 1960s around the area of Bukom Square, hence the name. In many ways the movement reflected in microcosm similar responses in Harlem and other urban areas. Salm relies on interviews and newspapers from the time to draw his case, but says nothing about the possible preservation of posters, handbills, and other ephemeral forms of advertising. If these do happen to exist—and admittedly it is not likely—they would provide a rare glimpse of unmediated communication about this aspect of Ghanaian society

Dennis Cordell has longstanding experience in the demography of colonial and post-colonial Africa, so it is no surprise that in his contribution he turns to a discussion of sample surveys—a standard expedient much used to determine the whole from a part, particularly in areas where logistics were a perennial issue. As he points out, there is no lack of these available for the last fifty years or so, covering the bulk of Africa, if hardly to the same degree. In the event, he concentrates on a sample survey that he and his colleagues organized and carried out in Burkina Faso in 1974/75. Although the survey was not intended for the purpose, they came to realize that, viewed diachronically, it shed light, when compared with earlier ones, on the history of internal and external migration. Eventually, the survey comprised nearly 100,000 individuals drawn representatively from various parts of the country and various ethnic groups. By asking questions about past activity, Cordell and his associates learned that these 100,000 individuals participated in nearly ten times that many migrational movements (defined as moving from one sub-national entity for a minimum of three months). As Cordell points out, this information was gathered from participants rather than from observers, and in sum provides "an aggregate of individual African migrant perspectives on how mobility transformed life in Burkina Faso in the twentieth century."

Since the recollections of these migrations extended back about 75 years, Cordell and Victor Piché found it useful to divide the period into four eras: 1900–31, 1932–46, 1947–59, and 1960–73. They discovered that migratory patterns correlated well with economic and political phenomena. While this is hardly earth-shaking, being able to add evidence to intuition enables abstract hypotheses to be turned into working ones, and allows prudent forms of extrapolations to take place over time and places. The sheer magnitude of these migrations also points to what might otherwise be overlooked or denied—that the colonially governed peoples of Africa actually retained a great deal of flexibility and freedom of action. This provides another nail in the coffin of the belief in many quarters that the colonized were also the paralyzed.

Cordell is careful not to over-wring his claims for the value of this sample survey in particular and the technique in general. He realizes that, despite all efforts, the sampling was not as representative as desirable, even if more so than usual. No process involving human beings exercising free will can ever be. He calls for more such studies with a historical perspective. He closes by urging the development and implementation of further sample surveys, as well as collecting data in one place on those carried out elsewhere, and points to some existing resources in that direction.

It would not be easy to conjure up a more disparate group of sources than the four discussed in the papers in this section. Bundling together might seem capricious, but doing so makes an important point, one stressed by most of the contributors to the conference from which these papers emanate. There is a far greater diversity of sources than we might intuitively realize. This only reflects life more generally. The day before I wrote this, biologists decided to divide African elephants into two species, thereby doubling in a trice the variety there. Astronomers not only discover new examples of known phenomena but also examples of things heretofore unimagined. Archaeologists no sooner make a claim than the next excavation refutes or modifies it. More to the point of the conference theme, more routes to the summits of more mountains are being negotiated all the time. If all these things, and a myriad more, were not the case, the study of any branch of knowledge would be doomed to terminal—yet eternal—ennui. The cases cited throughout the present volume remind us that we are scholars practicing in a field with no visible boundaries, and we and that field are much the better for it.

20

BEN AND MAGGIE: CONSUMING DATA REASSESSING SCIENTIFIC AND ANTHROPOLOGICAL EVIDENCE: HISTORICAL PERSPECTIVE ON NUTRITION STUDIES

Cynthia Brantley

The title of this chapter means no disrespect in its familiarity. Its intention is to humanize and personalize the historical actors and to point out both the control they had over the information they gathered and its interpretation and availability. The Ben and Maggie of the title refers to Benjamin Platt, the medical researcher who was director of the 1939 Nyasaland Nutrition Survey and who collected all the data from the various scientists on the team, and to Margaret Read, the anthropologist for the survey. Never were they Ben and Maggie; their relationship was extremely formal and filled with friction. In fact, they had a falling out early in the undertaking that resulted in Read working separately and providing her own report which was appended to Platt's main report. Because of this separation of the data, it is possible and useful to distill the two distinctive interpretations. In addition to their being the main collectors of the data that focused on how people in three Nyasaland villages fed themselves, for various reasons, these data, with two exceptions,[1] remained in their personal possession and was neither published nor distributed and thus, never really interpreted.[2] This chapter is an effort to provide a dialogue between Ben and Maggie.

The arguments of this chapter are twofold. The major one concerns the value of comparing Read's anthropological data with the scientific measurements made by the team and then her further comparisons that emerge from her own reanalysis in a period up to the 1970s, when she produced a draft manuscript of a more extensive examination of the situations in the three villages.[3] The other argument is an underlying one—the issue of the data itself, and our presumption that all colonial data is in colonial archives and that projects undertaken exist at least in some sort of report.

I raise these concerns against the prevailing presumption that colonial documents of Africa are tainted by the ignorance, arrogance, and racism of their producers. I argue that when we seek to learn of the nature, form, and content of the European colonial project in Africa and the nature of the life of colonial subjects, these reports can be used to illuminate aspects of the social history of the colonized. Evidence from anthropological investigations of Africa in the 1930s is particularly suspect due to the collaboration anthropologists had with the colonial effort, the focus on "tribe" and function, and the privilege often given to the particular ethnic group studied over neighboring peoples who were probably not studied and whose lives are interpreted through the eyes of the particular society of the anthropologist's interests. This criticism certainly applies to some of the work of Margaret Read, who studied Ngoni society in Nyasaland in the 1930s.[4] I myself have criticized Read particularly for her efforts which presumed not only that patriliny was preferable to matriliny as ideological and organizational modes, but that patriliny would ultimately overtake matriliny and prevail over it. I argued that her own evidence belied such a conclusion, and that many aspects of Ngoni and their neighbors were exchanged and interchanged. The end result was not necessarily "Ngonized" neighbors.[5] However, all anthropological evidence should not be discarded out of hand as tainted, but must be used as we would oral evidence, in relation to a wider body of material, with complex comparisons, and with hindsight over time. In the case of Read's work as the "sociologist" for the 1939 Nyasaland Nutrition Survey, where the three villages had different core ethnicities, we have available to compare with her anthropological evidence the scientific data of the agricultural, medical, and nutritional investigations. As well, in the 1970s she provided a subsequent reanalysis of her own sociological data. In hindsight, she changed her mind about some of her initial conclusions, and this analysis becomes extremely valuable for our understanding of the colonial venture and the lives of the Africans under colonialism.

Scientific Goals and Findings[6]

The main concerns of the team of scientists were the staple crops and the availability of vitamins and minerals. The three study villages were within sixty miles of each other, and men in all villages had spent some time away as emigrant laborers. The main distinguishing conditions of the three villages were different ecological circumstances (lakelevel, escarpment, plateau) and different staple crops (maize on the plateau and escarpment versus cassava at lakelevel). Additional contributing factors to nutritional conditions included some cattle kept on the plateau, some cotton grown on the escarpment, and (theoretical) access to fish at lakelevel, which is important because of the limited nutrients available in cassava. The fact that the lakelevel and escarpment villages were matrilineal and the plateau village patrilineal seemed not to matter at all to the scientists.

The interdisciplinary team worked in tandem and collected evidence for almost an entire agricultural year (December 1938–October 1939). The doctor needed to know about the diseases and the measurements of weight and height. Soon he learned that he needed to pay attention to seasonal variations. The agriculturalist measured the size of plots, the crops grown, the amount of labor expended, and the resulting yield. He soon learned that he needed to deal with failed crops and the difficulties of measurements. The botanist identified the cultivated and wild plants and the nutritionist measured the amount of food consumed—an almost impossible task.

They discovered the average workable size of a family farm was 3½ acres, and that the initial clearing and planting of maize as well as harvesting was accomplished through communal beer parties. They found the beer had sufficient nutritional value to sustain these workers in the periods when this was all they consumed.

The scientists' calculations showed that the work of women in all three villages was stretched to the maximum of their time and energy, and that the vitamins and minerals derived from collectible edibles that formed the side dish for the porridge were extremely beneficial. Their basic findings were to discover that cumulatively, people in all three villages had sufficient calories to maintain their height and weight. Those who grew cassava could harvest it throughout the year, so they were not so locked into agricultural seasons. However, fish was not as readily available to everybody, mostly because men did the fishing and so many of them were away. The people in the cassava village were the most discontent about their plight because they were all Christians and thus more individualized and focused on education, they longed for their previous diet of maize and sorghum, and they disliked cassava. Ironically, however, of all the villages, the individuals who had the least amount of food were the widows in this village and some of the women whose husbands were away.

Both of the other two villages experienced hunger seasons before the new maize crop was ready for harvest. The hunger period was one or two months on the plateau but, because this village had different classes of wealth, some people escaped any hunger period, and those who faced it often worked for the others for food. The escarpment village, where people had to work fields on an incline as much as 45 degrees, had to spend more time producing the same amount of food that could be grown on flat land. They had a longer hunger period, which was attributed to their lack of organization and initiative.

Anthropological Findings[7]

Margaret Read came to this nutrition study from her "tribal" study of Nyasaland's Ngoni, with a special interest in their political chiefdom, which had originally derived from Swazi and Zulu and in the mine experience in Rhodesia and South Africa lived by emigrant Ngoni from Nyasaland. She collected evidence only during the first four months (December 1938 through March 1939). Her assessment was that, although the lakelevel village was Yao, the escarpment village was Chewa, and the plateau village was Ngoni, few tribal traditions remained. It seemed that any distinctive features of the people of the three villages had been blurred by historical events:

> Round the town of Kota Kota was a welter of tribes from Zanzibar to the Zambezi. . . . Chewa chieftains ruled over family groups along the lakeshore and the hills . . . and an offshoot of the Mzimba Ngoni settled in the hills to the southwest. . . . But the wars and raids destroyed any strong tribal tradition in the area, and it is the most confused and mixed tribal region in the whole of Nyasaland.

In fact, all villagers spoke the same language (Nyanja) of the Chewa. No tribal aspects of diet remained evident: they ate the same diet of stiff porridge (cassava or maize) accompanied by a side dish, mostly of vegetables but sometimes with fish or meat.

Villagers told Read about the hunger seasons. In the escarpment village, complaints about hunger were common. In the plateau village, the reports were more of empty grainstores. In the cassava village, she heard more general complaints of discontent. It was clear that, although widows got sufficient cassava, they struggled to get ingredients for their side dish and rarely, if every, had fish. Their nutritional quality suffered because cassava calories were insufficient for good nourishment. She found traditional wealth discrepancies on the plateau, new-wealth discrepancies at the lakelevel (where, by far, more men had emigrated and for a longer time) and a general evenness of wealth on the escarpment, where few families had more than just the bare minimum of material goods.

In her initial evaluations, efficient organizational principles and receptiveness to modernization prevailed as the main criteria for villagers to be feeding themselves effectively. Only on the plateau, in her mind, existed "viable" chiefs who could trace their position to a "traditional" leader. The chief of this village was a designated Native Authority and responsible for the nearby court. Here there was some marked discrepancy in wealth, reflecting the internal power differences that had been part of the system of chiefdom. Therefore, she viewed the Ngoni village to have a more effective form of organization. The Yao village, similarly (in this case, modified because of Christianity and based on individualism), was headed in the right direction (though the village size was diminishing over the years as more and more people moved out). She did not expect this village to survive as a village. The escarpment village was isolated, quarreling, and more distanced from the entire colonizing effort with its demands and lures. Fewer people had gained access to any wealth of note. Cotton as a cash crop was minimal. She viewed the escarpment village to be feeding itself least well because they were always complaining about hunger and seemed to be unwilling to make the effort to work to ameliorate their low production (in contrast to other neighboring Chewa villages). She alluded to the fact that matrilineal practices might be less efficient than patrilineal ones.[8] She definitely argued that social organization contributed to nutritional success, but underlying her position were her preconceived notions about which kinds of social organization were most effective.

Main Scientific Evaluations, March 1940[9]

In contrast, Platt's compilation of the scientists' findings was based on careful measurements—of land held, crops planted and harvested, labor expended, height and weight, and food eaten. The scientists stressed the nutritional benefits of beer and noted the sociological significance of food being produced by communal labor, via beer parties. Platt calculated the calories that were expended to produce food versus the calories that the people consumed in each village for every month. He found it startling that the Chewa in the escarpment village, despite their complaints about hunger and despite evidence of their producing insufficient food to last until the next harvest, measured more calories overall and had fewer months in which labor expended exceeded calories consumed. He concluded that he simply had underestimated the amount of calories needed to produce the food in the first place. His report, however, remained unfinished. The medical portion was never completed. Platt worked on subsequent drafts, but as general nutritional and medical scientific data expanded exponentially during World War II, he discarded some of the baselines he had begun with, and ultimately, he produced neither final calculations nor a final report.

Despite the inconclusiveness of the evidence, Platt and the Nyasaland Government launched a development project (Nutrition Development Unit [NDU], 1940–43), aimed to relieve the hunger season and to increase the intake of vitamins and minerals from new fruits and vegetables. Since this project focused on growing enough food to eliminate the hunger period, the cassava village was viewed as needing no help. Besides, this particular cassava village was regarded as self-motivated and modernizing. The only evidence they had of actual hunger—that of widows in the cassava village—was not taken into account. At some point, the decision was made that the escarpment village was hopelessly lacking in initiative and its inhabitants were too steeped in their beliefs in witchcraft, *chinimwali* (female puberty rituals), and *nyau* (male dance society) to benefit from the development efforts. Therefore, any development work that would provide more food, more vitamins, and more minerals would be wasted there. The better organized, more efficient plateau village seemed to be ripe for help because they were more likely to accomplish the suggested changes of the NDU. A pilot project which constructed a nearby dam had seemed to be successful. The scientists did not see that the dam pilot project required additional labor from the already limited village resources and that villagers had failed to appreciate the value that the technological experts saw. Still, the NDU development project focused on certain villages on the plateau and more progressive villages on the escarpment. (The development project failed, mostly due to the disruptions of the war, with its drain on personnel and funds, but also because it had been too ambitious and had not taken into consideration other human factors.)

Anthropological Reassessment[10]

As Read reassessed her material during the subsequent thirty years of inter-national teaching and as a consultant to the Food and Agricultural Organi-zation (FAO) and the World Health Organization (WHO) of the United Nations, she eventually produced a manuscript analysis. She saw the teleol-ogy of placing either the receptivity to new ideas and modern changes or the degree of incorporation into the trade networks as valuable criteria for nutritional success without dealing with the reality of limited or expanded opportunities and without valuing the benefits of retaining conservative practices. Over time, she focused much more on the importance of village- and neighborhood-sharing mechanisms (*chibale*—real or fictitious blood relations; *chibwenzi*—special pact of friendship between relatives or non-relatives; *chinansi*—neighborliness; *chinzawe*—companionships).[11] For in-stance, the escarpment village activated more forms of these, which helped to deal with food shortages. In this way, complaints about hunger failed to result in experiences of hunger. Prior sharing mechanisms of the cassava village had fallen away, but some were replaced with forms of Christian charity. Though sharing was selective and was associated with increased power derived to the giver, nonetheless sharing mechanisms were in place, even if they were insufficient to relieve the widows' plight. In the plateau village, which was not organized on the basis of kinship, sharing encom-passed women who were away from their natal homes and overcame the dissonance of co-wives. Food success was based neither on the crop nor the organizational principles of each village.

Another important change was that she no longer viewed "work for food," undertaken so often by escarpment villagers, merely as a humiliat-ing admission that one had not produced enough themselves. She saw it as a valuable alternative to feeding families in the context of unworkable vil-lage cooperation. She argued that the specific criteria and the arenas of measurements used by the Nyasaland Nutrition Survey could be much too limiting and that they failed to reflect the complexities of these villages and the significance of their human ecologies. They each needed to be viewed as villages with their own integrity and problems.

For instance, Read's main initial assessment surrounding the escarp-ment village included its isolation and its lack of powerful chiefly author-ity. Yet later, she came to see that the village was legitimately divided. The basic friction was between one hamlet (Biwi's) and two others that had been divided over an old, unresolved murder case. This division was exacerbated by two additional factors. The colonial (and subsequent Malawian) government had forced the three hamlets into an official village and given Biwi the tax book and the position of headman. It had been Biwi's grandfather who had committed the murder and Biwi's hamlet had been the latecomers, welcomed by the "owners of the land" from the other two hamlets. There was a correlating division between Biwi hamlet, which had become Christianized under the Dutch Reformed Church and the other two hamlets whose people still believed in the localized indigenous religion and its practices connected with the fertility of the daughters, the fertility of the land, harvest rituals, female puberty rites, and the male secret dance society. Since the Dutch Reformed Church opposed fermented beer, communal agricultural work was divided between those in Biwi's Christianized hamlet, who hoed for sweet beer, and those in the other two hamlets who hoed for fermented beer. The main result was that this village *produced* less because people were unwilling to work together to produce and share food on a village level. When people ran out of food, they would rather hoe for other neighbors for baskets of food than to hoe together as a village. The main reason the scientific measurements showed a discrepancy between work expended to produce food and the caloric value of the food consumed was that the team measured not only food produced in the village but also food consumed that was brought from outside, but did not measure the labor required to obtain the latter. The team recorded the highest calorie intake here of all three villages, though the hunger season of empty grainstores was also real, as were complaints about hunger. Few people actually went hungry, as distinct from some of those widows in the lakeshore village. Sharing of food remained a strong practice, though lazy people were shunned. In her reassessment, Read no longer viewed the fact that this village was matrilineal nor the fact that they acquired fewer material goods as aspects detrimental to their ability to feed themselves.

For the lakelevel village, Read argued that it had to be identified as more than a cassava, Christian, or Yao village (though all of these factors mattered considerably), or even as a village that was no longer controlled by matrilineal principles. The significant role of Christianity in peoples lives there facilitated increasing patrilineal authority, but at the same time the church had great authority and the most powerful members were the senior women of the villages' matriline. Despite Christianity and the fact that this village represented a single matrilineal family, the village remained divided between those who were descended from slave wives and those were descended from free wives of the founder, who represented the matriline. The man of greatest wealth was descended from a slave mother.

The village chief, the legitimate guardian of the matriline, was disrespected and weak. A new form of nuclear family prevailed. Men gained extensive control as husbands over wives and as fathers over children, while matrilineage claims to children fell by the wayside, as did brothers' responsibilities for their sisters and their sisters' children. The desire for education, the pattern of individualism, and the reality of increasing male emigrant labor placed a heavy burden on those women remaining in the village. These factors also meant that young daughters remained unmarried, since they were required to marry Christian husbands, but prospects were few since they lived in a primarily Muslim region. The administration had basically applauded this "modernization" and Christianization as the wave of the future, but the village could not serve as a model of nutritional success. By 1992, when I had a chance to see what had happened to this village, I found that Christian Chewa men had moved in to marry these Yao daughters. The village had declined even further in size, land was short, and only four of the original Yao families remained. By 1992, even more families had no fish to complement their cassava because fish had become scarce and expensive. Numerous emigrant older men had returned to the area to live after many years away with little to show for it, claiming matrilineal land rights through their natal home, and increasing pressure on the land.

The plateau Ngoni village was in some ways ultimately the greatest puzzle of all. This village had three mechanisms besides that of individuals working elsewhere for baskets of food to take care of the hunger months. First, though few people benefited nutritionally from the cattle, many men and their families benefited from polygamy, whereby more than one wife was always cooking for different eating groups, several of which overlapped. In addition, all village families belonged to one of two "houses," which were headed by the chief's two senior wives and which controlled some of the grain storage and distribution. More importantly, Read found that the plateau village was really half a village—the other half being the new village created by the current chief on the death of his father. This new village, twenty miles away, often provided food for the plateau village and was in a tobacco region that provided work for some of the plateau villagers. Overlapping food distribution mechanisms and access to food that was not produced directly from the village's labor overcame the direct problems of hunger during the hunger months. Yet even this was insufficient to promise nutritional success. The dam built near the village fell quickly into disrepair because the chief failed to commandeer labor to maintain it. The NDU's efforts left no lasting results. Unfortunately, both Read's recorded notes from her 1967 visit and my own observations in the village in 1992 show that many villagers, men and women, spent their days drinking. Read's preconceived notions of this village's advantages failed to hold.

Conclusion

Colonial records cannot answer all of the questions, but they can be extremely useful. Comparative data collected from a scientific and from an anthropological perspective both help to illuminate the other. Reflections on earlier findings illuminate ways to understand the colonial effort, the colonial mindset, and colonial interpretations of African lives. For a nutritional study in 1938, it proved much too simple to think that a specific crop and its attachment to an agricultural season would be the main determinant of successful feeding or nutrition, as the scientists believed. Adding crops that would provide more vitamins and minerals had greater labor costs and insufficient commitment by the people whom the colonial project was designed to help. It also proved to be somewhat misleading to rely on perceived organizational capabilities of villages, as the anthropologist did initially. These study villages in these seemingly similar environments were in fact quite different, but that difference cannot be measured in terms of willingness to modernize or receptiveness to the goals of colonialism or development. Instead, differences must be noted as ways people relate to and respond to their human and ecological environment and how they have dealt with changes—both the changes they chose and the changes that happened to them. Finally, as a historian of Africa, and as one who lives in an age where data emerges elusively on computer e-mails and telephone conversations, I want to remind us all that important records for Africa's colonial era exist outside official colonial records and that we must be diligent in finding them. At the same time we must produce, preserve, and make available our own reassessments, which can be valuable historical records for the future.

Notes

1. Margaret Read, "Migrant Labour in Africa and Its Effects on Tribal Life," *International Labour Review* 45, no. 1 (1942): 605–31; C. K. Ricardo Bertram, E. Trewavas, and H. J. H. Borley, *Report of the Fish and Fisheries of Lake Nyasa* (Zomba: Nyasaland Government, 1942).

2. The two sets of documents that I am exploring here are Benjamin Platt's drafts of the findings of the Nyasaland Nutrition Survey scientific data in 1940 (including some

subsequent, unfinished revisions), and Margaret Read's own compilation of sociological data of the Survey in 1940 (including her subsequent analysis derived from this material in the 1970s). The original draft of Platt's Survey report sent to the Colonial Office did not survive the bombing of London. In 1992, Veronica Berry and Celia Petty printed a major portion of documents and the first draft report of the survey: Veronica Berry and Celia Petty, *The Nyasaland Survey Papers, 1938–1943: Agriculture, Food, and Health* (London: Academy Books Limited, 1992).

3. Margaret Read Papers, British Library of Political and Economic Sciences at the London School of Economics, London, READ 1/36: "Human Ecology and Social Behavior Notes for MS."

4. Leroy Vail and Landeg White, "Tribalism and the Political History of Malawi," in *The Creation of Tribalism in Southern Africa,* ed. Leroy Vail, 151–92 (Berkeley: University of California Press, 1989).

5. Cynthia Brantley, "Through Ngoni Eyes: Margaret Read's Matrilineal Interpretations from Nyasaland," *Critique of Anthropology* 17, no. 2 (1997): 147–70.

6. Nyasaland Nutrition Survey Papers, Centre for Human Nutrition, London School of Hygiene and Tropical Medicine, University of London, NNS: Survey Report Draft (1940) [Carbon Copy].

7. Nyasaland Nutrition Survey Papers, Centre for Human Nutrition, London School of Hygiene and Tropical Medicine, University of London, NNS: Box 1: Margaret Read: "Notebook re: Survey Villages."

8. This issue is discussed in Brantley, "Through Ngoni Eyes."

9. Nyasaland Nutrition Survey Papers, NNS: Survey Report Draft (1940).

10. Margaret Read Papers, READ 1/36: "Human Ecology and Social Behavior notes for MS."

11. Nyasaland Nutrition Survey Papers, NNS: Box 1: Margaret Read: "Notebook re: Survey Villages."

21

ELECTRICITY NETWORKS IN AFRICA: A COMPARATIVE STUDY, OR HOW TO WRITE SOCIAL HISTORY FROM ECONOMIC SOURCES

Catherine Coquery-Vidrovitch

Electricity in Africa has been very little studied. Bibliographical material is nearly nonexistent. Works that treat the history of urban electricity are rare. There is one good recent study on electricity in South Africa (Christie 1984), and a shorter one on West Africa (Sarfoh 1990). As for the rest of Africa, one finds occasional analyses of electricity in the countryside of underdeveloped countries issued by the World Bank (1975) or, very recently, by AFREPEN (African Energy Policy Research Network, 1999), in particular on Central and Eastern Africa. There is not much, and everything is in English. As for works in French, one finds a slim prewar survey (François 1937), and several unpublished master's theses, either finished or in progress (Ardurat 1999, Saupique 2000, Stéphanie Robert 2001) under the aegis of the Association pour l'Histoire de l'Electricité en France; more rarely there are brief allusions to the existence of some published or unpublished dissertations (Seck 1970, Danfakha 1990). Everything else has yet to be done, since the documentation is not lacking; it can be gleaned from the depths of varied and very complete archives—notably the series "Travaux Publics" and, after the war, those of FIDES (Fonds d'Investissement et de Développement Économique et Sociale) and of FAC (Fonds d'Aide et de Développement)—and in numerous technical reviews of the period, colonial or otherwise.[1]

This work should absolutely be undertaken, as the study of electricity in the colonies opens multiple avenues of research. Obviously it is, essentially, an area of economic history that is still quasi-virgin. It includes the history of production of large metropolitan companies in this area, and the role that they have played in the equipment: mining production and improvement of the rail network (especially in South Africa), etc. But the implications go far beyond that; an example is a brief visionary study in urban history about public lighting in Tunis (Belaid forthcoming), and several reports of the history of dock workers in Durban after electricity was brought to the port (Atkins 1993); one could go much farther in social history, asking about the incidence of electricity in everyday life and the changes of mentality, something that seems not to have been attempted overseas. We know, for example, that an event that is often seen in French-speaking cities like Dakar or Lomé—where central sections contain both colonial "bourgeois" homes and islands of poorer housing—is that of the school children working on their lessons under a public lamppost.

What was, and what still is, the impact of domestic electricity on social transformations in a time when international organizations are promoting electricity in the countryside, while a number of urban neighborhoods are still deprived of electrical equipment? All of this appears to be an immense unfinished project, where the combined work of historians and anthropologists could show itself to be extremely efficient for what little we record in the research plans that are discussed. This is the result, for example, that we are waiting for from concerted action being undertaken by the SEDET Institute,[2] which aims to compare the development and the implications of the construction of networks of urban services (water, power, and transport) in various francophone port cities overseas: Maghreb and sub-Saharan Africa (excluding South Africa), but also Madagascar and the Caribbean.

This project, for which we have high expectations, is in progress. As far as what we are concerned with here, it aims to examine and compare the social effects of electricity in a certain number of African cities. Counting the meager sources before the Second World War, and the very limited electricity in small and middle-sized tropical villages in the interior of the continent at that time, we have focused on port cities, often, but not always, also capital cities, all of them metropolitan cities, starting with the year 1945. The study thus permits us to show the actions taken in the last colonial phase. It also allows us to see in what measure and how national politics have followed or transformed the programs after independence. The object is not to make economic history an end in itself; it is not a question of staying in the safe territory of macroeconomic research, with the priority being recording the cost of programs, the investments made, the cost price, and the consuming sectors. It is to grasp, throughout, among other things, these indices, which are the only prevalent ones in the available sources, the impact that the introduction of this new technology had on Africans. The foremost question is not therefore that of industrialization and economic development that might or might not have resulted from it, but that of the action of the material culture on the consumer: who, in the cities, was equipped first? What was the effect, in daily life of, for example, public lighting and of the introduction of a light bulb in a house? Who profited from it? Who could not, and why? What changes were thus engendered in the way of life, and, consequently, the way of thinking? When, to use the same example, would the school child go from the gas, and later electric street lamp, and from public lighting, to the lamp at home to do his lessons?

One of the only writers to have approached this type of question is Keletseo Atkins: he explains how the appearance of electric power in the port of Durban at the end of the nineteenth century transformed working-class life (as, contrary to tropical Africa, electrification in South Africa happened nearly in advance of that of Great Britain). Until then, the dockworkers obstinately refused to work at night, essentially for religious reasons, the night being the domain of evil spirits. But the use, beginning in the 1880s, of electricity on the wharf of Durban accelerated the progression of things. For several years already, drawn by higher-paying night work, the dock workers had kept less to this natural curfew: it was thus left to whites to worry, hence the establishment of an official curfew of 9 P.M. at Petermaritzburg in 1871, and in Durban three years later. These laws were reinforced with public electricity, and were maintained until the end of apartheid (Atkins 1993). It is in this beginning of modernization of their living conditions that the workers, taking into account the lengthening of the workday, also started, beginning in 1881, to claim the weekend for themselves.

Our task is therefore to note and analyze transformations of the same type, but which took place with a half-century delay in sub-Saharan Africa. The investigation involves a Franco-African team, it being understood that many of the existing documents, and, of course, eyewitnesses are available only on site. The points of concentration currently are the cities of Dakar (Senegal), Cotonou (Benin), Conakry and Fria (an aluminum city) in Guinea, Abidjan (Côte d'Ivoire), Douala (Cameroon) and, in East Africa, the corridor of Mozambique along the Malagasy coast. We have added to these for comparison and, among other reasons, to measure the delay between the cities under European influence and secondary cities, that is, several examples in the interior of the continent: Ouagadougou (Burkina Faso) and also Bouaké and Bondoukou (Côte d'Ivoire). Our researchers are now in the field, the investigation is in progress, and it is still premature to draw conclusions (in 2003).

I will therefore be content here to point out our meager knowledge about black Africa on this subject, and to indicate several of the avenues of research offered by the located documents.

The Situation before the Second World War

Generally, before the 1950s, the quasi-totality of electric power was of thermal origin, in both the most advanced countries, like South Africa where the coal mines were abundant, and in the rest of sub-Saharan Africa, which appears to be the Cinderella of electricity. This remains true if we limit ourselves to the French empire, where Africa south of the Sahara appeared very far behind Indochina and above all the Maghreb. The fuel imported (gas, petroleum, and diesel and fuel oil) here remains comparatively nonexistent (see table 21.1).

Table 21.1: Importation of energy sources in the French colonies (average 1933–1935)

Territory	Gasoline (tons)	Refined Oil (tons)	Diesel (tons)
Algeria	120,000	47,000	95,000
Tunisia	45,000	26,000	24,000
Morocco	92,000	12,000	12,500
Maghreb T.	257,000	85,000	131,500
% Magreb	80.6%	64.5%	85%
AOF	15,000	3,000	3,000
Togo	700	800	500
Cameroon	3,000	900	600
AEF	5,000	1,000	2,000
Sub-Sahara T. 23,700	5,700	6,100	
Madagascar	6,000	2,500	3,000
Réunion	2,500	900	—
Indian Ocean T. 8,500	3,400	3,000	
Indochina	29,500	37,000	14,000
% Indochina	9%	28.1%	1.9%
TOTAL	318,700	131,600	154,600
% AOF	4.7%	2.3%	1.9%

Based on the *Annuaire du Comité d'Études minières pour la France d'outre-mer,* published 1936, cited in François 1937, p. 2.

Otherwise, contrary to Indochina, black Africa then had neither coal nor lignite. As opposed to those of Nigeria, the lignite reserves of Niger (estimated at 4 million tons in the Agades region) would not be exploited until much later. The only local fuel, used both for machines and for the boilers of trains, boats, or vehicles (mainly gas trucks), was wood and charcoal. In other words, the steam engine was preferred for a long time at the expense of electrical production. Moreover, the multiplication of mobile charcoal ovens, hardly different in operation from those already in use by the local people, did not happen without having an impact on the environment, and was clearly becoming problematic in the non-forested areas. One is surprised at the rudimentary character of the solutions that were envisioned, which went from the mandatory use of a percentage of alcohol in the gas used as motor fuel[3] to inconclusive experiments on vegetable oil motor fuels (Francois 1937: 9–12). The attempts to use these ersatz metropolitan products, moreover, would be intensified during the Second World War. One is also struck by the fact that the planned usage remained almost exclusively that of transport vehicles, with electrical production for industry a distant second.

The delay seems enormous compared to that of North Africa, probably due to the absence of a colonizing population: the early use of electricity in Tunisia for public lighting, for example, is due to the presence of colonizing settlers; already in 1872, lighting of the city of Tunis had been granted to an English company that had installed a certain number of gas nozzles. The French Compagnie du Gaz , which also took care of the water supply, bought back the right in 1884; despite its opposition, beginning in 1898 the municipal council unanimously adopted the principle of electric lighting, already in use by the Résidence and the postal service. The plan was supported by a petition of French and Tunisian city dwellers who held professions that required the use of electricity: printers, photographers, café owners, merchants, industrialists, pharmacists, etc. The Compagnie du Gaz had to give in, and, by a contract in 1900, renewed in 1922, obtained the rights of the distribution of electric power intended for both lighting and industrial use. Gas lighting would disappear at the beginning of the 1930s, and in 1937 the number of consumers of electricity was estimated at 33,000 (Belaid 2001).

This is a far cry from Dakar, where electrification of the Medina, the "native" quarter, which was nevertheless central, was not planned until the 1950s.

The only part of West Africa where the use of electricity was even moderately widespread before the Second World War was Nigeria, where coal was discovered in the east in 1909 and began to be used in 1914. The production grew to 610,000 tons in 1948–49, a level that was maintained until 1966–67 (630,000 tons), and which peaked on the eve of independence (905,000 tons in 1973–74; 203,000 in 1977–78).[4] From the beginning this coal was locally used to furnish electrical energy, but also for steam locomotives (that changed to diesel with the emergence of petroleum).

This miserable picture seems to be the polar opposite of what happened in South Africa, which appeared at the beginning of the century as one of the premier electrified powers. From 1905, South Africa was without a doubt the country where the cost of thermal electricity was the lowest, and one of those where the role of electricity as a source of energy was the highest for at least three reasons: the coal mines, with thick and shallow seams, were particularly easy to exploit; African labor—based on "compounds" (work camps reserved for migrant workers under contract), the system of passes or work permits, and the politics of the reserves where the families lived—was exceptionally cheap; and finally, the furnishing of electricity to the businesses was assured by the state, which guaranteed favorable prices for the mines, transports, and industry: From 1923 electricity was provided at cost by a state-run enterprise. In 1948, with the rise to power of apartheid, the biggest remaining private provider of electricity was nationalized. In the early 1960s the municipalities lost the right to construct power plants. In 1975, the state provided 87.5% of all the electricity produced in the country at cost.

On the other hand, the distribution of electricity was, and remains, particularly uneven in South Africa: the Orlando power plant is surrounded by a million city dwellers who do not have domestic electricity. Electricity reaches almost everywhere in South Africa, except to the blacks. Nowhere more than in South Africa was electricity synonymous with the industrial revolution, as it served before all else to augment productivity and to further the accumulation of capital.

The electricity boom was, in effect, inseparable from the mining boom, by the joint exploitation of coal, which stocked the thermal power plants, which in turn governed the permanent modernization of the production of gold and diamonds. Public lighting was provided in 1882 in Cape Town, where dock work was then extended into the night. Also, in Kimberley, public lighting, they say, attracted diamond miners, who called it magic. The choice was clear: in 1905, the least expensive industrial tariff was a penny per unit of consumption, which is to say the same price as in England; on the other hand domestic electricity cost more by a shilling, versus only seven pence in Great Britain. At that time at least nine huge power plants existed. A decade later, the principal company, VFTPC (Victoria Falls and Transvaal Power Company), created in 1906 by the BSA (British South African Company) of Cecil Rhodes with German capital and technology from the AEG (Allemeine Elektrisitäts Gesellschaft) had made the price of a unit fall by half, to .5 penny. Benefiting from the proximity of most of the mines to each other, the Rand energy system was integrated even before that of London. It owed this to the enormous expansion of the mining industry of Johannesburg, mechanization conducted speedily by the Chamber of Mines, a coalition of gold mine owners, in response to the successive strikes of white and black miners from 1906 to 1922. The result was that in 1923, the VFTPC sold more electricity than London, Birmingham, and Sheffield could have consumed together. As for the nationalist state, in order to make the strategic installations, like the rail network, safe from social movements, it created in 1923 (at the end of the great strike of 1922) a state agency, ESCOM. The municipality of Johannesburg, in addition, owned its own power plant that serviced the urban trolleys.

It is electrical energy that permitted South Africa to produce, in less than a century, almost half of the gold produced in the world in six thousand years, and to sell it throughout the entire world (Christie 1984: 158–59). Since the period between the two wars, the evacuation railway lines of SAR (South African Railways) were electrified, at least in part. In 1933, the Natal line was the longest electrified railway in the empire. Rural electricity in western Cape Town (the most white and "colored" province in South Africa) was working. The urban industrialization that shot up in the 1930s brought an extremely profitable boom for the VFTPC. The production of electricity quintupled between 1933 and 1948. But the company succeeded in concealing the enormity of its profits by using huge reserves and accrued capital to avoid augmenting salaries or lowering tariffs.

Profiting from the great strikes of 1946, the government nationalized again, and negotiated the nationalization of the business two years later. The VFTPC was a company with largely foreign capital, mainly British, which abnormally elevated the profits because of its quasi-monopoly of furnishing electricity to the gold industry. The state thus inherited a major tool of advanced technology, of social control, and of accumulation of capital.

Postwar: The Boom of Hydro-Electricity

Transvaal and Natal have coal deposits likely to last for centuries. In the 1900s, nevertheless, they dreamed of the tremendous hydro-power that

Victoria Falls on the Zambezi, 1,100 km to the north, might provide. But the project was not followed through, because of the cost that high-tension lines would have represented, and above all the fact of the huge irregularity in rainfall that rendered the dry season particularly dangerous. It was not until after the Second World War that South Africa, like everywhere else in Africa, began to convert seriously to hydroelectricity. In fact, between 1960 and 1975, regardless of the energy source, ESCOM entirely unified the electric network of the territory, close to 2,000 miles from Cabora Bassa to Cape Town; this is about the same distance as from London to Moscow. This allowed, notably, for thermal power plants to be constructed above the coal mines, allowing considerable savings on transport. The hydroelectric power plants, like the one in Cabora Bassa in Mozambique, served above all as reserves in times of need: in 1977, despite the immensity of Cabora Bassa just having started and of other dams constructed at that time, 97% of the electrical energy of ESCOM still came from coal power plants, which allowed South Africa to suffer hardly at all from its lack of petroleum. Also, the oil crisis of 1973 prompted it to precipitate the completion of the electrical railroad network in order to eliminate diesel locomotives, and to make the transition to nuclear energy.

Until the end of apartheid, electrical production remained closely tied to the maximum industrialization of the country. However the large majority of the population, blacks, did not have electricity. In the countryside and in townships, it was and remains common practice to use candles and oil lamps for lighting, and coal, wood, or paraffin for heat. In 1977 still, only 38,000 of 100,000 white farms had electricity. Some did not use electricity except for lighting, others were completely modernized. The narrowness of the interior domestic market was compensated for by the militarization of the government, a large consumer of electric power for its political and police apparatuses (Christie 1984: chap. 2).

Electricity became a major industry in South Africa in the beginning of the century because it was at the very foundation of the total industrialization of the country. We are far from a report in sub-Saharan Africa (excluding South Africa), where industrialization was still barely on the agenda at the eve of independence. Even if the transition towards hydroelectric production was made in principle after the war, it was generally necessary to wait for independence to see the first large-scale realizations take form.

Previously, the few power plants continued to use all sorts of thermal fuels. To avoid importing too much heavy, and therefore very expensive, materials like coal or petroleum, they set themselves to using local products, like wood or all the possible agricultural wastes—notably peanut shells or rice hulls—which were used late in certain Senegalese power plants, in Djourbel or Ziguinchor.

Since before the war, some thought of exploiting the enormous potential represented by West African rivers, which were supposed to offer great electrical possibilities at very low cost: the Niger, Senegal, Volta, Bandama. But the plans had until that time concerned irrigation more than electricity; this was the case for the Niger River in the years 1919–20, which ended by the French creating the Office du Niger in 1932. However, the Samsanding dam, finished in 1947, was not used at that time except to cultivate irrigated land.

The second attempt made by the French administration concerned the Senegal River. It was in 1927 that the Governor General of French West Africa had set up the Union hydro-électrique africaine (UHEA) in Bordeaux, in order to study the possibilities of both irrigation and electrical production. A Mission d'Études du Fleuve Sénégal was created in 1935 to collect all the necessary data. Transformed into the Mission d'Aménagement du Sénégal (MAS), it was suspended with the Second World War. On the British side, there was no metropolitan encouragement. On the other hand, local authorities promoted the initiative of private companies: thus in 1923 the installation in Nigeria, at the falls of the Kwali river near the tin mines of the Jos plateau, of a small hydroelectric plant. Similarly, in 1919 the first project on the Volta saw the daylight in Côte d'Ivoire.

Things started gathering speed again after the Second World War: it was the rise of importation prices in these apparently fuel-deprived countries that led the colonial powers to value the natural potential of the continent as a motivating force. The British provided the model by developing, in 1940 and then again in 1944, their Colonial Development and Welfare Fund, which allowed the Colonial Office to directly intervene in these infrastructure projects.

The British recommended the project on the Volta, motivated by the lack of aluminum from which Great Britain was suffering after the war. Basic to the project was the industrial production planned in Côte d'Ivoire and picked up, after independence, by Kwame Nkrumah's Ghana. The Colonial Office began by wanting to interest the British Aluminium Company (BACO) in the enterprise. They approached the French at the Anglo-French conference of 1947 to organize a common project on the Niger, a plan that was not followed through. Nkrumah wanted to make the project the foundation of the industrialization of his country by exploiting the bauxite of Kibi. This idea had been around since the lode was discovered in 1915, and whose exploitation had already been explored beginning in 1924 by a South African business man, Duncan Rose, who succeeded in interesting the British government after the Second World War. He hired a British firm to evaluate the project; it was judged viable in 1951,[5] and the estimation was reconfirmed after a new study in 1956. But a report from the Colonial Office in 1948, the Watson report, taken up again on that occasion, suggested that, considering the size of the project, it would considered as national, thus including, besides private capital, a portion of public investments. The idea made the interested firms, BACO and ALCA (Aluminum Company of Canada), step back, as they did not want to create an integrated industry in Ghana. In the end, the consortium of American capital, VALCO, which took the business in hand decided otherwise: the bauxite in question was imported and the aluminum factory was created in the port of Tema, 15 miles east of Accra. The affair turned into disaster for Ghana, which nationalized the construction of the dam entrusted to the government agency VRA (Volta River Authority), and had to agree in 1961 to sell its electricity cheaply to a foreign firm: 70% of the electrical consumption is done by VALCO, the price of kilowatts being fixed for thirty years at 2.6 US mills,[6] that is to say a twentieth of the world market price! The price was so low that, despite the accord, it was raised several times, but it stayed very low: 17 mills in 1984, compared to a world market price of 50 mills. Despite the beginning of the exploitation of national bauxite deposits, the industrialization of Ghana had failed.

The French, for their part, reactivated the missions of the UHEA and the MAS, which had gone dormant because of the war. The UHEA was charged with studying the hydroelectric potential of the basin of upper Senegal, and recommended the construction of a dam. The work was taken up again in 1950, and in 1953 the UHEA made more precise recommendations, proposing the Guira dam between Kayes in Mali and the mouth of the Senegal River. It was nevertheless rejected as too expensive, and a new mission was entrusted to the Commission Consultative des Études pour l'Aménagement du fleuve Sénégal, which made more reports.

Around the same time, in 1947, the French government had charged the EDF (Électricité de France) to study all the hydroelectric potential of French West Africa (Thompson & Adloff 1969). At the end of the same year, the report was submitted to the Minister of France Overseas. The EDF recommended the construction of five dams: on the Konkouré river not far from Conakry in Guinea; on the Niger river downstream from Bamako in Mali; on the Bia river near Abidjan; on the Comoé in the Banfora region of Upper Volta (today Burkina Faso), and at the Felou Falls of the Senegal River.

A new ministerial mission was then set up to create details for the plans: the Société d'Énergie–AOF was charged with initiating and pursuing the electricity program proposed by the EDF for a series of cities in Sudan, Côte d'Ivoire, Niger, Upper Volta, and Mauritania. The society carried out the provisioning of water and electricity in some cities, but without realizing the hydroelectric plans proposed by the EDF. Only one dam was built between 1957 and 1959, and was finished after the end of the referendum: the factory of the Great Falls on the Samou river in Guinea, for which the first study had begun in 1948. We must add here that it is in Cameroon that the only finished hydroelectric project of importance was realized by the French before independence: the dams of Edéa. As in South Africa—and it is probably the only point in common—the program succeeded because it corresponded to a precise industrial plan: the one, again here, of aluminum production using bauxite imported from Guinea.

It is thus only after independence that a certain number of large dams were going to be finished, with the technical and financial aid of international organizations like the European Community, USAID, the World Bank, and the West African Development Bank. Several countries did undertake a systematic inventory of their hydroelectric resources: Côte d'Ivoire, Liberia, Nigeria, Senegal, Niger, and Ghana. Large dams were constructed: Akosombo in Ghana (1962–64), Kainji in Nigeria (1969), Mt. Coffee in Liberia, Kossou in Côte d'Ivoire (1969–71), all meant to provide for specific industries and the principal urban and port centers. These projects took on a new significance with the oil crisis of 1973, which underlined the extreme destitution of these countries—then all non-petroleum countries except Nigeria—which had to import at great cost the only fuel that they could use. They were comforted by the conferences that took place in 1981, the one in Nairobi on New and Renewable Energy Sources and the one on Energy for Survival held in Freetown in Sierra Leone under the aegis of the Economic Community of West African States (ECOWAS). Unfortunately, the work also occurred at a time when a long dry spell was casting doubt, for investors, on the capacity of the hydroelectric equipment to reliably cover needs.

Between 1960 and 1980, the landscape of electric production had completely changed also in West Africa, because of the more or less fortunate construction of these huge dams (cf. map). Since then, however, the prolongation of the depression and the absence of the growth of real industrialization made the projects sit idle. In Côte d'Ivoire, for example, where in the beginning of the 1980s hydroelectricity covered more that 90% of needs, at the worst point in the drought of 1984–85 four factories out of

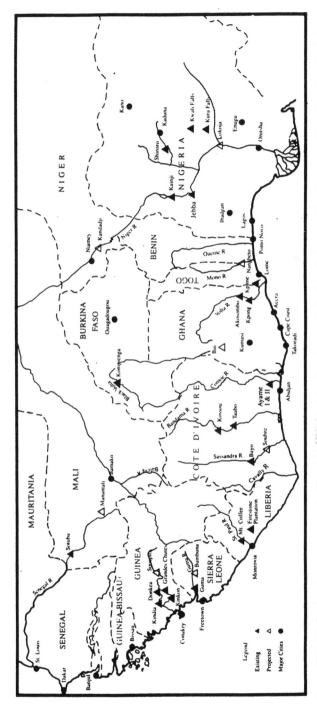

Figure 21.1. Hydroelectric power stations in West Africa, 1990. Map from Joseph A. Sarfoh, *Hydropower Development in West Africa* (New York: Peter Lang, 1990). Used by permission.

five rhat assured the production of electricity had to be temporarily closed, and the percentage fell to 23%; in Ghana, it fell from 90% to around 60%. Due to repeated droughts, the electricity deficit remains today, and translates into an unburdening detrimental to both industry and the everyday aspect of domestic life in almost all West African cities. As for the countryside, many cities still have, at best, only generating units.

In other words, in West Africa as in South Africa, one can see the close correlation between the industrial boom and electricity in the colonies. The difference is that development went hand in hand very early in South Africa. In West Africa, to the contrary, the lack of willingness and industrial prospects plunged the colonial powers into extended delays, generating expensive study missions which gave rise to quantities of reports often without followup. It was not until independence that the national governments started to occupy themselves with domestic consumption and that of the highly populated quarters, even—though only in a few countries (Côte d'Ivoire, Togo . . .)—with electricity for certain rural areas. But the movement was late: in Ghana, for example, for a quarter century the Akosombo dam had furnished electricity only for the south of the country, and the northern countryside had to wait until 1987 to be equipped.

Ironically, it was the oil crisis that accelerated the arrival of electricity in the countryside. The peasants, still unable to buy kerosene or gas necessary for their domestic needs, wanted to return to the traditional use of wood and charcoal. Deforestation and the intensification of the erosion of the soil provoked taking protective measures: a program of small hydroelectric power plants was undertaken, especially in Côte d'Ivoire and Ghana, where the construction of forty-one small power plants was launched in 1981. However, this development was hindered by the relatively elevated cost of construction, with almost all the necessary material being imported. This cost is more by $2,500 per installed kilowatt. It oscillates from $4,000 to $11,000 in Côte d'Ivoire, and from $2,500 to $5,000 in Ghana.

Urban lighting remains nonexistent in the borderline neighborhoods, and is often insufficient elsewhere. Even in 1972, only two large arteries of the old white quarter were lighted in Djamena (in equatorial Africa, especially poor, in Tchad), but this is not an isolated case. Today in Dakar, only main streets are lighted in the Medina, which is now part of the core of the city. Poor countries like Mali have astonishingly little access to electricity. A recent report on French television[7] showed the difficulties encountered by a Non-Governmental Organization made up of French electrical workers full of good will who had come to equip the inhabitants of a sizeable village: Nioro du Sahel. It was not sufficient just to install the wires. The good-natured efficiency of the French workers came up against the problems of mutual comprehension of negotiations with the municipal authorities and with the inhabitants, which rendered the enterprise fragile and difficult. Also, the domestic connection encounters the insoluble problem of cost, outside of the range of most of the grants. Now there remains a great deal to do: what still strikes the traveler, when the plane arrives at night, is the depth of the darkness that reigns as far as the eye can see everywhere but around the big cities.

Notes

1. The archives of French West Africa are nevertheless poor before the Second World War. At the National Archives of Dakar, the specific documents (strictly electricity and water: series 7P) are now classified. But most dossiers concerning electricity are classified in other subseries—P: Urbanism (4P), Roads and Bridges (5P). Many dossiers are in fact very technical. Before 1945, only Senegal is active. There is mention of concessions in several cities, for example to the CEEIA (Compagnie des Eaux et de l'Électricité de l'Ouest africain), in the towns of Saint Louis, Louga, Rufisque, Thiès, Diourbel, Kaolack, Zinguinchor, a dossier on Saint Louis in the 1930s. In other words, only the towns with full citizenship (Dakar, Rufisque, and Saint Louis) and towns with a mixed municipal regime are considered in the electrification plans (there are in principle forty-four for all of French West Africa on the eve of independence in 1960, a figure highly augmented from 1955 onwards).

2. Sociétés en Développement dans l'Espace et le Temps, Université Paris-7 Denis Diderot/CNRS, ACI, program "Politique d'équipement et services urbains dans les villes du Sud," 1999–2002.

3. Decree of 9 December 1933, promulgated by the *Jounal official de l'Indochine,* 13 June 1934, prescribing the addition of 10% of alcohol to imported gasoline destined to be used as fuel.

4. E. I. Oliver, UK Board of Trade, Nigeria, "Economic and Commercial Conditions," in *Nigeria Overseas Economic Survey* (London: HMSO, 1957), 132, and Central Bank of Nigeria, 1980, cited in Sarfoh 1990: 27.

5. R. W. Steel, "The Volta Dam: Its Prospects and Problems," in Rubin and Warren 1968.

6. The mill, equal to 1/10 of a cent (1/1000 of a dollar), is the unit used to calculate the price of electricity.

7. TV5, March 2000.

References

Annuaire du Comité d'études minières pour la France d'outre-mer (1936).

Ardurat, Sophie. 1999. *L'électrification en AOF avant 1945.* Dissertation, Maitrise en Histoire, Université Paris-1.

Atkins, Keletseo E. 1993. *The Moon is Dead! Give Us Our Money! The Cultural Origins of an African Work Ethic, Natal, South Africa, 1843–1900.* London: James Currey.

Barjot, D. *et al.* 2002. *l'Électrification Outre-mer de la fin du XIXè siècle aux premières décolonisations.* Paris, Publications de la Société française d'Histoire d'Outre-mer.

Bhagavan, M. R. 1999. *Reforming the Power Sector in Africa.* London: Zed Books.

Belaid, Habib. Forthcoming. *L'éclairage public en Tunisie à l'époque coloniale: L'exemple de la ville de Tunis.* Paris, Publications de la Société française d'Histoire d'Outre-mer.

Christie, Renfrew. 1984. *Electricity, Industry and Class in South Africa.* Albany, N.Y.: SUNY Press.

Cie Energie électrique de Côte d'Ivoire. 1980. *20 ans au service de la nation.* Abidjan: EECI.

Danfak, Papa Waly. 1990. *Equipement public et aménagement de la ville de Dakar, 1930–1957.* Thesis, Université Paris-7.

François, Marie-Thérèse. 1937. *La production de la force motrice aux Colonies, et plus particulièrement en Afrique française.* Paris: Association Colonies-Sciences.

Nigeria Overseas Economic Survey. 1957. London: HMSO.

Raganathan, V., ed. 1992. *Rural Electrification in Africa.* London: Zed Books.

Robert, Stéphanie. 2001. *La SONABEL, société d'électrification du Burkina Faso.* Thesis, Maitrise en Histoire, Université Paris-7.

Rubin, Neville, and William Warren, eds. 1968. *Dams in Africa.* New York: A. M. Kelly.

Sarfoh, Joseph A. 1990. *Hydropower Development in West Africa: A Study in Resource Development.* New York: Peter Lang.

Sarraut, Albert. 1923. *La mise en valeur des colonies françaises.* Paris: Payot.

Saupique, Thomas. 2000. *L'électrification de Dakar depuis 1945.* Dissertation, Maitrise en Histoire, Université Paris-7.

Seck, Assane. 1970. *Dakar, métropole ouest-africaine.* IFAN-Dakar.

Thompson, Virginia, and Richard Adloff. 1969. *French West Africa.* New York: Greenwood Press.

World Bank. 1975. *Rural Electrification in Developing Countries.* Washington, D.C.: World Bank.

22

"RAIN OR SHINE WE GONNA' ROCK" DANCE SUBCULTURES AND IDENTITY CONSTRUCTION IN ACCRA, GHANA

Steven J. Salm

This essay reconstructs the history of youth subcultures in Accra in the early independence era by examining how unique group identities emerged and how they were closely integrated with the creation, adoption, and adaptation—from both within and outside of the continent—of popular culture forms such as *kpanlogo,* highlife, and rock 'n' roll music. The creation of these subcultures was closely linked to their economic, political, and social environment, but it was also connected increasingly to an expanding global cultural system carried by changing technology and increased international mobility of people and ideas. Urban underclass youth successfully merged aspects of Western, diaspora, and African influences into new networks of association and created a new urban cultural milieu that both was a reflection of, and acted as an agent on, their changing identity constructs.

Subcultures, by definition, exist beneath the upper layer of society and, therefore, the references to them in traditional sources are scarce. In those instances where they do appear, the picture of them is more often than not skewed toward an image of "troublesome delinquents" and "social deviants" representing the decay of modern society. The Ghanaian historiography on urban history is limited; that of youth subcultures even more so. Recent works such as Claire Robertson's *Sharing the Same Bowl* (1984), Emmanuel Akyeampong's *Drink, Power, Cultural Change* (1996), and most recently, Jon Parker's *Making the Town: Ga State and Society in Early Colonial Accra* (2000) discuss various aspects of Accra history and have done much to expand our knowledge.[1] Only Akyeampong, however, delves into issues of Accra underclass culture with his focus on the social history of drinking; still, he touches only cursorily on the existence of youth cultures.

Youth culture is essential to understanding the development of an urban environment. Johan Fornäs sees youth as "what belongs to the future," and associates them with "what is new in culture."[2] In the African context, a large percentage of the population was (and is even more so today) younger than the age of twenty-five. A study of youth provides insights not only into the historical identity construction of urban society, new genres of popular culture, and their role in social reorganization, but it also contributes to a better understanding of variances in larger, global cultural trends, both past and present.

Today in Ghana, the most popular type of music among youth is hiplife, a combination of Ghanaian highlife and American rap and hip hop. It is usually sung in vernacular, often to a sample (playback) of American music, but with an underlying highlife offbeat. A typical performance features a single individual on stage, singing and dancing to play back. For someone wanting to be a hiplife performer, there is no need to learn to play an instrument, nor is there a need to form a band. The emphasis is on the visual presentation and the attraction of the lyrics for youth. Many people see hiplife as a negative sign of Ghanaian youth in general:

> Why this wholesale importation of foreign cultures? . . . Our entertainment industry has deteriorated to an extreme degree. Our rich and original highlife music is being corrupted by a Western style of music (both in lyrics and rhythm). . . . This so-called hip-life for instance is nothing but irritating noise. It is in, only to destroy the society. Those who write, sing, produce these songs are morally incorrect and sexually obsessive. They are lustful and hedonists. Their lyrics are provocative, vulgar and obscene. It is made up with insults.[3]

Such comments sound similar to those made about previous music forms that reflected emerging youth identities, especially rock 'n' roll in the late 1950s and early 1960s. Although the liberalization of the airwaves and pervasive impact of films and music videos during the last few decades has enhanced the dissemination of Western cultural influences, the hiplife generation was certainly not the first youth generation to focus more on external forms of popular music and dance. When I began the research, I expected to find a genre of popular culture like *milo jazz,* a form of hybrid music that *ode lay* youth groups in Sierra Leone incorporated into their clubs and performances.[4] *Kpanlogo,* a Ga dance and drum style created in the early 1960s, came closest to this. It caught on quickly with Accra youth, and *kpanlogo* groups sprung up all over the coastal region. Yet, there was something about *kpanlogo* dancing and the characteristics of the participants that caught my eye. There was a movement in the dance that was very foreign.

The "Bukom Boys"

The rapidly growing population of Accra during and after the Second World War helped to create conditions that led to a rapid downturn in the quality of life.[5] James Town and Ussher Town, the central and oldest areas of Accra, began to deteriorate into slum environments. Recovery from the devastating earthquake of 1939 was slow; a large part of the shipping industry was now going through the new, deep-water port of Sekondi-Takoradi, rather than the shallow waters of Accra;[6] and other areas of the city began to grow more quickly and receive more of the government's attention.[7] In central Accra, buildings that survived the earthquake grew more decrepit, jobs became difficult to find, and the cost of living increased rapidly. This contrasted with an increase in education throughout the mid-1940s and 1950s. Young men and women completed their primary school education and then, unable to meet the fees or unable to allot the necessary time because of family financial obligations, abandoned further studies.

The concept of youth as a distinct group, separate from both the world of adults and that of children, grew with the development of formal education, and the belief that children required a period of schooling before they could take on adult roles. In the Western world, this took place in the late nineteenth and twentieth centuries with the development of mass schooling. In Ghana, the boost in education after the Second World War contributed to the growth of adolescence during the 1950s and 1960s. In the United States, the emphasis on consumption, style, and leisure during the 1950s led to the development of goods and services (magazines, record shops, clothing, and entertainment) that were specifically marketed to young people. This, Tracey Skelton and Gill Valentine argue, led to the invention of "the teenager."[8] Ghana experienced a similar process of invention during the 1950s. Youth moved away from the culture of their parents, seeing it as too "colo"—colonial or old-fashioned. Whereas the Western influences of previous generations came mainly from the British, youth began to look more toward cultural stimuli coming out of the United States.

The rapidly changing technological and global cultural climate of the period under review must be briefly illuminated. The increasing availability of a larger and more diverse array of cultural stimuli heightened the rift between generations and acted as an agent on the development of subcultures. This is especially pertinent to African cities in the 1940s, 1950s, and 1960s. The increasing availability of Western movies and music, gramophones and records, radios, and even clothing served as the basis for rapid cultural change. Modern advances in radio and recording technology facilitated the dissemination of foreign music and helped produce hybrid musical genres.[9] These changes, and perhaps even more important to this project, the nature of these changes, had a profound effect on the cultural development of Accra youth.

By the mid-1950s, there were sharp differences between the concept of leisure for older and younger generations. In 1955, youth and those looking for nightlife saw Accra as a "sleepy town" and drew little excitement from current club life. The major draw was highlife music, but many of the highlife bands also played Western ballroom dances like the fox-trot, waltz, and quickstep. The youth saw the formal dancing of their parents' and grandparents' generations as restrictive; they desired something more: "Night Life in Accra today is dull; very dull. . . . Except at one or two hotels and occasionally at week-ends, there is no social life of any kind. There are no dances, not even radiogram programmes."[10] In 1954, Richard Wright described highlife dancing at one of the most popular Jamestown outdoor dance bars, Weekend in Havana: "The specialty of this establishment, as with all the dance spots in the Gold Coast, was a shuffling, lazy kind of somnambulistic dance step called High Life."[11]

The nightlife crisis was exacerbated by early closing times during the first quarter of 1955. The Accra Municipal Council, with enforcement by the Accra Divisional Police, forced all night clubs to close at 8 pm. One member of the Council explained the motivation behind the measure: "the main reason for trying to restrict the night clubs is to check school girls and teen-agers from attending dances at night clubs," even though the law already forbade people under the age of sixteen from attending them. One observer commented that, "the authorities seem to tell the youth, 'scorn delight and live laborious days.'"[12] After leaving school, many of the youth found jobs and had some disposable income, but there was little attractive nightlife on which to spend it.

This began to change in the late 1950s, when youth living in and around Bukom Square began to transform the cultural characteristics of James Town rapidly. By 1965, a reporter for a popular magazine described the now energetic area and its performers:

The Bukom Boys: Not the name of any particular group or spot [drinking bar]. However the interested party looking for authentic Accra night life will be amply rewarded by a trip to the back streets of James Town—Bukom Amaamo—where spontaneous bands spring up within minutes and some real dancing can be seen. The birth place of many new tunes and dances."[13]

Bukom was also the center of resistance to the Convention Peoples Party (CPP), and their leader, Kwame Nkrumah, in the 1950s and early 1960s. The area always drew the highest attendance for opposition rallies and was the breeding ground for anti-CPP groups like the Tokyo Joes. It was also subject to frequent curfews and bans on political rallies. In 1958, after a seven-day curfew, 273 people received fines for violations, ranging from one to four pounds. Outside of direct government curfews, living in central Accra, being young, and attending nightclubs was seldom a safe proposition during the days of the Preventive Detention Act, especially if you were a Ga male. There were numerous cases of police arresting young people and charging them with "loitering and assembling for idle purposes," usually outside of night clubs.[14]

How, then, did this area become a center of cultural activity in this short time? The deteriorating economic climate and changing political and social facade of the city provided the impetus for cultural transfer. Beneath the surface, there was an exploding subculture scene driven by dynamic youth groups. Existing on the margins of their own society, feeling inhibited by older generations, and embracing the growing availability of outside cultural stimuli, youth reacted by creating new types of associations to address their specific conditions.

Rock 'n' Roll Comes to Ghana

By 1957, when the country was preparing for independence celebrations, James Town youth embarked on a different path of change. Rock 'n' roll arrived in Ghana through the medium of the cinema. Youth viewed rock 'n' roll movies and were enticed by the dancing movements, the dress, and the language. They set out to adopt these elements. The popularity of rock 'n' roll movies caught on quickly and a steady stream of them continued for the next five years, during which time new rock 'n' roll dancing clubs sprang up all over the city, particularly in the James Town and Ussher Town areas.[15] The music and dance swept through the youth generation, and by 1959 it commanded a strong presence, even making front page headlines in the *Sunday Mirror*: "Rock 'n' Roll—Everywhere its rhythm fills the air. . . . You see flashy attired youngsters twirl, whirl and clap . . . they jump and shout as the step out to dance to its frenzied rhythm. YES, THAT'S ROCK 'n' ROLL. . . ."[16]

The Black Eagle Rock 'n' Roll Club was the first club of its kind. Its founding members, Lucky Thompson, Gary Davies, and Count Basie, first encountered rock 'n' roll dancing in February 1957 while seeing *Rock around the Clock,* the film recognized as the first true rock 'n' roll film.[17] The name "Black Eagle" came from the film. The three founders told six of their male friends about their plans and trained themselves for two weeks before officially establishing the club. Soon, many young women joined them, and they began to practice at the Park Cinema three times per week. Reports of the new dance craze spread quickly; within two months, the club had a membership of about 150 people, including fifty females, ranging from sixteen to twenty-eight years of age.[18]

Members came from a variety of professions. They were carpenters, mechanics, clerks, shop workers, tradesmen, traders, market women, and some were unemployed. Club members participated in different activities, including reading, fishing, boxing, and of course all members were taught how to "shake, rattle, and roll." Black Eagle had their inauguration ceremony at the Accra Community Centre in August of the following year. Soon after, they were even invited to the Castle to perform for Kwame Nkrumah and guests.[19] New clubs formed quickly by the early part of 1959. A breakaway group, Black Star, split from Black Eagles after less than one year because of conflict over money issues. Others were established as well, including the Rockin' Aces, Harlem, Teen Town, and All Yankees. In early 1959, the Rockin' Aces held their "outdooring," which received mainstream press coverage, including pictures of the club Secretary and dancing tutor, Gene Domino, on the cover page as he "digs it crazy with his partner Vivian Blaine." Another photo showed a couple with "Feet astride, gaping mouths and frenzy gestures," and the claim: "that's time to rock and roll."[20]

After separating from Black Eagle, Black Star rose to become one of the preeminent clubs. They had strict rules regarding membership. Before allowing prospective members to enter, they often did a background check on them, seeking information about their behavior and societal standing from friends and family. The club stressed cleanliness and said, at least publicly, that they did not allow smoking and drinking before or during a practice. It is clear that drinking and smoking were common in other clubs, and, as there are pictures of members drinking beer while dancing, there is some doubt that Black Star enforced these conditions wholeheartedly.

Black Star plugged into an already-existing organizational structure after breaking away from Black Eagle. Their leader, Count Basie, worked as a mechanic at the Accra Metropolitan Association (AMA). A European working there, "Wash," had a boxing club that he ran inside the workshop and agreed to manage the rock 'n' roll club as well. Pete Myers, a broadcaster with Radio Ghana (and later the BBC), also helped them out by loaning them records and playing long sets of rock 'n' roll on the radio. They started out by going to dances with a variety of people. During intervals, when others were resting, they demonstrated their rock 'n' roll steps. Basie recalled the experience: "They were thinking that we were going crazy. . . . But immediately you heard the music, you acted as if you are crazy. . . . The rhythm, the music that kicks you. You can't sit down when they put it on."[21]

Most clubs had a very organized structure, including a Director, Treasurer, and Secretary. Members paid dues and the cost of a membership card, with club rules written on the back. The money was sometimes kept in the bank, and often required three signatories to avoid any potential embezzlement. Dues were used to print posters, pay fees for the use of locales, and rent or buy gramophones. Money was also used to help a member who ran into trouble or suffered a family death. Clubs often performed at the funeral ceremony and, after receiving money from the audience, donated their earnings to the family as well. Within each club, there were divisions according to one's dance specialties. During a performance, the leaders would call a subgroup out to the floor by calling out their names and "challenging" them to perform.

Rock 'n' roll culture caught on quickly and permeated aspects of youth life such as language, dress, and nicknames. The new language accompanied it to distinguish new fashions from local idioms and customs. Youth began to employ words and phrases like "cool," "the Hep Turn," and "digging it."[22] One no longer talked of his friend "Kofi" but of "Jack." Each group also had a motto. Black Eagle's was "Rain or shine we gonna' rock!" Black Star's was, "High Stars, we're gonna' knock it." The dress was unique to each group and not inexpensive, generally consisting of a club T-shirt with its logo, "dungarees" (jeans, often with a wide bell-bottom), and *cambu* (white, leather-bottom shoes). Unlike (and in opposition to) the Western-style ballroom dancers who always wore black shoes, rock 'n' roll dancers always wore white shoes so that people watching could see the movement of their feet without missing anything.[23]

Rock 'n' roll dancing gave youth fame and formed an essential part of their identity formation. They assumed nicknames, names that they continue to use today. These included: Count Basie, Frankie Laine, Cab

Calloway, Pall Mall, Chris Turner, Betty Coloured, Elvis, and Johnny Walker, all drawn from some aspect of American culture, from jazz music to rock 'n' roll to Western films. Most members chose their names based on music that they had heard or films they had seen. Women, however, sometimes had their names chosen for them by the group leaders, although many of them later selected and adopted a different one.

New activities sprang up that catered to the rock 'n' roll crowd. Starting in 1959, Kash Register of the American Embassy and Pete Myers created the Disc Jockey Jamboree at the Metropole every Friday evening.[24] They wanted to gather youth onto one dance floor and play for them the latest rock 'n' roll records, and allow the best dancers to demonstrate new forms.[25] The atmosphere was relaxed, but participants earned prizes for the best dancing. Rock 'n' roll also created global connections. Frankie Laine, who excelled as a rock 'n' roll dancer and later as a *kpanlogo* dancer, traveled to Algeria for a dance contest, while another received correspondence and materials from the parents of Buddy Holly after his death.

The government encouraged rock 'n' roll clubs by organizing competitions. The first one was held in 1960 at the General Post Office grounds in central Accra. A boxing ring was brought from Wash's club to be used as a stage. The courtyard and surrounding streets were packed with people, awaiting the awarding of prizes for the best rock 'n' roll club, as well as a Mr. and a Miss Rock 'n' Roll."[26] One of the judges was the Principal Secretary for the Ministry of Social Welfare. It soon became clear, however, that the government was not completely supportive of the rock 'n' roll clubs. They requested that all clubs register with the Ministry of Social Welfare, but when the clubs tried they were denied. They also called the leaders of various clubs to come to Social Welfare. One member described the occurrence: "You will be here [practicing at a house] and see a messenger come with a letter, 'you are wanted at social welfare.'" When they arrived at the Ministry, however, the clubs received words of admonishment: "The girls are getting spoiled. They go to dance. They go to rock 'n' roll, all these things." Clearly, the government saw some danger in their activities. Aware of the tight reigns that the government was placing on them, groups such as Black Star practiced strict rules, at least on the outside, so as not to give them any reason to crack down on club activities: "We know some big men don't want it. We don't want to fall into their trap. So, you just read the back of the membership card and you will see everything."[27] Given that the Preventive Detention Act was in place and was used often to suppress activity around Bukom Square, the area where the opposition drew the highest numbers for their rallies, such overt rules and regulations were necessary.

Class and Generational Conflict

It is no great surprise that older generations were averse to rock 'n' roll dancing. There are always conflicts between generations in terms of cultural likes and dislikes. Younger generations tend to be more dynamic and willing to adopt and adapt new forms much more quickly than older generations.

All over the world the reception to the rock 'n' roll was mixed, generally receiving more negative opinions than positive ones. The Indonesian government banned it, reported one newspaper writer in Accra, and "the Indonesian cats looked down their whiskers and cursed beneath their breath."[28] In the United States, there was a great deal of discussion about the "evils" of rock 'n' roll. Columbia University's Dr. A. M. Meerio concluded: "If we cannot stem the tide of rock and roll with its waves of rhythmic narcosis and vicarious craze, we are preparing our own downfall in the midst of pandemic funeral dances."[29] Other government, religious, and educational leaders reiterated those sentiments, calling the music "immoral and sinful" and its participants "lazy and shiftless juvenile delinquents."[30]

Ghanaians, too, debated the merits of rock 'n' roll. One newspaper questioned Ghanaians' attitudes about the new music and dance:

> Some say the youths are getting crazy . . .
> Others fear rock 'n' roll lowers the morals of our youngsters
> ROCK 'n' ROLL
>   Is it good? Is it a menace?
> Does it throw you in ecstasy?
> Does it do more harm than good?

The opinions ranged from "Its rhythm fascinates me" and "It reflects the buoyancy of our present day youth" to "The dance is not decent enough" and "Youngsters can't lead disciplined lives if they dance rock 'n' roll." A Reverend of a Presbyterian Church said: "I've seen the rock 'n' roll but once—and I've been disgusted. The manner in which they do it is indecent enough. Of course, youngsters may dance—but not rock 'n' roll."[31] Others believed that rock 'n' roll reflected "the riotous pursuits of the youth" and that "the present Ghanaian youth is heading towards a moral loss.[32] Some saw the music as too sexually expressive. One writer referred to it as "rotten roll" and added, "I definitely object to converting its rhythmic movement to 'vertical expressions of horizontal wishes. . . .' Lousy!"[33]

Rock 'n' roll youth, however, were not "lazy and shiftless juvenile delinquents." They contributed positive activities in which peers could involve themselves. Rock 'n' roll dancing was a catalyst for youth to form new group identities. They viewed it as an expression of rebellion against the rigidity of other popular culture forms, especially the strict-tempo ball-room dancing. It gave them a sense of community in the face of declining hope for a better economic future. Some youths maintained "that with independence there's freedom—freedom of movement, freedom of actions, freedom of drinking and freedom of enjoyment. Some even go further to contend that life is now too short and one must enjoy himself."[34]

Rock 'n' roll dancing represented a fundamental shift in youth leisure activities. It revealed the affinity that the youth were developing for American culture in general, and rock 'n' roll music in particular. In contrast to older generations, they had little use for British culture, and certainly had a very unfavorable attitude toward British performers like Cliff Richards.[35] They saw rock 'n' roll as a product of the United States and did not, there-fore, find anything alluring in British rock.[36] The influence of cultural stimuli from the United States was enhanced during the Second World War with the presence of American soldiers in Accra, but the youth of the indepen-dence era increased their exposure through newly available cultural medi-ums.

Rock 'n' roll culture helped to increase the independence of youth, break down gender barriers, and separate their identities and interests from that of their parents. One story, in particular, deserves mention. At a 1958 New Year's Eve party at the Rodger Club, a social center built by the one-time colonial governor of the Gold Coast in 1904, youth expressed their new identity in the face of generational and police pressure:

> This particular night, the whole floor was crowded with teen-agers—the girls had their hair plaited and the boys in rock n' roll shirts and what they themselves described as "balloon pants" [bell bottoms]. . . . Then I saw that anytime the band started playing, about six policemen headed by a sergeant, would rush to the floor. And what would you see . . . a hide and seek, tip and run, catch-me-if-you-can and yells . . . then two or three boys would be held by their shirts, three or four girls their hands clutched together . . . off to the gates they went. . . . This went on and on until it was the end of the dance but yet these teenagers continued to surge in and refused to be treated or termed as being under-age.[37]

Rock 'n' roll dancing matched a woman with a man on the floor. There was no space between them. Indeed, it involved frequent contact between a man and a woman, and even included active tosses, dips, and slides. Though the original impetus was taken from the rock 'n' roll movies, youth adapted the steps to their own cultural environment. They incorporated steps from traditional ballroom dances like the waltz, fox-trot, and quick step and combined them with other movements that they learned by watching Ga fetish priests. One dancer described watching the fetish priests to learn their steps:

> They always dance when they are performing their customs. They dance on the street, beating drums, dancing, and their footsteps are very fast. If you don't watch them properly, you won't see it. . . . Their rhythm goes with rock 'n' roll. . . . He will just make some style with his foot that you haven't seen and if you watch it properly and you enter into the rhythm, it goes in straight. That means you have got a style.[38]

The best dancers practiced regularly and mastered many different steps. Their popularity grew with their skill level. For this reason, until 1962 and the influence of Chubby Checker's "Twist," rock 'n' roll dancing clubs in Accra were mainly limited to the subcultural level. Whereas early rock 'n' roll dancing in Ghana was seriously practiced and performed, with many difficult elements and rehearsed steps, the Twist offered a chance for those who did not want to spend the time to perfect their dancing. One newspaper raved about the new dance: "The Twist . . . has become so much the rage of the country. In the dance halls and night spots all around the cities, you'll find youngsters going through the motions of this dance!" One of the reasons that it became so popular was because it required no practice, no mandatory steps: "Anybody can twist. All you have to do is wriggle and wriggle hard. The more you can wriggle, the better 'twister' you are."[39]

Youth used the rock 'n' roll clubs as voluntary associations. If a member of the club needed money to start a business or to take care of a death in the family, the treasurer, with the approval of the entire executive board, disbursed the funds. Members with connections at workplaces also helped others to acquire jobs if they were able. They popularized rock 'n' roll dancing to the extent that they were paid to perform at funeral ceremonies and outdoorings. Only recently, one of the original members of Black Star died, and the surviving members performed rock 'n' roll dancing at his funeral. Some participants began to see dancing as their trade. Indeed, many believed that because they supported a rival party to the CPP, they could not get any other jobs.

Why was rock 'n' roll music and dance attractive to Accra youth? Rock 'n' roll music and dance expressed antiestablishment worldviews, it provided youth with the catalyst to form their own group identity, and it came with its own culture of dress, nicknames, and language. The history of rock 'n' roll subcultures in Accra reveals government attempts to control, or at least co-opt, popular culture, and the ability of the subculture to remain outside of that control, while utilizing government resources to their advantage. For youth of the early independence era, rock 'n' roll provided an alternative to the leisure activities of the older generation. Club activities represented manifestations of the youth's rejection of undue formalism in commercialized recreation and an active search for a more global identity.

There are many more paths to pursue in the analysis of early independence era subcultures in Ghana. Fashion, politics, and cultural offspring could provide legitimate and revealing areas of research. Subsequent dress styles, like the "sack" and "fish" dresses and mini-skirts, were fashions that raised the level of generational conflict. Hairstyles, too, delineated one group from another. In politics, some of the same youth who participated in the rock 'n' roll clubs also supported anti-CPP groups like the Tokyo Joes. Although, the popularity of rock 'n' roll music and dance began to decline by the early 1970s, one product of the rock 'n' roll subcultures continues to play an important role in Accra cultural life: *kpanlogo.*

One of the most visible products of the early rock 'n' roll dance subcultures, *kpanlogo* drumming and dance developed in Bukom in 1962. Some of the dance steps were incorporated from rock 'n' roll. In its immediate reception by lower-class youth, the resistance to it by older generations and authorities, and the types of associations that were formed by youth, the study of *kpanlogo* music and dance can shed more light on the importance and influence of the rock 'n' roll clubs. When asked today, most people will speak of *kpanlogo* as a "traditional" form of drumming and dancing that has existed in Ghana for a very long time. *Kpanlogo,* however, is a neo-traditional music and dance form that became the focus of subcultural identity and protest. *Kpanlogo* incorporated elements of previous Ga drumming styles such as *oge* and *kolomashie,* but the dancing was updated to reflect contemporary movements. The dance steps reflected the highly energized elements of rock 'n' roll dancing and, therefore, received similar derisive comments from older generations during its early days. One informant even called it "*kpanlogo* rock 'n' roll."[40]

Methods, Concepts, and Sources

This paper asks historians to think in a fundamentally different way. Too often, historians ignore the underclass in favor of more accessible and salient figures. Even those who approach their topics with the ideas and actions of the masses in mind frequently do so at the expense of youth culture and subcultures. So too, people who study popular culture often choose to write about the band leaders and the artists rather than the processes, patterns, and motivations of the audience, or the participants on the non-headliner side of the cultural environment.

The popular culture of Accra underwent a transformation because of the attitudes of youth and increasing external cultural influences created by the expanded availability of radio, music recordings, and films. The rapidly changing technological and global cultural climate increased the availability of a larger, and more diverse, array of cultural stimuli and forced a shift in attitudes toward leisure and entertainment that heightened the rift between generations and acted as an agent on the development of subcultures.

Identity is a key concept for research into youth and subcultures. Identity within subcultures includes self-presentation, cultural consumption, and creative adaptation of global stimuli. Popular music and dance function as major contributors to the creation and maintenance of new social images and identities. These subcultural identities developed in response to conditions engendered by urban living. Accra served as a "bridge-head" for foreign cultural influences, and the participants of these cultural offspring were "cultural brokers" who helped to redefine urban consciousness and characterized the aspirations of urban subcultural youth.[41] There is a need to find new sources for the history of subcultures in general.

It is also important to document the trans-Atlantic movements and characteristics of rock 'n' roll, a music and dance genre that grew out of African roots and, after multiple permutations, returned to be incorporated and manipulated as a key element in the identity formation of a developing Accra youth class during the late 1950s and early 1960s.[42] Rock 'n' roll and *kpanlogo* became pervasive in Ghana because they represented a fundamental shift in youth leisure activities. The research challenges the paradigm of highlife music as the dominant genre during this period. Although many popular bands still characterized themselves as highlife bands, many of them incorporated rock 'n' roll songs into their performances because they knew that, by doing so, they would attract a larger audience.

The development of urban subcultures in Accra interacted with other socio-historical variables that gave meaning to an entire group of marginalized youth and helped to provide a sense of belonging during the early independence era. The analyses provide insights into group identity transformation; they also expand on the broader divisions between the African elite and the mass of the population, between older and younger generations with a different worldview, and between African and Western cultural production. The creation of rock 'n' roll clubs was an act of revolt against class, gender, and generational divides, and an effort by the youth to merge their culture and identity into a new hybrid form that incorporated aspects of both global and local influences.

Notes

1. Claire C. Robertson, *Sharing the Same Bowl? A Socioeconomic History of Women and Class in Accra, Ghana* (Bloomington: Indiana University Press, 1984); Emmanuel Akyeampong, *Drink, Power, and Cultural Change: A Social History of Alcohol in Ghana c. 1800 to Recent Times* (Portsmouth, N.H.: Heinemann, 1996); and John Parker, *Making the Town: Ga State and Society in Early Colonial Accra* (Portsmouth, N.H.: Heinemann, 2000).

2. Johan Fornas and Goran Bolin, eds., *Youth Culture in Late Modernity* (Thousand Oaks, Calif.: Sage Publications, 1995).

3. W. H. Acquah, "Watch This Moral Decadence," *Graphic Showbiz,* 8 December 1999, 2.

4. See John Nunley, *Moving with the Face of the Devil: Art and Politics in Urban West Africa* (Urbana and Chicago: University of Illinois Press, 1987).

5. The population of Accra increased dramatically between 1948 and 1970: 136,000 in 1948, 492,000 in 1960, and 848,548 in 1970. During the same period, there was a severe increase in the cost of living and an acute housing shortage.

6. The shipping industry in Accra suffered a fatal blow when Tema Harbor opened in 1962, resulting in the loss of virtually all jobs for "pilot boys" and those who helped carry goods and people from the boats to the shore.

7. Many new immigrants, among them many young males, settled in areas around the Accra center, such as Adabraka, Nima, and Lagos Town (now called New Town).

8. Tracey Skelton and Gill Valentine, eds., *Cool Places* (London and New York: Routledge, 1998), 4.

9. See also C. F. Delgado and J. E. Munoz, eds., *Everynight Life: Culture and Dance in Latin/o America* (Durham, N.C.: Duke University Press, 1997).

10. "Low-Down on the Bright Spots," *Sunday Mirror* (Accra), 6 March 1955, 11.

11. Richard Wright, *Black Power: A Record of Reactions in a Land of Pathos* (Westport, Conn.: Greenwood Press, 1954; reprint, 1974), 107–8.

12. "Low-Down on the Bright Spots," 11.

13. *What's On in Ghana* 3 (April 1965): 31.

14. See Bob Fitch and Mary Oppenheimer, *Ghana: The End of an Illusion* (New York and London: Monthly Review Press, 1966). Numerous contemporary newspaper articles and government reports also document the frequent disruptions in and around Bukom Square in James Town.

15. A few examples of rock 'n' roll movies include: *Shake, Rattle and Rock* with Fats Domino (August 1957); *Rock, Rock* with Alan Freed (May 1958); *Disc Jockey Jamboree,* with more than twenty rock 'n' roll artists (August 1959); and much later, *Twist around the Clock,* with Chubby Checker (February 1964).

16. "Is This Crazy?," *Sunday Mirror,* 1 March 1959, 1.

17. See *Sunday Mirror,* 20 February 1957, 16. The song "Rock around the Clock," by Bill Haley, was recorded in 1954 (Decca), and the movie *Rock around the Clock,* was released in the United States in 1956. The song first appeared, however, in a 1955 movie, *Blackboard Jungle* (MGM), a movie about the spirit of teenage rebellion.

18. Interview with Count Basie, 28 April 2000.

19. "Rock 'N Roll 'Cats' at Govt House," *Sunday Mirror,* 7 December 1958, 6.

20. "'Cats' Rolled at the Accra Beach," *Sunday Mirror,* 18 January 1959, 14.

21. Interview with Count Basie, 28 April 2000.

22. "Rock 'N Roll Comes to Ghana," *Sunday Mirror,* 22 June 1958, 1; "Amon Okoe Discusses Discs: GBS Must Let Peter Dig 'Rock' Now," *Sunday Mirror,* 17 January 1960, 2; and "It's Music," *Sunday Mirror,* 23 August 1959, 11.

23. Interview with Count Basie, 28 April 2000.

24. The Metropole was described by the magazine *What's On in Ghana,* as a place for "local hep cats." See vol. 3 (April 1965): 31.

25. "A Boon for Teenagers," *Sunday Mirror,* 6 December 1959, 18.

26. "A Big Day for Rock 'n' Roll Fans," *Sunday Mirror,* 16 October 1960, 10.

27. Interview with Count Basie, 28 April 2000.

28. "A Nobody's Diary," *Sunday Mirror,* 27 March 1957, 3.

29. In Jerry Hopkins, *The Rock Story* (New York: Signet Books, 1970), 31.

30. Paul Friedlander, *Rock and Roll: A Social History* (Boulder, Colo.: Westview Press, 1996), 27.

31. "Is This Crazy?" 1.

32. "Are Our Youths Too Gay?" *Sunday Mirror,* 22 March 1959, 1.

33. "West Africa Whispers," *Drum* (Ghana), No. 77 (September, 1957): 16.

34. "Are Our Youths Too Gay?" 1.

35. Although the Beatles did become more popular later in the 1960s, it was with a younger crowd than the original rockers.

36. Interview with Frankie Laine, 13 April 2000.

37. Onua Francis, "Let's Save Our Teenagers from Bad Practices," *Sunday Mirror,* 18 January 1959, 2.

38. Interview with Count Basie, 18 May 2000.

39. "Twist—the New Craze in Ghana," *Sunday Mirror,* 15 April 1962, 16.

40. Interview with Fuzzy Lee, 21 May 2000, Jamestown, Accra.

41. See Ulf Hannerz, *Cultural Complexity: Studies in the Social Organization of Meaning* (New York: Columbia University Press, 1992), 230; and David Coplan, "The Urbanisation of African Music: Some Theoretical Observations," *Popular Music* 2 (1982): 113–29.

42. John Collins refers to the movement of musical cultures from Africa to the West and back to Africa as "jazz feedback." See John Collins, "Jazz Feedback to Africa," *American Music* 5, 2 (1987): 176–93.

23

SAMPLE SURVEYS: UNDEREXPLOITED SOURCES FOR AFRICAN SOCIAL HISTORY

Dennis D. Cordell[1]

Since the period between the two world wars, social scientists have conducted sample surveys among a variety of populations in Africa in an effort to formulate strategies to meet perceived contemporary challenges such as underdevelopment, rapid population growth, high levels of morbidity and mortality, excessive malnutrition, and so on. The retrospective nature of much of this research has led to the inadvertent collection of large bodies of historical data. For the most part, however, once these surveys have been completed and projects designed to help cope with these immediate problems, the data have been relegated to storage. The social scientists who developed the surveys have, on the whole, not been preoccupied with historical questions, and historians who might make use of their data are either unaware of these studies or do not know how to access and use them for their research.

This paper explores surveys as historical sources, both surveys that collected then-current data and those that assembled retrospective data, with a particular focus on demographic studies. The essay opens with a discussion of the characteristics of surveys and an overview of the range of survey data. The paper then features as a central case study the National Migration Survey conducted in today's Burkina Faso (formerly Upper Volta) in 1974–1975. My colleagues Victor Piché and Joel Gregory of the Université de Montréal initially conceived the National Migration Survey as a study whose conclusions would aid in the formulation of development projects that might stem the emigration of burkinabè men and women to the Côte d'Ivoire, Ghana, and other countries. Later, they and I realized that the survey was, in addition, an invaluable source for tracing the history of burkinabè migration in the twentieth century. We mined the National Migration Survey as a major source for the social history of burkinabè migration in several articles and a major monograph.[2] The essay concludes with a brief mention of specific surveys, including the extensive World Fertility Survey (WFS) and the Demographic and Health Surveys (DHS), that might be marshaled as historical sources in our efforts to understand the social history of Africa in the twentieth century.

What Are Sample Surveys?

Sample surveys collect information on a topic or set of topics from a representative fraction of a defined population, as opposed to censuses, which aim at recording data about every individual included in a population.[3] In Africa, from the interwar period through the 1970s, sample surveys rather than censuses were the most common instruments used by social scientists to collect data from and about people on a large scale. Most surveys in Africa have involved direct face-to-face questioning, rather than interrogations by mail or by telephone, which are much more common in Europe and North America. Sample surveys offer three major advantages over censuses. First, censuses are much more complex to organize; the smaller scale of a sample survey makes it easier to administer in the absence of a highly developed bureaucracy—which was the case in most parts of colonial and immediately post-colonial Africa. Second, the immense scale of a census makes it very expensive to prepare, administer, and analyze. And third, locating the large numbers of interviewers required to carry out a census and providing them with adequate training is extremely difficult—witness, for example, the difficulties that the United States Bureau of the Census experienced in recruiting interviewers for the 2000 enumeration. Taken together, these challenges impose limits on the complexity and the length of the census questionnaire. A sample survey, on the other hand, allows individual scholars, teams of researchers, or agencies to hire smaller numbers of interviewers who can be trained in greater depth. Smaller numbers of better-trained interviewers are, in turn, able to administer longer and more complex questionnaires to the smaller sample population. Obviously, the use of a sample population rather than the larger target population introduces the possibility of sampling errors. However, this disadvantage is much more often than not offset by the greater accuracy of data collected by more highly skilled interviewers from a smaller number of people.

Most population surveys collect two broad categories of information. The first includes basic descriptive data about the current "state of the population"—its size, age and sex structure, and geographical distribution. This category may also include data on specific characteristics of the population targeted by the survey—employment, consumption patterns, housing quality, proximity to government services, the frequency and characteristics of migration, and so on. The second category includes information on "trends in the population"—the direction and dimensions of change.[4] In seeking to document trends in the population, social scientists open the door to history, for they need to record data about previous "states of the population" to understand how various characteristics of the population evolved to produce its current profile.

In Africa, demographic sample surveys developed first in the French colonies south of the Sahara immediately after the Second World War. At that time in francophone Africa, demographic data was limited to information collected in the course of "administrative censuses," whose quality was questionable at best. Given the truncated structure of the colonial state, and the limited training of colonial officials in demography, the French opted for a series of sample surveys launched in Guinea in 1954 and concluded in Madagascar in 1966.[5] These operations collected the first substantial bodies of survey data on the state and evolution of colonial populations that conformed to criteria set by the emerging international demographic establishment.[6] Given that these surveys collected data that are now nearly a half-century old, they constitute a very valuable source for African social history in the mid-twentieth century. Moreover, many of the questionnaires used in these surveys asked questions about earlier periods, and thus include data from as early as the 1910s and 1920s.[7] Confined for many decades to the cellars of government agencies in the French capital, components of these surveys—including some of the raw questionnaires themselves, instruction manuals distributed to interviewers, and a wealth of tables that were prepared but never published—have recently been restored and are now available to researchers.[8]

Retrospective Sample Surveys

Growing out of the need to understand trends in population change, retrospective surveys focus on the collection of information about demographic events in the past in order to understand the overall evolution of a population or any of its specific characteristics. Armed with questionnaires, interviewers collect information from people about their individual demographic pasts, information that is first combined to produce the demographic history of the larger sample population to which these individuals belong, and then extrapolated to the entire population of which the sample is but a fraction.

In the last few decades, retrospective sample surveys in Africa have tended to focus on two dimensions of the demographic history of African populations. First, given the dearth of census data—the first "modern" censuses in most of Africa date only from the 1970s—many retrospective surveys focused on demographic events that occurred in the previous twelve months in the life of an individual or a household, and in particular on births and deaths. Second, a very substantial body of retrospective survey research has collected data on the reproductive histories of women—an outgrowth of the preoccupation by international funding agencies with the perceived "population explosion" on the continent. By asking women how many children they have had, how many boys and how many girls, and where they live, as well as by recording their names and dates of birth (and, all too frequently, dates of death), interviewers assemble bodies of data that researchers can cross-check to produce a quite accurate set of reproductive histories of individual women, the sample, and the larger population.

While the bulk of retrospective surveys in Africa have indeed focused on topics related to reproduction, a not insubstantial number have also collected data on other topics easily related to social history—studies of employment in the formal or informal sectors, agricultural production, consumption of goods of various provenance, housing, schooling, mobility both within colonies and countries or between them, and so on. The National Migration Survey carried out in Burkina Faso (then Upper Volta) in 1974–1975 offers an excellent example of how a data collection operation conceived to meet contemporary needs for information may also serve as an invaluable source for social history.

The National Migration Survey, Upper Volta, 1974–1975

The National Migration Survey, conducted in 1974 and 1975 in Upper Volta, as Burkina Faso was called at that time, is an excellent example of a retrospective sample survey whose objective was the collection of data to illuminate an issue of great contemporary importance to the country, but which also serves as a source for social history. In a note on the survey published while it was still going on, the principal investigators Sidiki Coulibaly, Joel W. Gregory, and Victor Piché enumerated their initial aims:

> The survey has a double purpose. First, the study will permit the estimation of the current volume and direction of migration as well as its recent evolution, at both the national and regional levels. Furthermore, these data will provide answers to the following types of questions: 1) Is rural-urban migration as important as international migration? 2) What is the quantitative importance of "spontaneous" migration? 3) How much migration has been caused by the drought [of the late 1960s ands early 1970s]? 4) Have the various migratory streams changed in the recent past?
>
> A second and equally important purpose is the study of the motives for, and the results of migration. The data collected will permit the direct study of economic, social, and socio-psychological causes and effects of migration based on more detailed interviews of a large sub-sample of individual respondents.
>
> Briefly, [then,] the survey has three major objectives: the *measure* of migration; the explanation of *why* migration happens, and the study of some of the major *effects* of migration.
>
> Four different forms of data collection are being used: 1) a household sample survey, with short interviews collecting both current and retrospective data, covering a population of approximately 100,000 people; 2) a sub-sample of these individuals with lengthened questionnaires on causes and effects; 3) a series of tape-recorded group discussions with open-ended questions; and 4) a socio-economic and historical study of the towns and villages where the survey is taking place.[9]

The survey collected retrospective data on mobility from a representative sample of residents throughout Burkina Faso. Survey agents elicited migration histories from all residents in the sample aged five years and older who were present at the time of the operation. The sample was a representative national sample, and, at the same time, representative of each of eleven cities in the country,[10] and each of two rural zones. Of the two rural zones, one was a representative rural sample of the "rural Mossi," the predominant ethnic group in Burkina Faso, and the other a representative rural sample of everyone else, termed the "rural non-Mossi." The urban samples of the survey totaled 41,093 people, while the rural samples of Mossi and non-Mossi included 52,304.[11] In order to assure that a large enough number of migrants were included in the urban sample, the urban areas were "oversampled" relative to the two rural zones. Subsequently the urban and rural samples were weighted to eliminate this imbalance.[12] Overall, then, the total national sample came to nearly 100,000 people—a large number of respondants, even by survey standards.

The National Migration Survey of 1974–1975 defined a migration as a move across a "sous-préfecture" boundary or an international border by adult men and women, and boys and girls five years of age and older, for a period of at least three months. For each such move, survey agents recorded the following information, all of it very useful for social history: destination, length of stay, age at migration, marital status at migration, motive(s) for moving, people (if any) with whom the person migrated, where she or he stayed upon arrival, and economic activity at destination (including occupation, occupational status, and employer).

The National Migration Survey of 1974–1975 as a Source for Burkinabè Social History in the Twentieth Century

From the point of view of historical research, two characteristics of the National Migration Survey are very exciting: First, the already large sample of nearly 100,000 people had made nearly 1,000,000 moves defined as migrations, which represents a corpus of information that is extraordinary for social history. Second, even though these burkinabè men and women, and both migrants and non-migrants, were responding to questionnaires and interview schedules prepared by researchers, and, therefore, not always able to describe their experiences in their own own terms of reference, the survey data nonetheless represent a set of burkinabè views of migration. Given that the written historical sources on burkinabè migration consist almost exclusively of reports by European officials and social scientists, or European documents in European archives, the National Migration Survey represents, in a very important sense, an aggregate of individual African migrant perspectives on how mobility transformed life in Burkina Faso in the twentieth century.[13]

During the course of analyzing the data from the National Migration Survey, Gregory and Piché became aware of the potential importance of the data for understanding the history of burkinabè migration. Indeed, they presented a paper outlining the methodology for using the survey data for historical analysis in 1979, the year before the survey results appeared; the paper appeared as an article five years later.[14]

However, it was not until the late 1980s, following the death of Joel Gregory, that Victor Piché and I tackled the task of truly reshaping the survey data to enable an historical study of burkinabè migration in the twentieth century.[15] The earliest migrations recollected by burkinabè informants dated from around 1900, shortly after the imposition of French colonial rule in the territory that would become the colony of Upper Volta. The most recent migrations dated from 1973, the year before the survey. The history of Upper Volta/Burkina Faso in the first three-quarters of the twentieth century falls into four periods that seemed to us to be meaningful. We worked with a programmer, who transferred the survey data from the computer tapes on which it had been recorded in the 1970s to computer disks, and then grouped the collected responses by historical period. We limited our study to moves by migrants over fifteen years of age. We also separated the responses of men from those of women to try to capture gender perspectives on migration over the four periods.

The first period covers migrations in *the years 1900–1931,* an era associated with colonial penetration and the creation of the colony of Upper Volta. The migration sample was small—230 moves by women and 791 by men—but the period is coherent from a historical point of view. It spans the years from the beginning of colonial rule through the foundation of the colony of Upper Volta in 1919, and comes to a close with the suppression of the colony in 1931. The second period focuses on *the years 1932–1946,* from the dismantling of Upper Volta to the decision to abolish forced labor in 1946. During this era, the largest part of the colony was annexed to Côte d'Ivoire to facilitate the supply of labor to the emerging sector of commercial agriculture. Over these years, the survey recorded more moves—839 by women and 3,110 by men. The third period takes up the story in *the year 1947,* which marked the reconstitution of the colony, and terminates in *the year 1959,* on the eve of independence. Migrations captured by the survey were much more numerous for this more recent period: women interviewed by survey agents had migrated 2,101 times, while men made 5,699 moves. The fourth and final period covers *the years 1960–1973,* from independence to the date of the survey. The numbers of moves were greater still, with women migrating 6,289 times and men crossing sous-prefecture boundaries on 11,439 occasions.

This reformatting and reclassing of survey data by historical period allowed us to trace the evolution of internal and international migration by men and women over the four periods into which we had divided the years 1900–1973. For each period we constructed tables recording the following information: destinations of migrants, lengths of time they stayed at those destinations, ages at migration, marital status at migration, motives for moving, people (if any) with whom they migrated, where they stayed upon arrival, and their economic activity at destination (including occupation, occupational status, and employer). This exercise produced very nearly one hundred tables documenting the characteristics of migration by burkinabè men and women.[16] This corpus of raw data is extraordinarily rich. Nonetheless, interpreting it in a way that truly contributed to our understanding of the social history of Burkina in the twentieth century presented a variety of challenges.

Some Methodological Challenges to Using Retrospective Data from the National Migration Survey for Social History

Up to now I have emphasized the great value of retrospective data from the National Migration Survey for understanding the social history of Upper Volta/Burkina Faso in the first three-quarters of the twentieth century. Such enthusiasm is not, however, meant to gloss over the fact that survey data have important limits. While some of these imperfections may be "corrected," in other cases, it is simply a question of recognizing and acknowledging the limits of the data, and accepting the fact that all historical data are imperfect. Virtually all historians have to learn to live with imperfect data, because the sources we use to answer the questions we ask were not created with our questions in mind. Although not exhaustive, the next several paragraphs describe some of the obstacles in using the Upper Volta survey data to write history. Discussion of these problems is useful because they are also likely to come up in attempts to use data from other surveys.

First, while the survey was the major single source used in our efforts to trace the history of burkinabè mobility, it cannot stand alone. We found it absolutely necessary to refer to other kinds of data to contextualize and interpret its findings. For earlier periods, about which less is known, for example, the addition of qualitative information is important for understanding the migration process. We also tried to complement the survey data with macro-level analysis of the historical and structural evolution of burkinabè societies since the late nineteenth century, paying particular attention to the interplay between policies at the level of the state (in the colonial and post-independence eras), and the internal dynamics of individual societies.

In addition, we incorporated the findings of other quantitative studies of burkinabè mobility into our analysis. Again, for the earlier periods, we compared survey data with studies based on statistics from the colonial archives. For recent decades, quantitative surveys are more numerous. A survey by the French Office de la Recherche Scientifique et Technique d'Outre-Mer (ORSTOM) was of particular significance, because it resembles the National Migration Survey in some respects.[17] In the end, then, statistical comparability and historical consistency were two measures against which we evaluated the survey's conclusions.

Second, we faced important questions of the validity of definitions over time. The designations "urban" and "rural" illustrate the problem. In this regard, two issues are particularly salient. First, urban sites changed over time. In 1925, for example, some centers defined as urban in 1974–75 were merely big villages. And second, town boundaries shifted. In the case of Ouagadougou, for example, the city has expanded to incorporate neighboring villages. For the migration survey, the names of all localities were recorded and then coded as rural or urban, using definitions current in the mid-1970s. For our historical study, we projected these definitions backward—over the four periods of the study.

This procedure undoubtedly led to some distortion. Some sites defined as urban in 1974–75 would not have been so labeled earlier. However, it seemed to us that such distortions only minimally affected *Hoe and Wage,* the book that resulted from our analysis. For the earlier periods, we aggregated our data into the two very broad categories of "urban" and "rural." Our conclusions were not based on the analysis of individual migration flows to or from the smaller urban centers. For these earlier periods, then, the aggregate data may include small flows erroneously classed as urban. However, these inaccuracies do not significantly affect the overall profile of migration to and/or from urban zones because most urban mobility at this time consisted of migration to and/or from Ouagadougou and Bobo-Doulasso, which were by far the two largest urban centers. By all definitions, both cities were "urban" over the entire period.

Third, we faced methodological problems. If the survey samples were representative for burkinabè populations in 1974–75, such was not necessarily the case for earlier periods. We thus decided to limit our analysis to multidimensional cross-tabulations of the independent variables recorded by the survey. We did not use multivariate analysis precisely because our data set was not representative of all migration flows for all periods.

Two phenomena were responsible for the possible lack of representivity. First, some migrants—and the proportion increased with age—obviously died between their last migration and the survey. Hence, their histories were not captured by the study. The death of this subpopulation may have biased our data set insofar as their migration histories differed from those who survived to the time of the survey. This would be the case, for example, if the migration experience itself had had a specific impact on mortality. And such is not improbable for certain types of migration. For instance, harsh conditions associated with forced migration, military service, or labor on colonial work sites may have provoked higher levels of mortality. If such were the case, these types of migration would be underestimated in our data set, and the more so as we go back in time. By the same token, the levels of return migration of these individuals would also be underestimated if they died abroad. Another bias is introduced by the age of the migrants at the time of the survey. By definition, people who were older in 1974–75 contributed more to migrations in the earlier periods than younger people; and yet, a larger proportion of migrants from these years would have died before the study.

Another bias is produced by absent migrants, those outside Burkina Faso at the time of the 1974–75 survey. These people fall into two categories: (1) those who settled permanently elsewhere; and (2) those who eventually returned after the survey. Estimates of "permanent" migration are not easy to obtain; given that migrants may decide to return at any time, it is not certain when migration becomes permanent. According to the research of Capron and Kohler, however, a minority of burkinabè migrants— a maximum of 20 percent—settled in 1973.[18] Our analysis suggests that this proportion becomes smaller as we move back in time. If such is indeed the case, we may conclude that the migration histories of migrants who did not return were not appreciably different from those who did.

As for the second population, made up of migrants would eventually return, inasmuch as lengths of stay have not changed markedly over time, their migration histories are probably similar to those of return migrants interviewed in Burkina Faso in 1974–1975. While there is evidence that migrants were staying longer in Côte d'Ivoire in the latter decades of the twentieth century, this increase is very recent and not large enough to influence our conclusions for the period up to the survey.

Other characteristics of the survey data raise other, less important, conceptual and methodological issues. They also make it evident that the results of the 1974–75 study are not absolutely representative of the burkinabè population in earlier eras. Nonetheless, when supplemented by other kinds of data, the survey is of great value in helping frame a migrant-centered analysis of mobility and its impact on individual burkinabè men and women, their families, and their societies. Such were the topics that we tackled in *Hoe and Wage*. While the volume offers one illustration of how contemporary or near-contemporary survey data may be used to study the social history of African populations, the National Migration Survey is by no means the only such study susceptible to being recast as a historical source.

By Way of Conclusion: Surveying the Survey Literature

For scholars in search of survey sources for African social history, the terrain is both familiar and new. Because many surveys were commissioned by government entities and international organizations, locating them often requires navigating through a plethora of official agency publications and documentation centers. For historians, accustomed to finding their way along circuitous paths to information conserved in official archives, the challenge is familiar, even if the particular itineraries are not.

Since very few survey results are published in their entirety, one way of proceeding is to search out articles and books published by social scientists that are based on survey data. These publications often identify the office or agency that sponsored the original survey and make it easier to locate them. In an exercise to test the feasibility of this option, I surveyed the articles included in a bibliography on African historical demography that two colleagues and I published some years ago; among the 2,550 entries, I located nearly one hundred that might lead to promising survey data.[19]

However, rather than pursuing leads willy-nilly through the literature in the social sciences, a more systematic strategy for topics that broadly relate to population is to consult the *Population Index,* a publication that I have described elsewhere as "an extraordinary ongoing bibliography."[20] Published four times a year by the Office of Population Research at Princeton, *Population Index* surveys demographic research published as monographs, official reports, working papers, compact disks, and articles from about 4,000 periodicals in dozens of languages for all disciplines of the social and natural sciences. It is available in printed form that includes published summaries cross-indexed by topic and geographical area; moreover, a web-based searchable version of the bibliography is available for volumes published since 1985.[21]

Other options include searching out the raw data and even the published summary results from known survey operations. Earlier in this essay, I cited the example of the series of sample surveys conducted in francophone Africa in the 1950s and 1960s (see note 7). But apart from returning to questionnaires or unpublished tables, even published data from these survey operations offer insights for social history. For example, in the case of the *Enquête démographique en République centrafricaine, 1959–1960* cited earlier, not only do the data provide a "snapshot" of the fertility levels of women in the mid-twentieth century, but the study recorded the numbers of births from women whose reproductive lives had begun as early as the 1910s. Such information as been of assistance to scholars attempting to discover the causes behind the often very low birthrates in this part of Africa, located in the center of the "low fertility belt" that stretches from southern Cameroon to western Uganda and northern Tanzania.[22] Or, in the case of the *Enquête démographique au Tchad, 1964,* the survey provides tabular data on the size and constitution of households by age of the household head among several ethnic groups in the southern half of the country.[23] Other tables from this survey include retrospective information on migration. Hence, the search for useful information for social history does not necessarily require the major reformatting and reanalysis of survey data such as that described for the National Migration Survey of 1974–1975 in Upper Volta/Burkina Faso.

Several sets of global surveys have also collected substantial bodies of retrospective survey data in the years since African independence. These sources are useful both for research on the social history of a single country or population, and for comparisons on a continental or even inter-continental scale. In the area of population studies, the oldest of these series of surveys is the World Fertility Survey (WFS). At the beginning of the 1970s, several governments and international institutions became concerned about the high levels of fertility characteristic of many developing countries. Financed largely by the United Nations Fund for Population Activities and the United States Agency for International Development (USAID), with additional funding from the governments of the United Kingdom, France, Canada, and Japan, the surveys were executed by the International Statistical Institute in collaboration with the International Union for the Scientific Study of Population. Between 1974 and 1982, forty-two countries in the developing world participated in the WFS program. Twenty developed countries also carried out surveys, without international financial and technical assistance.[24] Apart from collecting retrospective data on fertility levels from women around the world—including a dozen countries in Africa—the mandate of the WFS included research on the relationship between fertility and women's participation in the workforce.[25] By all accounts, this is the stuff of social history.

A second, even more ambitious, and still on-going series of surveys took up where the WFS program left off. Launched in 1984 by the Office of Population and the Office of Health in USAID, and administered by IRD/Macro International in Calverton, Maryland, the mission of the DHS program has led to the collection of substantial survey data, retrospective and otherwise, useful for social historians of twentieth century Africa:

> […] the Demographic and Health Surveys (DHS) program has assisted countries in conducting national surveys on fertility, family planning, and mater-

nal and child health. The DHS program is a primary source of information on the reproductive and health behavior of women throughout sub-Saharan Africa, the Near East, North Africa, Asia, and Latin America. DHS data give policymakers information necessary for making crucial decisions about how to allocate scarce resources and provide family planning and health services to those who need them. In addition, DHS plays a major role in furthering international understanding of global population and health trends. The DHS program provides an unparalleled body of comparable data on demographic, health, and family planning indicators.[26]

As of fall 2001, DHS program surveys numbered 145, conducted in more than seventy countries and regions around the world.[27] In many countries, the program has administered multiple surveys over time, which allows researchers to track changes over the last two decades of the twentieth century. And in most cases, the surveys include retrospective questions that provide data on earlier periods.

Apart from administering standardized surveys to representative samples of between 4,000 and 8,000 women (and, more recently, men) in countries and subnational regions around the world, the DHS program has also allowed for more specialized research. Some surveys have included special components, or, in some cases, entirely separate questionnaires, on specialized topics of interest to individual countries. Topics of such research have included knowledge and attitudes about AIDS, male attitudes concerning reproduction, causes of child deaths, and female genital cutting.[28] DHS data are readily available in printed form or on disk at no, or little, charge. Moreover, in the fall of 2000, the DHS program launched an online database tool called DHS STATcompiler that enables researchers "to select from numerous countries and hundreds of indicators, and to create customized tables to serve their specific data needs."[29] This tool should enhance the efforts of historians and historically oriented social scientists to conduct research on topics in African social history.

Channeled by my own areas of expertise, this essay has necessarily focused on studies about population and related topics in an effort to demonstrate the wealth of survey sources that are available for research on social history. However, social scientists from other fields have also collected survey data—most notably in the field of economics—since the middle decades of the twentieth century. As Toyin Falola has written, "African history is written using many different sources and methods. Decades ago, Africanists played a crucial role in the development of oral history within the discipline. Today, Africanists are still at the forefront of incorporating new ideas into the historical method."[30] Sample surveys, retrospective and otherwise, have fostered the collection of large bodies of data about African societies for a half-century and more. Historians need to incorporate these sources into their research, for they, too, open "pathways to Africa's past."

Notes

1. I wish to dedicate this essay to my colleague and extraordinary friend Victor Piché of the Département de Démographie at the Université de Montréal, with whom I have worked for two decades on questions of migration and African historical demography. Please direct comments and questions regarding this essay to me at my electronic mail address (dcordell@mail.smu.edu).

2. Dennis D. Cordell, Joel W. Gregory, and Victor Piché, *Hoe and Wage: A Social History of a Circular Migration System in West Africa* (Boulder, Colo.: Westview, 1996).

3. For a more exhaustive discussion of sample surveys in Africa, see Francis Gendreau, *La population de l'Afrique: Manuel de démographie* (Paris: Karthala/CEPED, 1993), 46–57. Also see Arthur Haupt and Thomas T. Kane, *The Population Reference Bureau's Population Handbook. International Edition,* 2nd edition (Washington, 1986), 57, 63; Henry S. Shryock, Jacob S. Siegel and Associates, *The Methods and Materials of Demography* (New York: Academic Press, 1976), 13–14, 29–38, 54–55, 297–312, 484, 497.

4. United Nations Economic and Social Commission for Western Asia and the International Union for the Scientific Study of Population, *Trilingual Demographic Dictionary. Arabic-English-French. English-French-Arabic. French-English-Arabic* (Baghdad: ESCWA, 1988), 92, 98.

5. Gendreau, *La population de l'Afrique,* 49–50.

6. For a history of this establishment, one of the first truly international networks of agencies and scholars in any field, see Oscar Harkavy, *Curbing Population Growth: An Insider's Perspective on the Population Movement* (New York: Plenum Press, 1995), 1–92, and Eric B. Ross, *The Malthus Factor: Poverty, Politics and Population in Capitalist Development* (London and New York: Zed Books, 1998), 69–104, 200–223.

7. See, for example, République centrafricaine, Service de la statistique générale, *Enquête démographique en République centrafricaine, 1959–1960* (Paris: Institut National de la Statistique et des Études Économiques or INSEE, 1964), whose tables include information on women whose reproductive histories began in the early decades of the twentieth century.

8. For more information on these surveys and how to access them, see Richard Marcoux, "Les enquêtes démographiques des années 60 en pays sahéliens francophones," *Newsletter: Canadian Association of African Studies/Bulletin: Association Canadienne des Études Africaines* (Winter/Hiver 1990): 14–21; Raymond R. Gervais and Richard Marcoux, "Saving Francophone Africa's Statistical Past," *History in Africa* 20 (1993): 385–90; William Brass, "The Demography of French-Speaking Territories Covered by Special Sample Inquiries: Upper Volta, Dahomey, Guinea, North Cameroon, and Other Areas," in *The Demography of Tropical Africa,* ed. William Brass et al. (Princeton: Princeton University Press, 1968), 342–439; Pierre Cantrelle, "Pour un inventaire des archives des recensements et enquêtes démographiques réalisés en Afrique d'expression françaises," *Bulletin de liaison: La démographie en Afrique d'expression française* 14 (December, 1974): 40–51.

9. Sidiki P. Coulibaly, Joel W. Gregory, and Victor Piché, "A Note on the Migration Survey in Upper Volta," *International Migration Review* 9, 1 (1975): 57–58.

10. The eleven urban areas were so designated by the Institut National de la Statistique et de la Démographie (INSD), and included all towns that served as headquarters for Regional Development Offices: Ouagadougou, Bobo-Dioulasso, Kaya, Koudougou, Koupéla, Ouaghiouya, Dori, Fada N'Gourma, Banfora, Dédougou, and Gaoua. For descriptions of these centers, see Cordell, Gregory, and Piché, *Hoe and Wage*, 37.

11. See Coulibaly, Gregory, and Piché, *Les migrations voltaïques*, vol. 1, *Importance et ambivalence de la migration voltaïque* (Ouagadougou: Centre Voltaïque de la Recherche Scientifique [CVRS] and Institut National de la Statistique et de la Démographie [INSD]; Ottawa: Centre de Recherches sur le Développement International [CRDI]; 1980), 141–42, Table A.1, column 5; Table A.2, column 5. Along with volume 1, the survey results were reported in the following volumes (all 1980): vol. 2, Coulibaly, Gregory, and Piché, eds. *Méthodologie*; vol. 3, Coulibaly, Gregory, André Lavoie, and Piché, *Mesure de la migration, 1969–1973*; vol. 4, Coulibaly, Gregory, and Piché, *Caractéristiques des migrants et des non-migrants*; vol. 5, Coulibaly, Gregory, and Piché, *Motifs de la migration*; vol. 6, Coulibaly, Gregory, and Piché, *Opinions sur le phénomène migratoire*; vol. 7, Coulibaly, Gregory, and Piché, *Opinions sur le rôle du gouvernement en matière de migration*; vol. 8, Coulibaly, Denise Desrosiers, Gregory, and Piché, *Appréciation collective du phénomène migratoire*. The survey results also provided the raw data for the preparation of one dissertation and more than a dozen master's theses in the Département de Démographie at the Université de Montréal between 1978 and the late 1980s.

12. For a description of weighting procedures, see Coulibaly, Gregory, and Piché, *Les migrations voltaîque* 1 :139–44.

13. For these sources, see the bibliography and footnotes to Cordell, Gregory, and Piché, *Hoe and Wage*, 343–65; Cordell and Gregory, "Labour Reservoirs and Population: French Colonial Strategies in Koudougou, Upper Volta, 1914–1939," in *African Historical Demography II*, ed. Centre of African Studies (Edinburgh: University of Edinburgh, Centre of African Studies, 1981), 51–104; Cordell and Gregory, "Labour Reservoirs and Population: French Colonial Strategies in Koudougou, Upper Volta, 1914 to 1939," *Journal of African History* 23: 205–24.

14. Victor Piché, Joel Gregory, André Lavoie, "L'analyse historique des migrations: La pertinence de l'analyse longitudinale à partir des histoires retrospectives," *Genus: Rivista fondata da Corrado Gini* 40, 3–4 (July–December 1984): 25–45.

15. Indeed, we published our first article on the history of burkinabè migration in an issue of the *Canadian Journal of African Studies/Revue canadienne des études africaines* (CJAS/ RCEA) dedicated to Joel's memory. See Joel W. Gregory, Dennis D. Cordell, and Victor Piché, "La mobilisation de la main-d'oeuvre burkinabè: Une vision rétrospective," *CJAS/ RCEA* 23, 1 (1989): 73–105.

16. See Cordell, Gregory, and Piché, *Hoe and Wage*, vii–xi.

17. Jacques Vaugelade, "Les migrations des Voltaïques en Côte d'Ivoire: Bilan comparatif des résultats de l'enquête Mossi et de l'enquête nationale, 1974–1975," in *Les migrations voltaïques*, 2:134–62. ORSTOM is now called the Institut Français de Recherche Scientifique pour le Développement en Coopération (IRD).

18. Jean Capron and Jean-Marie Kohler, "Migrations de travail vers l'étranger et développement national," paper presented at the Séminaire sur les méthodes de planification du développement rural, organized by the Ministère du Plan et de la Fonction Publique et

du Travail, Ouagadougou, March 1976. On the effects of retention on the numbers of burkinabè emigrants in Ghana and Côte d'Ivoire, see Aka Kouamé, "Contribution à la démographie historique ouest africaine: Une étude des migrations burkinabè vers le Ghana et la Côte d'Ivoire de 1900 à 1960," *African Population Studies* 4: 69–94; André Quesnel and Jacques Vaugelade, *Les mouvements de population mossi: Démographie et migration* (Ouagadougou: Ministère du Travail et de la Fonction Publique, 1975), dossier 2, fasicule 1, section 3.9.

19. Joel W. Gregory, Dennis D. Cordell, and Raymond Gervais, *African Historical Demography: A Multidisciplinary Bibliography* (Los Angeles: Crossroads Press of the African Studies Association, 1984), items 11, 16, 19, 64, 67, 255–58, 261–63, 278, 325, 346, 807, 838, 889, 981–83, 1027, 1096, 1107, 1128, 1153–54, 1159–60, 1163, 1169, 1193, 1207, 1209, 1214, 1243, 1282, 1285, 1306, 1325, 1335, 1342, 1344–45, 1355, 1363, 1379, 1408, 1421, 1467, 1492, 1499, 1514, 1544, 1564, 1569, 1567, 1587, 1604–6, 1613, 1645, 1659, 1678, 1682, 1692, 1713, 1729, 1743, 1749–56, 1771, 1774, 1791–92, 1796, 1799, 1803–5, 1809, 1822, 1824–26, 1830–31, 1841, 1850, 1956.

20. Dennis D. Cordell, "African Historical Demography in the Years since Edinburgh," *History in Africa* 27 (2000): 62.

21. See the Popindex website <*http://popindex.princeton.edu*>. Concerned about the cost of maintaining Popindex, the Office of Population Research has recently discontinued it. However, professional organizations in the field of population studies such as the Population Association of America and the International Union for the Scientific Study of Population responded by urging the investigation of alternative means of financing this extraordinary bibliography.

22. For more on this topic, see, for example, Anne Retel-Laurentin, *Un pays à la dérive: Une société en régression démographique. Les Nzakara de l'est centrafricain* (Paris: Jean-Pierre Delarge, 1979); Dennis D. Cordell, "Où sont tous les enfants? La faible fécondité en Centrafrique, 1890–1960," in *Population, reproduction, sociétés. Perspectives et enjeux de démographie sociale: Mélanges en l'honneur de Joel W. Gregory*, ed. Dennis D. Cordell, Danielle Gauvreau, Raymond R. Gervais, and Céline Le Bourdais (Montréal: Les Presses de l'Université de Montréal, 1993), 257–82.

23. République du Tchad, Service de Statistique/République française, Sécretariat d'État aux Affaires Étrangères chargé de la Coopération, *Enquête démographique au Tchad, 1964. Résultats définitifs*, vol. 1, *Analyse des résultats* (Paris: INSEE, 1966).

24. See J. Cleland and J. Hobcraft, eds., *Reproductive Change in Developing Countries. Insights from the WFS* (Oxford: Oxford University Press, 1985); J. Cleland and C. Scott, eds., *The World Fertility Survey: An Assessment* (Oxford: Oxford University Press, 1987).

25. Gendreau, *La population de l'Afrique*, Appendix IIIA, 59–60; Jean Poirier, Victor Piché, and Ghyslaine Neill, "Travail des femmes et fécondité dans les pays en développement: Que nous a appris l'Enquête mondiale de la fécondité," *Cahiers québécois de démographie* 18, 1 (1989): 159–84.

26. Macro International, *DHS: Demographic and Health Surveys* (Calverton, Md.: Macro International, n.d.).

27. See *DHS+ Dimensions. A Semiannual Newsletter of the Demographic and Health Surveys Project* 3, 2 (Fall, 2001): 6–7.

28. See, for example, Dara Carr, *Female Genital Cutting: Findings from the Demographic and Health Surveys Program* (Calverton, Md.: Macro International, 1997*)* and *DHS+ Dimensions. A Semiannual Newsletter of the Demographic and Health Surveys Project.*

29. "Access DHS Data Instantly and Easily with New Internet Tool," *DHS+ Dimensions: A Semiannual Newsletter of the Demographic and Health Surveys Project* 2, 2 (Fall 2000): 1–2. See the DHS website <http://www.measuredhs.com>.

30. Toyin Falola, "Theme Statement," electronic mail message, Austin, Tx., 31 May 2001.

CONTRIBUTORS

Cynthia Brantley is Professor of History at the University of California, Davis. Her research has focused primarily on colonialism and social and economic change in East and Central Africa. Her special interests include family and gender, nutrition, and colonial cultural imperialism. Her scholarly articles and book reviews have appeared in journals such as *Africa, The International Journal of African Historical Studies, Agricultural History,* and *Critique of Anthropology.* She has published *The Giriama and Colonial Resistance in Kenya, 1800–1920* (1981). Her book *Feeding African Families: African Realities and British Ideas of Nutrition and Development* is forthcoming.

Matt Childs is Assistant Professor of Caribbean History at Florida State University. He earned his Ph.D. in history from the University of Texas at Austin. He has published articles in peer-reviewed journals and edited collections on Che Guevara's role in the 1959 Cuban Revolution, the gendered aspects of female education in nineteenth-century Cuba, the abolition of slavery in Brazil, the consequences of the Haitian Revolution for Cuban history, and African ethnicity in the Americas. Childs has received research grants from the Social Science Research Council, the Ford Foundation, the American Council of Learned Societies, and the Fulbright-Hays Program.

Gérard Chouin is a doctoral student in the Department of Anthropology at Syracuse University and the co-founder of the Association for the Protection of Historical and Archaeological Sites in Ghana. A former lecturer at the University of Ghana and at the University of Cape Coast from 1993 to 1999, he has investigated the history of environmental, social, and economic changes in precolonial Gold Coast. His research in Europe and in Ghana has led to a number of publications. His dissertation project focuses on an historical and archaeological study of sacred groves in southern Ghana. He is the author of *Eguafo, un royaume africain au 'coeur françois,' 1637–1687: Mutations socio-économiques et politique européenne d'un état de la*

393

Côte de l'Or au XVIIe siècle (1998) and Écrits d'entre-deux mondes: Un index analytique des sources manuscrites de l'histoire des états de la Côte de l'Or (Côte d'Ivoire, Ghana) dans les fonds de la Bibliothèque Nationale et des Archives Nationales de France (1996).

Catherine Coquery-Vidrovitch is Professor of Modern African History at the University of Paris 7–Denis-Diderot, and since 1981 has been Adjunct Professor in the Department of Sociology at the State University of New York at Binghamton. She has trained a large number of French-speaking African historians in Paris and at African universities. She has published half a dozen books, among which two have been translated into English: *Africa South of the Sahara: Endurance and Change* (1987) and *African Women, a Modern History* (1998). A third book *Histoire des villes africaines,* is being translated. She has edited about twenty books on African studies and the third world. In 1999, she was given the African Studies Association Distinguished Africanist Award. Since August 2000, she was elected a member (2000–2005) of the ICHS (Internationl Committee of Historical Sciences).

Dennis D. Cordell is Professor of History and Associate Dean for General Education and the University Honors Program at Southern Methodist University (Dallas). He is the author of *Dar al-Kuti and the Last Years of the Trans-Saharan Slave Trade* (1985); co-editor with the late Joel W. Gregory of *African Population and Capitalism: Historical Perspectives* (1987 and 1994); co-editor with Danielle Gauvreau, Raymond Gervais, and Celine LeBourdais of *Population, reproduction, sociétés: Perspectives et enjeux de démographie sociale* (1993); and co-author with Victor Piche and Joel Gregory of *Hoe and Wage: A Social History of a Circular Migration System in West Africa* (1996). Most recently he published "African Historical Demography in the Years since Edinburgh" in *History in Africa* 27 (2000), an overview of research in the field over the last two decades. Funded by the National Science Foundation, he and his colleague Carolyn Sargent are currently conducting fieldwork on the construction of transnational space and changing representations of the family and contraception among Malian migrants in Paris.

Christopher R. DeCorse is Associate Professor of Anthropology in the Maxwell School of Citizenship and Public Affairs, Syracuse University. His research interests include culture change, ethnicity, and material culture studies. His recent book, *An Archaeology of Elmina: Africans and Europeans on the Gold Coast, 1400–1900* (2001), examines culture contact and interactions in coastal Ghana over the past five hundred years. He is the author of *Record of the Past: An Introduction to Physical Anthropology and Archaeology* (2001) and co-author with Raymond Scupin of *Anthropology: A Global Perspective* (2001). His edited volume, *West Africa during the Atlantic Slave Trade: Archaeological Perspectives*, appeared in 2001.

James Denbow is Associate Professor at the University of Texas at Austin. He established the archaeology program at the National Museum of Botswana and has carried out archaeological investigations in both Botswana and the Republic of Congo. Recent publications include: "Heart and Soul: Glimpses of Ideology in the Iconography of Tombstones from the Loango Coast," and "Material Culture and the Dialectics of Identity in the Kalahari: A.D. 700–1700."

James Giblin is Professor of African History at the University of Iowa. He is the author of *The Politics of Environmental Control in Northeastern Tanzania, 1840–1940* (1993), and co-editor of *Custodians of the Land: Ecology and Culture in the History of Tanzania* (1996). Currently he is completing a book on the twentieth-century social history of Njombe in southern Tanzania, and is co-directing a collaborative research project on the Maji Maji war of 1905–7.

David Henige is Africana Bibliographer at the University of Wisconsin-Madison and the author of several books and papers on historical method in its various guises. He is the editor of *History in Africa* and has just completed a work entitled *Historical Evidence and Argument*.

Jan Jansen is a Research Fellow of the Royal Netherlands Academy of Arts and Sciences at Leiden University. He is the co-editor of *African Sources for African History*, published by Brill. His research has focused on oral tradition in Mali and Guinea. He has published two monographs and several text editions on the griots of the village of Kela. His articles have appeared in *Cahiers d'Études africaines*, *History in Africa*, and *Research in African Literatures*.

Russell Lohse is a Ph.D. candidate in History at the University of Texas at Austin. His dissertation focuses on the constitution of identities among enslaved Africans and their descendants in colonial Costa Rica. He is also contributing to another research project identifying the ethnic origins of some 10,000 enslaved Africans recaptured by the British Navy in the early nineteenth century. Lohse is the author of "Reconciling Freedom with the Rights of Property: Slave Emancipation in Colombia, 1821–1852, with Special Reference to La Plata," forthcoming in the *Journal of Negro History.*

Paul E. Lovejoy is Distinguished Research Professor of History at York University and is Director of the York/UNESCO Nigerian Hinterland Project (www.yorku.ca/nhp). He also holds the Canada Research Chair in African Diaspora History and is a Fellow of the Royal Society of Canada. His areas of specialization are West African economic and social history, slavery, the slave trade, and the African diaspora. He has written, edited, or co-edited twenty books, including *The Ideology of Slavery in Africa* (1981); *Workers of African Trade* (1985), co-edited with Catherine Coquery-Vidrovitch; *Africans in Bondage: Studies in Slavery and the Slave Trade* (1985); *Unfree Labour in the Development of the Atlantic World* (1994); and *Consuming Habits: Drugs in History and Anthropology* (1995), with Jordan Goodman and Andrew Sherratt. His *Transformations in Slavery: A History of Slavery in Africa* (1983; 2nd ed., 2000) was awarded the Social Science Federation of Canada Certificate of Merit. *Slow Death for Slavery: The Course of Abolition in Northern Nigeria, 1897–1936* (1993), co-authored with Jan S. Hogendorn, was awarded the Wallace K. Ferguson Prize of the Canadian Historical Association in 1994. His most recent books include *Identity in the Shadow of Slavery* (2000); *Slavery on the Frontiers of Islam* (2001); *Trans-Atlantic Dimensions of Slaving* (2001), with David Trotman; and *Pawnship, Slavery and Colonialism in Africa* (2001), with Toyin Falola.

Kristin Mann is Associate Professor of History at Emory University. She is author of *Marrying Well: Marriage, Status, and Social Change among the Educated Elite in Colonial Lagos* (1985), and co-editor of *Law in Colonial Africa* (1991) and *Rethinking the African Diaspora: The Making of a Black Atlantic World in the Bight of Benin and Brazil* (2001).

Meredith McKittrick is Assistant Professor in the Department of History and the Edmund A. Walsh School of Foreign Service at Georgetown University. Her research focuses on the social and environmental history of Namibia and Angola. Her scholarly works have appeared in the *Journal of African History, African Economic History, Social Science and History,* and several edited collections. Her book, *To Dwell Secure: Generation and Christianity in Ovamboland, Northern Namibia, 1855–1955,* is forthcoming in Heinemann's Social History of Africa series.

Laura J. Mitchell is Assistant Professor of History at the University of California, Irvine. Her research explores colonial interactions in eighteenth-century Southern Africa, particularly issues of forced labor, land tenure, and environmental change.

Jamie Monson is Associate Professor of History at Carleton College, where she teaches African History. Her research interests include agricultural and environmental history, memory, the Maji Maji rebellion, and the TAZARA railway. She is currently working on a book on the rural social history of TAZARA in the Kilombero valley region of Tanzania. Dr. Monson has published articles in the *Journal of African History, African Economic History*, and the *International Journal of African Historical Studies*, and has contributed chapters to edited volumes on Tanzanian agrarian history.

Akinwumi Ogundiran is Assistant Professor in the Department of History at Florida International University, Miami. He has conducted interdisciplinary fieldwork on the archaeology of landscape and community history in Nigeria. He is a co-author of *Cultural Resources in Ijesaland* (1992) and he is currently completing a monograph titled *Archaeology and History in Ilare District, AC 1200–1900*, for Cambridge Monographs in African Archaeology. His ongoing research focuses on history of ideas, cultural history, and regional interaction in Yoruba-Edo region.

Kevin Roberts is a Ph.D. candidate in History at the University of Texas at Austin. His dissertation examines the ethnoracial identities, kinship practices, and cultural institutions of enslaved Blacks in nineteenth-century Louisiana and Cuba.

Steven Salm is completing his Ph.D. in History at the University of Texas at Austin where he is currently an A. D. Hutchinson Fellow. He has performed fieldwork in several West African countries, focusing on twentieth century urban history and culture. His dissertation discusses the development of youth subcultures in Accra, Ghana, since the Second World War by addressing the changing dynamics of globalization, cultural consumption, and identity transformation. He has received a number of awards and fellowships for his work, including the Jan Carleton Perry Prize and various research grants. He has taught at the University of Monterrey, Mexico; presented research papers at various conferences; and published chapters and articles on a wide range of topics such as gender, youth, music, literature, alcohol, and popular culture. His writings have appeared in *Africa Today, African Economic History,* and *The Encyclopedia of African History,* as well as other journals and edited works. His book, *The Culture and Customs of Ghana,* is forthcoming.

Thomas Spear is Professor of African History and chair of the Department of History at the University of Wisconsin-Madison. He is the author or editor of a number of books and articles on eastern African history and historiography, including *The Kaya Complex* (1978), *Kenya's Past* (1981), *The Swahili* (with Derek Nurse, 1985), *Being Masaai* (edited with Richard Waller, 1993), *Mountain Farmers* (1997), and *East African Expressions of Christianity* (edited with Isaria Kimambo, 1999). He is also an editor of the *Journal of African History.*

Constanze Weise is currently writing her Ph.D. dissertation, "Memory and Embodiment in Rituals, Festivals and Ceremonies among the Nupe People of Nigeria" at the University of Bayreuth (Germany). Her current interests include ritual, history, memory, witchcraft, and African Kingship systems in Nigeria and West Africa. She wrote her M.A. thesis on the precolonial Hausa-Kingship of Kano and the role played by the non-Islamic Hausa religion within the kingship system before the nineteenth century.

Ed Wilmsen received his Ph.D. in Anthropology from the University of Arizona in 1967 after teaching and practicing architecture subsequent to receiving a Master of Architecture degree from MIT in 1959 with a thesis on community development at Shiprock on the Navaho Reservation. Since 1973, he has worked with Zhu, Herero, and Tswana peoples in Botswana and has represented them in petitions to District and Ministry agencies. In 1975–76, he served as consultant to the Rural Income Distribution Survey and, in 1981, wrote an analysis of "Remote Area" peoples for the National Migration Study, which served as a source for the subsequent sixth National Development Plan of Botswana. His book *Land Filled with Flies: A Political Economy of the Kalahari* was awarded the 1990 Herskovits Prize of the African Studies Association (U.S.A.) and the 1992 Graham Prize of the School of Oriental and African Studies (London); its companion book, *Journeys with Flies,* was published in 1999. He has recently edited *The Kalahari Ethnographies of Siegfried Passarge (1896–1898): Nineteenth Century Khoisan- and Bantu-Speaking Peoples* and co-edited *The Politics of Difference: Ethnic Premises in a World of Power.*

INDEX

Sources and methods have been an ongoing concern in African history since the early years of its development as a field of academic specialization. Pioneering Africanist scholars developed the first rigorous methodologies for the use of oral tradition as history, despite prevailing doubt and skepticism from many of their colleagues. Oral tradition was soon complemented as a source by the development of methodologies for carbon dating, allowing new archaeological evidence to be used in reconstructing African history, and glottochronology, which opened new lines of inquiry for historical linguists. Africanist historians also pioneered methodologies for the study of religious, environmental, ecological, military and gender history. Spurred in part by the ongoing re-evaluation of sources and methods in research, African historiography in the past two decades has been characterized by the continued branching and increasing sophistication of methodologies and areas of specialization. The rate of incorporation of new sources and methods into African historical research shows no signs of slowing.

This book is both a snapshot of current academic practice and an attempt to sort through some of the problems scholars face within this unfolding web of sources and methods. The book is divided into five sections, each of which begins with a short introduction by a distinguished Africanist scholar. The first section deals with archaeological contributions to historical research. The second section examines the methodologies involved in deciphering historically accurate African ethnic identities from the records of the trans-Atlantic slave trade. The third section mines old documentary sources for new historical perspectives. The fourth section deals with the method most often associated with African historians, that of drawing historical data from oral tradition. The fifth section is devoted to essays that present innovative sources and methods for African historical research. Together, the essays in this cutting-edge volume represent the current state of the art in African historical research.

Toyin Falola is the Frances Higginbothom Nalle Centennial Professor of History at the University of Texas at Austin. He is author of *Violence in Nigeria* (University of Rochester Press, 2000) and *Nationalism and African Intellectuals* (University of Rochester Press, 2002) as well as many other works.

Christian Jennings is a doctoral candidate in history at the University of Texas at Austin. His research includes East African pastoralists, environmental history, and the history of science. He has co-edited *Africanizing Knowledge: African Studies Across the Disciplines* and has written textbook chapters and encyclopedia entries on pastoralism and environmental history in Africa.